Second Edition

Australian Courts of Law

James Crawford

OXFORD
UNIVERSITY PRESS

Melbourne · Oxford · Auckland · New York

OXFORD UNIVERSITY PRESS AUSTRALIA

Oxford New York Toronto
Delhi Bombay Calcutta Madras Karachi
Petaling Jaya Singapore Hong Kong Tokyo
Nairobi Dar es Salaam Cape Town
Melbourne Auckland
and associated companies in
Berlin Ibadan

OXFORD is a trade mark of Oxford University Press

© James Crawford 1988
First published 1982
This edition published 1988
Reprinted 1989

This book is copyright. Apart from any fair dealing for the purposes of private study, research, criticism or review as permitted under the Copyright Act, no part may be reproduced, stored in a retrieval system, or transmitted, in any form or by any means, electronic, mechanical, photocopying, recording, or otherwise without prior written permission. Inquiries to be made to Oxford University Press.

Copying for educational purposes
Where copies of part or the whole of the book are made under section 53B or section 53D of the Act, the law requires that records of such copying be kept. In such cases the copyright owner is entitled to claim payment.

National Library of Australia
Cataloguing-in-Publication data:

Crawford, James, 1948-
    Australian courts of law.

    2nd ed.
    Includes index.
    ISBN 0 19 554675 X.

    1. Courts — Australia. I. Title.
347.94'01

Edited by Lynn Gemmel
Designed by Echidna Graphics, Surrey Hills, Victoria
Cover illustration by Michael Lodge
Typeset by Meredith Trade Lino Pty Ltd
Printed in Australia by The Book Printer, Victoria
Published by Oxford University Press,
253 Normanby Road, South Melbourne, Australia

Contents

Preface ix
Acknowledgements xii
Abbreviations xiii

PART ONE   GENERAL PRINCIPLES 1

1 The Development of Legal Systems 3

2 The Common Law Background 6

2.1 The Origins and Development of the Common Law   6
    (1) The development of the common law in England   6
    (2) The growth of equity   7
    (3) Parliament and the common law   8

2.2 The Development of the English Court System   8
    (1) The common law courts   8
    (2) The Court of Chancery   11
    (3) Other courts   11
    (4) The Council   12
    (5) The development of appellate courts   13

2.3 The Reception of Common Law, Statutes, and Courts in Australia   14
    (1) The reception of common law and equity   14
    (2) The reception of statute law   15
    (3) The reception of legal institutions   16

3 The Constitutional Background   22

3.1 The Constitution of State Courts   22
   (1) The development of colonial courts   23
   (2) The constitution of state courts   23
   (3) Appeals from state courts   24

3.2 The Constitution of Federal Courts   25
   (1) The constitutional settlement   25
   (2) The role of the High Court   26
   (3) The separation of 'judicial power'   26
   (4) Other constitutional guarantees   27
   (5) The Privy Council under the Constitution   32

3.3 State and Federal Jurisdiction   32
   (1) The distinction between state and federal jurisdiction   32
   (2) Investing state courts with federal jurisdiction   33
   (3) Investing federal courts with state jurisdiction   38

3.4 Courts in Federal Territories   38

4 The Organization of the Judicial System   52

4.1 The Role of Courts and the Adversary System   52
   (1) The role of courts   52
   (2) The adversary system   53

4.2 The Judiciary   54
   (1) The appointment of judges   55
   (2) Independence, tenure, and dismissal of judges   56
   (3) The role of Chief Justices and Chief Judges   60
   (4) Extra-judicial uses of judges   60

4.3 The Legal Profession   62
   (1) Legal representation and legal aid   62
   (2) The organization of the legal profession   64
   (3) The law officers of the Crown   64

4.4 The Layman in the Judicial Process   65
   (1) Trial by jury   65
   (2) Other forms of lay participation in the judicial process   67

PART TWO   COURTS OF GENERAL JURISDICTION   79

5 Criminal Jurisdiction in Inferior and Intermediate Courts   81

5.1 Inferior and Intermediate Criminal Courts in Australia   81

5.2 Summary Jurisdiction in Australia   83
   (1) Courts of summary jurisdiction   83
   (2) Summary jurisdiction over federal offences   85

        (3) Appeals from courts of summary jurisdiction   86
        (4) Other problems of summary jurisdiction   87

5.3 Committal for Trial in Intermediate and Supreme
    Courts   88
        (1) The committal procedure   88
        (2) Committal for sentence   89
        (3) Alternatives to committal   90
        (4) The status and future of committal proceedings   90

5.4 Trial on Indictment in Intermediate Courts   91
        (1) The jurisdiction of intermediate criminal courts   92
        (2) Appeals from intermediate criminal courts   92

6   Civil Jurisdiction in Inferior and Intermediate Courts   100

6.1 The Development of Minor Civil Courts   100
        (1) The personnel of inferior and intermediate civil
            courts   101
        (2) The civil jurisdiction of intermediate civil courts   102
        (3) The civil jurisdiction of inferior civil courts   103
        (4) Invested federal jurisdiction in civil cases   104

6.2 Some Problems of Limited Civil Jurisdiction   104
        (1) Limited equitable jurisdiction   104
        (2) Avoiding jurisdictional limits   105
        (3) Increasing jurisdictional limits   108
        (4) The role of inferior civil courts   108

6.3 Relations Between Courts Exercising Civil
    Jurisdiction   109
        (1) Remittal of cases to lower courts   109
        (2) Removal to higher courts   110
        (3) Appeal and review   110

7   State and Territory Supreme Courts   117

7.1 The Structure and Personnel of Supreme Courts   117
        (1) Judges and other personnel   118
        (2) Administration and regulation of Supreme Court
            business   118

7.2 The Original Jurisdiction of Supreme Courts   119
        (1) Supreme Courts — superior courts of general
            jurisdiction   119
        (2) Common law and equity   122
        (3) Admiralty jurisdiction of Supreme Courts   123
        (4) Other jurisdictions   124

7.3 Supreme Courts as Courts of Appeal   124
        (1) The organization of appeals   124

    (2) Appellate jurisdiction of Supreme Courts   125
    (3) The functions of intermediate appeal courts   126

7.4 Some Problems of Practice and Procedure   127
    (1) Procedure in Supreme Courts   127
    (2) A unified civil jurisdiction?   127

8 The Federal Court of Australia   136

8.1 The Establishment of the Federal Court of Australia   136
    (1) The Federal Court controversy   136
    (2) The organization of the Federal Court   138

8.2 The Jurisdiction of the General Division of the Federal Court   138
    (1) Original jurisdiction   138
    (2) Appellate jurisdiction   141
    (3) Pendent, 'associated', and 'accrued' jurisdiction   142

8.3 The Federal Court and Conflict with State Courts   146
    (1) Resolving jurisdictional conflicts between state and federal courts   146
    (2) The debate over the merits of the Federal Court   148

9 The High Court of Australia   156

9.1 The Establishment and Constitution of the High Court   156

9.2 The Jurisdiction of the High Court   157
    (1) Original jurisdiction   157
    (2) Appellate jurisdiction   160
    (3) Removal and remittal of cases   163
    (4) Accrued jurisdiction in the High Court   164

9.3 Changes in the High Court's Jurisdiction and Composition   165
    (1) Further reform of the High Court's jurisdiction   165
    (2) Advisory opinions   167
    (3) Appointments to the High Court   169

9.4 The Role of the High Court   170
    (1) The High Court in constitutional cases   171
    (2) The High Court as a general court of appeal   173

PART THREE SPECIALIST COURTS AND TRIBUNALS   185

10 Family and Children's Courts   187

10.1 The History of Family Jurisdictions in Australia   187

10.2 The Family Court of Australia 189
   (1) The scope of federal family law power 189
   (2) The Family Court of Australia 192
   (3) The jurisdiction of the Family Court 194
   (4) Other problems of the Family Court 198
   (5) Proposals for additional Family Court jurisdiction 200
   (6) Assessment 201

10.3 State Family Jurisdictions 202
   (1) The Family Court of Western Australia 202
   (2) Other state family jurisdictions 203

10.4 Children's Courts 205
   (1) The philosophy and functions of children's courts 205
   (2) Children's courts in Australia 206
   (3) Diversion of young offenders from judicial process 207
   (4) Young offenders and the ordinary courts 208

11 Industrial Courts and Commissions 218

11.1 The History of Industrial Jurisdictions in Australia 218

11.2 The Federal System of Conciliation and Arbitration 219
   (1) The ambit of federal industrial power 219
   (2) The Australian Conciliation and Arbitration Commission 221
   (3) The Federal Court of Australia (Industrial Division) 223
   (4) Other federal industrial forums 224

11.3 Industrial Regulation in the States and Territories 225
   (1) State industrial commissions 226
   (2) Conciliation committees and other tribunals 227
   (3) Industrial courts 227
   (4) Industrial regulation in the territories 228
   (5) Industrial magistrates 228

11.4 The Future of Industrial Arbitration 228
   (1) Conflict and co-operation between the federal and state systems 228
   (2) Industrial jurisdictions and the ordinary courts 229
   (3) The future of industrial arbitration 230

12 Small Claims Courts and Tribunals 240

12.1 The Development of Small Claims Courts 240

12.2 Small Claims Courts and Tribunals in Australia 241

12.3 Further Reform in Small Claims Jurisdictions 245

13   Other Specialist Courts and Tribunals   251

13.1 Other Specialist Courts and Tribunals — A
      Conspectus   251

13.2 Some Examples of Other Specialist Courts   252
      (1) Licensing courts   252
      (2) Mining courts   252
      (3) Land and environment and local government courts and
          tribunals   253
      (4) Coroner's courts   256
      (5) Courts of disputed returns   256
      (6) Other courts   257

13.3 Proliferation in the Court System — Desirable, Avoidable,
      or a Necessary Evil?   257

13.4 The Relations Between the Ordinary Courts and Specialist
      Courts and Tribunals   258
      (1) Judicial review of decisions of inferior courts and
          tribunals   259
      (2) Review of decisions of federal tribunals and
          courts   260

PART FOUR   PROSPECTS FOR CHANGE   269

14   Reform of Australian Courts   271

14.1 An Increasing Pace of Change   271

14.2 Structural and Constitutional Issues   271

14.3 Alternative Dispute Resolution and the Future of the
      'Ordinary Courts'   272

Select Table of Cases   278
Index   280

Preface

In the first place, this is a student's book. There is a need for a concise account of Australian courts for first-year law students and others seeking an introduction to legal institutions in Australia. In those law schools where there is an introductory course on legal institutions, this book may accompany existing works on precedent, statutory interpretation, judicial law-making, and federal jurisdiction. Where there is no such course, new students will still need to have a general understanding of the matters discussed here, as a background to their study of other substantive law subjects.

There are, however, further justifications for the study of our law courts and tribunals. The structure of Australian government is increasingly studied, but most of the emphasis has been on the overtly 'political' institutions of Parliament, the executive government, and the civil service. Australia is not, or not yet, subject to a regime of 'government by judiciary', but courts and tribunals do have a significant impact, direct and indirect, on the ordinary person and on the system of government. As a matter of public administration, there is a need for greater study of the way in which these institutions work. This need has already been felt in other countries both within and outside the common law tradition. Common problems include striking the right balance between judicial independence and judicial accountability; the cost of legal services and the impact of legal aid; the extent to which civil disputes should be determined by the formal and sometimes protracted adversary process in ordinary courts of law or by less formal means, such as administrative tribunals; whether legal services should be provided in a few centres or be more widely decentralized; the division of jurisdiction between superior, intermediate, and inferior courts; the desirability of specialist courts for such matters as family law; the extent and costs of appeal and (in the case of administrative jurisdictions) the nature and extent of judicial supervision or control, and the structure and functions of the legal profession itself. Added to these common difficulties are those presented by a court structure organized along federal lines: problems of overlapping jurisdiction, or uncertainties as to the extent to which federal jurisdiction has pre-empted state courts in particular matters, have led to renewed demands for a unified structure of Australian courts. Some brief examination of these issues is necessary, both to assist in understanding the present system and, perhaps, to stimulate students, and the general reader, to reflect on the social function of courts in Australian society.

A second justification, and one of the chief interests in the history of legal institutions in Australia, lies in the way in which borrowed or transplanted rules or systems have been adapted to local needs or, in some cases, have continued in force despite their inappropriateness. In this respect Australia has a dual heritage, since the original reception of English models has had superimposed on it a federal judicial structure substantially borrowed from the United States. The result is a mixture ('blend' would be too strong a word) of diverse elements. Quite apart from whether it works, its characteristics have a comparative interest of their own. Again, these themes can only be hinted at, but they may provide intrinsic interest to a subject which is often regarded as dreary.

* * *

In revising this book for the second edition, I have adhered as far as possible to the structure of the first edition, but have sought to reflect, at least in outline, the major debates about the courts, their personnel, and functioning which have taken place since April 1981 (the effective date of the first edition), as well as the many changes in detail. The principal changes from the first edition include an expanded discussion of the constitutional (Chapter 3) and policy (Chapter 14) implications of some form of integrated court system; more detailed discussion of judicial independence and discipline (Chapter 4), reflecting both the controversy over Justice Lionel Murphy and the debates in New South Wales over judicial improprieties and how to deal with them; a discussion (Chapter 8) of the proposed cross-vesting legislation, in the context of the debate about the Federal Court and its impact on state courts; the deletion of the chapter on the Privy Council (with the final abolition of appeals in 1986 the Privy Council is no longer in any sense an 'Australian court', although an understanding of its role in the Australian legal system remains necessary, and I have expanded the discussion of it in Chapters 2 and 3 accordingly); a more extensive discussion of the sadly bitter and divisive debate about the Family Court (Chapter 10); and a more extensive discussion of questions of reform (Chapter 14), much of it based on the work of the Australian Judicial System Committee of the Constitutional Commission.

* * *

One of the difficulties in writing, and revising, a book of this sort is that there is often a difference between the law on paper and the way in which the institutions actually work. Australian court systems are such a morass of detail that inaccuracies cannot have been avoided. I would be grateful if readers could draw my attention to any such mistakes, so that they can be avoided in future.

So far as possible, the text is correct as at 1 May 1987, but a few subsequent references have been added.

Sydney
1 July 1987

Acknowledgements

In addition to those who helped with the first edition, I owe a considerable debt of thanks to Ms Anne Duffield, for tireless and meticulous research assistance, to Lynn Gemmell, for editorial assistance, and to Marisa Crawford, for patience inexhaustible.

Abbreviations

Note: Conventional abbreviations for law reports and journals have been used as far as possible, and these are not included here. This list, as well as setting out less well-known law reports and journals, includes other abbreviations used in the interests of conciseness.

Abel-Smith & Stevens	R. Abel-Smith & B. Stevens, *Lawyers and the Courts* (1967)
ABLR	*Australian Business Law Review*
AJLH	*American Journal of Legal History*
ALLR	*Australian Labour Law Reporter*
ASCL	*Annual Survey of Commonwealth Law*
Baker	J.H. Baker, *An Introduction to English Legal History* (2nd edn, 1979)
Beeching Report	UK, *Report of the Royal Commission on Assizes and Quarter Sessions* (Cmnd 4153, 1969)
Bennett, *History*	J.M. Bennett, *A History of the Supreme Court of New South Wales* (1974)
Bennett, *Keystone*	J.M. Bennett, *Keystone of the Federal Arch. A Historical Memoir of the High Court of Australia to 1980* (1981)

Bennett & Castles	J.M. Bennett & A.C. Castles, *A Source Book of Australian Legal History* (1979)
Blackshield	A.R. Blackshield, *The Abolition of Privy Council Appeals* (Adelaide Law Review Research Paper No. 1, 1978)
Blom-Cooper & Drewry	L. Blom-Cooper & G. Drewry, *Final Appeal. A Study of the House of Lords in its Judicial Capacity* (1972)
Broun & Fowler	M.D. Broun & S.G. Fowler, *Australian Family Law and Practice Reporter* (1976)
Castles	A.C. Castles, *An Introduction to Australian Legal History* (1971)
CLB	*Commonwealth Law Bulletin*
Cowen & Zines	Z. Cowen & L. Zines, *Federal Jurisdiction in Australia* (2nd edn, 1978)
Crawford	J. Crawford,'The New Structure of Australian Courts' (1978) 6 *Adel LR* 201
DCR	District Court Rules
de Smith	J.M. Evans, ed., *de Smith's Judicial Review of Administrative Action* (4th edn, 1980)
FCR	Federal Court Rules
Finlay	H.A. Finlay, *Family Law in Australia* (3rd edn, 1983)
FLC	Australian Family Law Cases
FLR	Federal Law Reports
FLR	*Federal Law Review*
Ford, Hearn & Lansbury	G.W. Ford, J.M. Hearn & R.D. Lansbury, *Australian Labour Relations: Readings* (3rd edn, 1980)
Guilty, Your Worship	Legal Studies Department, La Trobe University, *Guilty, Your Worship. A Study of Victoria's Magistrates Courts* (1980)

Hart & Wechsler	Hart & Wechsler's *The Federal Courts and the Federal System* (2nd edn, 1973)
HCR	High Court Rules
Higgins Royal Commission	Victoria, *Report of Royal Commission for . . . the Administration of Justice* (Chairman, H.B. Higgins) (1899)
Holdsworth, HEL	W. Holdsworth, *A History of English Law*, vol I (7th edn, 1956)
Howard	C. Howard, *Australian Federal Constitutional Law* (2nd edn, 1972)
Howell	P.A. Howell, *The Judicial Committee of the Privy Council 1833–1976* (1979)
Isaac & Ford	J.E. Isaac & G.W. Ford, *Australian Labour Relations: Readings* (2nd edn, 1971)
Jackson	R.M. Jackson, *The Machinery of Justice in England* (7th edn, 1977)
Jacob	H. Jacob, *Justice in America. Courts, Lawyers and the Judicial Process* (4th edn, 1984)
Klein	F.J. Klein, *Federal and State Court Systems — A Guide* (1977)
Lane	P.H. Lane, *Australian Federal Constitutional Law* (2nd edn, 1979)
LRC	Law Reform Commission (thus ALRC — Australian Law Reform Commission, etc)
LSB	*Legal Service Bulletin*
Macken	J.J. Macken, *Australian Industrial Laws. The Constitutional Basis* (2nd edn, 1980)
McCallum & Tracey	R.C. McCallum & R.R.S. Tracey, *Cases and Materials on Industrial Law in Australia* (1980)
Morison	W.L. Morison, *The System of Law and Courts Governing New South Wales* (2nd edn, 1984)

MULR	Melbourne University Law Review
NZLJ	New Zealand Law Journal
NZRCC	New Zealand, *Report of Royal Commission on the Courts* (1978)
Portus	J.H. Portus, *Australian Compulsory Arbitration* (2nd edn, 1979)
Quick & Garran	J. Quick & R.R. Garran, *The Annotated Constitution of the Australian Commonwealth* (1901, repr. 1976)
Radcliffe & Cross	Radcliffe & Cross' *The English Legal System* (6th edn, ed. G.J. Hand & D.J. Bentley, 1977)
Russell	E. Russell, *A History of the Law in Western Australia and its Development from 1829 to 1979* (1980)
Sawer, *Australian Federalism*	G. Sawer, *Australian Federalism in the Courts* (1967)
SCR	Supreme Court Rules
Seymour	J. Seymour, *Committal for Trial. An Analysis of the Australian Law together with an Outline of British and American Procedures* (1978)
Shetreet	S. Shetreet, *Judges on Trial. A Study of the Appointment and Accountability of the English Judiciary* (1976)
SMA Papers	First Convention of the Stipendiary Magistrates of Australia, *Papers* (1978)
Stevens	R. Stevens, *Law and Politics. The House of Lords as a Judicial Body, 1800–1976* (1979)
Syd LR	Sydney Law Review
Taylor, 'Small Claims'	G. Taylor, 'Special Procedures governing Small Claims in Australia', in M. Cappelletti & J. Weisner, eds, *Access to Justice*, vol. 2, *Promising Institutions* (1979) 595

UWALR	*University of Western Australia Law Review*
Wright	C.A. Wright, *Handbook of the Law of Federal Courts* (4th edn, 1983)

PART 1
General Principles

CHAPTER 1

The Development of Legal Systems

Human societies, especially those with any degree of economic and technical sophistication, need organizing. Organizing means (among other things) rules, and the tasks of making and applying rules, beyond a similar level of development, share in the specialization that is a mark of such societies. Obviously, how that specialization occurs, what sorts of institutions are set up and maintained, varies with each society. This story shows how one society does it.

In the beginning, there was a community, ruled over by a 'lawgiver', a person we may call the sovereign. At first the sovereign determined disputes between members of the community, but judging can be a lengthy matter, if there are many disputes or if the ways of dealing with them become more complicated, and the sovereign had other more urgent things to do. So judging was delegated to specialists, with a power to refer difficult or important matters to the sovereign. The specialists, the judges (as they became), developed formal procedures, and asserted their jurisdiction over a range of matters which, since their pay depended on court fees, tended to expand. There were conflicts with other jurisdictions, set up for other purposes, more or less defined. Each group of judges (that is, each court) developed a group of specialist pleaders, or advocates, and of solicitors, so-called becuase they were able to solicit work from ordinary people who were involved in disputes but who were not familiar with the procedures and rules of the court. Not surprisingly, the specialists strongly resisted attempts at simplifying their procedures and rules. For a long time they used an antique language, to increase the difficulty. With their specialization came monopoly. The judges excluded the pleaders, the pleaders excluded the procurers, the procurers excluded the public: the public, one way or another, paid for it all. The ultimate extension of the monopoly was the exclusion even of the sovereign: when he tried to re-assert the ancient prerogatives of personal justice he was told that he no longer spoke the right language, that he lacked 'the artificial reasoning and judgment of the law'.[1] His role was formalized out of existence; his person was (except ceremonially) ignored. So the rules, still enforced in his name, were administered by others, and legislation came to be fully external to the system of courts.

By this stage, 'system' was an inexact description of the way things were. There were many different courts, with much conflict and competition between them, and the result, while it was vigorous, was not tidy. Formal and procedural rigidity tended to cause injustice, and since the courts — caught up in a procedural tangle of their own making — did not act to remedy it, some further body had to be called on. That body, set up to dispense 'fairness' rather than 'law', built up its own body of practices — by a similar line of development itself became a court. Far from remedying them, its own rigidities added to those it had been set up to remedy. The augmented disorder again required the intervention of the sovereign, not in his excluded role of dispenser of justice but in his exclusionary role as law-maker. (Actually, the sovereign's role as law-maker had been formalized in much the same way: legislation had become, if not a job for specialists, at least one for representatives. But that is a matter for another book.)

Despite the opposition of vested professional interests, there was, eventually, general legislative reform. It was extensive, but much of the earlier fabric was left — a result dictated by the limited zeal of the reformers and the strength of the opposition. The earlier structures retained an influence: the system became an overlay of legislative order on the historical disarray.

At least, that is, in exaggerated outline, how it happened in England, between the eleventh and the nineteenth centuries.[2] But the system which had taken so long to grow was, even before this process was completed at home, transplanted to new countries with no institutions or with unwanted or unsuitable institutions. Australia was such a country, and it required institutions both of government and of imperial control. At first, little or no distinction was drawn between them, as the governors were imperial officials, under imperial direction. Later, with the introduction of representative government, the distinction became important, but local choice no less than central direction led to the adoption of English institutions.

However hard they tried (and in some cases they tried very hard indeed) the colonists could not simply reproduce the system at home. A much smaller society, with different needs, led to different jurisdictional forms. The structure became largely statutory and constitutional as the basic rules of government for the new country were settled and the residual forms of imperial control were shed. But the historical influence remains strong, and it is with an outline of its development and transplantation that we must start.

Notes

1 *Prohibitions del Roy* (1607) Co. Rep. 63. There is some doubt as to whether these famous words really were spoken by Coke CJ to James I; see Usher (1903) 18 *Eng Hist Rev* 664. But they do now represent the law, whether or not Coke's report is accurate. For Coke's role in the development of constitutional thought in the seventeenth century see e.g. Hill, *Intellectual Origins of the English Revolution* (1982) ch. 5.
2 And cf. Shapiro, *Courts. A Comparative and Political Analysis* (1981) ch. 2, for a similar version of the English story, focusing on the limits and meanings of judicial 'independence'.

CHAPTER 2

The Common Law Background

2.1 The Origins and Development of the Common Law

English and Australian legal institutions are founded, historically and conceptually, on the common law. This was the system of law which grew up in the King's courts at Westminster from the twelfth century onwards. Much later, it was modified and supplemented by a distinct, though partial, body of law, called equity, developed in the Court of Chancery. Since the 'fusion' of the two in the nineteenth century, it is convenient to describe all the non-statutory law applied in English and Australian courts as the common law.[1] It contrasts with statutory law, that is, laws enacted by a Parliament (legislation) or regulations made by some official or body under parliamentary authority (delegated legislation).

(1) The development of the common law in England[2]

There was little or nothing in the nature of a common law in England before the Norman Conquest. The Romans, departing over 600 years earlier, had left Christianity but not their law. Before 1016, England was divided into a number of kingdoms, and their laws had little more in common than is usual among societies at such a level of development. Even after the unification of England under Cnut, and despite an increasing degree of administrative centralization, most law was administered informally by the local assembly.[3] Thus the claim that the common law was in origin a customary law is doubtful, since there was no general custom on which to build. It is judge-made law, the 'sources' for which included some customs (especially in relation to land holding), some importation of foreign influences,[4] but much more importantly, the notions of justice and fairness of the judges, consolidated by their shared culture, their professional collegiality, and a growing tradition. The beginnings of the growth of judge-made law were therefore dependent on the appointment of judges — first appointed as surrogates for the King in the twelfth century.[5] Judges were directed to tour the country deciding cases; others followed the King or remained in London.

The common law was in origin the King's law, and for a time it co-existed with the law of the local communities of England. For example, in disputes over land the tenant had first to seek justice in the court of the lord from whom (under the system of feudal land tenure) he held the land. The King's courts had jurisdiction only if the land was held directly from the King, or if the feudal lord's court in some way failed to act. But the jurisdiction of the lord's courts was gradually eroded, by their failure to act or by the fiction, encouraged by the common law courts, that the lord had waived his jurisdiction. By means such as these, the common law courts came to regard themselves as applying the law of the land, not only a general law but a law which controlled and limited the various local or special jurisdictions.[6] As Hale was to express it four centuries later, because of the uncertainties and limitations in the jurisdiction of particular courts, 'the jurisdiction returns now to its original namely the common law by a kind of eschete or jus'.[7]

(2) The growth of equity

Whatever their pretensions, the common law courts were not yet in command of the field. They had themselves been created by a royal delegation of power, and the possibility remained of further delegations, or of the personal exercise of justice by the King in his Council.[8] The most important such delegation was to the Chancellor, who was recognized as having the power to do justice in cases where the common law, through the rigidity of its formulas, was unable or unwilling to help. This led to the development, from the fifteenth century onwards, of a body of rules supplementary to the common law, a sort of law in mitigation. This was called 'equity': starting out as an instinctive, unfettered justice according to the Chancellor of the time (it varied, the common lawyers scornfully said, 'according to the length of the Chancellor's foot'[9]), it became in time nearly as rigid a code as the old common law had been. Its operation can be seen in matters such as trusts, where someone agrees to hold property on behalf of someone else. The common law courts treated the holder as owner for all purposes, so that, unless there was a contract with the person for whom the property was intended, or with the person who gave the property in the first place, the holder could refuse to comply with the original trust. The Chancellor stepped in here, directing the holder (the trustee) to administer the property in favour of the beneficiary.[10] In the early seventeenth century it was settled that in case of conflicts such as this the rules of equity prevailed over those of the common law.[11]

The administration of law and equity in separate courts remained a feature of English law until the 1870s, when, as part of the union of the English courts into a single High Court, the Judicature Acts of 1873 and 1875 provided for the concurrent administration of law and equity, without any need for a case to be transferred from one division or court to another. Equitable remedies could thus be granted for common law rights and so on: in case of conflict, the rules of equity were to prevail. This is called the 'Judicature Act' system. Its Australian history is outlined in Chapter 7.

(3) Parliament and the common law
The origins of Parliament as the paramount legislative authority are still rather obscure.[12] The term was first used in the thirteenth century: it came to refer to the meeting of the King with the most important men of the kingdom, and the representatives of the towns and shires, in an enlarged *Curia Regis*. Its functions were to redress grievances and to vote money: the redress of grievances took the form partly of judicial, partly of legislative action (though the distinction was clouded for a long time). By the sixteenth century, its structure was well established: the King, a House of Lords composed of the hereditary peers, and a House of Commons composed of two representatives of each shire and borough. The distinction between Parliament's role as legislature and the judicial function of the courts was by then clear enough, but Parliament retained certain judicial powers, most notably the power to review decisions of the ordinary courts as an ultimate court of error, a power which from the fifteenth century was exercised by the House of Lords alone.

The legislative powers of Parliament, though large, were still of uncertain scope. Throughout the seventeenth century the idea persisted that there were certain fundamental rules or institutions of the common law which Parliament had no power to change. The idea faded after the Revolution of 1688,[13] and in the eighteenth century it came to be accepted that Parliament's legislative authority was plenary.[14]

2.2 The Development of the English Court System[15]

(1) The common law courts
Although they are for convenience separated here, it is artificial to distinguish the development of the law from the development of the courts. The processes occurred together; indeed, in a way the courts came *before* the law.

By the time of Magna Carta (1215) there was a need for a fixed seat of justice, apart from the court which followed the King on his travels through England. Clause 17 of Magna Carta required King

John to maintain a court for common pleas in some fixed place (in practice, Westminster). This was an attempt to re-establish a practice which had grown up under Henry II but which John had discontinued. Later in the century the distinction had hardened into the existence of two separate courts, the court *coram rege* (before the King), which came to be called the Court of King's Bench, and the fixed court at Westminster, the Court of Common Pleas. But these two courts were not the only places where judicial matters were dealt with. The first separate central administrative department to emerge was the Exchequer (the medieval treasury), and it developed a jurisdiction in cases related to royal revenue. The King also retained judicial powers, which he exercised, personally or through trusted advisers, in his council, the *Curia Regis*.

These embryonic courts developed at Westminster, or travelled with the King, but there was also a need for some more widespread system of royal justice. In particular, the jury, the mainstay of common law procedure, was supposed to come from the locality where the dispute or crime occurred, and it was highly inconvenient for local jurymen to have to attend one of the central courts. Two main devices were adopted for the decentralization of royal justice. First, criminal cases were tried by judges specially commissioned by the King to go to specific towns to hear and determine them, and to clear the gaols of accused persons. These came to be called commissions of oyer, terminer, and general gaol delivery,[16] and the commissioners (judges or leading practitioners) were called commissioners of assize. Their rounds, or circuits, were organized in the thirteenth century into a fixed pattern: the six circuits established in 1328 remained in being until 1971.[17] The most common method of trying civil cases was by the summoning of juries to Westminster or the court *coram rege*, unless (*nisi prius*) the judges had previously visited the locality to take the juries' verdicts. Judges would then be directed into the counties to hear the cases and to bring the verdicts back to the central court in which the case had begun, for it to be formally recorded. The *nisi prius* jurisdiction, as it was called, came to be combined with the exercise of criminal jurisdiction by the circuit judges on assizes.

Even with the assize system, the King's judges could not decide every minor criminal case, and to relieve the pressure local commissioners, called justices of the peace, appointed in each county, were given certain police powers as well as the jurisdiction (exercisable by at least two justices) to hear criminal cases. Their sessions, held four times a year, were called quarter sessions: by this means even the lesser criminal jurisdiction came to be exercised on behalf of the King, and subject to the supervision of the central courts.[18] Much later, with the advent of summary offences (created by statute), the justices of the peace were given this numerous jurisdiction, which they exercised throughout the year at what were called petty sessions.[19]

By the fourteenth century, therefore, there were three distinct superior courts of common law, King's Bench, Common Pleas, and Exchequer, all of which (including the formerly peripatetic King's Bench) had come to reside permanently in Westminster Hall in London. Despite some degree of overlap, their jurisdictions were in principle distinct; the supposed division of labour was stated in the early sixteenth century by Christopher St Germain in his popular treatise, *Doctor and Student*:

fyrste I shall shewe the how the custome of the realme is the verye grounde of dyuers courtes in the realme that is to say of the Chaunceyre where among other things, are obtained the original writs directed to the king's other courts, according to the needs of plaintiffs; of the kynges Benche where tresons, murders, homicides, felonies and other things done against the king's peace are dealt with; of the common place where common pleas are dealt with, that is to say such, tenements, debts, chattels and the like: and the Escheker wherein are conducted divers affairs only concerning the king himself, as of sheriffs, escheats, receivers, bailiffs, other royal officers and the like the whiche be courtes of recorde bycause none may syt as Iuge in the courtes but by the kynges letters patentes.[20]

But jurisdiction meant business and court fees, and there ensued a tortuous competition between the courts for that business. The details are given elsewhere:[21] for present purposes it is enough to summarize the position reached at the end of the eighteenth century. By that time the three common law courts had acquired a substantially similar general jurisdiction. In a few matters the original division of functions was preserved,[22] but both the Exchequer and the King's Bench had virtually full jurisdiction, under cover of various fictions, to hear common pleas of debt and the like. Although Common Pleas retained a monopoly over the old real actions,[23] effectively the same jurisdiction was exercised, less cumbrously, in both its rival courts by the machinery of ejectment.[24]

This was the strange and untidy position when the Australian colonies were founded.[25] Thereafter legislation, in particular the Uniformity of Process Act 1832, the Common Law Procedure Acts of 1852 and 1854, and the Judicature Acts of 1873 and 1875, brought major, much-needed reform.[26] The old system of specific writs and the forms of action were abolished; litigation was greatly simplified, and improved procedures for enforcement introduced. A simpler, uniform process made the historical differences between the courts appear largely irrelevant to their present functions, and the Judicature Acts merged all the superior courts into a single Supreme Court of Judicature, consisting of a High Court in five divisions and the Court of Appeal.[27] Each old common law court became a division of the High Court: in 1881, the three divisions were fused, so that the ancient jurisdiction of the three common law courts was exercised by a single division, the Queen's Bench Division, of the High Court.[28]

(2) The Court of Chancery[29]

The Chancery, like the Exchequer, was a department of government: one of its functions was the issuing and sealing of public documents, including writs commencing actions before the common law courts. These writs were at first framed to take account of the particular grievance for which they were sought, but after a time the categories of writ were regarded as closed. Thus in some cases the common law courts were unable to do justice, and petitions were brought to the King to remedy the defect. By the fifteenth century these were usually referred to the Chancellor, and it was through his decisions in these cases that the rules of equity developed. The Court of Chancery, as it became, had procedural advantages: cases were begun by a simple bill of complaint; jurisdiction over the defendant could be effectively established, and its decrees were directly enforced against the defendant. It had the substantive advantage of flexibility and fairness as a 'court of conscience' (though this depended on the Chancellor of the time), but by the eighteenth century these advantages had been largely dissipated by the inordinate delay, expense and complexity of Chancery litigation, and the increasing rigidity of the rules of equity. As with the common law courts, reform had to wait until the nineteenth century.[30]

(3) Other courts

Although the most important, these four were by no means the only courts in England. A system of ecclesiastical courts, set up by the Church and administering canon law, existed: the Reformation's only direct effect on the structure was the abolition of the appeal to Rome and the substitution of the Crown as the Head of the English Church. The central courts through which this supervisory jurisdiction was exercised were the Court of Delegates and the High Commission.[31] These ecclesiastical jurisdictions were of considerable importance since they dealt, among other things, with matrimonial cases and wills and inheritances. Another significant special jurisdiction was that of the Court of Admiralty, which dealt with maritime matters — prize (goods taken at sea during war), piracy, wreck, and generally with 'things done upon the sea'.[32] The most lucrative aspect of its jurisdiction was over merchants' contracts made abroad; this included many shipping matters. The Admiralty jurisdiction attracted the interest and enmity of the common lawyers, who in a sustained campaign in the seventeenth century succeeded in obtaining much of its commercial business.[33]

Other courts, such as the Court of the Constable and Marshall,[34] are of lesser importance for our purposes. There was also a patchwork system of minor civil courts called courts of requests,[35] but there was no uniform or effective jurisdiction over minor civil matters until the County Courts Act 1846.[36]

(4) The Council

Although these various courts came to be established by delegation or commission of the sovereign, there remained a residual jurisdiction exercisable by the King in his council of advisers. By a process of evolution the early undifferentiated *Curia Regis*, the central governing body, had by the mid-fourteenth century become several distinct bodies, each revolving around the King. Parliament was an enlargement of the *Curia Regis*, and it took with it certain judicial functions, in particular the power to review decisions of common law courts for error. But it had no original jurisdiction, nor was it a suitable body for giving the King regular advice on confidential or pressing matters.

For that purpose the King retained his council of advisers, which also exercised judicial powers over particularly important or intractable disputes (e.g. those between lords, or matters, such as disputes with foreign merchants, with international implications). This jurisdiction was exercised by virtue simply of the King's inherent residual powers of government, in other words, by virtue of the prerogative, which is the legal term for the special powers of the Crown recognized by the common law and not superseded by statute. For a long time the Council's jurisdiction was exercised in collaboration with, rather than confrontation to, the common law courts: the Council could (like the Parliament) seek the advice of the judges on any matter, and the methods of transfer of cases from ordinary courts to Council seem to have been informal.[37] The number of petitions coming before the Council required some degree of delegation: apart from the Court of Chancery, which was created in this way, there developed a number of courts, such as the notorious Court of Star Chamber, the Court of High Commission, and the Court of Requests.[38] These became a crucial part of the machinery of government from 1629 to 1640 when Charles I attempted to rule England without any Parliament, and their fate was bound up with the constitutional crisis that resulted. When Parliament was eventually reconvened, it immediately abolished the Star Chamber and the High Commission, and forbade the exercise of any Council jurisdiction with respect to England.[39]

After the Act of 1641 the Privy Council (as it was called by now) retained only the most minor jurisdiction in English cases,[40] but the Act was not regarded as having abolished the jurisdiction which the Council had already asserted, to hear appeals from courts established in Britain's overseas possessions.[41] Throughout the eighteenth century such appeals were heard by a committee of at least three Privy Councillors, whose advice to the Crown was embodied in an Order in Council. In form, then, an executive committee determined a judicial matter, with the result an act of legislation. In practice it came to be a settled understanding (or 'convention') that the Council's function was judicial and that its advice would always be accepted.[42] But other aspects of the Council's practice were highly unsatisfactory. There was no requirement that any member of the Appeals Committee be a lawyer; in some cases the legal members were outvoted by non-lawyers. The Committee, despite its fluctuating and occasional membership, was overloaded with appeals, many of which had no prospect of being heard. It sat only a few days in the year, those its members could spare from their other duties.[43] As an early instalment of the general court reforms of the nineteenth century, substantial reform of the Privy Council's judicial work was carried out.[44] The Judicial Committee Act 1833 established a Judicial Committee of the Council to which all judicial business would be referred. The Committee was to consist only of specified Privy Councillors, mostly judges or former judges. There were also various procedural reforms.[45]

Despite these changes, the Privy Council was by no means an ideal appellate court for distant colonies. When a party appealed a case to the Privy Council, the effect was to suspend enforcement of the judgment appealed from pending the appeal, usually for years rather than months. The respondent could be placed under great pressure to compromise the case rather than face the expense and uncertainty of the appeal. In 1856 the South Australian Governor remarked that appeals were 'in general unsatisfactory in the issue, expensive and tedious';[46] this was only one among many such complaints. Not until the improved communications of this century were these inherent defects of the appeal partly overcome. By then, new criticisms were being made, leading to the eventual, if gradual abolition of Privy Council appeals from most Commonwealth countries. In the case of Australia, this process began in 1903 but was not completed until 1986:[47] it is described briefly in Chapter 9.

(5) The development of appellate courts[48]

Finally, something should be said about the development of appeals in England. Originally, decisions of superior common law courts were final and without appeal (though a case might be adjourned for further consideration by the judges before the actual decision was given). Where a decision was reached by a single judge and jury, for example at *nisi prius*, the judgment had to be recorded in the Court from which the judge came. At this stage a party could move in arrest of judgment, or for a new trial, and the other party might be called on to show cause why the motion should not succeed. This was a sort of 'appeal' before all the judges of the Court, but it took place before rather than after the formal decision. The only machinery for upsetting a decision once recorded was a writ of error, an original proceeding before another court (King's Bench for Common Pleas; Exchequer Chamber for Exchequer and King's Bench; Parliament as a final resort). This was a very limited form of review, restricted to errors apparent in the formal record of the decision. Only in the nineteenth century was jurisdiction in error replaced by more satisfactory statutory procedures of appeal (which enabled the substantive decision, and in particular any legal issues involved, to be considered). In the case of Chancery, where there was no formal record, a distinct review on the merits had always existed, in the form of a rehearing by the Chancellor: it was established in 1675 that a further appeal lay to Parliament. From early on the House of Lords alone exercised the error and appeal jurisdiction of Parliament. This jurisdiction was substantially reformed in 1875, when a single Court of Appeal was also established for all civil cases.[49] Only then did the appeal by rehearing become the normal method of review of decisions.

2.3 The Reception of Common Law, Statutes, and Courts in Australia

Eastern Australia was settled by a mixed force of soldiers, convicts, and camp-followers in 1788. Problems of the reception of English law may not have had a first claim on the attention of the first settlers, but they were then, and continue to be, necessary to an understanding of Australian legal development.

(1) The reception of common law and equity

By the middle of the eighteenth century English law had developed a distinction between conquered or ceded colonies on the one hand and settled colonies on the other.[50] The pre-existing law in a conquered or ceded colony continued in force until altered by Parliament or the Crown (and the extent of Crown legislative authority in such a colony was considerable). In a settled colony, the common law, so far as appropriate, occupied the land with the first settlers — a form of intellectual baggage.[51] The distinction between the two kinds of colony is usually said to reflect the distinction in international law between conquest or cession of territory and occupation of *terra nullius* (land not 'owned' by any group or State, in international law); if so, the reflection was inexact, since territory which in international law was treated as ceded might still, for the purposes of the reception of the common law, become a settled colony. This would be so if the pre-existing law was thought to be wholly inappropriate to regulate the lives of the settlers.[52] Australia had been inhabited for many thousands of years before 1788, but whether or not it was then *terra nullius* in international law, it was treated as a settled colony for these purposes. Into the propriety of that decision, in the circumstances — as into the propriety of the acquisition of Australia in international law — the courts would not, and did not, inquire.[53]

Thus, in each of the Australian colonies the common law and the rules of equity were received — if not lock, stock and barrel, at least substantially. A few rules were inapplicable because of local conditions — for example there was never an Established Church, and so the rules of ecclesiastical law, and the ecclesiastical jurisdictions, were not received.[54] But the local reception of the common law was much more extensive than the reception of British statute law. It was no objection that conditions were initially inappropriate: a common law rule might be subsequently attracted as the colony matured.[55] As English decisions in common law and equity were followed in Australian courts as a matter of course, the initial reception flowed without much distinction into the assumptions of precedent.

Most of the common law and equitable rules relating to the jurisdiction and powers of courts were thus received, becoming applicable when the appropriate courts were established. The extent to which this reception was not merely assumed but clung to, as a mark of Englishness in a strange land, is shown by the way in which common law and equitable jurisdiction, vested in the same Supreme Court rather than in separate courts as in England, was administered separately, as nearly as possible in the English mode. By such imitation the professional lawyers managed to avoid the Judicature Act system until its adoption in England in 1875 — and in New South Wales, for a century beyond that.[56]

(2) The reception of statute law

As well as the common law and equity, some part of British statute law was also applied in the Australian colonies. There were two categories of such statutes. In the first place, by a common law rule, all statute law appropriate to the new colony was received into it.[57] It is disputed whether the date of reception was the date of settlement or of the establishment of a local legislature: it makes no difference in Australia since in each state the date has been fixed by statute.[58] Received statutes became part of the body of colonial law, but they had no special status, and could be amended or repealed by the local legislature. (Conversely, their status as part of the local law was not affected by their repeal by the British Parliament, unless the repealing Act was expressed to apply to the colony.) British statutes later than the date of reception were not applicable in this way.

Secondly, any Act of Parliament which expressly or by necessary implication applied to the colony did so of its own force, by virtue of British dominion and control over the colony. It did not matter whether such 'paramount force' statutes (as they were called) were passed before or after the date of settlement. Unlike a received statute, a paramount force statute could not be amended or repealed by the local legislature.[59] Such statutes thus provided a more rigid framework of imperial control.

In the case of the colonial judicial systems, 'patchwork' might be a better word. The major constituent Acts of the nineteenth and early twentieth centuries — the Australian Courts Act 1828,[60] the Australian Constitutions Act 1850,[61] the Colonial Laws Validity Act 1865, and the Commonwealth of Australia Constitution Act 1900 are the most important ones — were empowering rather than restraining laws. Apart from these, the paramount force statutes dealing with the courts fall into three groups. The Judicial Committee Acts of 1833 and 1844 (with subsequent amendments) were the most significant. They provided the statutory basis for appeals to the Privy Council from state courts, and (subject to the Commonwealth Constitution) also from federal and territory courts, until the remaining possibility of Privy Council appeals was abolished in 1986.[62] A number of statutes, especially the Colonial Courts of Admiralty Act 1890 (UK), dealt with admiralty and prize jurisdiction.[63] And five Acts, of rather minor significance, dealt with questions of evidence and foreign law.[64]

It is less easy to detail the relevant statutes which were received at settlement.[65] Many — such as Magna Carta 1297, the Petition of Right 1628, and the Bill of Rights 1688 — stated basic constitutional precepts in rather general terms — in terms of emphasis rather than enactment.[66] The powers of justices of the peace in matters of public order still derive in part from a statute of 1361, although at this remove it is hard to tell whether the statute operates of its own force or by a form of 'merger' with the common law.[67] Other examples included the Habeas Corpus Acts,[68] but not, it seems, the Act of Settlement 1700.[69] A considerable number of other received Acts dealt with miscellaneous subjects of procedure or jurisdiction.[70] The Privy Council apart, it could not be said that Australian legislatures were very closely fettered by an imperial statutory incubus, in establishing their judicial systems.

(3) The reception of legal institutions

In new settlements such as the Australian colonies, institutions, as distinct from rules, are not so much received as enacted. The general law would vest courts, once created, with jurisdictions and powers, but the creation of courts required action, either under the prerogative or imperial legislation. Thus we move from the common law background to the developing framework — the constitutional framework — of the courts in the Australian colonies.

Notes

[1] Many other former British territories retain a broadly common law system (e.g. New Zealand, Canada (except for Quebec, where most of the private law is French-based civil law), India and Pakistan, many former British colonies in Africa and the Caribbean, etc.), though with many variations between them, depending on the pre- existing law of the territory, post-independence developments, and the accidents of history.

[2] See Milsom, *Historical Foundations of the Common Law* (1969); Radcliffe & Cross, *The English Legal System* (6th edn, 1977) chs 5, 6, 10, 11; Baker, *An Introduction to English Legal History* (2nd edn, 1979) ch. 2; Hanbury & Yardley, *English Courts of Law* (5th edn, 1979) 15–92.

3 Brooke, *From Alfred to Henry III 871–1272* (1974) ch. 4; Holdsworth, *A History of English Law* (7th rev. edn, 1956) vol. 1, 1–32; Baker, ch. 1.
4 The major foreign influence was that of Roman or 'civil' law, especially in the twelfth but also to some degree in the sixteenth century. But for various reasons English law (unlike Scots law) developed largely in isolation from European influence: cf. Baker, 27–8; Plucknett (1939–40) 3 *U Tor LJ* 24.
5 Holdsworth, 1 HEL 36–7; Radcliffe & Cross, 27.
6 See Capua (1983) 27 *AJLH* 54.
7 *A Disquisition touching the Jurisdiction of the Common Law and Court of Admiralty* (British Library, Harg MS 93, f39). An 'escheat' is a reversion of property to a feudal lord or the King when there is no member of the family left to inherit the land. Hale uses it as a metaphor to express the supremacy of the common law over other jurisdictions. Matthew Hale (1609–76) was successively Chief Baron of the Exchequer and Chief Justice of the King's Bench. He wrote extensively on English law and legal history.
8 The common lawyers argued that this power had either been fully exercised or that its further exercise was prohibited by statute (see Baker, 83), but the statutes in question were by no means clear on the point.
9 *The Table Talk of John Selden* (ed. Pollock, 1927) 43. Selden (1584–1654) was a common lawyer, antiquary, and historian.
10 On the growth of equity see Baker, ch. 6; Radcliffe & Cross, chs 8–9; Holdsworth, 1 HEL ch. 5; Plucknett, *A Concise History of the Common Law* (1956) Part 5. The Exchequer also had an equitable jurisdiction (abolished in 1841): see Bryson, *The Equity Side of the Exchequer* (1975) chs 2, 5.
11 The point was settled by James I in 1616, adjudicating on a dispute between Lord Chancellor Ellesmere and Coke CJ: Holdsworth, 1 HEL 461–3.
12 Spofford, *Origins of the English Parliament* (1967); Wilkinson, *Constitutional History of Medieval England 1216–1399* (1958) III, chs 5–7.
13 Cf. Blackstone, *Commentaries on the Laws of England* (1765) I, 160.
14 Baker, 177–83; and see Gough, *Fundamental Law in English Constitutional History* (1958).
15 Apart from the works cited already, see Harding, *The Law Courts of Medieval England* (1973); Turner (1977) 21 *AJLH* 238; Baker, ed., *The Reports of Sir John Spelman* (1978) II, 51–82.
16 'Oyer' and 'terminer' from the French verbs 'to hear' and 'to determine'. A 'legal dialect' of French, called law French was used in the common law courts until 1732. See Baker (1984) 100 *LQR* 544.
17 On the circuit system see Abel-Smith & Stevens, *Lawyers and the Courts* (1967) s.v. 'Circuits'; Royal Commission on Assizes and Quarter Sessions (Beeching Report) (Cmnd 4153, 1969); Courts Act 1971 (UK); Jackson, *The Machinery of Justice in England* (7th edn, 1977) 75–80.
18 Holdsworth, 1 HEL 285–93.
19 Holdsworth, 1 HEL 293–8. See further Chapter 5.
20 *Doctor and Student, First Dialogue*, ch. vii (pub. 1523 in Latin; first pub. in English, 1531) (Plucknett & Barton, eds, 1974) 47. The speaker here is a student of the common law.
21 Baker, 36–43; Holdsworth, 1 HEL 219–22, 240.
22 Thus King's Bench retained its supervisory jurisdiction over inferior courts and officials by means of the prerogative writs of certiorari, prohibition, and mandamus: Holdsworth, 1 HEL 226–31, and see Chapter 13.

23 These were called 'real' actions because they dealt with title to 'real property', i.e. interests in land.
24 Baker, 252–5.
25 For an account of the position at about this time, given by the leading court reformer of the century, see Brougham's speech, 'The State of the Courts of Common Law', 7 Feb. 1828, *Hansard (NS)* XVIII, cols 127–247. Brougham (1778–1868) was a liberal politician, law reformer, and for a time (1830–4) Lord Chancellor, although he was unsuccessful in that office and never held office again.
26 Radcliffe & Cross, ch. 15; Holdsworth, 1 HEL ch. 8; Abel-Smith & Stevens, 29–76.
27 The five divisions were King's Bench; Common Pleas; Exchequer; Chancery; and Probate, Divorce, and Admiralty.
28 For the subsequent development of the English court system, see Jackson, Part II & 178–211; Abel-Smith & Stevens, Parts II & III. The divisions of the High Court at present are Queen's Bench, Chancery, and Family.
29 See the works cited above n10, and Jones, *The Elizabethan Court of Chancery* (1967); Ives (1968) 18 *TRHS* (5th ser.) 145.
30 Holdsworth, 1 HEL 467–9, 633–43.
31 See Duncan, *The High Court of Delegates* (1971); Houlbrooke, *Church Courts and the People during the English Reformation 1520–1570* (1979); Holdsworth, 1 HEL 580–632; Baker, ch. 8.
32 Holdsworth, 1 HEL 544–68, 656–8; Baker, 107–9; Wiswall, *The Development of Admiralty Jurisdiction and Practice since 1800* (1970); ALRC 33, *Civil Admiralty Jurisdiction* (1986) ch. 2.
33 Cf. Yale, in *Legal History Studies 1972*, 87. For the background to these 'civil law' jurisdictions, as they were called, see also Levack, *The Civil Lawyers in England 1603–1641* (1973).
34 Baker, 106–7; Holdsworth, 1 HEL 573–80; Squibb, *The High Court of Chivalry* (1959).
35 Many such local 'courts of requests' were established after 1660 by private Act of Parliament. They were courts of 'equity and good conscience', with jurisdiction in cases of debt up to 2 pounds, or in some cases 5 pounds. Though popular, their effectiveness was highly variable, and many litigants were not within the territorial jurisdiction of a court of requests. They were abolished in 1846. See Winder (1936) 52 *LQR* 369; Holdsworth, 1 HEL 187–91.
36 See Holdsworth, 1 HEL 187–91.
37 On the early Council see Baldwin, *The King's Council in England during the Middle Ages* (1913); Holdsworth, 1 HEL 477–525; Radcliffe & Cross, chs 7, 20.
38 Cf. Baker, 101–6. The Court of Requests was a sort of 'poor man's Chancery' which grew up in the late fifteenth century. Though not suppressed with the other conciliar courts in 1641 in fact it ceased to exercise any jurisdiction shortly thereafter: Holdsworth, 1 HEL 412–16. But its name, and purpose, were taken over by the local courts of requests: above n35.
39 By the Act 16 Charles I c.10 (1641).
40 Holdsworth, 1 HEL 524–5.
41 For the uncertain process by which this jurisdiction was asserted after 1641 see Smith, *Appeals to the Privy Council from the American Plantations* (1950) chs 1–3; Blackshield, *The Abolition of Privy Council Appeals* (1978) 20–3.

42 Cf. *Ibralebbe v R* [1964] AC 900, 919–23; *Commonwealth v Queensland* (1975) 134 CLR 298; Howell, *The Judicial Committee of the Privy Council 1833–1976* (1979) 35–8. But the formal nature of the Committee's judgment as 'advice' to the sovereign is still reflected in its practice of delivering a single judgment embodying that advice. Indeed, until the Judicial Committee (Dissenting Opinion) Order in Council 1966 allowed them, no dissenting opinions were given, nor was the existence of any dissent disclosed. See Blom-Cooper & Drewry, *Final Appeal* (1972) 110–11, 401–2.
43 Cf. Brougham, *Hansard (NS)* XVIII, 154–62 (1828).
44 On these reforms see Howell, chs 1, 2; Stevens (1964) 80 *LQR* 343; Swinfen (1974) 90 *LQR* 396.
45 For an account of the later nineteenth-century statutes dealing with the Privy Council see Howell, 48–71.
46 Quoted by RM Hague, *The Court of Appeals* (1940) 17. See also the opinions set out in Bennett & Castles, *A Source Book of Australian Legal History* (1979) 241–6.
47 See the Australia Act 1986 (Cth) s11; Australia Act 1986 (UK) s11; (1986) 60 *ALJ* 253.
48 Baker, 116–23; Radcliffe & Cross, ch. 13; Holdsworth, 1 HEL 222–6, 242–6, 357–94, 642–5.
49 The Judicature Act 1873, which established the Court of Appeal, abolished the appellate jurisdiction of the House of Lords. However, a reprieve was given by the Judicature Act 1875 and the abolition never came into effect. Instead the Appellate Jurisdiction Act 1876 provided for judges, called Lords of Appeal in Ordinary, to sit as an Appellate Committee of the House to hear appeals. Proposals to merge the appellate jurisdiction of the House of Lords and the Privy Council into one Supreme Court for the Empire came to nothing. See Stevens (1964) 80 *LQR* 343; Blom-Cooper & Drewry, 18–43. Criminal appeals were not established until as late as 1907: Jackson, 203–4.
50 Blackstone, *Commentaries* (1765) I, 108–9; *Blankard v Galdy* (1692) 4 Mod 222, 87 ER 359; *Anon.* (1722) 2 P. Wms 75, 24 ER 646. These principles were early affirmed in the High Court: *Delohery v Permanent Trustee Co. of NSW* (1904) 1 CLR 283.
51 See Windeyer, *Lectures on Legal History* (2nd rev. edn, 1957) 296–313; Castles, *An Introduction to Australian Legal History* (1971) 114–44; Castles (1963) 2 *Adel LR* 1; Bennett & Castles, 263–91.
52 As with the North Island of New Zealand: see Crawford, *The Creation of States in International Law* (1979) 177–84; Evatt, in Alexandrowicz, ed., *Grotius Society Papers 1968* (1970) 16.
53 Attempts on the part of Aboriginal people to litigate these issues have failed: *Coe v Commonwealth* (1978) 18 ALR 592, (1979) 24 ALR 118. The argument that after occupation certain land rights subsisted in the aboriginal inhabitants, recognized by the common law, was rejected in *Milirrpum v Nabalco Pty Ltd* (1971) 17 FLR 141, but is still open in the High Court: cf. (1979) 24 ALR 113, 129–30 (Gibbs J) 135–6 (Jacobs J); 137–8 (Murphy J). See also ALRC 31, *The Recognition of Aboriginal Customary Laws* (1986) ch. 5; Bennett & Castles, 247–63.
54 Campbell (1964) 4 *Syd LR* 343, 363–6.
55 *Cooper v Stuart* (1889) 14 App Cas 286 (PC).
56 And cf. *Dugan v Mirror Newspapers* (1978) 22 ALR 439 (HC); *SGIC v Trigwell* (1979) 26 ALR 67 (HC).

20 • *General Principles*

57 *Quan Yick v Hinds* (1905) 2 CLR 345; *Mitchell v Scales* (1907) 5 CLR 405; Castles, 145–66.
58 For the four eastern states, 25 July 1828 was fixed as the date of reception by the Australian Courts Act 1828 s24. See now Imperial Acts Application Act 1969 (NSW) s5; Constitution Act 1975 (Vic.) s3; Supreme Court Act 1867 (Qld) s20. For WA and SA it was fixed at settlement (1 June 1829 & 28 Dec. 1836 respectively): see Interpretation Act 1918 (WA) s43; Acts Interpretation Act 1915 (SA) s48.
59 Colonial Laws Validity Act 1865 (UK) s2. Earlier there had been controversy about the extent to which colonial legislatures could modify general common law principles. For the activities of Boothby J in South Australia see Castles, 155–6; Hague, 'Mr Justice Boothby' (MS, Adelaide Law Library, ?1961). It was to settle this doubt that the Act of 1865 was passed. The Statute of Westminster 1931 (UK) abrogated the 1865 Act so far as the British Dominions was concerned (it was applied to the Commonwealth from 1939 by the Statute of Westminster Adoption Act 1942 (Cth)). But the Statute had no application to the states, which remained bound by the Colonial Laws Validity Act until the passage of the Australia Acts 1986 s3. See Castles [1962] *Public Law* 175; Watts (1987) 36 *ICLQ* 132.
60 9 Geo 4 c.83; Bennett & Castles, 72–84.
61 13 & 14 Vic c.59; Lumb, *The Constitutions of the Australian States* (4th edn, 1986) 16–19. The Act was to provide a basis for the enactment of constitutions for each colony.
62 In the case of Australia the process of abolishing Privy Council appeals was an extraordinarily complex and lengthy one. Its principal stages were as follows: 1901 (appeals from the High Court in *inter se* questions required leave of High Court); 1903 (no appeals from courts exercising federal jurisdiction other than the High Court); 1968 (no appeals from federal courts, territory Supreme Courts, and the High Court exercising federal jurisdiction); 1975 (no appeals from the High Court in any case); 1986 (remaining appeals abolished by Australia Acts 1986 (UK & Cth) s11). See the first edition of this book, ch. 10; Blackshield, 16–23, and see further Chapter 9.
63 Admiralty Offences (Colonial) Act 1849; Admiralty Offences (Colonial) Act 1860; Colonial Courts of Admiralty Act 1890; Prize Courts Act 1894.
64 Evidence on Commission Act 1831; Foreign Tribunals Evidence Act 1856; Evidence by Commission Act 1859; British Law Ascertainment Act 1859; Foreign Law Ascertainment Act 1861.
65 Only Victoria and NSW have 'codified' the received statute law. See Victoria: Imperial Acts Application Act 1922 & Explanatory Paper (Sir Leo Cussen); Imperial Acts Application Act 1980; Imperial Law Re-enactment Act 1980; Statute Law Revision Committee, Report (PP 10/1979); NSW: Imperial Acts Application Act 1969; NSWLRC, *Report No. 4 on the Application of Imperial Acts* (1967). See also ACTLRC, *Report on Imperial Acts in force in the ACT and Supplementary Report* (1973).
66 For example, the famous clause 29 of Magna Carta (25 Edw I c.29, a re-enactment of the original Charter of 1215) provided that no freeman should be condemned 'but by lawful judgment of his peers, or by the law of the land'. For the controversy over the application of clause 29 to trial by jury in the Australian colonies see Castles (1975) 5 *Adel LR* 294.

67 34 Edw III c.1 (1361). See *R v Wright, ex p Klar* (1971) 1 SASR 103. In some states these provisions have been re-enacted as part of local law: e.g. Imperial Laws Application Act 1969 (NSW) s30.
68 Habeas Corpus Acts 1640, 1679, and 1816. See *Ex parte West* (1861) Legge 1475. Habeas corpus is the remedy used for procuring the release of someone wrongfully detained or imprisoned.
69 Cf. Lindell (1980) 54 *ALJ* 628.
70 See the works cited above n65, and SALRC, *61st Report relating to the Inherited Imperial Law and the Civil Jurisdiction and Procedure of the Supreme Court* (1980).

CHAPTER 3

The Constitutional Background

3.1 The Constitution of State Courts

'Constitution' is an ambiguous word. The United Kingdom has no constitution in the sense of a fundamental written instrument of government, but it has a constitution in the sense of a collection of common law rules and statutory provisions which are regarded as fundamental, even though they can be changed in the ordinary manner. A system of government could grow up in this flexible, unstructured way, but it could not be transplanted to colonies in a new country without some more rigid form of control. From the first, the Australian colonies were to be restrained in writing, and the enactment of colonial constitutions, though it increased the measure of responsible self-government and reduced the measure of imperial control, was another step towards constitutional government, not only in the second sense but in the first, more formal one.

On the other hand, the disputes which prompted these constitutions were — at any rate after 1823 — more about the extent of local legislative autonomy and the relations between the executive and Parliament or between the two Houses, than they were about the courts. General legislative competence, achieved for five of the six Australian colonies by the 1850s,[1] carried with it the power to legislate for the courts, but, apart from the tenure of Supreme Court judges, few judicial guarantees were thought necessary. With only a few exceptions, the constitutions of the Australian states continue to reflect this balance.[2] To this extent the 'constitution' of state courts remains flexible in the same way as the constitution of English courts on which they were largely modelled. Guarantees relating to the judicial system, in the first, strict, sense had to await the federal Constitution, when the balance between imperial control and constitutional self-government was shifted decisively to the latter.

(1) The development of colonial courts

Whatever the underlying or ultimate reasons for its foundation, the settlement of New South Wales was initially a military establishment, an 'open gaol' for transported convicts. Its institutions were adapted to this end: the very extensive, almost dictatorial power of the Governor; a criminal court manned by officers and with a procedure more like a court martial than a common law court,[3] and a civil court established under the prerogative (without statutory authority),[4] also with a very summary procedure. In neither civil nor criminal cases was there trial by jury.[5] In the fifteen or so years before 1823, the arrangements for civil and criminal jurisdiction were increasingly a matter of controversy and criticism, and they were to form one of the subjects of inquiry for Commissioner Bigge, appointed in 1819 to inquire into the affairs of the settlement.[6] The second of Bigge's three reports, on the *Judicial Establishments of New South Wales and Van Diemen's Land* in 1823,[7] led to the passing of the Act of 1823 'for the better Administration of Justice in New South Wales and Van Diemen's Land'. The Act established Supreme Courts in New South Wales and Tasmania, separated the Tasmanian courts from those of New South Wales, and provided for inferior courts more in line with the accepted English model.[8] Thereafter, the creation of the new Australian colonies was not attended by the same difficulties, and similar provision was made for a Supreme Court and inferior courts at the same time as, or soon after, their creation.[9] Trial by jury, in civil and criminal cases, followed, though in New South Wales not until the 1840s.[10]

(2) The constitution of state courts

The structure and jurisdiction of state courts, many of them legally continuous with the courts established in 1823 for New South Wales and Tasmania, or on the foundation of the other colonies,[11] are dealt with in later chapters. But an account of the constitutional background to the Australian courts would not be complete without some reference to the relevant state constitutional provisions.

As has been suggested, such an account can be brief. The first constitutions, apart from conferring a general legislative power extending to the judicial system, made provision only for the tenure of Supreme Court judges during good behaviour, with a power to remove them on an address of both Houses of Parliament, and for the payment of judicial salaries and pensions.[12] Moreover, until recently, state constitutions have been of a 'flexible' nature: that is, they could be amended without any onerous requirements of manner and form, such as a referendum or an intervening election.[13] As a result, no express guarantees of the preservation of the judicial system existed. Recently there has been a tendency to 'entrench' particular constitutional provisions, dealing with matters such as the constitution of Parliament, the electoral system, and so on, by requiring special majorities or referendums before they can be amended. But with one exception, this tendency has not extended to the judicial system. The Tasmanian and New South Wales constitutions do not deal with the judicature at all.[14] The Queensland, South Australian, and Western Australian constitutions provide only for the tenure of Supreme Court judges.[15] The exception is Victoria: its constitution of 1975 incorporates the basic provisions for the Supreme Court, which in other states are to be found in the Supreme Court Act, and these are (rather weakly) entrenched.[16] The difference is perhaps symbolic, and there has been no corresponding movement in other states to include in their constitutions more adequate provision for the integrity of the judicial system.

An alternative to constitutional protection under state constitutions would be to insert overriding protections in the federal Constitution. It is by no means unusual for federal constitutions to guarantee, at least in general terms, the integrity of the judicial systems of the constituent states or provinces: this is the case, for example, in Canada, the United States, the Federal Republic of Germany, Brazil, and Austria. Entrenchment of basic standards of judicial tenure and independence would provide a degree of legal, and perhaps psychological, protection to state judges that they may not enjoy now. At least this was the view of the Judicial System Committee of the Australian Constitutional Commission, which recommended that the federal Constitution contain effective guarantees of judicial tenure, appeal to the High Court, and trial by jury in respect of state and territory as well as federal courts.[17] On the other hand such proposals are regarded by state (and even territory) governments as yet another case of federal interference in their affairs, on the basis that the federal Constitution is a constitution of the federal government rather than of the nation. The combination of such states' rights arguments and arguments based on the need for administrative flexibility is likely to prevent any extension of constitutional protection to state courts.

(3) Appeals from state courts

During the nineteenth century providing an adequate appeal from Supreme Courts was a constant problem. In most states a 'Local Court of Appeals' was established in the form of the Governor in Council: it was hardly satisfactory.[18] The Privy Council heard appeals from state courts, as of right or by leave of the local Supreme Court or by special leave of the Privy Council itself. But the expense and delay of these appeals provoked much criticism. The need for a more accessible Australian court of appeal was one of the factors in the movement for federation,[19] and the federal Constitution (s73) guaranteed access to the High Court on appeal from state Supreme Courts. The present extent of that appeal (which is now, with the abolition of appeals to the Privy Council from all Australian courts,[20] the only form of appeal from state Supreme Courts) is dealt with in Chapter 9.

3.2 The Constitution of Federal Courts

(1) The constitutional settlement

The Commonwealth of Australia Constitution Act 1900, which brought about the federation of the six Australian colonies, was an Act of the Imperial Parliament. But it was almost entirely drafted by delegates from the colonies, at four conventions held in Australia from 1890 to 1898.[21] In formulating the judicial provisions of the Constitution, the delegates were confronted with two quite different models, which may be described as the unitary and the federal. The unitary model, a result of recent English influence, was represented by the six Supreme Courts, now based (for the most part) on the post-1873 English Supreme Court of Judicature. These were courts of general jurisdiction, with no very specific constitutional role. By contrast, the federal court system of the United States suggested a strict separation of 'federal' from 'state' matters in parallel, partial jurisdictions, together with a federal Supreme Court which (unlike the Appellate Committee of the House of Lords) would have an extensive original jurisdiction and a specific mandate to supervise and enforce the Constitution.

Like most conferences, what the Conventions produced was a compromise. On the one hand, the High Court of Australia, which was to be established under Chapter III of the new Constitution, was to have an extensive original jurisdiction in 'federal' matters, modelled closely on that of the United States. It was to have specific constitutional responsibilities. It could be assisted, in the application of federal law, by other federal courts which the Commonwealth Parliament was given power to establish. On the other hand state courts would continue to be courts of general jurisdiction, deciding federal as well as state matters (unless some federal court was given exclusive responsibility for a subject). The Commonwealth Parliament was given power to invest state courts with further jurisdiction in federal matters — something the US Congress could not do. And, unlike the US Supreme Court, the High Court was to be a general appeal court from state Supreme Courts, in state as well as federal matters. Under this compromise, whether the Australian system was to become more like that of Britain or the United States would depend on the way in which Parliament exercised its powers, on the one hand, to entrust federal matters to existing state courts, on the other, to establish federal courts with exclusive jurisdiction to determine cases arising under federal law. As will be seen in Chapter 8, the issue is with us still.

Providing for a system of courts was only a part — if an important part — of the general constitutional arrangements for federation. What concerned the delegates most was the financial arrangements between the new Commonwealth and the states. What proved to be more significant, in the long run, was the distribution of legislative powers: the Commonwealth Parliament was given a quite extensive list of powers to legislate on subjects such as interstate trade and commerce, taxation, defence, posts and telegraphs, banks, trading and financial corporations, external affairs, and so on. More important, for our purposes, was the addition of powers (not contained in the US Constitution) over a number of legal and commercial subjects which, as well as enabling uniform legislation to be applied throughout Australia, would call either for special courts, or jurisdictions, to apply the legislation. These powers included bankruptcy and insolvency, divorce and matrimonial causes (including related issues of custody of children and maintenance), and the conciliation and arbitration of industrial disputes extending beyond any one state.[22]

The purpose of a constitution is not merely to create the organs of power but to provide safeguards against its abuse. A number of safeguards, direct and indirect, were incorporated into Chapter III, the 'Judicature' section: these were the central role of the High Court, the separation of judicial from non-judicial power, and guarantees of judicial independence and trial by jury. They will be discussed in turn.

(2) The role of the High Court

Central to the constitutional scheme was the new High Court, which s71 said 'shall be' created. Although it was not stated in so many words, the High Court was to determine questions of constitutionality of legislation, arising between the states and the Commonwealth or in the course of ordinary litigation between private parties.[23] It was given a guaranteed original jurisdiction in a variety of 'federal' and 'national' matters (s75): these included cases arising under treaties, involving representatives of foreign countries, between the Commonwealth and the states or between states, between residents of different states, or involving claims against the Commonwealth or its officers. Jurisdiction over a variety of other matters (including cases arising under the Constitution or under federal laws, cases of admiralty and maritime jurisdiction, and cases involving interstate conflicts of laws) could also be given by federal law under s76. Even more importantly, s73 gave the High Court a broad appellate jurisdiction which, in the case of state Supreme Courts, also contained an irreducible minimum. The restriction on Privy Council appeals, brought about by s74, also depended on the availability of the High Court as the primary Australian court of appeal.

(3) The separation of 'judicial power'[24]

(A) THE SEPARATION OF POWERS UNDER THE CONSTITUTION

Section 71 of the federal Constitution requires 'the judicial power of the Commonwealth' to be vested in the High Court and other federal courts or courts invested with federal jurisdiction. The clear intention was to reserve the exercise of 'judicial power' to properly constituted courts (federal or state), so as to prevent the threat to liberty traditionally associated with uncontrolled legislative and executive power.[25] The need was all the greater because of the federal nature of the Constitution, which required some independent authority to decide disputes between the Commonwealth and the states. That only the courts listed in s71 can exercise federal judicial power has never been doubted.[26]

The converse proposition — that federal courts could only exercise judicial power — did not seem as obvious. True, s71, with its 'exhaustive statement of the manner in which the judicial power of the Commonwealth is or may be vested',[27] was paralleled by similar statements in ss1 (legislative) and 61 (executive power). The pattern was very much that of the US Constitution, with its strict separation both of powers and of the organs of power. But under the Australian Constitution the legislative and the executive were *not* separate and distinct: on the contrary, members of the executive government were required to be members of the House of Representatives or senators (Constitution s64), and the executive was not prevented from exercising legislative functions (usually under powers delegated by Parliament).[28] The Constitution, far from separating executive from legislature, intended to establish the British — and Australian colonial — system of ministerial responsibility. Legally, the executive was to be as much the servant of the legislature as, politically (given a party majority in both Houses), the legislature would be the servant of the executive. The effect was to weaken, if not destroy, the 'logical inferences from . . . the form and contents of sections 1, 61 and 71',[29] emphasizing instead the distinctive and separate role of the federal judiciary. The point is that, discarding any superficial symmetry of drafting, judicial power is not like legislative or executive power, if only in that it is, unlike them, inherently non-delegable. Judging is a personal responsibility, not a general mandate.[30]

For fifty years the decisions on judicial power bore out this analysis. It was always assumed that judicial power could be vested only in s71 courts, but beyond that there was no objection to federal courts exercising distinct non-judicial functions (provided that these were not in some way inconsistent with or destructive of the court's truly judicial functions). The point arose most often over the Commonwealth Court of Conciliation and Arbitration. Its functions, pursuant to s51(35) of the Constitution, were to settle interstate industrial disputes by making and enforcing industrial awards. To enforce an award was clearly a judicial exercise, but to make an award was more in the nature of legislation. In *Alexander's case* (1918),[31] it was held that the Commonwealth Court, if it was to exercise the judicial function of enforcing awards, had to be constituted under Chapter III, but there was no hint of any view that, so constituted, the Court could not also exercise the non-judicial power of making awards.[32]

This was to reckon without Dixon CJ. He had earlier indicated his adherence to the strict separation of judicial from other powers, and in *R v Kirby, ex parte Boilermakers' Society of Australia* he persuaded a majority of the High Court to his view — a view endorsed by the Privy Council on appeal.[33] Thus it was held that the Commonwealth Court could not exercise both judicial and non-judicial power, and since, despite its being constituted a court under s72, its primary function was the non-judicial one of making awards, it could not validly enforce them.

The Commonwealth's immediate response was to separate the conciliation and arbitration function (vested in a Conciliation and Arbitration Commission) from the enforcement function (vested in the Commonwealth Industrial Court).[34] This solved the particular problem, at least for the time being,[35] but with the decision in the *Boilermakers' case*, the definition of 'judicial power' took on a new importance.

(B) THE DEFINITION OF 'JUDICIAL POWER'
As the cases demonstrate, classifying a power as 'judicial' is not a simple matter. The question arises in two distinct ways: in determining whether a power, classified as judicial, is invalidly vested in a body which is not a s71 court; and in determining whether a power, classified as non-judicial, is invalidly vested in such a court. The core issue may be the same, but the two contexts provide a different — in practice very different — direction to the inquiry.

The core of 'judicial power' probably lies in two things: the determination between parties of disputed issues of law with binding effect on those parties, and the enforcement by court order or decree of rights or liabilities ascertained according to a pre-existing standard. The making of an arbitral award, though a binding settlement of a dispute between parties, was held not to be judicial because it involved broad elements of discretion, and because there was no pre-existing rule which the arbitrator could be said to apply.[36] On the other hand, the making of an eviction order between landlord and tenant on specified grounds was a form of enforcement, and was judicial.[37] To restrain parties to an agreement in restraint of trade from performing the agreement was not a judicial power, where the order operated only prospectively, and was made on an assessment of general considerations of public policy.[38] But to punish violation of such an order would be judicial. Many other examples could be given.

A power will be classified as judicial as it approximates to either of the paradigms of judicial power: the converse is true of non-judicial powers. But the cases have shown much more subtlety and flexibility than this brief summary might indicate. For example, a power which, vested in an administrative agency, would be held to be non-judicial, may still be properly vested in a court (even if the same words are used). This may be so because the power is 'neutral', 'colourless' or 'incidental', taking its character from the body which is to exercise it, or because the context — the vesting of the power in a court or a non-court — indicates the standards by which the power is to be exercised — and thus, classified![39] A choice of 'appeals' from an administrative decision, such as a tax assessment, to an administrator or to a court, has been upheld on the basis that the administrator is to review the decision on its merits, whereas the court is to review it 'judicially', by the application of legal standards.[40] Functions which have historically been exercised by courts have been upheld, even though they involved a very large element of discretion (e.g. the general powers of a court to award maintenance or to make orders affecting property on a divorce, and the powers of judicial management of the property of bankrupts and wards of court).[41]

Conversely, binding decisions by administrative agencies on questions of fact have been held non-judicial, at least where no very elaborate standard for the assessment of the facts was involved. Administrative determinations of 'jurisdictional facts' (preconditions for further action) have been upheld, where these were preliminary to clearly administrative decisions.[42] The effect has been that only in extreme cases is the judicial power doctrine likely to invalidate carefully drafted legislation, as the case-law of the last fifteen years has shown.[43]

(C) EXCEPTIONS TO THE 'JUDICIAL POWER' DOCTRINE
Apart from the flexibility introduced by these devices, a number of distinct exceptions exist to the separation of judicial power. State and territory courts do not have to comply with s72 in order to exercise judicial power under federal laws.[44] Parliament retains the apparently 'judicial' power to adjudicate on its privileges and to punish for contempt of Parliament, as a result of its inheritance of the powers and privileges of the British House of Commons.[45] Certain disciplinary powers, exercised within the police force, the army and similar bodies, though they involve 'pains and penalties', do not contravene the separation of powers. The extreme case is military court martial: even where the death penalty can be imposed, a court martial need not be constituted as a Chapter III court.[46]

A less dramatic exception, but one of considerable importance, is the so-called *persona designata* doctrine. Chapter III requires judicial power to be vested in a court, but it does not require that judges of a court only act in that capacity. A judge may be appointed to perform a non-judicial function — as an ambassador, or as a Royal Commissioner inquiring into some subject — in his or her personal capacity. The judge is then acting not as a judge but as a person designated to perform that function. This has been the basis for a quite extensive use of federal judges for other roles: as Presidential Members of the

Administrative Appeals Tribunal (a non- judicial body),[47] even as Director-General of ASIO. To what extent judges *should* be used in that way is another question (one which is discussed in the next chapter), but the constitutionality of the practice is established.[48]

(D) THE FUTURE OF THE 'JUDICIAL POWER' DOCTRINE

Despite these extensive qualifications and exceptions, the question has been raised whether the *Boilermakers'* rule should be maintained. Barwick CJ several times argued that the rule is 'unnecessary . . . for the effective working of the Australian Constitution or for the maintenance of the separation of the judicial power of the Commonwealth or for the protection of the independence of courts exercising that power'.[49] But the Court as a whole has avoided deciding the question. Indeed, in view of the flexibility that has been shown in applying it, it may be doubted how much practical difference there would be between the present rule and its alternative, or whether the case will ever arise requiring that choice to be made. The experience of the 1976 *Joske case*[50] — where a Full Court was convened to reconsider the rule, but the case went off on the 'incidental' ground — suggests that the *Boilermakers'* doctrine may remain intact, suspended as a sort of 'hypothetical question' above the administrative reality of the rule as actually applied.[51] It would be a nice irony.[52]

(4) Other constitutional guarantees

Several other guarantees of the integrity of the federal judicial process should be referred to.

(A) JUDICIAL TENURE

Section 72 of the Constitution, as enacted in 1900, provided that High Court and other federal judges should not be removed except 'on an address from both Houses . . . on the ground of proved misbehaviour or incapacity'. This fundamental guarantee of security of tenure was more stringent than the equivalent provisions for state judges in several ways: it clearly restricted Parliament's power of removal to cases of 'proved misbehaviour or incapacity', and it was interpreted to require life tenure. Appointment until a fixed retiring age, or for a fixed period of years, was not permitted.[53] It is hard to see how the independence of the judiciary could be affected by their having to retire at a fixed age, and in 1977 a constitutional amendment was passed to this effect.[54] Section 72 now provides that High Court judges hold office until the age of 70; other federal judges hold office until 70 unless Parliament provides some lesser age.[55] The retiring age of a federal judge may not be reduced after his appointment.[56]

The restriction on removal to cases of 'proved misbehaviour or incapacity' raises important issues, which were at the legal centre of the dispute over the attempted removal from office of Justice Lionel

Murphy. These questions are discussed in the context of removal of judges in Chapter 4.

(B) DIRECT LEGISLATIVE INTERFERENCE IN THE JUDICIAL PROCESS
The separation of judicial powers under the Constitution undoubtedly carries the implication that some forms of direct legislative interference in the judicial process are prohibited. For example, legislation directly incriminating a particular person might be held invalid on this basis,[57] if it was not held to be beyond power on other grounds.[58] No clear case of such interference has occurred at federal level in Australia,[59] although there have been a number of cases at state level.[60] As these cases show, even a rather formal guarantee of separation of powers can direct the legislature's attention to the constitutional proprieties.[61]

(C) TRIAL BY JURY
Section 80 of the Constitution provides that the 'trial on indictment of any offence against any law of the Commonwealth shall be by jury'. This was an attempt, following a similar United States provision,[62] to guarantee trial by jury for serious ('indictable') federal offences. However, s80 does not in terms require that any crime, no matter how serious, actually be tried on indictment,[63] and in a series of cases the High Court has refused to give any real content to s80: the choice of summary or indictable procedure is one for Parliament.[64] As a result of this interpretation, 'what might have been thought to be a great constitutional guarantee has been discovered to be a mere procedural provision'.[65]

The restrictive view of s80 has not gone unassailed. In a series of dissenting judgments, Murphy J, and later Deane J, have argued that it should be interpreted to apply to all 'serious' federal offences, thus operating as a real guarantee.[66] The same underlying question has arisen indirectly, and been answered in different ways by different majorities. On the one hand, s80 was held to be a constitutional guarantee and not a personal right of the accused, so that jury trial cannot be waived by the defendant;[67] on the other hand, it was held to be entirely a matter for Parliament to define the 'offence' to which s80 applies, so that it could define an offence in basic terms (e.g. possession of drugs) and leave it to the trial judge to decide vital issues of fact (e.g. the quantity of the drug or the defendant's intention) on which the classification of the offence depended.[68] There are good arguments for the minority view on both issues. If s80 is a real guarantee there must surely be some limits to the issues which Parliament can take away from the jury; on the other hand, the interests of economy and efficiency (e.g. in long and complex fraud cases) suggest that a defendant should be entitled to consent to some other form of trial. The Judicial System Committee of the Australian Constitutional Commission has recommended that s80 be amended so as to guarantee jury trial in all 'serious' cases, but with Parliament able to provide for waiver and majority verdicts.[69]

(5) The Privy Council under the Constitution

The status of the appeal to the Privy Council was a highly contentious issue during the Convention debates. After earlier disagreement, the draft Constitution approved in 1898 provided (cl 74) that no appeal should be allowed 'in any matter involving the interpretation of this Constitution or of the Constitution of a state, unless the public interests' of the Empire were involved. Clause 74 became the main subject of dispute between the Australian delegates and the Colonial Secretary, Joseph Chamberlain, during the passage of the Constitution Bill through the British Parliament.[70] Chamberlain, concerned for the protection of British investment in Australia and of imperial interests generally, forced a compromise: the prerogative appeal by special leave was preserved (s74(3), subject to two qualifications.

First, no appeal from the High Court was permitted in respect of any question

as to the limits *inter se* of the Constitutional powers of the Commonwealth and those of any State or States, or as to the limits *inter se* of the Constitutional powers of any two or more States, unless the High Court shall certify that the question is one which ought to be determined by Her Majesty in Council.

The limitation of *inter se* matters was intended to reserve for the High Court specifically Australian questions of the delimitation of federal and state power. It had a long and contentious history. The Privy Council dealt with inter se matters on only a handful of occasions, mostly with unfortunate results,[71] and the High Court thereafter refused, with increasing asperity, further applications for certificates under s74.[72]

Secondly, the Commonwealth Parliament was given power to 'make laws limiting the matters' in which special leave to appeal to the Privy Council from the High Court might be asked. This power to 'limit' (like the power in s73 to prescribe 'exceptions and regulations') might well have been thought to be itself a limited power, a power to limit but not to exclude. This turned out not to be so: in 1975 appeals from the High Court were eventually 'limited' to the point of abolition.[73]

These matters are now of historical interest only, since the effect of the Australia Acts 1986 (UK & Cth) was to abolish all remaining appeals to the Privy Council from Australian courts.[74]

3.3 State and Federal Jurisdiction

(1) The distinction between state and federal jurisdiction

We have seen that the Constitution gave the Parliament the choice between creating federal courts to exercise jurisdiction under Commonwealth law, and investing such jurisdiction in state courts. Had the United States pattern of distinct federal and state courts been adopted, there would have been no great problem in distinguishing federal from state jurisdiction. But the interlocking structure of federal and state courts, which would result from investing state courts with federal jurisdiction, required the two forms of jurisdiction to be distinguished from each other. For example, conditions have been attached to the exercise of federal jurisdiction by state courts which do not apply to their exercise of state jurisdiction.

The apparently obvious distinction — that deciding a matter of state law is state jurisdiction, a matter of federal law, federal jurisdiction — could not be supported, for several reasons. First, the better view is that the common law is one and the same throughout Australia, and is neither federal nor state. There is thus no subject-matter criterion to determine which jurisdiction a court deciding a common law matter is exercising. Secondly, a single case often involves distinct issues of state and federal law, yet it would obviously be undesirable to chop it up into state and federal bits for jurisdictional purposes. Thirdly, the same case might involve state or federal jurisdiction, depending on how it was commenced. An action between residents of different states would be a matter of federal jurisdiction if started in the High Court (s75 (iv)), but such a matter could have come before a state court quite apart from the Constitution or federal law, for example by an interstate plaintiff commencing proceedings in the state court. The Constitution Act itself (cl. 5) made the Constitution and federal laws binding on state courts and judges: in deciding such issues state courts would be applying laws binding them in the same way as other Imperial Acts. (Their power to do so is referred to as 'belonging' jurisdiction, a term taken from s77(ii) of the Constitution.)

The true distinction is that federal jurisdiction is the power to decide a case given to a court by or pursuant to Chapter III of the Constitution, whereas state jurisdiction is the power to decide a case given independently of Chapter III. The criterion is thus the source of power, rather than the subject matter of the case or the law to be applied (although these will often be relevant in determining whether the power to decide the case derives from Chapter III). As Menzies J remarked:

Resort to the source of the law conferring jurisdiction, as the means of determining whether the jurisdiction being exercised is or is not federal jurisdiction, is . . . less than an ideal method of determining the character of the jurisdiction being exercised by a court . . . This is, however, what the decisions require.[75]

(2) Investing state courts with federal jurisdiction

Section 77(iii) of the Constitution allows the Parliament to invest 'any court of a state with federal jurisdiction' in respect of any of the matters set out in ss75 and 76. This, the so-called 'autochthonous expedient',[76] was an important innovation, allowing efficient use of judicial resources and tending to prevent the jurisdictional problems associated with divided hierarchies. Despite this, the law relating to s77(iii) has developed its own refinements, intricacies and absurdities. Four areas of doubt or difficulty will be briefly described.[77]

(A) IMPOSING CONDITIONS ON THE EXERCISE OF FEDERAL JURISDICTION

Although s77(iii) makes no reference to conditions or restrictions on an investment of jurisdiction, it is settled that federal jurisdiction may be conferred subject to conditions or restrictions. In fact, general federal jurisdiction has been conferred on state courts, and a number of important restrictions have been imposed on that jurisdiction. The key provision is s39 of the Judiciary Act 1903 (Cth), which provides:

(1) The jurisdiction of the High Court, so far as it is not exclusive of the jurisdiction of any Court of a State by virtue of section 38, shall be exclusive of the jurisdiction of the several Courts of the States except as provided in this section.
(2) The several Courts of the States shall, within the limits of their several jurisdictions, whether such limits are as to locality, subject matter or otherwise, be invested with federal jurisdiction, in all matters in which the High Court has original jurisdiction or in which original jurisdiction can be conferred upon it, except as provided in section 38, and subject to the following conditions and restrictions:
(a) A decision of a Court of State, whether in original or in appellate jurisdiction, shall not be subject to appeal to Her Majesty in Council, whether by special leave or otherwise;
(b) . . .
(c) The High Court may grant special leave to appeal to the High Court from any decision of any Court or Judge of a State notwithstanding that the law of the State may prohibit any appeal from such Court or Judge;
(d) The federal jurisdiction of a Court of summary jurisdiction of a State shall not be judicially exercised except by a Stipendiary or Police or Special Magistrate, or some Magistrate of the State who is specially authorized by the Governor-General to exercise such jurisdiction, or an arbitrator on whom the jurisdiction, or part of the jurisdiction, of that Court is conferred by a prescribed law of that State, within the limits of the jurisdiction so conferred.[78]

Section 39 is perhaps the most litigated, certainly the most difficult, provision in this field. Although its validity and effect are now settled, a brief account is required of the controversies it has aroused.

Section 77(iii) of the Constitution empowers the Parliament to make the jurisdiction of a federal court (including the High Court) 'exclusive of that which belongs to or is vested in the courts of the States'. A number of provisions, notably s38 of the Judiciary Act 1903, confer exclusive jurisdiction under this power. But neither the High Court nor other federal courts have been given exclusive jurisdiction, or indeed any jurisdiction at all, over many of the matters listed in s76 of the Constitution, and (apart from s39 itself) the High Court's inherent original jurisdiction in s75 of the Constitution is to a large extent concurrent, not exclusive.

What s39(1) does is to deprive state courts of jurisdiction by making the High Court's jurisdiction exclusive. Section 39(2) then invests state courts with federal jurisdiction over all the matters listed in ss75 and 76 of the Constitution, subject to conditions. It will be seen that this investment covers two distinct categories. The first is those matters already covered by s39(1) (i.e. within the actual jurisdiction of the High Court under s75 and part of s76). The second is those matters which are not affected by s39(1), because the High Court has not been given any jurisdiction over them (the bulk of s76 matters). With respect to the first category, those subjects of jurisdiction shared with the High Court, it was at length held that s39(1) took away the 'belonging' jurisdiction of state courts, so that the only jurisdiction they had was that given by s39(2) (which was subject to the conditions stipulated).[79] But the second category (matters of potential but not actual High Court jurisdiction), was unaffected by s39(1), and in that case s39(2) simply invests in state courts an apparently cumulative or parallel jurisdiction, additional to their 'belonging' jurisdiction but subject to restrictions and conditions. For some time it was thought that the state jurisdiction coexisted with the invested jurisdiction and could be exercised without regard to those conditions.[80] This raised obvious problems of how one could tell which jurisdiction was being exercised. Litigants might be able to evade the conditions in s39(2) by requesting the court to exercise state jurisdiction rather than invested federal jurisdiction, but what if the litigants disagreed? How a court could have determined which jurisdiction it was exercising is quite unclear.

In the event, the High Court came to the rescue, holding, in *Felton v Mulligan*, that in this situation the invested federal jurisdiction was inconsistent with, and thus prevailed over, the 'belonging' jurisdiction of state courts.[81] That jurisdiction was suppressed, so that no option could arise.

Though welcoming the result, Cowen and Zines are critical of the majority's reasoning in *Felton v Mulligan*, on the ground that, even if s39(2) disclosed an intention to exclude state jurisdiction, the only way a state court could be deprived of its 'belonging' jurisdiction is by an exercise of power under s77(ii) and (as to the second category — cases not within actual High Court jurisdiction) s39 is not an exercise of that power.[82] But the High Court relied not on s77(ii), but on the clear inconsistency it found between the conditional federal jurisdiction of state courts and their unconditional 'belonging' jurisdiction. Once it is conceded that the power to confer federal jurisdiction in s77(iii) extends to all s75 and 76 matters (not merely those over which the state courts would not otherwise have had jurisdiction), and that it allows the imposition of conditions and restrictions, it follows that the investment of a restricted jurisdiction in a court must be assumed to exclude any unrestricted 'belonging' jurisdiction over the same matter. Otherwise the power to impose conditions is meaningless. It follows that s39(1) was, after all, unnecessary, a result which it took a mere seventy years to reach![83]

(B) SECTION 77(iii) AND THE STRUCTURE OF STATE COURTS
There are a number of limitations on the Parliament's power to impose conditions and limitations under s77. The first and most important of these relates to the 'structure' of state courts. The bodies in which federal judicial power can be vested are 'State courts'.[84] State courts do not have to have the judicial tenure prescribed by s72, nor are they restricted to the exercise of judicial power only. This is no objection to their exercising federal jurisdiction: on the contrary it is established that the Commonwealth, in investing jurisdiction in a state court, must take the state court as it finds it. More exactly, the Commonwealth may regulate the jurisdiction and procedure of the court in exercising federal jurisdiction, but must not interfere with its structure or 'constitution'. Thus in *Le Mesurier v Connor*[85] the Commonwealth attempted to make a Commonwealth public servant an officer of the state Supreme Court so as to be able to issue bankruptcy notices. The law was held to be invalid since, in adding to the personnel of the Court, it interfered with its constitution.[86]

It may be difficult to determine whether a particular regulation is 'procedural' or 'structural' for this purpose — a point demonstrated by the disagreement in *Russell v Russell*.[87] The Family Law Act 1975 required state judges exercising family law jurisdiction not to wear robes, and to sit in closed court. The High Court held (in each case by a 3–2 majority) that the requirement not to robe was procedural but that the closed court requirement was structural and therefore invalid. Two justices (Mason and Jacobs JJ) held that both were procedural; two (Barwick CJ and Gibbs J) that both were structural. Only Stephen J drew a distinction between the two requirements, and formed part of the majority on both questions. It is suggested, however, that there is a good deal to be said for this view. To treat the wearing of robes as part of the structure of a court is absurd: it is to confuse tradition with substance. But the idea that courts should be open to public scrutiny is much more than traditional. An obligation, as distinct from a power, to close a court might well be said to be fundamental or structural. At any rate it was this view which prevailed.[88]

Although the Commonwealth cannot itself restructure a state court for the purposes of s77(iii), there is no objection to the state agreeing to do so as a condition to the conferral of jurisdiction. Such an arrangement has been made, for example, in the establishment of the Western Australian Family Court.[89]

(C) SECTION 77(iii) AND THE DESIGNATION OF JUDGES TO EXERCISE FEDERAL JURISDICTION

Section 77(iii) allows the Commonwealth to designate a 'court' to exercise federal jurisdiction, but one would not have thought that it allowed the Commonwealth to pick and choose between the judges of a particular court. There are a number of provisions in which the Commonwealth has done something of the kind. The best known is s39(2)(d) of the Judiciary Act 1903, cited already, which invests federal jurisdiction in state courts of summary jurisdiction on condition that the jurisdiction be exercised only by a magistrate. The purpose of s39(2)(d) is to prevent untrained justices of the peace from exercising federal jurisdiction, even though JPs, sitting in pairs, may constitute a court of summary jurisdiction under state law. The purpose may be a reasonable one, but one could imagine many cases which would not be reasonable: for example a condition that no judge who had been a member of a (named) political party should exercise federal jurisdiction. The validity of s39(2)(d) has been upheld,[90] though no very convincing explanation of the source of the Commonwealth's power of selection has been given.[91]

(D) INVESTING STATE COURTS WITH NON-JUDICIAL POWER

The power in s77(iii) is limited to the matters listed in ss75 and 76, the basic matters of federal judicial power. Section 77(iii) thus provides no warrant for investing a state court with anything but judicial power (or power incidental to judicial power). In *Queen Victoria Memorial Hospital v Thornton* it was held that a conferral of non-judicial power on a state court is invalid, although no very clear reasons were given for this.[92] On the one hand, state courts are not limited by their own constitutions to the exercise of judicial power; on the other, although there is no express provision in the Constitution enabling the Commonwealth to confer power on state bodies generally, there are many instances in which the Commonwealth has done so, and (provided the subject-matter is included in s51) there is no reason why such provisions should be invalid. It may be that the Commonwealth cannot *require* a state authority to exercise any power, and that a conferral of power which expressly or impliedly conflicted with the constitution of the state authority would be invalid or inoperative (as it would also be under s77(iii)). But in cases of co-operative arrangements such an investment should be possible: it would be an odd federal constitution which prohibited it.[93] It is not enough, therefore, to explain *Thornton's case* on grounds of mere absence of power:[94] it must be the case that s77(iii) impliedly prohibits the conferral of any other than judicial power on a state court. Why this should be so is not clear, but the point seems settled.[95]

(3) Investing federal courts with state jurisdiction

The converse question is whether the states may confer state jurisdiction on a federal court. That question is raised by the proposed cross-vesting scheme, under which there would be a mutual vesting on federal and state superior and family courts of general residual jurisdiction, in an attempt to avoid cases of disputed or divided jurisdiction.[96] The details of the cross-vesting scheme are discussed in Chapter 8, but some reference should be made here to its constitutional validity.

The argument against the power to vest state jurisdiction in federal courts is based not so much on the failure of Chapter III of the Constitution to mention the possibility: the presence of s77(iii) (allowing federal jurisdiction to be vested in state courts) can be explained on other grounds,[97] and a federal constitution should be interpreted to allow co-operative schemes rather than to exclude them.[98] The difficulty arises, first, from the implication drawn by the High Court from the notion of federal supremacy, to the effect that the states cannot legislate so as to bind the Commonwealth,[99] and secondly, from the apparently exclusive or exhaustive language of ss75 and 76 of the Constitution in enumerating the possible scope of the original jurisdiction of federal courts. It would be curious if the Commonwealth Parliament could, by consenting to state legislation, give it an effect it could not otherwise have, and which the Parliament could not itself enact. Particular restrictions upon federal judicial power (e.g. the exclusion of advisory opinions, the prohibition on vesting strictly non-judicial power in federal courts) could thereby by evaded, since there are no such restrictions on state judicial power.

These are strong arguments, but it is likely that the High Court would uphold a vesting of state jurisdiction in federal courts, subject to judicially contrived limitations as to advisory opinions, non-judicial powers, and similar matters. Whatever the difficulties of rationalization, the desirability of co-operative federalism, and the difficulties of divided federal and state jurisdictions, are likely to prevail.[100]

3.4   Courts in Federal Territories[101]

Section 122 of the Commonwealth Constitution gives the Parliament power to legislate 'for the government of' the various Commonwealth territories.[102] This is a general power, not limited, in the way that the Parliament's 'federal' powers of legislation in s51 are limited, by reason of the existence and partial autonomy of state legislatures. But there is no mention in s122 of its relation to other parts of the Constitution, a matter which, likely to cause difficulties anyway, has been vastly complicated by the course of judicial interpretation. Obviously, the power to legislate for the territories was intended to be additional to the federal legislative powers of the Parliament, and thus was not to be limited by specific restrictions or exclusions in these powers.[103] But many of the provisions of the Constitution (e.g. ss55, 80, and 116) are in the nature of limits or controls on government generally, and are not to be attributed only to the requirements of a federal system. In particular, there might have seemed no reason for excluding the territories from the protection of Chapter III: an independent judiciary, trial by jury, and the separation of powers are values associated as much with the preservation of freedom as of federalism.

The trouble started early, in *R v Bernasconi*,[104] where it was held that s80 did not apply to the trial of an indictable offence under a New Guinea ordinance, on the quite general ground that 'Chapter III . . . has no application to territories'.[105] The reasoning was based not on anything in the terms of s80 or Chapter III, but on an implication from the 'structure' of the Constitution of the sort which was later to be condemned in the *Engineers' case*.[106] It might have been expected then that *Bernasconi's case* would be critically re-examined when next the problem arose, but in *Porter v R*, the court held, following *Bernasconi*, that the Northern Territory Supreme Court was not a 'federal court' within the meaning of s73, so that there was no right of appeal under that section to the High Court.[107] It followed also that territory judges did not have to have the judicial tenure laid down by s72, but could be appointed for a fixed term, or during the Governor-General's pleasure.

For a long time no effective challenge was made to these authorities; indeed, the logical extension of the view that territory jurisdiction is a 'disparate and non- federal matter'[108] was a decision of Fullagar J, in *Waters v Commonwealth*, that not even the High Court's inherent original jurisdiction under s75 applied in a territory.[109] Officers of the Commonwealth were thus, it was held, immune from the supervisory jurisdiction of the High Court under s75(v) when they acted in a territory (even the Australian Capital Territory, the seat of government).

When the challenge did come, it proved, in some respects at least, to be too late. In *Spratt v Hermes*,[110] the issues were, first, whether the High Court could be given jurisdiction to determine a case under the Australian Capital Territory Supreme Court Act 1933 (Cth); secondly, whether a magistrate comprising a Court of Petty Sessions in the territory was validly appointed, though he was not appointed for life under s72; and thirdly, whether territory courts had jurisdiction to enforce a law of Australia-wide application made under s51 (the Post and Telegraph Act 1901 (Cth)). The Court answered all three questions in the affirmative. It was agreed that *Bernasconi's case* had stood too long to be overruled, although there were differing degrees of enthusiasm at this conclusion. Three justices (Barwick CJ, Menzies, Windeyer JJ) wholly disagreed with the reasoning in *Bernasconi's case*: in their view, Chapter III could not be said to be, in principle, irrelevant to courts created under s122, although particular provisions might be found to be inapplicable to territory courts, because their language was inappropriate to apply to them. This was so of s72, which applied only to the 'federal' courts enumerated in s71, so that judges of territory courts did not have to be appointed for life.[111] But it was not true of ss75 and 76, relating to the High Court's original jurisdiction, since these provisions were capable of application in the territories (indeed, s75 demanded to be so applied). *Waters v Commonwealth* was thus wrongly decided.[112]

Kitto J (and, perhaps, Taylor J) reached the same result but by very different reasoning. The separateness of territory from federal jurisdiction, of s122 from Chapter III, underlying *Bernasconi's case* was accepted, so that territory courts did not have to be created in accordance with s72. But particular provisions in Chapter III might as a matter of interpretation extend or authorize the extension of the competence of federal courts to cases arising in a territory. This was true, at least, of s75, so again *Waters v Commonwealth* was wrong.[113]

In view of the eventual agreement reached, the difference between the two views might be thought to be of little significance. However, problems still arise when we ask whether it is possible for a territory court to exercise federal jurisdiction, or for a court established in a territory to be a federal court, for example for the purposes of the High Court's appellate jurisdiction under s73. These issues underlie the deceptively simple case of *Capital TV and Appliances Pty Ltd v Falconer*.[114] The Australian Capital Territory Supreme Court was established by Commonwealth Act: its judges (unlike the magistrate in the Court of Petty Sessions) seemed to have the tenure required by s72 (although the relevant provisions were obscure). The appellant sought to appeal 'by virtue of . . . s73' to the High Court from a decision of the Supreme Court dismissing his appeal from a conviction under a local planning ordinance. Whether he could so appeal depended, in the first instance, on whether the Supreme Court was a 'federal court' or was exercising 'federal jurisdiction' within the meaning of s73. The High Court held that it was neither.

Spratt v Hermes was regarded by some justices as indicating without more that the Supreme Court was a territory court, not a federal court.[115] However, no one went so far as to deny that it was possible for a court set up in a territory to be a federal court, and Menzies and Walsh JJ both examined in some detail the constitution and jurisdiction of the Supreme Court on the express assumption that it might have been intended as a federal court.[116] It is submitted that this view is correct (although the difficulties in arguing that the Supreme Court was such a court were considerable). If the Parliament's power over a territory is plenary, and not dissociated by some legal implication from Chapter III, it ought to extend to the creation of a properly federal court in that territory, with its attendant safeguards.[117]

The apparent corollary of this view is that a territory court might (provided it is properly described as a court) be empowered to exercise additional federal jurisdiction within the meaning of s76. This proposition seems to have been rejected by the Court, either on the ground that s73 refers only to state courts exercising federal jurisdiction,[118] or that jurisdiction invested in a territory court derives necessarily from s122.[119] The former argument adds the qualification 'State' to the term 'court exercising federal jurisdiction' in s73(ii), without any apparent justification. The latter involves an extension of *Bernasconi*, whereas if the majority approach in *Spratt v Hermes* meant anything it was that the *Bernasconi* 'principle' would not be applied to new situations. No doubt *Bernasconi* required that the term 'federal jurisdiction' in s73 be interpreted to exclude jurisdiction conferred pursuant to s122, and this was enough to defeat the appellant (who was convicted under a territory ordinance). But the Parliament has in fact purported to vest specifically federal jurisdiction in territory courts, in cases where s122 would have been available, and also (and more importantly) where it would not be available (because of the absence of any connecting factor between the jurisdiction and the territory).[120] The effect of *Capital TV and Appliances Pty Ltd v Falconer* is to deny to the Parliament the use of territory courts for jurisdictional purposes within Commonwealth power but not associated with the territory, an unnecessary restriction on the efficient use of Commonwealth resources. It is a pity that the opportunity was not taken to overrule *Bernasconi* once and for all.[121]

One final matter that requires mention is the extent to which the High Court and other federal courts can have appellate and original jurisdiction conferred on them under s122. It is usually said that no limit exists on the power to confer appellate jurisdiction,[122] although it is doubtful whether an appeal could be provided from a wholly non-judicial function of a territory court.[123] However, opinion has been divided over the power to confer original jurisdiction — a division of opinion which *Spratt v Hermes* failed to resolve.[124] If, as seems likely, the term 'law of the Commonwealth' in s76(2) is taken to include legislation (including delegated legislation) enacted by the Parliament or by federal officers under s122, few subjects within the ambit of s122 will fall outside the ambit of ss75 and 76 and the disagreement will be unimportant. But problems could still be raised, for example by the conferral of an advisory opinions jurisdiction on the High Court in respect of matters in a territory.

The position of judicial power under s122 may thus be summarized as follows:
1   The Commonwealth can create courts in a territory which do not have to comply with the tenure provisions of s72. The separation of powers has no application to such courts, which can have non-judicial functions conferred on them.
2   Such courts are not federal courts. In exercising jurisdiction de-

rived from s122 they are not exercising federal jurisdiction. To that extent there is no constitutional right of appeal from territory courts to the High Court under s73.

3   However, the Parliament may under s122 confer a general appellate jurisdiction on the High Court (and other federal courts) from territory courts, although such jurisdiction could not extend to decisions in wholly non-judicial matters.

4   Section 75 applies to acts done or matters arising in a territory in the same way and (subject to any questions of interpretation or description) to the same extent as it applies in a state.

5   It is unclear whether the Parliament can confer original jurisdiction on the High Court or other federal courts in respect of matters arising in a territory which go beyond the descriptions in ss75 and 76. The preferable view is that there should be no distinction between original and appellate jurisdiction for the purposes of s122. In any event, if the term 'laws made by the Parliament' includes (as it probably does) laws made by the Parliament under s122 there will in practice be few such matters.

6   Neither the Australian Capital Territory nor the Northern Territory is in any different position to other s122 territories.[125]

7   Section 80 does not apply to trials on indictment in courts (whether territory courts, or it seems, federal courts) exercising non-federal jurisdiction in a territory.

8   A federal law of general application which applies in the states by virtue of some s51 head of power will normally apply in the territories by virtue of s122, so that a territory court exercising jurisdiction under that law will not be exercising federal jurisdiction for the purposes of s73.

9   A federal court with a general jurisdiction in the states and territories would presumably still be a 'federal court' while exercising jurisdiction in a territory, for the purposes of Chapter III (unless the Act expressly provided to the contrary).

10   A federal law under s51 could, it seems, expressly create a federal court to exercise jurisdiction only in a territory, in which case Chapter III would apply to the court while it was exercising that jurisdiction. But the presumption is against this.

11   It seems that where a federal law expressly purports to confer federal jurisdiction on a territory court, that jurisdiction will, if possible, be treated as valid under s122: otherwise, it will be wholly invalid. Why this should be so is a mystery.[126]

Notes

1 See Lumb, *The Constitutions of the Australian States* (4th edn, 1977) ch. 1 for details. The establishment of a fully independent legislature in WA did not occur until 1893: id., 38–40. On early Australian constitutional development generally see Melbourne, *Early Constitutional Development in Australia* (ed. Joyce, St Lucia, 1963); McMinn, *A Constitutional History of Australia* (1979) chs 1–4.
2 Cf. Lumb, 113. There is, for example, no requirement that state courts exercise only judicial power, or that only state courts should exercise state judicial power: *Gilbertson v South Australia* (1977) 14 ALR 429, 434 (PC).
3 The Court of Criminal Jurisdiction, established in 1788, pursuant to the Act 27 Geo III c2 (1787), by the First Charter of Justice, 2 Apr. 1787: Bennett & Castles, 18–23.
4 First Charter of Justice. In 1814, pursuant to the 'Second Charter of Justice' (Letters Patent of 4 Feb. 1814), the Court of Civil Jurisdiction was replaced by a 'Supreme Court' with jurisdiction in civil cases up to £50, and a Governor's Court (in Van Diemen's Land, a Lieutenant-Governor's Court) with civil jurisdiction above £50. See Bennett & Castles, 27–42; Castles, 23–57. The legality of the creation of courts under the prerogative was disputed: see Evatt (1938) 11 *ALJ* 409; Campbell (1951) 25 *ALJ* 59; Windeyer (1962) 1 *U Tas LR* 635; Else-Mitchell (1963) 49 *JRAHS* 1; Campbell (1964) 4 *Syd LR* 343; Campbell (1964) 50 *JRAHS* 161.
5 Castles, 36–7. On the position of the Deputy Judge Advocates during this period, see Bennett (1958) 2 *Syd LR* 501.
6 On the Bigge Reports generally see Ritchie, *Punishment and Profit* (1970).
7 House of Commons Paper 33 (1823); Adelaide, Australian Facsimile Editions No. 69 (1966). For strenuous criticism of Bigge's Second Report as biased and unfair to Governor Macquarie, see Bennett (1971) 15 *AJLH* 85.
8 Castles, 58–67; Bennett & Castles, 42–69.
9 Castles, 68–113. WA was the exception: its Supreme Court was not established until 1862: Russell, *A History of the Law in Western Australia and its Development from 1829 until 1979* (1980) ch. 12.
10 Castles, 61–2, 72–5.
11 Later state constitutions have simply provided for the continuance of the Supreme Court and other courts already established. And see Bennett, *A History of the Supreme Court of New South Wales* (1974).
12 NSW: Constitution Act 1853 ss38–40, 42, 51; Victoria: Constitution Act 1855 ss38–41, 49; Queensland: Constitution Act 1867 ss15–17, 38; WA: Constitution Act 1889 ss54–5, 58. The Tasmanian Constitution Act 1854 contained no relevant provisions.
13 This compares with the federal Constitution, s128 of which requires a majority of voters in a majority of states for its amendment. Substantive amendment of the federal Constitution has proved difficult to achieve.
14 NSW: Constitution Act 1902 (cf. s43); Tasmania: Constitution Act 1934.
15 Queensland: Constitution Acts 1867 ss15–17; SA: Constitution Act 1934 ss74–5; WA: Constitution Act 1889 ss54–5.
16 Victoria: Constitution Act 1975 Pt III (ss75–87).
17 Constitutional Commission, Committee on the Australian Judicial System, *Report* (1987) para. 4.6, 5.67–9, 6.14.

18 A Local Court of Appeals existed in NSW and Van Diemen's Land only until 1828, and in WA from 1832–61: see Castles, 62–3, 71–2, 90; Bennett, *History*, 169–70. In SA the Local Court of Appeals was established in 1837 and not abolished until 1935 (though it heard its last case in 1882). See Castles, 93, 95–6; Hague, *The Court of Appeals* (1940).
19 An Australian court of appeal was proposed as early as 1849: Quick & Garran, 83–5, and the idea recurred frequently during the second half of the century.
20 Australia Act 1986 (Cth) s9; Australia Act 1986 (UK) s9.
21 Quick & Garran, 79–252; La Nauze, *The Making of the Australian Constitution* (1972).
22 Cf. Crawford, in Craven, ed., *Commentaries on the Convention Debates* (1987) 113.
23 This central principle of judicial review of legislation was established in the US in the landmark case of *Marbury v Madison* 1 Cranch 137 (1803). It is clearly assumed in the federal Constitution, ss74, 76(ii): cf. Quick & Garran, 791.
24 See generally Zines, *The High Court and the Constitution* (1981) 131–76; Sawer (1961) 35 *ALJ* 177; Finnis (1968) 3 *Adel LR* 159; Howard, *Australian Federal Constitutional Law* (3rd edn, 1985) ch. 4; Lane, *The Australian Federal System* (2nd edn, 1979) 403–508; Renfree, *The Federal Judicial System of Australia* (1984) ch. 1; Lane, *Commentary on the Australian Constitution* (1986) 329–50. On the values associated with the separation of powers see Vile, *Constitutionalism and the Separation of Powers* (1967).
25 This was Montesquieu's concern in *L'Esprit des Lois* (1748), which is regarded as the origin of the political theory of the separation of powers as a safeguard against despotism. Cf. *R v Trade Practices Tribunal, ex p Tasmanian Breweries Pty Ltd* (1970) 123 CLR 361, 392 (Windeyer J).
26 *Huddart Parker v Moorehead* (1909) 8 CLR 330, 355 (Griffith CJ); *NSW v Commonwealth* (1915) 20 CLR 54 (where the inference from s71 was used to read down the terms of s102 of the Constitution, emasculating the Interstate Commission).
27 *Boilermakers' Case* (1956) 94 CLR 254, 270 (Dixon CJ, McTiernan, Fullagar & Kitto JJ).
28 *Victorian Stevedoring & General Contracting Co. Pty Ltd v Meakes & Dignan* (1931) 46 CLR 73; *Radio Corporation Pty Ltd v Commonwealth* (1938) 59 CLR 170.
29 *Boilermakers' Case* (1956) 94 CLR 254, 275.
30 Cf. Detmold, *The Australian Commonwealth* (1985) 237–9.
31 (1918) 25 CLR 434.
32 Cf. *R v Taylor; ex p Roach* (1951) 82 CLR 587. No appeal lay from the Commonwealth Court exercising non-judicial functions to the High Court under s73: *Jacka v Lewis* (1944) 68 CLR 455; *Penton v Australian Journalists' Assoc.* (1947) 73 CLR 549.
33 *R v Kirby, ex p Boilermakers' Society of Australia* (1956) 94 CLR 254; on appeal (1957) 95 CLR 529 (sub nom *AG (Commonwealth) v The Queen*). See Galligan, *Politics of the High Court* (1987) 201–9; d'Alpuget, *Mediator. A Biography of Sir Richard Kirby* (1977) 142–8, for the political and personal background to the decision. Its aftermath, as d'Alpuget makes clear, was not a triumph for the independence of the judiciary.

34 This arrangement was upheld in *Seamen's Union of Australia v Matthews* (1957) 96 CLR 529.
35 But a much closer link between the federal industrial judicial work and federal conciliation and arbitration is again being proposed: Committee of Review into Australia's Industrial Relations and Systems (Chairman: K. Hancock), *Report* (1985) vol. 2, 380–98. On federal industrial jurisdiction see further Chapter 11.
36 Cf. *Alexander's Case* (1918) 25 CLR 434; *Boilermakers' Case* (1956) 94 CLR 254, 281–9.
37 *Silk Bros Pty Ltd v SEC (Victoria)* (1943) 67 CLR 1.
38 *R v Trade Practices Tribunal, ex p Tasmanian Breweries Pty Ltd* (1970) 123 CLR 361.
39 *Farbenfabriken Bayer AG v Bayer Pharma Pty Ltd* (1959) 101 CLR 652; *R v Quinn, ex p Consolidated Foods Corp.* (1977) 16 ALR 569; and see *R v Davison* (1954) 90 CLR 353, 369–70.
40 *Federal Commissioner of Taxation v Munro* (1926) 38 CLR 153; on appeal, *Shell Co. of Aust. Ltd v FCT* (1930) 44 CLR 530 (PC).
41 *Cominos v Cominos* (1972) 127 CLR 588.
42 *Tasmanian Breweries Case* (1970) 123 CLR 361; cf. *Rola Co. (Aust.) Pty Ltd v Commonwealth* (1944) 69 CLR 185; *R v Marks, ex p Australian . . . Builders Labourers' Federation* (1981) 35 ALR 241.
43 Other cases in recent years where judicial power arguments failed include: *R v Hegarty, ex p Salisbury City Corporation* (1981) 36 ALR 275; *Minister for Immigration and Ethnic Affairs v Gungor* (1982) 42 ALR 209; *Pioneer Concrete (Vic.) Pty Ltd v TPC* (1982) 43 ALR 449; *Victoria v Australian . . . Builders Labourers' Federation* (1982) 43 ALR 693 (a remarkable example of different ways of reaching the same conclusion); *Re Ludeke, ex p Australian . . . Builders Labourers' Federation* (1985) 62 ALR 407. Cf. also Lane (1981) 55 *ALJ* 6.
44 Strictly speaking, state courts exercise federal jurisdiction invested in them under s77(iii) of the Constitution, while territory courts exercise territory jurisdiction under s122. In neither case does the federal separation of powers doctrine apply (although the High Court has held that federal laws cannot confer non-judicial powers on state courts: *Queen Victoria Memorial Hospital v Thornton* (1953) 87 CLR 144).
45 Constitution, s49; *R v Richards, ex p Fitzpatrick & Browne* (1955) 92 CLR 157, 166–7.
46 *R v Cox, ex p Smith* (1945) 71 CLR 1 (mutiny). See now Defence Force Discipline Act 1982 (Cth), and for a critique of the exception, Brown (1985) 59 *ALJ* 309. Cf. *R v White, ex parte Byrnes* (1963) 109 CLR 665 (public service disciplinary tribunal).
47 *Drake v Minister for Immigration & Ethnic Affairs* (1979) 24 ALR 577, 584.
48 For an extreme example see *Hilton v Wells* (1985) 58 ALR 245, a 3–2 decision of the High Court, noted (1985) 59 *ALJ* 303. As the minority judgment of Mason & Deane JJ in that case suggests, there must be some limit to the *persona designata* exception, otherwise the basic principle of judicial separation would disappear. A new federal industrial court has been proposed, consisting of judges who are also members of a parallel Conciliation and Arbitration Commission: see n35. However, there would

still be a formal and procedural separation between the two bodies, a separation which is presumably necessary for the device to work (although in *Hilton v Wells* the majority required little or nothing of the kind). See also *Narain v Parnell* (1986) 64 ALR 561.
49 *R v Joske, ex p ABLF* (1974) 2 ALR 447, 449–50. Mason J agreed that it was a 'serious question': id., 459.
50 *R v Joske, ex p Shop Distributive & Allied Employees' Assoc.* (1976) 10 ALR 385.
51 A provision which might raise the question, is National Health Act 1953 s82ZD (giving the Court a general discretion to cancel or vary certain contracts of its own motion).
52 However, the Constitutional Commission's Committee on the Australian Judicial System recommended no change in this respect: *Report* (1987) para. 5.4–8.
53 *Waterside Workers' Federation of Australia v JW Alexander Ltd* (1918) 25 CLR 434 (Higgins & Gavan Duffy JJ dissenting).
54 Constitution Alteration (Retirement of Judges) 1977.
55 Retirement at 65 has been prescribed for judges of the Family Court (Family Law Act 1975 s23A), but not for judges of the Federal Court. The reasons given were the rigours of the family jurisdiction, and the need for judges to keep in touch with community mores in the family law area (which would, apparently, not happen after the age of 65).
56 The amendment is prospective only, so that it does not apply to judges appointed before 29 July 1977. All the present members of the High Court have been appointed (or, in the case of Mason CJ, reappointed) since that date, but there are a considerable number of judges of the Federal and Family Courts holding life tenure by virtue of pre-1977 appointments.
57 Cf. *Liyanage v R* [1967] 1 AC 529 (PC); Nettheim (1966) 40 *ALJ* 221.
58 As in the *Communist Party Dissolution Case* (1951) 83 CLR 1.
59 Cases in which such an argument has been rejected include: *Nelungaloo Pty Ltd v Commonwealth* (1948) 75 CLR 495, 503–4, 579–80; *Palling v Corfield* (1970) 123 CLR 52; *R v Humby, ex p Rooney* (1973) 2 ALR 297; *Sorby v Commonwealth* (1983) 46 ALR 237; *Australian . . . Builders Labourers' Federation v Commonwealth* (1986) 66 ALR 363.
60 E.g. *Building Construction Employees' and Builders' Labourers' Federation v Minister for Industrial Relations* (unreported, NSWCA, 31 Oct. 1986).
61 Cf. the terms of the Commonwealth and NSW legislation upheld in *Australian . . . Builders Labourers' Federation v Commonwealth* (1986) 66 ALR 363 and *Building Construction Employees' and Builders Labourers' Federation v Minister for Industrial Relations* (unreported, NSWCA, 31 Oct. 1986) respectively.
62 US Constitution, Art III s2(3), which refers to 'all crimes'. Minor penalties, such as fines, imposed without a jury trial have been upheld as 'civil' or 'administrative' sanctions: *Atlas Roofing Co. v Occupational S. & H. Rev. Comm'n* 518 F 2d 990 (1975).
63 A point made by Isaacs during the Convention debates: Quick & Garran, 807.
64 This interpretation of s80 was first adopted in *R v Archdall, ex p Carrigan & Brown* (1928) 41 CLR 128. More recent cases include: *Zarb v Kennedy* (1968) 121 CLR 283; *Li Chia Hsing v Rankin* (1978) 23 ALR 151. See also *R v King* (1978) 24 ALR 346, 354–5; Comans (1969) 3 *FLR* 51.

65 *Spratt v Hermes* (1965) 114 CLR 226, 244 (Barwick CJ).
66 This view was forcibly put by Dixon & Evatt JJ (dissenting) in *R v Federal Court of Bankruptcy ex p Lowenstein* (1938) 59 CLR 556, 580–5. For Murphy J's views see e.g. *Beckwith v R* (1976) 12 ALR 333, 345–6; *Yager v R* (1977) 13 ALR 247, 263–4. For Deane J's views see *Clyne v DPP* (1984) 55 ALR 9, 17–18; *Kingswell v R* (1985) 62 ALR 161, 185–202.
67 *Brown v R* (1986) 64 ALR 161 (Brennan, Deane, Dawson JJ; Gibbs CJ, Wilson J dissenting). See (1986) 60 *ALJ* 423.
68 *Kingswell v R* (1985) 62 ALR 161 (4–2, Brennan & Deane JJ dissenting).
69 Constitutional Commission, Committee on the Australian Judicial System, *Report* (1987) para. 6.12–20.
70 La Nauze, 248–69.
71 The Privy Council twice decided an *inter se* question, once without a certificate under s74 (*Webb v Outtrim* [1907] AC 81), and once with one (*A-G v Colonial Sugar Refinery Co. Ltd* [1914] AC 237). The reasoning in each case was untenable. More recent constitutional solecisms, by way of *obiter dicta*, include *Oteri v R* (1976) 11 ALR 142, 145 (where it was said, in a case involving a fishery offence on the high seas, that the Commonwealth Parliament had no power over criminal law).
72 In *Kirmani v Captain Cook Cruises Pty Ltd (No. 2)* (1985) 58 ALR 108 the High Court said it would never grant a certificate under s74.
73 Privy Council (Appeals from the High Court) Act 1975 (Cth), held valid in *A-G v T & G Mutual Life Soc. Ltd* (1978) 19 ALR 385.
74 Australia Act 1986 (Cth) s9; Australia Act 1986 (UK) s9. On the history and influence of the Privy Council in Australian law see the first edition of this book, 169–83, and works there cited, esp. Howell, *The Judicial Committee of the Privy Council 1833–1876* (1978).
75 *Capital TV & Appliances Pty Ltd v Falconer* (1971) 125 CLR 591, 607.
76 *Boilermakers' Case* (1956) 94 CLR 254, 268.
77 See further Cowen & Zines, ch. 5; Bailey (1940) 2 *Res Judicatae* 108, 184; Harvey & Thomson (1975) 5 *Monash ULR* 229; Howard, 230–49; Lane (1979) 693–716.
78 For s39(2)(d) (as amended in 1984) see below. Section 39(2)(b), omitted in 1976, provided for a direct appeal to the High Court from any decision of a state court which could be appealed to the Supreme Court. For the relation between s39 and s68 of the Judiciary Act (invested criminal jurisdiction), see Cowen & Zines, 214–23. Section 39A applies the s39 conditions to investments of federal jurisdiction under other federal Acts.
79 *Baxter v Commissioners of Taxation (NSW)* (1907) 4 CLR 1087, not following the decision of the Privy Council in *Webb v Outtrim* [1907] AC 81. See further *Lorenzo v Carey* (1921) 29 CLR 243; *Commonwealth v Limerick Steamship Co. Ltd* (1924) 35 CLR 69; *Commonwealth v Bardsley* (1926) 37 CLR 393.
80 *Lorenzo v Carey* (1921) 29 CLR 243, 252; *Booth v Shelmerdine Bros Pty Ltd* [1924] VLR 276.
81 (1971) 124 CLR 367. The point had been made long before, by Dixon J in *Ffrost v Stevenson* (1937) 58 CLR 528, 573. *Felton v Mulligan* was reaffirmed and applied in *Moorgate Tobacco Co. Ltd v Philip Morris Ltd* (1980) 31 ALR 161.
82 Cowen & Zines, 227–8.
83 If a state court was composed entirely of persons not qualified under s39(2)(d) to exercise federal jurisdiction (e.g. JPs), the court would have

a 'belonging' jurisdiction over many of the matters in s76, but could not exercise it, because s39(2) would operate to invest jurisdiction in the court, and it would never be properly constituted to exercise the jurisdiction! On the other hand s39(2)(d) does not prevent the exercise by JPs of administrative powers under federal legislation (e.g. issuing search warrants), even where the JP must act 'judicially' in exercising the power: *Westpac Banking Corp. v Barnes* (1983) 47 ALR 431.

[84] It is not necessary that, under state law, the body be described as a 'court', if it is properly so described: *Pearce v Cocchiaro* (1977) 14 ALR 440. The converse may also be true — a body described by state law as a court may not be able to exercise federal jurisdiction if in reality it is not a 'court': cf. *Tana v Baxter* (1986) 68 ALR 245.

[85] (1929) 42 CLR 481 (Knox CJ, Rich & Dixon JJ; Isaacs & Starke JJ dissenting).

[86] The law was amended to make Commonwealth officers available to the state court and subject to its directions, without making them officers of the court. In that form it was upheld in *Bond v George A. Bond & Co. Ltd* (1930) 44 CLR 11.

[87] (1976) 9 ALR 103.

[88] Cowen & Zines, 196–9, argue that both requirements were procedural: whether courts should be open or closed in a particular case is, in their view, a policy matter which the Commonwealth Parliament should be free to regulate incidentally to investing the jurisdiction. Another issue relating to the exercise of invested federal jurisdiction is whether persons other than judges may exercise judicial power. The High Court initially held that Masters and Registrars who did not, under state law, constitute part of the court could not exercise federal judicial power: *Kotsis v Kotsis* (1970) 122 CLR 69; *Knight v Knight* (1971) 122 CLR 114. But the dissenting view of Gibbs J in that case was unanimously approved by the Full High Court in *Commonwealth v Hospital Contribution Fund of Australia* (1982) 40 ALR 673, which overruled the earlier decisions. It is now clear that Masters and Registrars of both federal and state courts can exercise ancillary judicial powers: cf. *Letts v Commonwealth* (1985) 62 ALR 517. But the validity of the 1984 amendment to s39(2)(d), which allows federal jurisdiction to be exercised by 'an arbitrator on whom the jurisdiction, or part of the jurisdiction, of that Court is conferred by a prescribed law of that state, within the limits of the jurisdiction so conferred', is doubtful. This is intended to allow for court-annexed arbitration under state law (e.g. Arbitration (Civil Actions) Act 1983 (NSW)). But arbitrators under that Act are not part of the state court, even in the sense that court officials such as registrars and masters are.

[89] Family Law Act 1975 (Cth) s41. See further Chapter 10.

[90] *Queen Victoria Memorial Hospital v Thornton* (1953) 87 CLR 144, 152; and cf. *Kotsis v Kotsis* (1970) 122 CLR 69, 110–11 (Gibbs J). See Cowen & Zines, 191–5, to similar effect.

[91] The argument for validity must be that it is incidental to the effective exercise of federal jurisdiction that the judges be properly qualified: if so, lack of incidentality might exclude the grosser examples of selection. There can be practical problems with s39(2)(d), since it may not appear that a court of summary jurisdiction is exercising federal jurisdiction until the

defence case is put (or at all): e.g. *Sanderson & Co. v Crawford* [1915] VLR 568. The Constitution (s79) allows the Parliament to prescribe the number of judges who are to exercise federal jurisdiction in any case: this speaks against a power to prescribe qualifications.
On the related problems of the conferral of jurisdiction by proclamation or delegated legislation see Cowen & Zines, 181–4.

92 *Queen Victoria Memorial Hospital v Thornton* (1953) 87 CLR 144.
93 Cf. *Re Duncan; Ex p Australian Iron & Steel Pty Ltd* (1983) 49 ALR 19 (Commonwealth-NSW Coal Industry Tribunal).
94 As do Cowen & Zines, 181.
95 In *Pearce v Cocchiaro* (1977) 14 ALR 440, 445, the High Court upheld an investment of committal jurisdiction in a state magistrate: the provision was valid 'whether or not at that time [the magistrate] is conducting an inquiry that can properly be called judicial'. Ordinarily, committal jurisdiction is regarded as 'administrative' rather than judicial, but rather than casting doubt on *Thornton's case*, the Court was treating the jurisdiction as 'incidental' (cf. *Aston v Irvine* (1955) 92 CLR 353), as it made clear in *R v Murphy* (1985) 61 ALR 139. And see Cowen & Zines, 221.
96 See Jurisdiction of Courts (Cross-Vesting) Act 1987 (Cth), and the various state and NT counterparts. The scheme is planned to come into effect in 1988.
97 In particular s77(iii) allows the federal Parliament to vest federal jurisdiction in state courts, irrespective of the consent of the states.
98 Cf. *Re Duncan; Ex p Australian Iron & Steel Pty Ltd* (1983) 49 ALR 19.
99 *Commonwealth v Cigamatic Pty Ltd (in liquidation)* (1962) 108 CLR 372.
100 This was Zines' conclusion: 'Integrated Courts Scheme' in *Proceedings of the Australian Constitutional Convention, Brisbane . . . 1985* (1985) vol. 2, 27. Cf. also *Re Duncan; Ex p Australian Iron & Steel Pty Ltd* (1983) 49 ALR 19, where the High Court had no difficulty in upholding a joint scheme for a Coal Industry Tribunal (though one not involving judicial powers). On the other hand the Constitutional Commission's Committee on the Australian Judicial System doubted whether cross-vesting of state legislation in federal courts (other than by reference of power under s51(38)) is possible without a constitutional amendment, which it recommended: *Report* (1987) para. 3.114.
101 See Cowen & Zines, ch. 4; Comans (1971) 4 *FLR* 218.
102 The Commonwealth can acquire territories in a variety of ways: by transfer from the states (as with the NT, transferred from SA in 1911; the ACT, transferred from NSW in 1911 to be the 'seat of government of the Commonwealth'; and Norfolk Island, transferred from NSW in 1913); by transfer from another country (as with the Cocos (Keeling) Islands and Christmas Island, transferred from the UK in 1955 and 1958 respectively), or even from an international organization (as with Nauru and New Guinea, held as trust territories under the United Nations and now independent). Other federal territories at present are the Australian Antarctic Territory, and a number of small islands, mostly uninhabited (Heard & McDonald Islands, Coral Sea Islands, Ashmore and Cartier Islands).
103 Even where (as with the acquisitions power, s51(31)) the limitations extend to 'any purpose for which the Parliament has the power to make laws': *Tau v Commonwealth* (1969) 119 CLR 564.

104 (1915) 19 CLR 629. It had previously been held that s55 had no application to taxation laws for a territory: *Buchanan v Commonwealth* (1913) 16 CLR 315; Cowen & Zines, 149–50.
105 (1915) 19 CLR 629, 635 (Griffith CJ). Isaacs J added that s80 would impose on the (largely native) population of the territories 'what would be in the vast majority of instances an entirely inappropriate requirement of the British jury system': id., 638.
106 (1920) 28 CLR 129. The doctrine of 'implied prohibitions', rejected in the *Engineers' case*, was a doctrine of restrictive interpretation of Commonwealth powers so as to preserve the presumed powers of the states. *Bernasconi* might be thought to involve the reverse fallacy: an uncontrolled interpretation of Commonwealth powers where state powers were not in question.
107 (1926) 37 CLR 432. The Court held further (Knox CJ, Gavan Duffy J dissenting) that the High Court could be given additional appellate jurisdiction from a territory court under s122, despite the apparently exclusive terms of Chapter III.
108 *Attorney-General (Cth) v The Queen* (1957) 95 CLR 529, 545 (PC).
109 *Waters v Commonwealth* (1951) 82 CLR 188.
110 (1965) 114 CLR 226.
111 Id., 243–8 (Barwick CJ); 269–71 (Menzies J); 274–8 (Windeyer J).
112 Id., 242–3 (Barwick CJ).
113 Id., 253 (Kitto J). Owen J simply followed the previous cases without indicating agreement with either line of argument.
114 (1971) 125 CLR 591.
115 Id., 598 (Barwick CJ); 601–2 (McTiernan J); 613–4 (Owen J); 625–6 (Gibbs J).
116 Id., 603–4, 608–9 (Menzies J); 616–20 (Walsh J).
117 This is true, *a fortiori*, if one accepts the view that federal jurisdiction cannot be conferred on a territory court. Otherwise, despite the amplitude of its power, the Parliament is simply debarred from investing any federal jurisdiction in a court located in a territory.
118 (1971) 125 CLR 591, 602 (McTiernan J); 606–8 (Menzies J); 613 (Owen J); 627 (Gibbs J).
119 Id., 599–600 (Barwick CJ), echoing his surprising agreement with Kitto J on the federal/non-federal distinction in *Spratt v Hermes*: (1965) 114 CLR 226, 248 (Barwick CJ); 259–60 (Kitto J) (surprising because of Barwick CJ's disapproval there of the reasoning in *Bernasconi*). Walsh J, (1971) 125 CLR 591, 620–4, may also have favoured this view, at least on these facts (but see his reservation: id., 623–4). Windeyer J agreed generally in the result, without indicating a preference for one or the other line of reasoning.
120 See Cowen & Zines, 171, for examples.
121 *Bernasconi* may have the further corollary that the Parliament may not be able to invest state courts with jurisdiction under s122, even though a law may operate in a state under s122: *Lamshed v Lake* (1958) 99 CLR 122.
122 *Porter v R, ex p Yee* (1926) 37 CLR 432; Cowen & Zines, 152–3, 162–3.
123 Cf. *Minister for Works for WA v Civil and Civic Pty Ltd* (1967) 116 CLR 73.

[124] (1965) 114 CLR 226. The Court there was evenly divided on the question. See Cowen & Zines, 163–5.

[125] Despite arguments to the contrary, there is no third category of polity within the Commonwealth, apart from states and territories. For certain purposes, however, the NT is treated as if it were a state. Cf. Nicholson (1985) 59 *ALJ* 698.

[126] In this work only the courts of the two mainland territories (the ACT and the NT) will be dealt with. Three other territories have their own separate court systems:
Norfolk Island: The Supreme Court of Norfolk Island is constituted by the Supreme Court Ordinance 1960, pursuant to the Norfolk Island Act 1979 ss52–9 (replacing earlier legislation). The main inferior court is the Court of Petty Sessions (Court of Petty Sessions Ordinance 1960). See also Juries Ordinance 1960; Justices of the Peace Ordinance 1972; Coroners Ordinance 1927.
Cocos (Keeling) Islands: The law of Singapore (previously the Straits Settlements) as at 1955 was continued in force by the Cocos (Keeling) Islands Act 1955 s8. See now Singapore Ordinances Application Ordinance 1979 No. 5. Inferior Courts are established by the Courts Ordinance 1955 (Singapore) as amended by Comonwealth Ordinances 1955 No. 5, 1978 No. 2. The Cocos (Keeling) Islands Supreme Court is established by the Supreme Court Ordinance 1955.
Christmas Island: There is a Supreme Court of Christmas Island, constituted by the Supreme Court Ordinance 1958 (Cth), pursuant to the Christmas Island Act 1958 (Cth) ss11–12. Inferior courts established by ordinance are the District Court (District Court Ordinance 1958), Magistrates Court (Magistrate's Court Ordinance 1958), and Children's Court (Children's Court Ordinance 1972). See also Small Claims Ordinance 1983. The substantive law of Singapore (to the extent that it applied to Christmas Island as at 1958) remained in force: Christmas Island Act 1958 (Cth) s7.
Four small Commonwealth territories have had the jurisdiction of the courts of a larger territory applied to them: Ashmore and Cartier Islands Acceptance Act 1933 (Cth) s12 (NT); Australian Antarctic Territory Act 1954 (Cth) s10 (ACT); Coral Sea Islands Act 1969 (Cth) s8 (Norfolk Island); Heard Island and McDonald Islands Act 1953 (Cth) s9 (ACT).

CHAPTER 4

The Organization of the Judicial System

4.1 The Role of Courts and the Adversary System

The following chapters examine the main Australian courts and their functions. In the course of this examination a number of issues of judicial organization will be discussed: for example, in Chapter 7, the increasingly important topic of judicial administration; in Chapter 8, the relations between federal and state courts; in Chapter 9, the role of appeal courts; in Chapter 13, the relations between tribunals and courts; and in Chapter 14 the debate about an integrated court system. This chapter discusses certain basic features of the judicial system which are more or less common to all courts, or which are an important part of the common law heritage. These are the adversary system, and the role in that system of the three main classes of participants: judges, lawyers, and laymen.

(1) The role of courts

In any society there are disputes — disagreements between husband and wife, parent and child, businessman and client, employer and employee, official and member of the public. Many disputes are settled one way or another between the parties, without outside intervention. But if they cannot be settled, some outside intervention may be necessary to prevent the dispute festering and perhaps leading to violence. The intervention may take many forms, for example the mediation of a friend or adviser, the direction of a teacher or employer, someone with authority over the quarrellers. But if this does not succeed, and if the dispute persists, an official form of dispute settlement may be necessary. Very occasionally this may take the form of intervention by the legislature, laying down a new rule. Generally, though, it is the function of the courts, established by the state with powers of decision and enforcement.[1]

(2) The adversary system

Again, there are different ways in which courts can be established for these functions. A court might have a roving commission, to seek and settle disputes, to search out and destroy disagreements. But unasked-for intervention is unpopular, and may make matters worse rather than better. So courts sit back and wait for disagreements to come to them.

In the common law system, this simple rule of efficiency is taken far indeed: it becomes a basic principle of organization. The courts will decide only what parties in disagreement ask them to decide. Their function is not to find out the truth but to decide, between conflicting versions of the truth, which is to be preferred. Normally it is irrelevant that there may be a third version, truer than that presented by either party.

This principle was established for civil cases at an early stage. The development of a group of specialist pleaders, who alone had the right to argue cases before the superior courts, was a necessary condition.[2] They acquired the remarkable power of being able to determine the grounds on which the dispute would be argued, and thus decided. This was done primarily through the pleadings, the formal documents setting out each party's case, and from which it was not permitted to stray.[3]

In criminal cases, the adversarial method seems to have remained an abstract theory for much longer. Until the eighteenth century legal representation in ordinary criminal cases was a rarity: the prosecution was organized informally, and the accused, in cases of felony, was not even entitled to counsel. The excuse was that the judge would protect the accused's interests, and judge and jury were active in calling and questioning witnesses. The introduction of legal representation in the eighteenth and nineteenth centuries led to the extension of civil adversarial methods to criminal cases. Here too the 'tribunal of fact', the jury, became a passive arbitrator between conflicting arguments.[4] The result, in Lord Denning's words, is that

> In the system of trial which we have evolved . . . the judge sits to hear and determine the issues raised by the parties, not to conduct an investigation or examination on behalf of society at large . . . So firmly is all this established in our law that the judge is not allowed in a civil dispute to call a witness whom he thinks might throw some light on the facts. He must rest content with the witnesses called by the parties . . .[5]

In that case the Court ordered a retrial on the ground that the judge had intervened so much in argument that the case was taken out of counsel's hands, and could not be fairly presented. Australian courts have taken a very similar line.[6]

It follows from this system that a court may have to decide a case on grounds which, if other arguments had been presented, would be wrong or irrelevant. That the accused was insane when he committed the offence is no excuse if insanity is not pleaded. That the plaintiff's claims in contract should fail because the contract was not, but should have been, in writing, or because the claim is out of time under the Statute of Limitations, does not matter if those defences are not relied on. Even in constitutional cases, legislation may be declared invalid on one ground when another, unargued, may have been available.[7] Such decisions acquire binding force between the parties, although future courts are protected to some extent by the rule that a decision on a question conceded or not argued is no authority (i.e. is not a 'precedent') on that question.[8]

The adversary system is not the only way of organizing trials. Most European systems practise a form of inquisitorial method, in which, once a case comes to court, the judge exercises general control over it, calling and examining witnesses, actively inquiring after the truth of the matter, with assistance from the lawyers for the parties but in principle free to direct and decide the case on whatever ground seems best. Like most arrangements of a *laissez-faire* kind, the adversary system works best when the parties are on an approximately equal footing, with sufficient resources to prepare and present their case. It is, as a result, considerably more expensive than the inquisitorial method, at least in the cases that actually reach the court.[9]

When the parties are not on an equal footing, or when the question does not warrant the cost of full-scale legal representation, the adversary method tends to break down. Steps can be taken to restore equality — most notably, by the provision of legal aid or by other forms of assisted legal representation. Alternatively, forms of administrative or judicial intervention can be adopted, along 'inquisitorial' lines: for example, in small claims courts and tribunals (where the parties are usually not entitled to legal representation) or in a more rigorous control of pre-trial procedures in both civil and criminal cases. But the delay and expense of litigation are leading to experiments with forms of mediation, counselling, and compulsory pre-trial conferences, to encourage the settlement of cases without trial. Major litigation, criminal and civil, is likely to remain strongly adversarial in nature, but in other cases, and in matters of pre-trial procedure, hybrid forms of adversarial and inquisitorial methods are starting to emerge.[10] A number of these are outlined in later chapters: for example, attempts to streamline criminal trials (Chapter 5), reform of civil procedure (Chapter 7), small claims courts and tribunals (Chapter 12), and the move to 'alternative dispute resolution' (Chapter 14).

4.2 The Judiciary

Central to the constitution and operation of a court system is the judiciary: in a real sense, the judge is the court. How judges are appointed, how their independence is maintained, how and on what grounds they can be removed, and what other (non-judicial) functions they can properly perform are thus important questions. In recent years many of these issues have become very controversial, as a result of disputes about the appointment and, especially, the removal of judges.[11]

(1) The appointment of judges

In Australia the appointment of judges is, by constitution or statute, universally the responsibility of the executive, that is, the federal government in the case of the High Court and other federal courts, state governments in the case of state courts. Formally, appointments are made by the Governor-General, or the Governor, in Council. The reality is that they are matters for Cabinet decision. There are statutory criteria of eligibility, but these are usually limited to a period of admission or practise as a barrister and/or solicitor within the relevant jurisdiction. Once these not very exacting requirements are met, the appointment is at the discretion of the executive.

This system contrasts, in different ways, with that adopted in the United Kingdom and the United States. In the United Kingdom, the responsibility for advising judicial appointments is an individual one — the Prime Minister in the case of the most senior appointments, the Lord Chancellor in other cases. They are not a matter for Cabinet discussion.[12] In Australia (where there is no equivalent to the Lord Chancellor) the initial nomination would usually be made by the Attorney-General, but the decision is a collective one and the Attorney-General's agreement with it is not required.

On the other hand, in the United States many state judges are elected (some for fixed terms, requiring re-election); of those that are not, certain major appointments are subject to legislative concurrence. For example, Supreme Court judges are nominated by the President but require the advice and consent of a majority of the Senate.[13] These forms of public accountability have led to much greater scrutiny and criticism of candidates before appointment. In Australia, public criticism usually has to wait until after appointment, when it is arguably too late to be effective.

The opportunity the Australian system presents for political influence in judicial appointments has led to proposals for appointment by, or pursuant to a recommendation from, some form of Judicial Appointments Committee composed of judges and lawyers and (perhaps) laymen.[14] Formal consultation with the profession and other interested governments or parties has been developed, along these lines, in the United States and Canada, but with two exceptions no such consultation is required in Australia.[15]

The arguments for the present system are nevertheless strong. In practice, party-political appointments have been rare, and those which may have originated in party manoeuvres have usually been defensible on other grounds.[16] The danger of an 'independent' commission is that it would produce 'safe', uncontroversial appointments and that it would tend to limit the range of candidates. Domination of such a commission by judges and senior professionals would tend to self-perpetuation, whereas, in courts as in executive government, changes of course from time to time may be desirable.[17] No adequate system would have failed to appoint a Griffith, an Isaacs, or a Dixon, but would a judicial committee have nominated Ninian Stephen, John Bray, Felix Frankfurter, or Bora Laskin? Fundamentally, to assert that judicial appointment is a non-political function is to exclude the judiciary from the processes of democratic responsibility. The character and quality of the judiciary is no less a matter of public concern than the character and quality of the laws it administers.[18]

(2) Independence, tenure, and dismissal of judges

On the other hand, it is a fundamental principle that a person once appointed a judge should be independent of executive direction or control. This is the undisputed core of the notion of separation of powers. Judges decide legal disputes between government and government, between government and private citizen, and it is essential that they be independent of any party. Even in cases between subject and subject, there would be no point in the elaborate presentation of evidence and argument if the decision depended on external direction. Judicial independence is fundamental to any system of justice, as distinct from power.[19]

Such independence was not always secured. Until the end of the seventeenth century English judges could be appointed, suspended, and dismissed at the pleasure of the Crown. The use of these prerogatives was a marked feature of the forensic successes the Stuarts enjoyed before 1688.[20] In 1700 the Act of Settlement established the rule that superior court judges should be appointed during good behaviour, though they could be removed by the Crown on an address of both Houses of Parliament.[21] The effect was that the Crown could not simply get rid of unfavoured or even incompetent judges. The Act of Settlement still left open the possibility of impeachment by Parliament or removal for misbehaviour in appropriate legal proceedings,[22] but in practice an address of both Houses was the only method by which judges within the United Kingdom would be removed. Only one removal by address has ever been necessary.[23]

Unlike other fundamental legislation, s3 of the Act of Settlement was not received on the establishment of the Australian colonies. Colonial judges were at first appointed at pleasure, and were liable to removal by the Crown, or to what was termed 'amoval' by the Governor in Council under the provisions of Burke's Act 1782.[24] The establishment of responsible government brought with it security of judicial tenure — sometimes described as Act of Settlement tenure.

But amoval under Burke's Act remained a possibility, at least until 1964. The only three Australian superior court judges who have been dismissed from office — Willis, Montagu, and Boothby — were all amoved by the Governor in Council rather than removed on an address of Parliament.[25]

(A) TENURE AND REMOVAL OF JUDGES: THE MODERN LAW

There is a basic difference in the tenure of federal judges under s72 of the Constitution, compared with that of state and territory superior court judges. Inferior court judges and magistrates form yet a third category for this purpose.

(I) FEDERAL JUDGES

Legally, the most straightforward position is that of federal judges. Section 72 of the Constitution provides that High Court justices and other federal judges

> shall not be removed except by the Governor-General in Council, on an address from both Houses of Parliament in the same session, praying for such removal on the ground of proved misbehaviour or incapacity.[26]

Section 72 provides a stricter guarantee of tenure than provisions based on the Act of Settlement, since it is the only way by which federal judges can be removed. On the other hand the political implications of attempts at removal of a federal judge can be very considerable, especially if, as was the case in the lengthy proceedings against Justice Lionel Murphy, the judge involved is a High Court justice and the major political parties take differing views about the conduct alleged. Murphy, who had previously been a Labor Cabinet Minister and Attorney-General, is the only Australian superior court judge to be convicted during tenure of office of a serious criminal offence, although that conviction was quashed on appeal as a result of an obvious misdirection, and Murphy J was then acquitted on retrial.[27] Parliamentary inquiries involving allegations against Murphy J (partly but not wholly related to the two charges on which he was tried) were also established: a Parliamentary Commission examining whether there were grounds for removal under s72 had only begun its investigations when Murphy was taken fatally ill.[28] Sharply differing views are held as to whether the lengthy proceedings against Murphy J were justified,[29] but an incidental effect of the controversy was to clarify some aspects at least of the meaning and operation of s72.

The Parliamentary Commission of Inquiry took the view that the words 'proved misbehaviour or incapacity' in s72 were not restricted to serious criminal offences or misconduct in office, but extended to any conduct which, judged by the standards of the time, was so serious as to demonstrate the judge's unfitness to hold office.[30] In determining whether misbehaviour existed, Parliament was obliged to allow the judge a full opportunity to be heard.

However, some issues were not resolved. It can be argued that s72 is directed at misbehaviour of a person after appointment as a judge, rather than at misbehaviour before appointment. It is not clear whether Parliament can delegate the power to determine 'proved misbehaviour or incapacity',[31] nor by what standard a decision to remove a judge under s72 would be reviewed by the High Court. On the one hand, s72 constitutes the Houses of Parliament as the primary judges of misbehaviour or incapacity, neither of which are terms of art, and this would suggest that judicial review of a removal under s72 would be restricted to grounds such as denial of natural justice, or the absence of any evidence at all on which the Houses could have acted.[32] On the other hand it could be argued that Parliament is not competent to decide unaided such legal issues as whether particular conduct constitutes 'misbehaviour' or whether that conduct has been 'proved'. In a representative democracy the latter argument (which has some influential supporters) is more persuasive for the requirement of 'proof' than for setting the standard of 'misbehaviour': judges are judges of the community, rather than of themselves.

(II) STATE AND TERRITORY SUPERIOR COURT JUDGES

Section 72 of the Constitution does not apply to judges of territory courts,[33] although a comparable degree of tenure has been conferred on judges of the Australian Capital Territory and Northern Territory Supreme Courts.[34] The position in the states is variable and, in most, uncertain. In all states, Supreme Court judges are appointed during good behaviour. However, it seems that in no state (with the exception of New South Wales, discussed below) is the removal of a judge on an address of Parliament conditioned upon misbehaviour or incapacity, as it is under s72. A representative provision is the Constitution Acts 1867 (Qld). Section 15 provides for tenure during good behaviour. Section 16 then provides that

It shall be lawful nevertheless for Her Majesty to remove any such judge or judges upon the address of the Legislative Assembly.[35]

The power of removal is expressed as a reservation upon tenure, not as a method of determining an appointment upon misbehaviour. It follows that (except in New South Wales) the Houses may in law move an address for removal on any ground at all, a power which would exclude judicial review for denial of natural justice no less than lack of evidence. Except in Tasmania, it is also likely that the constitutional and statutory provisions, based on the Act of Settlement, do not exclude alternative methods of removal at common law, although even if these remain in theory, in practice they are obsolete.[36] A similar level of protection is offered to acting justices of the Supreme Court for the duration of their appointment.[37]

The controversies which surrounded the trial of Murphy J at the federal level were paralleled in New South Wales, where a District

Court judge was acquitted, and a former chief magistrate convicted and jailed, for attempting to pervert the course of justice.[38] The state government responded to these and associated concerns about the administration of justice by rushing through Parliament the Judicial Officers Act 1986 (NSW), despite strenuous protests from the Supreme Court and the legal profession.[39] The Act governs the tenure of 'judicial officers' at all levels (including magistrates). Judicial officers hold office 'during ability and good behaviour'. They may be removed only on an address of both Houses of Parliament, and only if a Conduct Division of the Judicial Commission, established by the Act, has reported that 'a matter could justify parliamentary consideration of . . . removal'. The Judicial Commission (in which the heads of the relevant courts have a major role) is given the power to receive complaints of misconduct which, if apparently justified, can be referred to a Conduct Division, consisting of judges or retired judges. The Act strengthens the independence of inferior court judges and magistrates, and has other positive features,[40] but it goes too far in allowing a Conduct Division to investigate minor complaints (that is, those which could not justify removal), and in vesting in the presiding officers of each of the courts the power to suspend judges, even in respect of minor complaints.

(III) INFERIOR COURT JUDGES AND MAGISTRATES
Historically judges of inferior and intermediate courts and magistrates and justices of the peace have enjoyed a lesser degree of protection than that provided for Supreme Court judges.[41] In recent years South Australia, Victoria, and New South Wales have conferred more secure tenure on magistrates and inferior court judges,[42] and this reflects a general trend. Moreover, magistrates in all jurisdictions except Queensland are no longer part of the public service or subject to public service discipline and removal provisions.[43]

(IV) JUDICIAL INDEPENDENCE AND TENURE: PROPOSALS FOR REFORM
Despite these changes, tenure is by no means as secure as it might appear. One possibility, increasingly resorted to, is the abolition of a court, or its reconstitution under new legislation accompanied by a refusal to reappoint some of the previous judges.[44] Complaints procedures, unless carefully designed, can also lead to insecurity, as has been said to be the case under the Judicial Officers Act 1986 (NSW).[45] The government of the day necessarily has a majority in the lower House, frequently in both Houses. (In Queensland and the Northern Territory there is only one House.) Security of tenure thus depends as much on the values of judicial independence, supported by public opinion and by certain conventions of parliamentary behaviour,[46] as on adequate legislative guarantees. There are concerns that, at times of high political pressure, both may be missing in some jurisdictions.[47]

(B) SOME ASSOCIATED ISSUES

Certain other guarantees of judicial independence may be briefly mentioned. It is usually provided that judicial salaries may not be decreased during tenure of office.[48] More significant are problems of orderly increases in judicial salaries, and of provision of accommodation and facilities, all of which have at some time caused strident disagreement between the judiciary and governments in Australia.[49] One result has been a growing demand for administrative independence, at least at the level of Supreme Courts. The substantial administrative independence of the High Court under the High Court of Australia Act 1979 (Cth) has been taken by some as a model, but the High Court as the final court of appeal is by no means in the same position as other courts, especially trial courts.[50]

(3) The role of Chief Justices and Chief Judges

The titular head of the High Court and of each Supreme Court is the Chief Justice. In the case of federal courts and of some intermediate state courts, the equivalent is the Chief Judge. The powers of Chief Justices and Chief Judges are purely statutory or conventional, and vary from court to court. They may include a special role in making Rules of Court, a 'casting vote' in some cases of even division of opinion,[51] and most importantly, the organization of the work of the court (for example, in determining the composition of benches and the work to be done by particular judges).[52] The Chief Justice, when present, presides over the court and is its official spokesman in non-litigious matters.

Less formally, a court, especially an appeal court, often takes its popular name — even its 'image' — from its Chief Justice. Divergences of approach to the Bill of Rights in the United States are analyzed, more or less misleadingly, in terms of the Warren Court or the Burger Court.[53] Australian versions, at a much lower forensic temperature, are the Dixon and the Barwick courts. If the Chief Justice does not always provide leadership, he does sometimes provide a label.

(4) Extra-judicial uses of judges

Reference has already been made to the use of judges in investigative or administrative roles distinct from their judicial work, as an 'exception' to the separation of powers under the federal Constitution. At common law a judge could not, without forfeiting his judicial appointment, undertake an incompatible office. But the performance of specific designated functions — such as royal commissions and other inquiries — was not prohibited.[54] Statutory authorization would be required, and in Australia, has been given, where judges have undertaken distinct offices rather than specific, temporary functions.[55]

Although its legality is settled, there has been a continuing debate in Australia over the desirability of the differing kinds of extra-judicial tasks of judges. At one extreme is the view, generally adhered to by the Victorian Supreme Court and set forth in the so-called Irvine memorandum, that no such tasks should ever be performed. In refusing to make a judge available to inquire into charges of corruption in certain harbour works, Irvine CJ had stated that

> The duty of His Majesty's Judges is to hear and determine issues of fact and of law arising between the King and a subject, or between subject and subject, presented in a form enabling judgment to be passed upon them, and when passed to be enforced by process of Law. There begins and ends the function of the Judiciary. It is mainly due to the fact that, in modern times at least, the Judges in all British Communities have, except in rare cases, confined themselves to this function, that they have attained, and still retain, the confidence of the people. Parliament, supported by a wise public opinion, has jealously guarded the Bench from the danger of being drawn into the region of political controversy. Nor is this salutary tradition confined to matters of an actual or direct political character, but it extends to informal inquiries, which, though presenting on their face some features of a judicial character, result in no enforceable judgment, but only in findings of fact which are not conclusive and expressions of opinion which are likely to become the subject of political debate.[56]

The same position has been taken by the High Court.[57]

On the other hand, other federal judges and other Supreme Courts have not accepted these arguments, and in fact judges have been employed on a wide variety of tasks, by no means all of an investigatory nature. Representative of the 'libertarian' view is this comment of Brennan J:

> The answers depend upon where the balance is struck between the necessity to draw upon judicial skills in non-traditional ways, and the risk of thereby diminishing confidence. An undue timorousness in drawing upon judicial skills leads to the development of problem-solving machinery that is less satisfactory than it should be, and to a sense that the judiciary is unduly irrelevant to many issues of community concern. Too adventurous an approach requires the judges to expose themselves to an assessment — political or otherwise controversial — and to a consequential loss of confidence in the judiciary and in judicial institutions.[58]

One of the difficulties with the Australian debate has been the tendency to treat the problem exclusively in terms of such imponderables as 'public confidence' and 'judicial prestige'. No doubt these concepts are relevant, but they are not helpful. It may be better to consider the problems in more functional terms. Not all extra-judicial activities are of the same kind; not all courts are structured in such a way as to free judges for other tasks.

In the first place, there must be certain prerequisites to any such uses of judges. There should be no substantial disturbance to the work of the court in question. This consideration alone is enough to exclude High Court justices: in an evenly balanced court of seven which sits together to hear the most important cases, the prolonged absence of any one judge can have a marked impact.[59] Other courts, not sitting in banc, do not have the same problem. As Brennan J has suggested, a judge should not undertake an inquiry or investigation unless the principles of natural justice can be applied, so that persons affected have the opportunity to be heard and to answer charges against them. And it is hard to justify the use of an acting judge in any extra-judicial role at all, since the inference would always be that subsequent permanent appointment was contingent upon (or a reward for) 'satisfactory' performance.[60]

Subject to this, the problem would appear to be one of assessment and balance rather than the application of any rule. Clearly relevant are the expertise (or otherwise) of the judge for the task; the proximity of the task to matters within ordinary judicial functions (Brennan calls this determinacy of data and result); and any exceptional need, in war-time or emergencies, for judicial impartiality. Certain factors will count against acceptance. These include the possibility (e.g. in the Petrov case[61]) of the inquiry being instituted for ulterior, party-political motives, so exposing the judge to a form of manipulation. Another reason for non-acceptance is that the court in question may have to decide issues arising out of the inquiry. Thus a spectrum of cases emerges. Few would doubt the propriety of judges undertaking functions of a quasi-judicial kind, or judicial functions under other legal systems.[62] The acceptability of ordinary forms of inquiry and mediation and the like may depend upon their subject matter: inquiries relating to the legal system itself (e.g. chairmanship of law reform commissions) are obviously desirable. On the other hand, traditional or categorical executive positions — such as the head of the Australian Security Intelligence Organization or an ambassador — are much less appropriate. If such functions are to be performed by judges at all (and there is much to be said for the view that they should not be), some mechanism of secondment with suspension of judicial office should be devised, to avoid misleading impressions of judicial, as distinct from personal, competence.[63]

4.3 The Legal Profession

This is not a study of the legal profession, but some brief reference is required to the various ways in which the profession contributes to the functioning of the courts.

(1) Legal representation and legal aid

The importance of legal representation for the common law adversary system has been emphasized already. A party to civil or criminal proceedings, at first instance or on appeal, can represent himself,[64] and in certain very restricted circumstances a friend or agent can appear on his behalf. With these exceptions, legal practitioners have a statutory monopoly of representation on behalf of parties in litigation, and in all serious cases it is usual for the parties to obtain legal representation. This can be an expensive business, especially in long cases. In civil litigation the successful party will normally be awarded his costs, but these will not cover the full expense of the action.[65] The losing party, in consequence, pays the winner's costs and all his own. In criminal cases the general rule is that the defendant pays his own costs.[66] Unaided litigation has always been a risky and expensive business.[67]

Various palliatives have been developed. Small claims courts and tribunals (which are discussed in Chapter 12) usually do not allow legal representation: costs are therefore minimal and are borne by the parties whether they win or lose. Provision has been made in all states and at the federal level for certain costs to be paid if they result from an error of law on the part of the judge, or from the miscarriage of a trial through no fault of the parties.[68] In some cases, public bodies or officials are authorized to conduct litigation on behalf of private parties.[69]

However, the most significant form of assistance is organized legal aid. Until the 1970s, legal aid was arranged on a piece-meal basis in each state, mostly through the local legal professional organization. In 1973 a much more ambitious national system of legal aid — the Australian Legal Aid Office — was instituted. The lack of a statutory charter, questions of the independence of the Office from the Commonwealth executive, local opposition, and other problems led in each state to its replacement by a co-operative scheme.[70] Legal Services Commissions set up under state legislation receive funding from both federal and state governments for legal aid in matters within their respective jurisdictions. (For example, the Commonwealth pays for family law cases, the states for most criminal cases.) Commissions provide legal aid for eligible persons either through their own salaried legal staff or by assignment to the private profession. The balance to be struck between the two methods is one of a number of problems, but, as always, the most pressing problem is that of funding, especially in areas of state jurisdiction.[71]

Different views are held as to how freely available legal aid should be, even in criminal cases. In *McInnis v R*, Murphy J (dissenting) declared:

> Every accused person has the right to a fair trial, a right which is not in the slightest diminished by the strength of the prosecution's evidence and includes the right to counsel in all serious cases. This right should not depend on whether an accused can afford counsel. Where the kind of trial a person receives depends on the amount of money he or she has, there is no equal justice.[72]

In that case the High Court majority held that McInnis, who had been denied legal representation on a rape charge, had no right to legal aid and, though unrepresented, had not been unfairly convicted.

The fairness of the conviction, to that extent, took priority over the fairness of the trial.

(2) The organization of the legal profession

The legal profession, like the courts it services, is separately and differently organized in each state and territory.[73] But, unlike the courts, there is as yet no separately organized federal legal profession.[74] Questions of the organization of the profession have attracted considerable attention, in both England and Australia, in recent years. A brief account must suffice.

In New South Wales, Victoria, and Queensland, the profession is divided, by law or convention, into two distinct branches, barristers and solicitors. The division, inherited from England (where it is still maintained), is said to reduce costs through specialization. Barristers have the right of audience in superior courts, and confine themselves to advocacy, drafting and giving legal opinions. Solicitors are concerned with general advice to clients, with most of the preparation for litigation, and with non-litigious matters such as wills and land transactions (conveyancing).[75] In Tasmania, Western Australia, South Australia, and the two territories the profession is fused: that is, the same person usually acts both as barrister and solicitor, though a measure of specialization, formal and informal, does occur.

The Supreme Courts have a general oversight of matters of admission to practice and professional discipline: subject to this, the legal profession is substantially self-regulating.[76]

(3) The law officers of the Crown

Apart from the judiciary, the members of the legal profession with the most important role in the working of the courts are the law officers of the Crown. The term itself is English, and refers to the Attorney-General and the Solicitor-General, both Members of Parliament, who act as the primary legal advisers and counsel to the Crown.[77] Neither have any exact equivalent in Australia. Attorney-Generals here (unlike the British one) are members of Cabinet, and combine some of the functions of Lord Chancellor (judicial appointments, administration of the court system, and law reform) with those of Crown legal adviser.[78] The office of Solicitor-General presents an equally marked contrast: in Australia the Solicitor-General is not a Member of Parliament but an independent public servant whose principal function is to act as Crown counsel.[79]

The Attorney-General has other important responsibilities. These include the general oversight of criminal cases, the power to terminate any case by entering what is called a *nolle prosequi*, and the right to intervene on behalf of the government in certain cases, or to commence proceedings — either independently or at the request ('relation') of a private citizen — to vindicate public rights.[80] The Attorney-

General also has a variety of statutory powers and functions relating to the legal system, although in the area of the criminal law these are increasingly shared, and in practice exercised, by the Director of Public Prosecutions.[81]

4.4 The Layman in the Judicial Process

(1) Trial by jury

Although the operators of the court system are usually professionals — judges, lawyers, court officials — in several important ways laymen continue to play a role. The most obvious is by serving on juries in criminal or civil cases.

(A) THE ORIGINS OF TRIAL BY JURY

The interesting and complex history of the common law jury has been described elsewhere.[82] There is still dispute over the origins of the jury, which may have been diverse: in criminal cases, the presentment of suspected offenders by at least twelve men of good standing in the locality, which developed into the grand jury; in civil cases, the inquisition or inquest by local witnesses under official supervision. After 1215, with the decay of older methods of trial such as combat and ordeal, a second, small or *petit* jury was added in criminal cases, to decide whether the accused was guilty or not guilty. By the fifteenth century the jury was established as the essential tribunal of fact in all common law cases, and it became a decider of facts brought before it rather than a body which itself was expected to witness to the facts. In giving a wrong verdict, the jury could no longer, therefore, be charged with perjury: the jury verdict, given without reasons, became practically unimpeachable, unchallengeable by appeal or other procedure except where the jury was misdirected or must have made a mistake in law.[83]

True to its diverse origins, the jury took on a variety of forms: the grand jury, usually of 23 so that a majority of 12 could be obtained to present an accused; the petty jury of 12 in criminal cases and its civil counterpart, which were required to be unanimous; the coroner's jury; and two splendid variations, the mixed-language jury (jury *de medietate linguae*) to try foreigners, and the jury of matrons (jury *de ventre inspiciendo* — literally, to inspect the womb) which had to investigate whether a woman convicted of felony was pregnant and could therefore escape execution. In all, the jury was one of the most remarkable common law inventions.

(B) TRIAL BY JURY IN AUSTRALIA

The adoption of trial by jury in Australia was a slow and controversial process, but at least it maintained the jury's record for liveliness and diversity. New South Wales, not being a free colony, was said not to have inherited civil and criminal juries, the introduction of which was not achieved until the 1840s.[84] But there are much earlier records of other forms of jury being used: a jury of matrons in 1789 (the woman was hanged),[85] a coroner's jury of 24 in 1810,[86] even a grand jury. The jury *de medietate linguae*, alas, was not received, New South Wales not then being recognized as a 'multi-cultural society'.[87] And the grand jury, after a brief, uncertain career, has now disappeared everywhere.[88]

Throughout Australia, trial by a jury of 12 remains the normal method of trying indictable (i.e. serious) offences. Much of the law and lore of juries remains, although in four jurisdictions majority verdicts are allowed in all but 'capital' cases (such as murder and treason),[89] and in some states the defendant may elect to be tried by judge alone.[90] In criminal cases the jury's verdict is conclusive as to the facts; except in Tasmania, it is also conclusive as to the defendant's innocence.[91] Appeals from a jury verdict of guilty require a defendant to show some error of law or serious misdirection by the trial judge.

Except for serious criminal cases the jury is in decline. Four jurisdictions have abolished the coroner's jury; in the other four it is a rarity.[92] In all except two states, juries in civil cases are almost as rare, even where the parties are entitled to claim trial by jury. South Australia has gone furthest in this respect: there has been no civil jury trial since the late 1920s.[93] Civil jury trial is said to take longer, to be more expensive and less efficient; the parties are said to be less inclined to settle cases (since juries are less predictable than judges); it is far more difficult to sustain an appeal on any ground involving assessment of the facts. In personal injuries cases, damages awards made by juries are said to be inconsistent, and often lower than a judge would have awarded.

Surprisingly, in the two busiest jurisdictions, Victoria and New South Wales, civil jury trial has substantially survived, even flourished. In New South Wales, in the Common Law Division about 35 per cent of all civil cases are tried without a jury: an important exclusion is motor accident cases (about 50 per cent of all cases), which are tried by judge alone.[94] In Victoria the proportion of civil jury trials is even higher: they include both motor accident and industrial accident cases. But the introduction of a Personal Injuries list, of cases tried without a jury, has substantially increased the number of non-jury civil trials.[95] A movement away from civil jury trials has already occurred in England,[96] in the High Court,[97] and elsewhere in Australia, and it is hard to believe that New South Wales and Victoria will not follow.[98]

Civil jury trial in cases not involving personal integrity or reputation thus seems to have little future. The position of criminal jury trial, on the other hand, is unresolved. In one English survey it was concluded that 'juries reached, with considerable frequency, verdicts that could not be regarded as true verdicts according to the evidence'; that 'trial by jury is a relatively crude instrument for establishing the truth'.[99] In complex cases such as company frauds, it is often doubted whether juries can understand or properly assess the evidence: a New South Wales proposal for trial by judge alone in such cases was hotly opposed and amended so as to require the defendant's consent.[100] There are other dangers to the integrity of criminal jury trial, such as plea bargaining,[101] jury vetting,[102] defective procedures for impanelling juries, and problems of the public disclosure of jury deliberations.[103]

Despite these problems, the proposition that an accused should not be deprived of his 'life or liberty' but by 'lawful judgment of his peers' remains a valued one. Hale was confident that 'the Trial by a Jury of Twelve Men . . . upon all Accounts, as it is settled here in this Kingdom, seems to be the best Trial in the World',[104] and this still represents dominant opinion.[105] In Australia, it is still the case that little research has been done,[106] so that maintaining such a high degree of confidence in criminal jury trial may have to be put down to intuitive experience. It remains to be seen whether this strong consensus will be maintained, given the increasing number of lengthy and complex trials, and the enormous costs to the public of trials and retrials.[107]

(2) Other forms of lay participation in the judicial process

In a variety of other ways laymen may play a part in deciding issues of law or fact in the courts. For example, in each jurisdiction there is provision for the court to order an inquiry into a case or an issue, or indeed the trial of the case, by referees or arbitrators, and for assessors to sit with the court to advise it (usually in technical matters).[108] In some courts, a judge and lay assessors are required to sit together to constitute the court.[109] Lay justices of the peace continue to exercise minor criminal jurisdiction in some states, as outlined in Chapter 5.

A very significant method of lay trial, this time as an alternative rather than an addition to trial in a court, is private arbitration. It is competent for the parties to a contract to agree that disputes under the contract be referred not to a court but to an arbitrator or arbitrators chosen by the parties (or by some other named person or institution), and in some contexts, such as building or shipping disputes, or international trade contracts, reference to arbitration is extremely common. Arbitrators will often be experts in the field of the dispute, rather than lawyers. The aim of arbitration is to settle the dispute by an award, which is enforceable on registration in a court and from which there is no appeal. But the courts retain supervisory jurisdiction over the arbitral process and there is provision, more or less restricted, for cases to be stated to the court on questions of law.[110]

Notes

1. In different cultures the extent to which disputes are settled by official adjudication, rather than by less official forms of conciliation or coercion, varies markedly. For examples of different cultural techniques see e.g. Aubert, ed., *Sociology of Law* (1969) Parts 1 & 3.
2. On the evolution of the legal profession in England, see Baker, 133–50.
3. On the system of pleadings see Baker, 67–82.
4. For these developments see Langbein (1978) 45 *U Chic LR* 263. Full rights to counsel in serious criminal cases were not established in England until 1836.
5. *Jones v National Coal Board* [1957] 2 QB 55, 63–4.
6. On excessive intervention by a judge in proceedings see *R v Watson, ex p Armstrong* (1976) 9 ALR 551. In criminal cases a judge may call a witness only in the 'most exceptional circumstances': *R v Apostilides* (1984) 53 ALR 445. But the English cases which are said to preclude a trial judge from calling a witness in civil cases have not been followed in Australia. Instead the rule in civil cases appears to be the same as in criminal cases: *Obacelo v Tavercraft* (1986) 66 ALR 371 (Wilcox J). See also Sheppard (1982) 56 *ALJ* 234.
7. In *Minister for Justice ex rel ATI (Ops) Pty Ltd v ANAC* (1977) 12 ALR 17, the High Court held certain legislation invalid in part. Argument was confined to the trade and commerce power (s51(1)): although it might well have supported the legislation in full, the corporations power (s51(20)) was not referred to. But a court is required to satisfy itself that it has jurisdiction, irrespective of the arguments of the parties: *Cockle v Isaksen* (1957) 99 CLR 155, 161. Cf. also *Tana v Baxter* (1986) 68 ALR 245.
8. Cross, *Precedent in English Law* (3rd edn, 1977) 148–50. A point assumed but not argued in such cases is said to have passed *sub silentio*.
9. See the interesting account by Devlin, *The Judge* (1979) 54–83, and for an exchange of Australian views, Eggleston (1975) 49 *ALJ* 428; Connolly, id., 439, 685. See also Brouwer (1981) 55 *ALJ* 207; Zeidler (1981) 55 *ALJ* 390; Certoma (1982) 56 *ALJ* 288.
10. Cf. Devlin, 67, 74–82. Recent procedural reforms have aimed at increasing the courts' control at the interlocutory or pre-trial stage, to reduce costs and delay: e.g. Barwick (1979) 53 *ALJ* 487, 493–4.
11. There has correspondingly been much more written in recent years about (and indeed, by) the Australian judiciary. In addition to the works cited below, see Kirby, *The Judges* (1983); Fricke, *Judges of the High Court* (1986).
12. Shetreet, *Judges on Trial. A Study of the Appointment and Accountability of the English Judiciary* (1976) 46–83, 393–404; Jackson, 456–81; Lord Chancellor's Department, *Judicial Appointments — The Lord Chancellor's Policies and Procedures* (1986). The English system is based on an extreme centralization of judicial appointments, which tends to vitiate the comparison with a federation such as Australia: but cf. Gibbs (1987) 61 *ALJ* 7.
13. Jacob, 94–123; Abraham, *Justices and Presidents. A Political History of Appointment to the Supreme Court* (2nd edn, 1985); Lively (1986) 59 *Calif LR* 551. A feature of the Canadian system is that the federal government appoints many of the provincial judges (including the Supreme Court and Court of Appeal judges), as well as all the federal judges. For reform in

the Canadian system of judicial appointments see Lederman (1979) 57 *Can BR* 687, 696–700; Canadian Bar Association, *The Appointment of Judges in Canada* (1985). On the impact of the Canadian Charter of Rights on judicial independence see *Valente v R* (1985) 24 DLR (4th) 161. Generally on the Canadian judiciary see Russell, *The Judiciary in Canada: The Third Branch of Government* (1987).

[14] Barwick (1977) 51 *ALJ* 480, 494; Basten (1980) 52 *Aust Q* 468. Gibbs CJ, on the other hand, was less specific in his proposal: (1987) 61 *ALJ* 7, 11. See also Hurlburt (1963) 6 *Alberta LR* 174; Note [1974] *NZLJ* 86; NZRCC, 32–4, 195–206.

[15] The exceptions relate, first, to the appointment of High Court justices (High Court of Australia Act 1979 (Cth) s6), and secondly to the appointment of judges to state family courts (Family Law Act 1975 (Cth) s41(4)(a)). These are discussed in Chapters 9 and 10 respectively.

[16] For the case of Piddington (1913) who resigned without sitting as a justice, see Bennett, *Keystone*, 33; Sawer, *Australian Federal Politics and Law 1901–1929* (1956) 105–6. Piddington was criticized for answering questions asked by Attorney-General Hughes about his attitude to federal-state rights before his appointment.

[17] To similar effect, Durack (1980) 5 *Cth Rec* 991; Editorial (1977) 51 *ALJ* 506. Cf. also King (1980) 39 *AJ Pub Adm* 1, 4–5; Brennan (1979) 53 *ALJ* 767 (though both propose mandatory consultation before appointments are made).

[18] Cf. Constitutional Commission, Committee on the Australian Judicial System, *Report* (1987) para. 5.21–33 (rejecting a Judicial Commission for appointment but proposing informal consultation).

[19] For a range of views on judicial independence see Stephen (1982) 13 *MULR* 334; Green (1985) 59 *ALJ* 135; Kirby, in Shetreet & Deschênes, *Judicial Independence: The Contemporary Debate* (1985) 8; Shetreet, id., 590; Brown (1986) 58 *Aust Q* 348. On the status of judges generally see Holdsworth (1932) 48 *LQR* 25; Wade (1932) 173 *LT* 246; Shetreet (1975) 27 *Admin LR* 185.

[20] On the 17th century conflict over judicial independence see Jones, *Politics and the Bench* (1971); Keeton (1962) 7 *JSPTL* 56; Havighurst (1950) 68 *LQR* 62, 229, (1953) 69 *LQR* 522; Shetreet (1976) 2–9.

[21] 12 & 13 Wm III ss2, 3; Shetreet (1976) 10–11.

[22] Shetreet (1976) 85–159 for a full account.

[23] Barrington (1830), an Irish judge. See Shetreet (1976) 143–4.

[24] The Colonial Leave of Absence Act 1782 (22 Geo III c75). The Act provided for appeal to the Privy Council against amoval. Cf. Cowen & Derham (1953) 26 *ALJ* 464. On the non-reception in Australia of the Act of Settlement see *Terrell v Secretary of State for the Colonies* [1953] 2 QB 482; Lindell (1980) 54 *ALJ* 628.

[25] *Willis v Gipps* (1846) 5 Moo PC 379, 13 ER 536; *Montagu v Van Diemen's Land* (1849) 6 Moo PC 489, 13 ER 773. On Montagu see Howell (1966) 2 *U Tas LR* 253. On Boothby, see Hague, 362–89. The British government had previously declined a parliamentary address for Boothby's removal: Castles, 155–6. There have been a number of other judges suspended under the Act. Burke's Act was repealed for the UK in 1964, but it is doubtful whether the repeal extended to Australia: see NSWLRC, *Report No. 4 on the Application of Imperial Acts* (1967) 115.

26 For an analysis of the Convention debates about s72 and some issues of interpretation see Thomson [1984] ACL 36033, 36055.
27 Proceedings in relation to the two trials are reported as follows: *Murphy v DPP* (1985) 60 ALR 299 (Toohey J) — application for judicial review in respect of Murphy's committal for trial on two charges refused; *R v Murphy* (1985) 61 ALR 139 (High Court) — motion in arrest of judgment on guilty verdict, and removal of questions of law reserved for the Court of Appeal rejected on certain legal grounds; factual issues reserved to the Court of Appeal; *R v Murphy* (1985) 63 ALR 53 (NSWCA) — new trial ordered on remaining count; *R v Murphy* (1985) 64 ALR 498 (Hunt J) — intervention of amicus in second trial in relation to evidence given before Senate Committee. See also (1986) 60 *ALJ* 56.
28 The main pre-trial inquiry was Senate Select Committee into Allegations concerning a Judge, *Report* (Cth Parl. Paper 1984/271), although the report of an earlier Senate Committee inquiry was also published: Senate Select Committee on the Conduct of a Judge, *Report* (Cth Parl. Paper 1984/168). The post-trial inquiry, established under the Parliamentary Commission of Inquiry Act 1986 (Cth), issued Special Reports on 5 & 19 Aug. 1986 and was then dissolved: Parliamentary Commission of Inquiry (Repeal) Act 1986 (Cth): for its *Report* see Cth Parl. Paper 1986/443. A challenge to one of the Commissioners on grounds of bias failed: *Murphy v Lush* (1986) 65 ALR 651. Murphy J sat on two further occasions in the High Court (60 ALJR 685, 698), and died on 21 Oct. 1986.
29 Apart from the material in the 1984 Senate Select Committee Reports, see (1985) *Law Inst J* 892; Brown *et al.* (1985) 10 *LSB* 153, (1986) 11 *LSB* 147; Whitton, *Can of Worms* (1986) 165–99, for a range of views.
30 Report of 19 Aug. 1986 (Lush, Blackburn, Wells); Cth Parl. Paper 1986/443.
31 The Murphy case demonstrated that Parliament itself is not an appropriate body to hold a factual inquiry, but the High Court left the delegation issue open in *Murphy v Lush* (1986) 65 ALR 651.
32 Cf. *Ex p Ramshay* (1852) 18 QB 174 (an inferior court judge). Generally see Quick & Garran, 728–34.
33 *Spratt v Hermes* (1965) 114 CLR 226.
34 ACT Supreme Court Act 1933 (Cth) s7; Supreme Court Act 1979 (NT) s40.
35 Similarly Supreme Court Act 1867 (Qld) s9. In other states: SA: Constitution Act 1934 ss74–5; Tasmania: Supreme Court (Judges' Independence) Act 1857 s1; Victoria: Constitution Act 1975 s77(1); WA: Constitution Act 1889 ss54–5; Supreme Court Act 1935 s9. See Wheeler (1980) 14 *UWALR* 305.
36 Shetreet (1976) 90–109. The question is still controversial in the US: for opposing views see Berger (1970) 79 *Yale LJ* 1475; Kaufman (1979) 88 *Yale LJ* 681.
37 Acting judges are temporarily appointed to relieve pressure of work in a court when a judge is unavailable. They also enable assessment of a potential judge 'in action'. A similar device is the appointment of senior barristers as commissioners to hear criminal cases on circuit. Acting judges cannot be appointed in federal courts, because of s72. For appointment and tenure of acting judges, see: Supreme Court Act 1970 (NSW) s37; Supreme Court Act 1979 (NT) s32(2); Acting Judges Act 1873 (Qld);

Supreme Court Act 1935 (SA) s11(3), although the provision is ambiguous; Supreme Court Act 1887 (Tas.) s3; Constitution Act 1975 (Vic.) s81; Supreme Court Act 1935 (WA) s11. There is no provision for acting judges in the ACT.

[38] For details see Whitton (1986) s.v. 'Foord', 'Farquhar'. See also *Foord v Whiddett* (1985) 60 *ALR* 269.

[39] For the Supreme Court's protest see *Sydney Morning Herald* 1 Oct. 1986. The judges argued for delay and proper consideration of the proposal, rather than against the principle of a Judicial Commission as such. See also Rogers (1987) 17 *Qld L Soc J* 21.

[40] E.g. the Commission's powers to collect and publish information about sentencing (s8), and to encourage measures of 'judicial education' (s9). See further Goldring (1986) 11 *LSB* 275.

[41] E.g. in Queensland the Governor may remove District Court judges for incapacity or misbehaviour without an address of Parliament: District Courts Act 1967 s13.

[42] NSW: Judicial Officers Act 1986 (NSW) ss3(1), 4; SA: Magistrates Act 1983 ss9–12; Victoria: Magistrates' Courts Act 1971 ss8, 8A.

[43] E.g. County Court Act 1958 (Vic.) s9; Magistrates' Courts Act 1971 (Vic.) s7(5). These provisions are discussed in more detail in Chapter 5.

[44] Under a flexible constitution, abolition of a court entails lapse of any judicial appointment to it: *Reilly v R* [1934] AC 176. There is some doubt whether this result would follow under Chapter III of the federal Constitution. For the machinery used to dissolve the Australian Industrial Court and the Federal Court of Bankruptcy, see Chapter 8. In NSW a similar procedure was followed with the reappointment of magistrates in 1983: see NSWLRC, Report 38, *First Appointments as Magistrates under the Local Courts Act, 1982* (1983), but the decision not to reappoint five magistrates was later quashed by the Court of Appeal on the ground of denial of natural justice: *Macrae v A-G (NSW)* (unreported, 24 June 1987). The constitutionality of the analogous practice of 'sidelining' a federal judge in the US is unresolved: *Chandler v Judicial Council of the Tenth Circuit* 398 US 74 (1970); *Hastings v Judicial Conference of the United States* 770 F 2d 1093 (1985). For the debate on the Judicial Councils Reform and Judicial Conduct and Disability Act 1980 see Baker (1985) 94 *Yale LJ* 1117.

[45] Nonetheless the case for formal judicial control over complaints procedures is strong: see Basten, 479–81; NZRCC, 216–23; Braithwaite, *Who Judges the Judges?* (1971). One corollary of complaints procedures is likely to be an increasing formalization of standards of judicial conduct, as has already happened in the US: see American Bar Association, Special Committee on Evaluation of Judicial Performance, *Guidelines for the Evaluation of Judicial Performance* (1985). A first step in Australia is Thomas, 'Judicial Ethics in Australia' (Supreme Court Judges Conference, 1987). See also Demack (1987) 17 *Qld L Soc J* 13. For a comparative survey of judicial accountability see Cappelletti (1985) 31 *Am J Comp L* 1.

[46] Cf. Pettifer, ed., *House of Representatives Practice* (1981) 23–4, 463–7; Odgers, *Australian Senate Practice* (5th edn, 1976) 250–4, 598–9. And see Shetreet (1976) 161–267 for some of these 'checks and balances'.

[47] For this reason the Constitutional Commission's Committee on the Australian Judicial System recommended that s72 tenure be extended, by

constitutional amendment, to all state and territory superior court judges, and that no judge should be removed except on a finding by a Judicial Tribunal that facts which could support a finding of misbehaviour or incapacity warranting removal have been proved: *Report* (1987) para. 5.55–69.
48 E.g. Constitution s72(iii). Cf. Supreme Court Act 1935 (SA) s12.
49 See Cowen & Derham (1956) 29 *ALJ* 705; Bennett, *Keystone*, 46–8, 101–3, for prominent examples. And cf. Green (1985) 59 *ALJ* 135, 143–8.
50 On the administration of the High Court see Chapter 9. See also AIJA Seminar, *Constitutional and Administrative Responsibilities for the Administration of Justice: The Partnership of Judiciary and Executive* (1975).
51 E.g. Judiciary Act 1903 (Cth) s23(2)(b). The constitutional validity of this provision is not beyond question.
52 E.g. Australian Capital Territory Supreme Court Act 1933 (Cth) s7B. On the administrative functions of the Chief Justice of the High Court, cf. Marr, *Barwick* (1980) 211–17, 221–2.
53 E.g. Bickel, *The Supreme Court and the Idea of Progress* (1978); McCloskey, *The Modern Supreme Court* (1972).
54 *Dyer's Case* (1557) 2 Dyer 158b, 73 ER 344; *Milward v Thatcher* (1787) 2 TR 82, 100 ER 45; Note (1962) 47 *Iowa LR* 1026, 1026–32.
55 E.g. Judiciary (Diplomatic Representation) Act 1977 (Cth), which authorized Fox J to accept appointment as ambassador-at-large in relation to nuclear safeguards.
56 Victoria, *Parl Debs* 1923–4, I, 523. The Victorian history is informatively set out by McInerney (1978) 52 *ALJ* 540.
57 Bennett, *Keystone*, 44–5. More recently the Queensland Supreme Court has apparently taken the same view: Thomas, 'Judicial Ethics in Australia' (Supreme Court Judges Conference, 1987) 47.
58 (1978) 9 *FLR* 1, 3–4. See also McGregor, in AIJA, *Judges as Royal Commissioners and Chairmen of Non- Judicial Tribunals* (1986) 172.
59 Similar considerations apply to the US Supreme Court, which with very few exceptions has refused all extra-judicial assignments: (1953) 67 *Harvard LR* 193; Bell (1970) 22 *Stan LR* 587.
60 This criticism can be levelled at the SA government's use of White AJ to investigate Special Branch Files: see Cockburn, *The Salisbury Affair* (1979) 162–96. Cockburn's criticism of the White Report is however substantially unfounded, as another judicial inquiry, this time by Mitchell J, indirectly found: SA, *Royal Commission into the Dismissal of HH Salisbury* (1978) 25–7.
61 Whitlam & Stubbs, *Nest of Traitors* (1974) 96–8.
62 Australian judges have frequently been seconded to courts of developing countries in the region: e.g. Judicial Office (Papua New Guinea) Act 1979 (NSW). Sir Garfield Barwick acted as judge *ad hoc* (and dissented) in the International Court of Justice in the *Nuclear Tests Case*: ICJ Rep. 1974, 253, 391–455.
63 The restrictive view is supported by McInerney, 552 (on loss-of-public-confidence grounds) by Hillyard (1971) 6 *Irish Jur (NS)* 93 (on grounds of judicial incompetence in questions of social policy) and by Barwick (1979) 53 *ALJ* 487, 490–1, and McInerney & Maloney, in AIJA, *Judges as Royal Commissioners and Chairmen of Non-Judicial Tribunals* (1986) 5 (on a variety of grounds). Connor is critical of the use of judges in

'frankly executive appointments': (1978) 52 *ALJ* 482. Both the NSW and SA Supreme Courts adopt a more flexible approach than the Victorian Supreme Court: Street (1978) 52 *ALJ* 661; King (1980) 39 *AJ Pub Adm* 1, 15–17. On similar uses of judges in the UK see Rhodes, *Committees of Inquiry* (1975) 83–4, 219–22; Cartwright, *Royal Commissions and Departmental Committees in Britain* (1975) 72. On the relation between royal commissions and courts cf. *McGuiness v A-G (Victoria)* (1940) 63 CLR 73; *Victoria v Australian . . . Builders Labourers' Federation* (1982) 152 CLR 25.
64 But not, it has been held, on applications for special leave to appeal to the High Court: HCR O70 R2(6); *Hass v R* (1975) 133 CLR 120; Barwick (1979) 53 *ALJ* 494.
65 A distinction is drawn between 'party and party' and 'solicitor and client' costs. The latter are normally met by the party in question, whatever the outcome of the case: see Cairns, *Australian Civil Procedure* (2nd edn 1985) ch. 16.
66 But cf. Costs in Criminal Cases Act 1967 (NSW); Costs in Criminal Cases Act 1976 (Tas.); Official Prosecutions (Defendant's Costs) Act 1973 (WA), which entitles a successful defendant to his costs.
67 Generally on the costs of litigation see Disney *et al.*, *Lawyers* (2nd edn, 1986) 295–376.
68 Federal Proceedings (Costs) Act 1980 (Cth); Suitors' Fund Act 1964 (WA); Appeal Costs Fund Act 1964 (Vic.); Suitors' Fund Act 1951 (NSW); Appeal Costs Fund Act 1973 (Qld); Appeal Costs Fund Act 1979 (SA); Appeal Costs Fund Act 1968 (Tas.). These Acts have, in some cases at least, been rather restrictively applied: *Zappulla v Perkins (No.2)* [1978] Qd R 401; cf. *Bullock v Federated Furnishing Trades Society of Australasia (No.2)* (1985) 58 ALR 373. And see WALRC, *Report on the Suitors' Fund Act (Parts A & B)* (1976).
69 E.g. Public Defenders Act 1969 (NSW); Public Defence Act 1974 (Qld). In consumer matters, a commissioner may support or initiate proceedings on behalf of a consumer who applies for assistance: e.g. Consumer Protection Act 1969 (NSW) ss16G–K.
70 Evans, ed., *Law, Politics and the Labor Movement* (1980) 149–77, esp. the paper by Armstrong. An example of the state schemes is Legal Services Commission Act 1977 (SA). The last merger of the ALAO with a state scheme occurred in NSW in 1987: (1987) 61 *ALJ* 108, 160.
71 On legal aid in Australia see further Disney *et al.*, *Lawyers* (2nd edn, 1986) 377–458; Hanks in Tomasic, ed., *Understanding Lawyers* (1978) 394; Jones (1980) 54 *ALJ* 502; Commonwealth Legal Aid Commission, *Legal Aid in Australia: An Annotated Bibliography* (1979); Boer, ed., *Legal Aid Research in Australia* (1981); Else-Mitchell (1983) 57 *ALJ* 439; Attorney-General's Department (Cth), Legal Aid Task Force, *Final Report* (1985); Hutchison (1985) 38 (17) *Canberra Survey* 1.
72 (1979) 27 ALR 449, 456–7. Cf. (1980) 5 *LSB* 307; International Covenant on Civil and Political Rights 1966 Art. 14(3)(d) (criminal cases only).
73 Generally see Disney *et al.*, *Lawyers* (2nd edn, 1986); Bennett, *A History of the New South Wales Bar* (1969); Tomasic, ed., *Understanding Lawyers* (1978); Disney (1979) 53 *ALJ* 348; NSWLRC, Report 31, *First Report on the Legal Profession. General Regulation and Structure* (1982); Sexton & Maher, *The Legal Mystique* (1982). On the English legal profession,

Abel-Smith & Stevens, *Lawyers and the Courts* (1967); Abel, *The Legal Profession in England and Wales* (1987).

[74] Lawyers admitted at state level are entitled to practise in federal courts, and in courts of other states exercising federal jurisdiction: Judiciary Act 1903 (Cth) s55B. This right will be extended under the proposed cross-vesting legislation: Jurisdiction of Courts (Cross-vesting) Act 1987 (Cth) s5(8).

[75] The NSWLRC proposed substantial modifications to the division of the profession in that state, a proposal which has not been implemented: NSWLRC 31 (1982) 59–79. See also Disney *et al.*, *Lawyers* (2nd edn, 1986) 59–77; Zander, *Lawyers and the Public Interest* (1968) 270–332; Forbes, *The Divided Legal Profession in Australia. History, Rationalization and Rationale* (1979); Mann (1977) 93 *LQR* 367. For the Benson Commission's very cautious account, see UK, Royal Commission on Legal Services, *Report* (1979) I, 187–202.

[76] See also Malcolm (1981) 55 *ALJ* 401.

[77] Edwards, *The Law Officers of the Crown* (1964); Archer, *The Role of the Law Officers* (1979).

[78] On the problems of the Attorney-General's independence from political control (in Australia, a tenuous tradition) see Plehwe (1980) 11 *FLR* 1. Cf. Edwards in Glazebrook, ed., *Reshaping the Criminal Law* (1978) 364.

[79] There is a Commonwealth Solicitor-General, and a Solicitor-General in each state. In Tasmania and NSW there is also a Crown Advocate with special functions in criminal cases. In Queensland and WA a Minister of Justice acts as Attorney-General.

[80] On the role of the Attorney-General in such cases see ALRC 27, *Standing in Public Interest Litigation* (1985) 55–61, 85–95.

[81] See Temby (1985) 59 *ALJ* 197, and see Chapter 5.

[82] Forsyth, *History of Trial by Jury* (2nd edn, 1878); Baker, 18–19, 63–6, 415–8; Turner (1968) 7 (2) *J Brit Stud* 1. A good general review is Cornish, *The Jury* (1971). Cf. also Williams, *The Proof of Guilt* (1955) 190–272; Devlin, *Trial by Jury* (1966).

[83] The jury's right to arrive at a verdict without coercion or punishment was established in *Bushell's case* (1670) Vaughan 135. The modern distinction between law and fact derived from the attempt to distinguish the function of the jury from that of the judge. But some degree of judicial control was maintained by manipulating the formulas: thus, whether a particular conclusion was *possible* in the circumstances was — and is — a question of law: cf. Baker, 81–2. See also Williams (1987) 61 *ALJ* 134.

[84] Bennett (1961) 3 *Syd LR* 463; Evatt (1936) 10 *ALJ Supp* 49. In the other Australian colonies jury trial was more rapidly introduced: Castles, 61–2, 72–5, 90–2.

[85] Castles, 35, 72.

[86] Bennett, 464.

[87] *R v Valentine* (1871) 10 SCR 113. The reasoning here may not have applied to the 'free' settlements such as SA, where such juries have been abolished by statute: Juries Act 1927 (SA) s85; cf. s86 (jury of matrons).

[88] Grand juries existed for General and Quarter Sessions in NSW: (Bennett, 482–5) and in SA and WA (Castles, 90, 93). But the system of criminal prosecution on the Attorney-General's information superseded the grand jury, which lapsed in NSW and was abolished in SA (1852) and WA

(1883). Cf. *R v Walton* (1851) 1 Legge 706. In Victoria, an Act of 1874 introduced grand juries, which were occasionally used: e.g. *R v McInnes* [1940] VLR 416. However the reaction to the actual use of a grand jury in 1986 led to a decision to abolish grand juries altogether: Crimes (Grand Juries) Bill 1986 (Vic.). Grand juries were abolished in the UK in 1933, but are still active in the US. See Frankel & Naftalis, *The Grand Jury* (1977); Hemholz (1983) 50 *U Chic LR* 613.

89 For majority verdicts see Jury Act 1899 (Tas.) s48; Juries Act 1927 (SA) s57; Juries Act 1963 (NT) s48; Juries Act 1957 (WA) s41.

90 Juries Act 1927 (SA) s7; Crimes Act 1900 (NSW) ss475A–B. There is no right of election for federal offences to which s80 of the Constitution applies: *Brown v R* (1985) 64 ALR 161.

91 Cf. *Storey v R* (1978) 22 ALR 47. Appeals and references from not guilty verdicts are discussed in Chapter 7. It is not clear whether majority verdicts or appeals from not guilty verdicts are consistent with the guarantee of jury trial for federal offences under s80 of the Constitution: cf. *Brown v R* (1985) 64 ALR 161.

Section 80 is discussed in Chapter 3.

92 Coroner's juries are abolished in ACT, NT, SA, Queensland. Limited provision is made for them in NSW (jury of 6), Tasmania (4–6), Victoria (5–12), WA (3).

93 Juries Act 1927 (SA) s5(1)(a) allows a judge to order civil jury trial where a question may arise whether a person has committed an indictable offence. There is no record of any successful application since 1927. Even before 1927 civil jury trial was a rarity: (1936) 10 *ALJ Supp* 75. In the NT and the ACT the court has a general discretion to allow civil jury trial, but there has been no such trial in the NT for at least 12 years, in the ACT, apparently never: Juries Act 1963 (NT) s7; Australian Capital Territory Supreme Court Act 1933 (Cth) s14. In the other three jurisdictions the parties may require or a judge may order jury trial. See as follows: Queensland: Supreme Court Act 1867 s61, SCR 039; District Courts Act 1967 s75, DCR R234. (Of 990 civil cases heard during 1979–80, 3 were tried by jury in the Supreme Court. Of 1721 cases heard in District Courts, 3 were jury matters. Tasmania: Supreme Court Civil Procedure Act 1932 ss27, 29, SCR 039; Local Courts Act 1896 ss64–6. (Only a very few civil cases are tried by jury in the Supreme Court (0.2%); virtually none in Courts of Requests. WA: Supreme Court Act 1935 s42; District Court of Western Australia Act 1969 s52. (Of 481 civil trials heard in the Supreme Court from 1976–9, only 2 were by jury. There has only ever been one civil jury trial in the District Court. And see Hales (1973) 11 *UWALR* 99.) The Federal Court may order trial by jury in civil cases, but is most reluctant to do so: cf. *Insurance Commissioner v Australian Associated Motor Insurers Ltd* (1982) 45 ALR 391.

94 Supreme Court Act 1970 (NSW) ss85–9; District Court Act 1973 (NSW) ss77–9. See Samuels (1980) 54 *ALJ* 586. In 1978, 39% of common law actions in the Supreme Court were jury matters; in 1979, 32%. Respectively, 93% and 78% of these were industrial accident cases. The proportion of District Court jury matters is much less: in 1979, 5.5% overall (in Sydney, 7.5%). Again, industrial accident cases predominate.

95 Victoria, General Rules of Procedure in Civil Proceedings 1986 O47.02; County Court Act 1958 (Vic.) ss67–72.

96 *Ward v James* [1966] 1 QB 273; *Williams v Beesly* [1973] 3 All ER 144; Jackson, 84–6, 499–504.
97 Judiciary Act 1903 (Cth) ss77A–D; HCR 036 rr3–6; *McDermott v Collien* (1953) 87 CLR 154.
98 There is, however, strong support for civil jury trial on the part of trade unions and the lawyers who appear on behalf of plaintiffs in personal injury cases. Compare the reticence shown, in the face of strong evidence that civil jury trial is wasteful and costly, by two recent reports: Cranston, Haynes, Pullen & Scott, *Delays and Efficiency in Civil Litigation* (AIJA, 1985) 146–51, 211–12; Civil Justice Committee, *Report concerning the Administration of Civil Justice in Victoria* (1984) I, 186.
99 Baldwin & McConville, *Jury Trials* (1979) 53, 67. They concluded that 36% of all acquittals and at least 5% of convictions in their sample were unsatisfactory. See id., 6–15, for an assessment of earlier research. No similar research has been conducted in Australia, but long-running disputes about the justice of jury convictions in a few major trials have thrown doubt on the jury system: e.g. *Chamberlain v R* (1984) 51 ALR 225; *Alister v R* (1983) 50 ALR 41. In both cases those charged and convicted were subsequently pardoned after new evidence was discovered.
100 Crimes Act 1900 ss475A–B (inserted 1979). There is also provision for waiver of jury trial in SA (Juries Act 1927 (SA) s11) inserted in 1984 following a recommendation of the Mitchell Committee, *Third Report* (1975) 80–94. Cf. also (1980) 6 *CLB* 1434; Sallmann, *Report on Criminal Trials* (AIJA/Victorian Bar, 1985) 164–5, 199; NZRCC, 122–5. An English committee has recommended trial by judge alone in complex fraud cases: Home Office, *Report of Fraud Trials Committee* (Chairman: Lord Roskill) (1986). Cf. (1986) 60 *ALJ* 193; Phillips (1983) 57 *Law Inst J* 1214.
101 Baldwin & McConville, *Negotiated Justice* (1977). In Australia, cf. Willis & Sallman (1977) 51 *Law Inst J* 498.
102 *R v Sheffield Crown Court ex p Brownlow* [1980] 2 WLR 892; *R v Mason* [1980] 3 WLR 617; (1980) 6 *CLB* 1517; (1980) 5 *LSB* 303; harman & Griffith, *Justice Deserted. The Subversion of the Jury* (1979).
103 This has been a particular problem in recent years (e.g. in the Murphy case: (1986) 60 *ALJ* 56): see Phillips (1985) 59 *L Inst J* 1330; Reid, in Challenger, ed., *The Jury* (1986) 45, 52–3; Chesterman, id., 129. Legislation has been enacted or proposed in several states to penalize jury room disclosures: Juries (Amendment) Act 1985 (Vic.); ALRC 35, *Contempt* (1987) ch. 7; NSWLRC, Report 48, *The Jury in a Criminal Trial* (1986) ch. 11; Vic. LRC, Background Paper 1, *The Role of the Jury in Criminal Trials* (1985) ch. 5; cf. (1986) 11 *LSB* 138. See further Campbell (1985) 11 *Monash LR* 169; McHugh (1986) 2(2) *Aust Bar Rev* 114. On the question of impeachment of jury verdicts based on jury fraud or misunderstanding cf. *Lalchan Nanan v State* [1986] 1 AC 860; Campbell (1985) 9 *Crim LJ*, 132, 187.
104 Hale, *The History of the Common Law of England* (3rd edn, 1739) 160.
105 See Devlin, *The Judge* (1979) 117–76; Jackson, 481–99; Dickey (1974) 11 *UWALR* 204; Brown, id., 256; Green, *Verdict according to Conscience. Perspectives on the English Criminal Trial Jury* (1985); McInerney (1985) 59 *Law Inst J* 1084; Harding, in Challenger, ed., *The Jury* (1986) 237; Murphy, id., 13; *Kingswell v R* (1985) 62 ALR 161, 185–9 (Deane J).

[106] Cf. Scutt (1980) 18 *Law Soc J* 119; Willis & Sallman (1977), and the summary in Victorian LRC, Background Paper 1, *The Role of the Jury in Criminal Trials* (1985) ch. 4.
[107] The NSWLRC recommended in favour of retaining jury trial (and unanimous verdicts) on the basis that it had not been shown that jury trial was undesirable: NSWLRC 48 (1986) 13–17. Given the absence of Australian research, this implies something of an act of faith. Cf. QLRC WP 28, *The Role of Juries in Criminal Trials* (1985).
[108] E.g. Supreme Court Act 1935 (WA) ss51 (inquiries by referees), 52 (trial by referees or arbitrators), 56 (assessors).
[109] See Dickey (1970) 33 *MLR* 494; Rogers (1984) 58 *ALJ* 608, 616–8; ALRC 33, *Civil Admiralty Jurisdiction* (1986) 238–41.
[110] See e.g. Sharkey & Dorter, *Commercial Arbitration* (1986); Lucke (1976) 5 *Adel LR* 244; O'Keefe, *Arbitration in International Trade* (1975); McPherson (1982) 12 *Qld L Soc J* 219. For developments in court-annexed arbitration and in commercial arbitration centres in Australia see Chapters 6 and 14.

PART 2
Courts of General Jurisdiction

CHAPTER 5

Criminal Jurisdiction in Inferior and Intermediate Courts

In this and the next four chapters, the various courts of general jurisdiction in Australia will be examined. These contrast with specialist courts and tribunals, set up to perform specific, more or less limited functions, and dealt with in Part Three. Formally, the courts of general jurisdiction will be discussed in ascending order, from the 'bottom' of the court hierarchy to the 'top'. In one sense, however, the 'inferior' courts are the most important ones. They are the only courts which the vast majority of people are likely to have to face. Together they deal with hundreds of thousands of cases a year, compared with the High Court's hundred or so. It is a natural consequence that the High Court has been extensively discussed and analyzed, while research into the courts of summary jurisdiction has hardly begun.[1]

5.1 Inferior and Intermediate Criminal Courts in Australia[2]

At common law there were, and are, two classes of criminal offence — felonies and misdemeanours. Felonies were the more serious, capital offences; misdemeanours were punishable only by fine or imprisonment, and the other consequences of conviction were less. Both felonies and misdemeanours were tried by jury on the basis of an indictment, a formal accusation of the crime.[3] Criminal proceedings could be commenced by presentment of a grand jury or (in the case of misdemeanours) by a criminal information.[4] However, many minor cases of breach of statutes did not warrant trial by jury, and the local justices of the peace could determine such minor offences in a 'summary' way. This was the origin of summary jurisdiction, which was eventually regulated, largely in accordance with existing practice, by the Summary Jurisdiction Act 1848 (UK).[5] So a further distinction developed between crimes, not by reference to penalty but to mode of trial — summary or simple offences, triable before justices at petty sessions, and indictable offences, felonies and misdemeanours triable at quarter sessions or assizes by jury.

The judicial functions of justices of the peace at petty and quarter sessions were only some of the very many tasks given them. Until the nineteenth century they were in effect the main organs of local government, responsible for the administration of the poor law, the maintenance of public order, much of the investigation of crime, and so on. Crown appointees commissioned from the propertied classes, they mostly had no legal qualifications, relying for legal advice on the justices' clerk. Indeed, in England this is still the case. Lay justices continue to hear a high proportion of all summary criminal cases in Magistrates Courts, and they still sit with a judge in the Crown Court (which in 1972 replaced quarter sessions) to hear appeals from Magistrates Courts and to assist with sentencing.[6]

In busy criminous cities, unpaid lay justices could not cope, and in 1792 the first 'stipendiary' or paid magistrate was appointed in London. Some other larger cities did the same, but these appointments remained exceptional outside London. In 1983 there were only some 58 legally trained stipendiary magistrates.[7]

In Australia, justices of the peace, appointed on the English model, from the first exercised criminal jurisdiction: their powers were in some respects greater than in England, especially over convicts. But stipendiary or police magistrates were also appointed (the first in 1826). In South Australia, most minor criminal cases were heard by Resident Magistrates' Courts rather than by justices. Where — as in the eastern states — an 'intermediate' criminal court sat, along the lines of quarter sessions, it was usually chaired by a legally trained judge, though justices might also sit.[8]

The three-tier English arrangement (petty sessions, quarter sessions, assizes) was at first followed with some fidelity, especially in New South Wales and Victoria. But attempts to establish courts of quarter (or general) sessions foundered in South Australia, and in most colonies there was relatively little difference between the summary jurisdiction of justices in and out of sessions. Queensland abolished quarter sessions in 1891; their replacements, District Courts, were themselves abolished in 1921.[9] In smaller jurisdictions a three-tier criminal structure was simply unnecessary: instead the Supreme Court took a much more active role in trying the serious cases, and in hearing appeals from, or reviewing, decisions of courts of summary jurisdiction.

However, the very great increase in crime in the last 35 years has led, in five jurisdictions, to the reconstitution of intermediate criminal courts. These were set up, or criminal jurisdiction was conferred on them, in Queensland in 1958,[10] in Victoria (replacing courts of general sessions) in 1968,[11] in Western Australia (replacing courts of sessions[12]) and South Australia[13] in 1969, and in New South Wales (replacing quarter sessions) in 1973.[14] These new courts have an extensive criminal jurisdiction over indictable offences, exercised by judge and jury. But the continued increase in crime and the increasing length of criminal trials have been major factors leading to further transfer of criminal trials to courts of summary jurisdiction.

It is proposed to discuss first, the courts of summary jurisdiction; second, the procedures of committal or preliminary examination, by which magistrates or justices send persons for trial in the higher courts; and thirdly, the criminal jurisdiction of County, District, and District Criminal Courts. In each case the provisions in the eight states and territories vary considerably, and only a general account can be given here.

5.2 Summary Jurisdiction in Australia

(1) Courts of summary jurisdiction

With only a few exceptions,[15] the hearing of the numerous simple offences created by statute is a matter for the courts of summary jurisdiction, variously named, in each state and territory.[16]

(A) MAGISTRATES AND JUSTICES IN COURTS OF SUMMARY JURISDICTION

In all states summary jurisdiction has at some stage been exercised by lay justices of the peace, but this is now the case only to a very limited degree. In the Australian Capital Territory and Queensland, justices do not sit judicially at all.[17] Elsewhere in Australia they have only a minor role. In New South Wales, for example, they are excluded from exercising jurisdiction in the Sydney and Newcastle police districts and in other proclaimed areas.[18] In South Australia they sit only in the less important cases or where no magistrate is available, and cannot imprison for more than seven days.[19] Even in Victoria, where until 1984 justices continued to hear a significant number of all criminal cases in Magistrates' Courts, only magistrates can now hear criminal cases or committal proceedings.[20] Throughout Australia, justices still exercise ancillary powers such as attesting documents, signing warrants, and admitting to bail.

Different views are held in England about the merits of lay justices in courts of summary jurisdiction, but there is no likelihood that they will be replaced.[21] In Australia they have been almost entirely excluded from exercising criminal jurisdiction, in state as well as in federal jurisdiction.[22] Arguments based on the supposed advantages of lay participation in the court system have thus not prevailed, in Australia at least. On the other hand the triviality of many minor cases in summary jurisdiction suggests that alternative methods will have to be found of handling the multitude of very minor offences — for example, extended use of 'on-the-spot' or 'expiation' fines, or the processing of minor cases 'on paper' by court officers or justices, without oral evidence and in the parties' absence.[23]

The decline in lay justices has coincided with an increase in status and security of tenure of magistrates in almost all Australian jurisdictions. The older description of 'police magistrate' has vanished, and with it, to some extent, the image of magistrates as partial to the police/prosecution rather than independent.[24] At one stage many Australian magistrates were part of the state public service, and were recruited from within the public service and qualified by examination rather than legal practice.[25] This created the potential for executive control of magistrates under these Acts — a problem underlined, for example, in South Australia, when magistrates were placed in the same government department as Crown prosecutors. That move was rapidly reversed when the Supreme Court held that it disqualified magistrates from sitting on grounds of bias.[26] The position now is that magistrates in all jurisdictions except Queensland hold office under separate legislation, with distinct security of tenure.[27] This is clearly a more desirable arrangement.

So far no federal magistrates have been appointed. Instead the Commonwealth has made extensive use of legally qualified magistrates in exercising federal jurisdiction both in civil and criminal matters. Whether this situation will continue for much longer remains to be seen. There are pressures for the appointment of federal magistrates to relieve the pressure on courts (for example in the family law area).[28]

(B) JURISDICTION OVER SIMPLE OFFENCES
Courts of summary jurisdiction have exclusive power to hear and determine complaints of simple offences — that is, statutory offences which are expressed to be triable summarily or which are not expressed to be triable on indictment. There are very many such offences scattered through the statute book — traffic and parking offences, drunkenness offences, offences against public order or safety, public health offences, and so on. These are tried without a jury, usually at a single sitting. Very frequently the defendant pleads guilty and the case is disposed of in minutes, although there is power to adjourn, and the occasional contested case may take longer.[29] Penalties are specified for each offence, but the court usually has considerable discretion in sentencing (or not sentencing), within the maximum limit set.[30]

(C) MINOR INDICTABLE OFFENCES
In addition to this numerous jurisdiction, there is in each state and territory power to try summarily a range of felonies and mis-

demeanours, usually described as 'minor indictable offences'. These are variously defined: typically, they include minor thefts, obtaining by false pretences, receiving stolen property, 'simple' assaults, housebreaking, and the like. These are among the most common crimes, so that summary trial relieves the higher criminal courts of a great deal of work. In most jurisdictions, offences against property are only triable summarily up to a certain value (which may be greater if the court consists of a magistrate, or if the defendant consents or pleads guilty). But these values vary greatly: in South Australia $400 (before a magistrate),[31] in Victoria, $10 000.[32] This last figure was increased from $2000 in 1980, in an attempt to reduce the delays before trial on indictment in the County Court. This is typical of the tendency to extend the ambit of summary jurisdiction, caused by the increases in housebreaking, shoplifting, and car-stealing, and in the length of trials on indictment in higher courts.

In all jurisdictions, the defendant must consent to summary trial (or may elect trial on indictment) for the more serious offences: in four states, the defendant may require any minor indictable offence to be tried by jury.[33] The court also has the discretion not to proceed to summary trial but to commit the defendant for trial or (in some jurisdictions) for sentence in a higher court.[34] Indeed, in the Northern Territory the court lacks jurisdiction to hear a minor indictable offence, even where the defendant consents, if it appears 'that the offence, having regard to its seriousness or the intricacy of the facts or the difficulty of any question of law likely to arise . . . or any other relevant circumstances, ought to be tried by the Supreme Court'.[35]

There are usually advantages for the defendant in having charges of indictable offences tried summarily. The case is dealt with speedily, and (unless there are prior convictions) the court can in most cases only impose lesser penalties than would have been available to the District or Supreme Court.[36] On the other hand a defendant who wishes to defend the charge may well prefer jury trial but be, in a sense, coerced into consenting to summary trial by the prospect of waiting nine months or more before the hearing. Acquittal rates in jury cases are much higher than in courts of summary jurisdiction. The choice is an invidious one, emphasizing the corrosive effects of delay in criminal trials.[37]

(2) Summary jurisdiction over federal offences

Section 68 of the Judiciary Act 1903 (Cth) confers summary jurisdiction on state and territory courts of summary jurisdiction with respect to offences against federal law. The law and procedure of the state or territory applies, except that justices of the peace may not sit.[38] Section 68 applies also to minor indictable offences: most Commonwealth offences are triable summarily, under s68(8) of the Judiciary Act or otherwise.[39] As Barwick CJ said in *Peel v R*, the effect of these provisions is that the value of uniformity of federal criminal law is subordinated to that of the uniform administration of all the criminal law in each state or territory.[40]

(3) Appeals from courts of summary jurisdiction

More than any other aspect of summary jurisdiction, the provisions for appeal from decisions of courts of summary jurisdiction are extraordinarily divergent and complex. Forms of review and appeal have undergone a considerable evolution since the nineteenth century,[41] but while new and simpler machinery for appeal from superior courts has tended to replace the earlier forms, in the case of courts of summary jurisdiction the process has usually been one of addition. In no state are there less than two methods of statutory review or appeal; in some there are as many as four or five. To this extent, the various provisions give an interesting cross-section of modes of appeal. That is all one can say in their favour.

In all states and territories there is at least some provision for appeal from decisions of courts of summary jurisdiction. In South Australia and the Northern Territory,[42] such appeals (to the Supreme Court) are the normal way of challenging decisions, but elsewhere this is not necessarily so. In some states (e.g. Western Australia), appeals are available on very restricted grounds, and orders to review or other similar procedures take priority.[43] Where an appeal is available in the case of a simple offence, it goes to the Supreme Court (and is heard by a single judge) in Western Australia,[44] the Northern Territory,[45] South Australia,[46] and the Australian Capital Territory,[47] and to the County or District Court in Victoria,[48] Queensland,[49] and New South Wales.[50] In Tasmania, in some circumstances an order to review becomes a rehearing, indistinguishable from an appeal, in the Supreme Court.[51] Appeals from conviction or sentence in the case of minor indictable offences go to the Full Supreme Court or Court of Criminal Appeal, in some states, in the same way as if the case had actually been heard on indictment.[52] In the remaining jurisdictions they are treated as summary convictions.

In five jurisdictions, the court can state a case for consideration by the Supreme Court: this is sometimes an interlocutory proceeding and sometimes a form of appeal, but it differs from ordinary appeals in being confined to questions of law. The Supreme Court cannot, therefore, draw inferences of fact, but is restricted to the case as stated or amended.[53] Unless the point of law obviously or clearly arises, the case stated can therefore be an unsatisfactory procedure.[54]

In five jurisdictions, there is a procedure by which the complainant or defendant can apply to the Supreme Court (in Queensland, a

District Court) for an order to review a decision of a court of summary jurisdiction.[55] Like the case stated, the order to review is restricted to points of law or jurisdiction. In each case it takes priority over any appeal. In Western Australia, at least, it is the usual method of challenging summary decisions. In New South Wales, a rather similar statutory procedure exists in the form of applications to set aside or to restrain proceedings.[56] In Tasmania, there is also an appeal from a decision of justices exercising summary jurisdiction to a magistrate.[57] A court of summary jurisdiction may also have power to set aside a decision where some procedural or other defect exists.[58]

For some time the only method of correcting summary decisions of justices in England was through the supervisory jurisdiction of the Court of King's Bench, especially the writs of certiorari, prohibition, and mandamus. In some states this jurisdiction still exists; in others it has been supplanted by the procedures referred to above, or by analogous statutory forms.[59]

It is difficult to justify the multiplicity of forms of review and appeal which exist in most states. As the Western Australian Law Reform Commission stated:

the existing dual system of appeals, each applicable only in certain circumstances, is unnecessarily cumbersome. The difference in statutory wording setting out each mode has tended to raise doubts as to the permissible grounds of appeal and as to the powers and functions of the appellate court. It has also led to separate procedures, with different forms, time limits, bail provisions and documentary requirements generally. The . . . present dual mode system should be replaced by a single system of appeals and procedure, with emphasis on clarity and simplicity.[60]

These comments are at least as true for most other states and territories, with even more complex provisions.

(4) Other problems of summary jurisdiction

Apart from the complexity of the provisions for appeal and review, other problems are apparent. These include the recruitment and training of magistrates,[61] reduction of the workload in trivial cases, and improved ways of listing cases for hearing.[62] But it is likely that other problems are not so apparent, since so little research has been conducted on the workings of courts of summary jurisdiction. A study of Victorian Magistrates' Courts concluded that magistrates 'showed a degree of professional competence considerably greater than that displayed by the Justices' and that many of the usual criticisms of such courts were exaggerated or unfounded.[63] The methods employed in the study have, however, themselves been criticized,[64] and much remains to be done.[65]

5.3 Committal for Trial in Intermediate and Supreme Courts[66]

(1) The committal procedure

Simple offences are brought before the courts by a straightforward procedure of complaint. The procedure for indictable offences is more elaborate. In every case someone must decide whether there is enough evidence to proceed, and in which court the case should be prosecuted. With certain exceptions, in the case of an indictable offence these decisions are not made informally (as with simple offences) or (as in Scotland) by a special prosecuting authority,[67] but by an 'examining' magistrate or two justices in a pre-trial procedure known as a preliminary examination (or committal proceedings).

The origins of committal proceedings are not judicial but executive. Local justices were required to examine persons suspected of indictable offences so that, if enough evidence was available, they could be brought before a grand jury to be presented for the offence.[68] With the growth of police forces this function gradually became more a judicial one, of examining the evidence to see if it was sufficient to put the defendant upon trial, and its purpose now was more to protect the defendant than to assist the prosecution.[69] In England the procedures which evolved were largely enacted in the Indictable Offences Act 1848, on which the Australian committal provisions were modelled.[70] But the origins of preliminary examinations can still be seen in the fact that they are carried out not by courts of summary jurisdiction as such but by examining justices or magistrates, who in doing so are deemed not to constitute an 'open court'.[71]

Until recently, the procedures for preliminary examination in Australia were fairly uniform. The prosecution's evidence was given and taken down in writing in the form of depositions, which could be used at the trial, if the witness was unavailable or to establish any inconsistency or change in the evidence. The magistrate then determined whether there was sufficient evidence to justify the defendant being put on trial. If not, the defendant was discharged without having to plead (though this did not constitute an acquittal: if, for example, the prosecutor obtained new evidence new proceedings could be commenced, either by way of a second committal hearing or an *ex officio* indictment). If a sufficient case was made out, the defendant was given an opportunity to plead, and on a plea of not guilty, to present evidence to refute the prosecution case. A defendant who pleaded guilty was committed for sentence (and the depositions, including any evidence on the defendant's behalf in mitigation of penalty, formed the basis for sentencing). If the evidence warranted it, a defendant who did not admit guilt would be committed to the appropriate court for trial. It then became the task of the Attorney-General or a Crown prosecutor to frame and file an indictment in the court, on the basis of which the defendant would be tried.[72] But the Attorney-General had no duty to file an indictment, and could refuse to proceed, or proceed in another court having jurisdiction, or charge some (lesser or greater) offence disclosed by the evidence.[73]

In each state and territory this can still be described as the 'normal' way in which a defendant is brought to trial on an indictable offence.[74] But considerable variation exists in this basic model. In the first place, as we have seen, the defendant can elect or be subjected to summary trial for a minor indictable offence. Any election or discretion to try such an offence summarily is made or exercised at the end of the prosecution's case, or upon an earlier plea of guilty.[75] The magistrate then becomes a court of summary jurisdiction for that purpose.

Secondly, in some jurisdictions the defendant can consent to be committed without the evidence being considered, even though he wishes to plead not guilty at the trial.[76] This reduces the cost of committal, but adds to the risk of the trial misfiring. It is desirable that the defendant be legally represented, so as to ensure an informed consent to committal.

A related change, which now exists in some form in each jurisdiction, is the so-called 'hand-up brief'. Introduced in England by the Criminal Justice Act 1967, this procedure allows the submission and consideration of evidence in written form.[77] It frees witnesses from attendance and thus saves the time taken in recording evidence in writing before the examining magistrate. It also gives the defendant better notice of the prosecution case, and thus a better opportunity to take advice. In England the procedure is extensively used; in Australia much more variably.[78] One argument against it is that, combined with the provision for committal by consent, it has increased the proportion of weak or untenable cases going to trial and having then to be withdrawn: some sceptics, unimpressed, say that committal proceedings never were very effective in filtering out weak cases.[79]

Other changes have included improved procedures for suppressing evidence given at committal proceedings, so as to avoid prejudicial pre-trial publicity,[80] and special provisions for sexual offences[81] and committal of corporations.[82]

(2) Committal for sentence

In most jurisdictions a defendant who pleads guilty at a preliminary investigation will be committed to the appropriate court for sentence. A change of plea is still possible, though this may require the trial court's consent.[83] Where there is a change of plea the defendant is treated as if committed for trial. In Victoria the problem is dealt with more simply: a defendant who pleads guilty is committed for trial, but the plea may be admitted in evidence at the trial.[84]

In four jurisdictions, a court of summary jurisdiction which finds a defendant guilty of a minor indictable offence may also commit for sentence if there is some special reason to do so (for example, the lower court's incapacity to impose an appropriate sentence).[85]

(3) Alternatives to committal

Despite these elaborate procedures, committal is neither a sufficient nor a necessary precondition to trial on indictment. It is not sufficient, because the Attorney-General may decline to file an indictment. It is not necessary, because the Attorney-General (or, in those jurisdictions where the office exists, the Director of Public Prosecutions) has the power to proceed by *ex officio* information. For example, s71A of the Judiciary Act 1903 (Cth) provides:

> Notwithstanding anything contained in this Part . . . the Attorney General of the Commonwealth may file an indictment for any indictable offence against the laws of the Commonwealth without examination or commitment for trial.[86]

Unlike the English position, no consent of a judge is required for the filing of an *ex officio* information or indictment.[87] The High Court has held that there is no power directly to prevent, or review, any such action.[88] The Courts have, however, been extremely critical of this 'anomalous procedure', in cases where it has been used to circumvent the detailed procedures for committal. If the defendant has been prejudiced, the trial judge can adjourn or even stay a trial until committal procedures or some equivalent to them have been provided.[89] This is some security against abuse of *ex officio* informations, although there is something to be said for adopting the English requirement of judicial consent to *ex officio* informations.[90]

In addition, there is provision in some states for informations to be filed, with the permission of the Supreme Court, by a private prosecutor. This is a quite legitimate alternative to official prosecution, although the Supreme Court will not act as a court of appeal from an Attorney-General's refusal to prosecute, in giving leave under these provisions.[91]

(4) The status and future of committal proceedings

The indeterminate nature of committal proceedings — poised between executive inquiry and judicial determination — creates problems in a number of ways. For example, the discharge of a defendant against whom no sufficient case is shown does not involve an 'order in favour of the defendant', and (in the absence of express statutory provision) no order for costs can be made.[92] This is unfair to a defendant who may have been put to great expense in preparing a defence. There has been a long-standing dispute over whether the prerogative orders such as certiorari lie in respect of committal proceedings: since these are not decisive of anything at all, it has been said they neither affect 'rights' nor involve 'judicial' action, and are therefore immune from common law powers of review.[93] There is no appeal from decisions at committal proceedings, and only in Western Australia[94] and in respect of federal offences[95] do they attract statutory review procedures.

Much of the case-law proceeds on too categorical a view of committal. There is no point in having an appeal on the merits, since if the case has been committed for trial the trial itself will determine the question, and if it has not, new committal proceedings can be begun (or, perhaps, an *ex officio* information filed). But review on questions of law or jurisdiction is another matter: whether a particular offence is known to the law is a question which can be determined at this preliminary stage, without exposing the defendant to an unnecessary trial. In *Sankey v Whitlam*,[96] the High Court granted a declaration that the offence in question was not known to the law, and the better view is that prohibition (or, after an order for committal, certiorari) would also be available in similar circumstances.[97] Committal proceedings still constitute part of the 'criminal process . . . of the States' for the purpose of compelling the attendance of an interstate witness, even if they are not judicial in some narrower sense.[98] To deny a defendant his costs after he has successfully contested committal proceedings is to proceed on too abstract a view.[99]

The continued need for formal committal proceedings is another matter. Several of the purposes of committal — the perpetuation of evidence in written form, and notice to the defendant of the real case against him — could be met in other ways.[100] With the introduction of a Director of Public Prosecutions at federal level and in three states, there is now a more regular and centralized procedure for making and reviewing prosecution decisions, one which is distinct from the investigatory role of the police.[101] Both the Canadian and New South Wales Law Reform Commissions, while suppporting new forms of pre-trial hearing and discovery in criminal cases, have proposed the abolition of committal procedures.[102] The case for their retention depends on their effectiveness as a filter for weak or unsound cases, about which different views are held. Perhaps the best position is a compromise: availability of genuinely independent scrutiny of the prosecution's evidence in contested cases, with provision for the laying of a charge without formal committal proceedings in cases where the defendant consents or the defence is reserved.[103]

5.4 Trial on Indictment in Intermediate Courts

As we have seen, all but the most serious crimes tried on indictment (approximately 90 per cent of all crimes tried on indictment) are tried before District, District Criminal, or County Courts, in the five states where these exist. The provisions for juries, and the criminal law and procedure generally, are the same as for Supreme Courts.

Judges of these intermediate courts are appointed by the Governor from legal practitioners. In addition to criminal trials, they also exercise the civil jurisdiction of the Court. In Queensland, the judges are appointed during good behaviour but are removable by the Governor in Council for cause.[104] In South Australia, New South Wales, Victoria, and Western Australia, they have, in effect, Supreme Court tenure.[105]

(1) The jurisdiction of intermediate criminal courts

In each state the Supreme Court has general jurisdiction to try indictable offences, and the intermediate criminal court shares a concurrent jurisdiction with respect to most of these. Only the most serious felonies are excluded from the intermediate court's jurisdiction: these usually include treason, murder, piracy, and rape, although the exclusions are variously defined.[106]

Where the intermediate court shares jurisdiction with the Supreme Court, the decision as to which will try the case may be made by the committing magistrate, or by the prosecutor in filing the indictment in the particular court. In South Australia the discretion to commit is structured: all Group III offences (punishable by up to four years' gaol) are committed to District Criminal Courts, all Group I offences (over which only the Supreme Court has jurisdiction) to the Supreme Court. Group II offences, the intermediate class, may be committed to either court depending on their seriousness.[107]

In Queensland and Western Australia, at the Chief Justice's request a case committed to the Supreme Court may be tried by the District Court. But only in Queensland is there provision for removing criminal cases from the District Court into the Supreme Court.[108]

In Victoria, New South Wales, and Queensland criminal appeals from courts of summary jurisdiction are taken to County or District Court. In Queensland this appeal is final.[109] However, as we have seen, these appeals are only one way of challenging summary convictions: in each state, applications for review and similar proceedings take priority over appeals. In South Australia and Western Australia the District (Criminal) Courts have no appellate jurisdiction.

(2) Appeals from intermediate criminal courts

In each state, the provisions for appeal from criminal trials on indictment are the same as for the Supreme Court, and are briefly described in Chapter 7.

Notes

[1] As with other aspects of judicial administration, Victoria is a partial exception. But even in Victoria work on inferior courts has largely been limited to their civil jurisdiction. See Victoria, Civil Justice Committee, *Report concerning the Administration of Civil Justice in Victoria* (1984) I, ch. 6; Attorney-General's Advisory Committee, *Report on the Future Role of Magistrates' Courts* (1986). The NSWLRC has conducted only a limited

amount of empirical work in its inquiry into criminal procedure: see NSWLRC, DP 14/1, *Procedure from Charge to Trial: Specific Problems and Proposals* (1987) para. 1.35. Cf. Sallman & Willis, *Criminal Justice in Australia* (1984) 136–43, documenting the 'general lack of interest in the lower courts'.

[2] Technically all courts which are not 'superior courts' are 'inferior courts': this is a legal category, not a description of actual performance. The category 'intermediate courts', on the other hand, is a reference to a court 'intermediate' between the Supreme Court and courts of summary jurisdiction. Australian intermediate courts are technically all 'inferior courts'. For the category 'superior court' see Chapter 7.

[3] On the distinction between felonies and misdemeanours see Howard, *Criminal Law* (4th edn, 1982) 8–9.

[4] Baker, 418–9.

[5] 11 & 12 Vic c43 (Sir John Jervis's Act).

[6] On the English history of justices see Holdsworth, 1 HEL 285–98. On their present status, Skyrme, *The Changing Image of the Magistracy* (2nd edn, 1983); Jackson, 285–323; Burney, *JP. Magistrate, Court and Community* (1979). On the controversy about 'representativeness' of the English magistracy see King & May, *Black Magistrates* (1985). On the administration of magistrates courts see also Samuels (1984) 128 *Sol J* 73 & works there cited.

[7] Skyrme, 184–95.

[8] See Castles, 41–4, 63–6, 71, 92–6, 105; Bennett & Castles, 50–1, 83–6, 96–8, 107–9, 125–6, 133–5, 175–80; La Trobe Legal Studies Department, *Guilty, Your Worship. A Study of Victoria's Magistrates' Courts* (1980) ch. 2; Weber (1980) 13 *ANZJ Crim* 142.

[9] Fry, 91–4; Castles, 111.

[10] District Courts Act 1958, replaced by District Courts Act 1967.

[11] County Court Act 1958 (Vic.) Part II Div. 1A.

[12] Under the Courts of Session Act 1921 (WA).

[13] Local and District Criminal Courts Act 1969 (SA).

[14] District Court Act 1973 (NSW).

[15] Superior courts have extensive powers to punish for contempt of court: this is a summary jurisdiction, triable by the judge in question, or a Full Court, without a jury. In a few cases Supreme Courts may also have jurisdiction of a summary kind under specific legislation: e.g. Supreme Court (Summary Jurisdiction) Act 1967 (NSW). See further Chapter 7.

[16] These are: ACT, Magistrates Court (until 1985, Court of Petty Sessions) (Magistrates Court Ordinance 1930); NSW, Local Courts (Local Courts Act 1982 (in force 1985, replacing Courts of Petty Sessions under Justices Act 1902)); NT, Court of Summary Jurisdiction (Justices Act); Queensland, Magistrates Courts (Magistrates Courts Acts 1921); SA, Courts of Summary Jurisdiction (Justices Act 1921); Tasmania, Courts of Petty Sessions (Justices Act 1959); Victoria, Magistrates' Courts (Magistrates' Courts Act 1971); WA, Courts of Petty Sessions (Justices Act 1902). See generally Ward & Kelly, *Summary Justice* (looseleaf, 1983); Nichols (1986) 6 *Cth Judicial J* 23.

[17] Magistrates Court Ordinance 1930 (ACT) s18(2); Cahill, *SMA Papers*, 1; Justices Acts 1886 (Qld) s30(2); Jacobs, *SMA Papers*, 1. Cf. Justices of the Peace Act 1975 (Qld) s19.

18 Justices Act 1902 (NSW) s13; McLennan, *SMA Papers*, 1, 7. In practice all judicial jurisdiction is now exercised by magistrates: see Smail, Miles & Shadbolt, *Justices Act and Summary Offences (NSW)* (looseleaf, 1980) 119–21, 203, 1024.
19 Justices Act 1921 (SA) ss5 (as amended in 1983), 43. Only magistrates can hear minor indictable offences: s120; Ward & Kelly, para. 5101–13. Cf. the position in Tasmania: Justices Act 1959 (Tas.) ss20, 113A; Burkett, *SMA Papers*, 5; and WA: WALRC, Report 55, *Courts of Petty Sessions. Constitution, Powers and Procedure* (1986) 25–9.
20 Magistrates' Courts Act 1971 (Vic.) s18A. For the earlier situation see *Guilty, Your Worship*, 17, 20; Griffin, *SMA Papers*, 1. They have also been excluded from exercising civil jurisdiction: Magistrates' Courts (Civil Jurisdiction) Act 1979 s51(1).
21 Cf. Skyrme, 232–8; Jackson, 285–7, 314–5; Mcmanus, Bankowski & Hutton, *Lay Justice?* (1987).
22 Cf. *Guilty, Your Worship*, 91; O'Connor, in Aust. Institute of Criminology, *The Magistrates Court 1976: What Progress* (1978) 3, 7. But the WALRC recommended only that they be limited to imposing sentences of one month's imprisonment or a fine of $500: WALRC 55 (1986) 28–9. In New Zealand, cf. NZRCC, 35–7, 185–95.
23 This is already done (by magistrates) in Victoria: Magistrates (Summary Proceedings) Act 1975 ss84–9 ('alternative procedure'). Cf. Justices Act 1902 (WA) s135(2). And see Sallmann & Willis, *Criminal Justice in Australia* (1984) 92–3.
24 *Guilty, Your Worship*, 19, 98–100.
25 In practice all magistrates are appointed from clerks of the court after examination in Queensland: Jacobs, *SMA Papers*, 3. This was also the case in Victoria, but magistrates are now required to have a law degree (*Guilty, Your Worship*, 19, cf. 22–7) and appointments are now made from the legal profession as well as from clerks of courts.
26 *Fingleton v Christian Ivanoff Pty Ltd* (1976) 14 SASR 530, not followed in *Falconer v Howe* [1978] WAR 81. Cf. *R v Moss, ex parte Mancini* (1982) 29 SASR 385.
27 See Magistrates Court Ordinance 1930 (ACT) ss10A–L (magistrates have judicial tenure under s10D(1) though they may be suspended for cause by the Governor-General); Judicial Officers Act 1986 (NSW) ss3(1), 4 (Supreme Court tenure); Magistrates Act 1983 (SA) ss10, 11 (removal by Governor after judicial inquiry); Magistrates' Courts Act 1971 (Vic.) ss8, 8A (removal by Governor on determination by Supreme Court judge of sufficient cause); Magistrates Act 1969 (Tas.) ss4, 9(1); Stipendiary Magistrates Act 1957 (WA) s5. By contrast in the NT magistrates were until 1981 removable only on an address of Parliament: Magistrates Act 1977. The Magistrates Amendment Act 1981 substituted a power to dismiss for cause by the Administrator — in theory, at least, a reduction in security of tenure. For the position on Queensland see Justices Act 1886 (Qld) s11; Justices of the Peace Act 1975 (Qld) s13.
28 It is not clear whether federal magistrates would have judicial tenure under s72 of the Constitution. The Constitutional Commission's Australian Judicial System Committee recommended a constitutional amendment to confer a modified form of tenure on federal magistrates: *Report* (1987) para. 5.73–6.

29 *Guilty, Your Worship*, 35–97.
30 See e.g. Fox, *Victorian Criminal Procedure* (1978) 62–70; Daunton-Fear, *Sentencing in South Australia* (1980); Miller, in *The Magistrates Court 1976*, 34.
31 Justices Act 1921 (SA) s120; cf. Justices Act 1928 (NT) s120. The figures are, respectively, $20 and $10 before JPs.
32 Magistrates' Courts Act 1971 (Vic.) s69(1). In other jurisdictions: Magistrates Court Ordinance 1930 (ACT) s92(1); Crimes Act 1900 (NSW) (as it applies in the ACT) ss476–7 (no consent <$500; consent <$2000); Crimes Act 1900 (NSW) s476 (<$10 000 with consent); Justices Act 1928 (NT) ss120, 121A (no consent <$400; consent <$2000 or in the case of motor vehicle offences $10 000); Criminal Code 1899 (Qld) ss443, 480; Justices Act 1959 (Tas.) ss71–2 (no consent <$100; consent <$1000); Criminal Code Act 1924 (Tas.) ss445, 308; Criminal Code 1913 (WA) ss426–7A, 465–7 (<$500 with consent).
33 Justices Act 1921 (SA) s122(2). For NSW, Victoria, and WA see n32.
34 E.g. Justices Act 1959 (Tas.) ss71–2 (discretion to refuse summary trial); Magistrates Court Ordinance 1930 (ACT) s92A (committal for sentence).
35 Justices Act 1928 (NT) s122A.
36 E.g. Crimes Act 1900 (NSW) s476(7) (2 years/$2000).
37 On this general problem cf. Sydney University, Institute of Criminology, *Problems of Delay in Criminal Proceedings* (1980); Cole, *Remands in South Australian Criminal Courts* (1980); Victoria, Legal and Constitutional Committee, *Preliminary Report. Delays in Courts* (1984); Sallmann, *Report on Criminal Trials* (AIJA/Victorian Bar, Shorter Trials Committee, 1985).
38 Judiciary Act 1903 (Cth) s68(3) (which repeats the effect of s39(2)(d), discussed in Chapter 3). Cf. Durack (1979) 53 *L Inst J* 421; Cowen & Zines, 214–23.
39 Cf. Crimes Act 1914 (Cth) ss12–12A; *R v Waddington* (1979) 26 ALR 503.
40 (1971) 125 CLR 447, 453 (dissenting).
41 On the development of criminal appeals in Australia see O'Connor (1983) 7 *Crim LJ* 262.
42 Justices Act 1921 (SA) s163; Justices Act 1928 (NT) s163.
43 In WA an appeal is available only in the case of a defendant imprisoned after pleading not guilty: Justices Act 1902 s183. In all other cases the appeal is by way of order to review. Between 1976–8 there were only 5 appeals but 233 orders to review: WALRC, *Report on the Review of the Justices Act 1902. Part 1 — Appeals* (1979) 6. In other jurisdictions appeal and review overlap, but review takes priority: this is so in Victoria, Queensland, and the ACT.
44 Justices Act 1902 (WA) s183 (which applies to all offences tried summarily). The decision of the Supreme Court is final: s190(3), subject to the remote possibility of special leave to the High Court under Judiciary Act 1903 (Cth) s35(2).
45 Justices Act 1928 (NT) s163(1), including minor indictable offences.
46 Justices Act 1921 (SA) s163(1).
47 Magistrates Court Ordinance 1930 (ACT) ss207–8. Minor indictable offences heard summarily under s92(1) are treated as if they were summary offences for the purposes of s208(1)(a): see s108A.

48 Magistrates' Courts Act 1971 (Vic.) ss73–4, which apply to all summary convictions.
49 Justices Act 1886 (Qld) s222 as modified by District Courts Act 1967 s95.
50 Justices Act 1902 (NSW) s122, which applies to all offences tried summarily.
51 Justices Act 1959 (Tas.) s111, which, like s107, applies to any 'order of justices'.
52 Criminal Code 1899 (Qld) s673, which excludes any other appeal under the Justices Act; Justices Act 1921 (SA) s163(1b), but the appellant may request that the appeal be heard by a single judge: s163(1c); Criminal Code Act 1924 (Tas.) s308, which applies only to summary trials by order of the Supreme Court.
53 The case stated procedure is available in NSW, Victoria, SA, NT, and Tasmania. See e.g. Justices Act 1902 (NSW) ss101–11 (appeal by way of case stated); Justices Act 1921 (SA) s162 (case stated during hearing or within one month after).
54 Cf. *White v Ridley* (1978) 21 ALR 661, esp. 678 (Murphy J).
55 Magistrates Court Ordinance 1930 (ACT) ss219A–F; Justices Act 1886 (Qld) ss209–21 (simple offences only); Justices Act 1959 (Tas.) ss107–13; Magistrates' Courts Act 1971 (Vic.) s88; Justices Act 1902 (WA) ss197–206I.
56 Justices Act 1902 (NSW) ss112–15 (restraint of proceedings by Supreme Court), ss118–21 (Supreme Court proceedings to set aside order).
57 Justices Act 1959 (Tas.) ss113A–B.
58 E.g. id., s31(5); Justices Act 1902 (NSW) ss100A–HA.
59 E.g. Justices Act 1921 (SA) ss188–93.
60 WALRC, 12. In SA, the Criminal Law Reform Committee rejected a suggestion for a dual system of appeals on the WA model: *Third Report. Court Procedure and Evidence* (1975) 192–8.
61 In 1978 there were approx. 300 full-time magistrates in Australia. Generally see O'Connor, in Aust. Institute of Criminology, *The Magistrates Court 1976: What Progress* (1978) 3, 7–10; Cameron, id., 14.
62 Wallace, *SMA Papers*, 1.
63 *Guilty, Your Worship*, 91, 98–103.
64 Tomasic (1980) 5 *LSB* 298; Rees (1980) 5 *LSB* 301.
65 Cf. Sallmann & Willis, 138–43.
66 See esp. Seymour, *Committal for Trial* (1978); Frohlich (1975) 49 *ALJ* 561; Devlin, *The Criminal Prosecution in England* (1958) 121–33; SA Criminal Law Reform Committee, 64–79; Fairall (1986) 10 *Crim LJ* 24.
67 Seymour, 94–5.
68 Langbein (1973) 17 *AJLH* 312; Langbein, *Prosecuting Crime in the Renaissance* (1974) 63.
69 Cf. O'Connor (1984) 8 *Crim LJ* 301.
70 Frohlich, 563; Bennett & Castles, 101–7.
71 Magistrates Court Ordinance 1930 (ACT) s52; Justices Act 1902 (NSW) s32; Justices Act 1928 (NT) s107; Justices Acts 1886 (Qld) s71; Justices Act 1959 (Tas.) s56(1); Magistrates (Summary Proceedings) Act 1975 (Vic.) s43(1); Justices Act 1902 (WA) s66. But the SA equivalent (Justices Act 1921 s107) was repealed in 1984. (References to legislation in this section are to these Acts unless otherwise stated.)

72 In this respect the Attorney-General substituted for the grand jury's presentment which, as was seen in Chapter 4, has never been firmly established in Australia.
73 In each jurisdiction the Attorney-General or Director of Public Prosecutions may decline to file an indictment (usually by certifying to the Supreme Court whereupon the defendant is discharged). Only SA and the NT provide in so many words that there is a duty to present a person committed for trial unless the relevant authority so certifies: Criminal Law Consolidation Act 1935 (SA) s276(2); Criminal Code 1983 (NT) s297A. A decision not to file an indictment (or a certificate to that effect where one is required) would not be reviewable by the courts. After the indictment is filed, the Attorney-General or (in some jurisdictions) the Director of Public Prosecutions may terminate the prosecution by a *nolle prosequi*.
74 In all jurisdictions but NSW and Victoria a coroner may commit for trial a person suspected of an indictable offence the subject of the inquest or inquiry (i.e. murder, arson, or related offences) but such committals are rare. Tasmania, unusually, allows for a 'guilty plea' before a coroner: Coroners Act 1957 s16(6). In NSW a coroner has no committal power, but must adjourn an inquest or inquiry once a prima facie case appears to exist against a known person for an indictable offence arising: Coroners Act 1980 (NSW) s19. In Victoria the coroner reports to the DPP who decides whether to prosecute: Coroners Act 1985 (Vic.) ss21, 38.
75 In the case of most indictable offences an initial guilty plea is provided for in the ACT (s90A); NSW (s51A); NT (s106A, minor indictable offences only); SA (s122(1), minor indictable offences only; also Criminal Law Consolidation Act 1935 s57a, certain sexual offences) and Tasmania (s56A(3)(a)). See Seymour, 5–7.
76 Consent to committal is possible in Queensland (s110A(6), on a 'hand-up' brief only); Tasmania (s56A(6), but the defendant can require that specified witnesses give evidence); Victoria (s51); WA (ss101B–C). See Seymour, 9.
77 NSW was the last jurisdiction to introduce 'paper committals': Justices (Procedure) Further Amendment Act 1983 (NSW). See Fairall (1986) 10 *Crim LJ* 24.
78 Seymour, 7–9; Bennett (1971) 45 *ALJ* 363. For other Australian provisions see ACT ss90, 90AA; NT ss105A–B; Queensland s110A; SA s106(2); Tasmania s57(2); Victoria ss45–6; WA ss69, 101A.
79 Seymour, 22–3. And cf. James Report (1975) 103–6; Bishop, 49–55.
80 E.g. Victoria s44; WA ss101C(c), 101D; and cf. SA Criminal Law Reform Committee, 73–9; Victoria, Statute Law Revision Committee, *Report upon Section 44 of the Magistrates (Summary Proceedings) Act 1975* (1978).
81 E.g. SA s106(6a); Victoria s47A, and cf. *R v Byczko* (1977) 16 SASR 506, 518–9 (Bray CJ); *R v Tortomano* [1981] VR 31.
82 E.g. Crimes Act 1900 (NSW) s360A(2); Victoria s169. See also Kilduff [1978] *ACLD* DT 59.
83 Seymour, 6–7. The provisions are: ACT s90A(7); NSW s51A(1)(e); and cf. Criminal Appeal Act 1912 (NSW) s8A; NT ss141–2; Criminal Code 1899 (Qld) s600; SA ss141–2; Tasmania s63(b); Criminal Code 1913 (WA) s618.
84 Victoria s57(1)(a).

85 ACT s92A; NT s121C (electable offences only); Tasmania s72B(2)(b); Criminal Code 1913 (WA) s427(b)(ii).
86 Cf. *R v Rocher* (1966) 9 FLR 275; *R v Bright* (1980) 31 ALR 496. The equivalent state provisions are: Australian Capital Territory Supreme Court Act 1933 (Cth) s53; NSW: Australian Courts Act 1828 (UK) s5; Criminal Code 1983 (NT) s300; Criminal Code, 1899 (Qld) s561; Criminal Law Consolidation Act 1935 (SA) s275(1); Criminal Code Act 1924 (Tas.) ss310(2), 42; Crimes Act 1958 (Vic.) s353; Criminal Code 1913 (WA) ss579, 729. In some states a defendant indicted without committal proceedings has a right to be tried at the next criminal sittings unless the Court orders: e.g. Criminal Code 1899 (Qld) s590.
87 Cf. Administration of Justice (Miscellaneous Provisions) Act 1933 (UK) s2(2)(b); Devlin, 125.
88 *Barton v R* (1980) 32 ALR 449, disapproving dicta of Fox J in *R v Kent ex p McIntosh* (1970) 17 FLR 65.
89 In *Barton v R* the majority remitted one case to the Supreme Court to consider whether a stay should be granted. Three judges (Gibbs, Mason, Aickin JJ) thought that in principle a stay should be granted where there had been no committal: (1980) 32 ALR 449, 463. Murphy & Wilson JJ dissented, and Stephen J, while agreeing in the result, was less committed to the value of committal: id., 466–7. The whole Court agreed, in a second case where committal proceedings had been commenced and all but one prosecution witness called, that there was no unfairness to the defendant warranting a stay.
90 And see Seymour, 73–9, 104–5; Edwards, *The Law Officers of the Crown* (1964) 262–7.
91 *R v McKaye* (1855) 6 NSWR(L) 123; *Gouldham v Sharrett* [1966] WAR 129. The Australian provisions are: NSW, Australian Courts Act 1828 (UK) s6; Criminal Law Consolidation Act 1876 (NT) s336; Criminal Code 1899 (Qld) s686; Criminal Code Act 1924 (Tas.) s420; Criminal Code 1913 (WA) s720 (non-capital offences). In most cases any individual can institute committal proceedings by complaint, but only in this way can a 'private' prosecution be brought for an indictable offence. Cf. also Queensland ss102A–3A (special committal procedures on private complaint). On private prosecutions see ALRC 27, *Standing in Public Interest Litigation* (1985) ch. 7; Hay (1983) 21 *Osgoode Hall LJ* 165.
92 *R v Melbourne Magistrates' Court ex p Hiscock* [1977] VR 569; *R v Nicholl ex p Webster* (1979) 26 ACTR 19. The ACT Ordinance was amended in 1984 to allow an award of costs in favour of a defendant in committal proceedings: ACT s97. In some states existing general provisions have been treated as conferring this power: e.g. *Healey v Williams* (1985) 64 ALR 140.
93 The leading case for the restrictive view is *Ex p Cousins; Re Blacket* (1946) 47 SR (NSW) 145. See also *Wentworth v Rogers* [1984] 2 NSWLR 422, 434; Seymour, 41–71; Fairall (1986) 10 *Crim LJ* 63.
94 Justices Act 1902 (WA) s197(1)(a) combined with s4 (definition of 'decision'). The WALRC, 7, 13–14, proposed no change in this respect.
95 It was established in *Lamb v Moss* (1984) 49 ALR 533 that the Administrative Decisions (Judicial Review) Act 1977 (Cth) extends to committal proceedings. However, jurisdiction will be exercised only in the clearest

case, especially where the essential issue is one of fact: e.g. *Seymour v A-G* (1984) 57 ALR 68.
96 (1978) 21 ALR 505, esp. 561 (Mason J).
97 The Administrative Review Council recommended that committal proceedings be exempt from review under the Administrative Decisions (Judicial Review) Act 1977 (Cth) but subject to review by state courts under common law or state statutory procedures: ARC Report 26, *Review of the Administrative Decisions (Judicial Review) Act 1977 — Stage One* (1986) para. 28–9, 96.
98 *Ammann v Wegener* (1972) 129 CLR 415. Cf. *Aston v Irvine* (1955) 92 CLR 353, 365.
99 Cf. *Green v James* [1979] 2 NSWLR 812 (Attorney-General's right to intervene in committal proceedings under Judiciary Act 1903 (Cth) s78B).
100 On the inadequacy of committal proceedings in providing discovery of the prosecution case see Campbell (1985) 9 *Crim LJ* 270.
101 There is now a DPP in Victoria (1982), the Commonwealth (1983), Queensland (1984), and NSW (1987). On the office and role of the DPP see Temby, in Potas, ed., *Prosecutorial Discretion* (1984) 53; Temby (1985) 59 *ALJ* 197; ALRC 27 (1985) para. 355–61; Clark (1986) 60 *ALJ* 199.
102 Canada LRC, WP No. 4, *Criminal Procedure — Discovery* (1974) 28–9; NSWLRC, DP 14/1, *Criminal Procedure. Procedure from Charge to Trial: Specific Problems and Proposals* (1987) vol. 1, 314–25. Similarly the UK Royal Commission on Criminal Procedure proposed replacing committal proceedings by an accused's right to apply to be discharged for want of a case to answer: *Report* (1981). The QLRC, on the other hand, was equivocal, but recommended a right to waive committal proceedings: QLRC WP 28, *The Role of Juries in Criminal Trials* (1985) 30–42, 76–9. On pre-trial review of cases see Baldwin, *Pre-Trial Justice* (1985); NSWLRC DP 14/2 (1987) ch. 9; Sallmann, *Report on Criminal Trials* (AIJA/Victorian Bar, Shorter Trials Committee, 1985) ch. 4.
103 Seymour, 103–18. Cf. the difference of opinion in the High Court in *Barton v R* (1980) 32 ALR 449. See further Napley [1966] *Crim LR* 490; Gardner & Carlisle [1966] *Crim LR* 498; Dean (1974) 58 *Marquette LR* 159.
104 District Courts Act 1967 (Qld) s13.
105 Judicial Officers Act 1986 (NSW) s3(1), 4; Local and District Criminal Courts Act 1926 (SA) s5f; County Court Act 1958 (Vic.) s9 (amended 1986); District Court of Western Australia Act 1969 (WA) s11.
106 District Court Act 1973 (NSW) s166; District Courts Act 1967 (Qld) s58; Local and District Criminal Courts Act 1926 (SA) ss4(3), 328; County Court Act 1958 (Vic.) s36A(1); District Court of Western Australia Act 1969 (WA) s42.
107 Justices Act 1921 (SA) s112(3). On the problems of directing cases to the appropriate trial court see Beeching Report, 68–73, James Report 81–94.
108 District Courts Act 1967 (Qld) s28. The equivalent SA provision (Local and District Criminal Courts Act 1926 ss335–6) was repealed in 1981.
109 *Exton v White* [1976] Qd R 126.

CHAPTER 6

Civil Jurisdiction in Inferior and Intermediate Courts

6.1 The Development of Minor Civil Courts

The patchy development of minor civil courts in England was referred to in Chapter 2. Not until the County Courts Act 1846 was there an effective country-wide system of minor civil courts. This pattern, or lack of it, presented problems for the early Australian colonies when they attempted to establish inferior civil courts: they had nothing (or not much) to copy! In eastern Australia, Courts of Requests were established as courts of 'good conscience' like their English counterparts.[1] In South Australia, civil jurisdiction was exercised by Resident Magistrates' Courts, in Western Australia, by a Civil Court, and later by Courts of Petty Sessions or Courts of Requests. After 1846 there was considerable pressure to set up District or Local Courts on the model of English County Courts, and this was done, replacing Courts of Requests and similar bodies, in South Australia in 1849–50 (Local Courts), in Victoria in 1852 (County Courts),[2] in New South Wales in 1858 (District Courts),[3] and in Western Australia in 1863 (Local Courts). Only in Tasmania did Courts of Requests continue throughout the nineteenth century: reconstituted under the Local Courts Act 1896, they are still called Courts of Requests.[4]

But in some colonies minor civil jurisdiction was also conferred on, or continued in, courts of summary jurisdiction and exercised by police magistrates or justices. This was so, for example, in Victoria, where Courts of Petty Sessions had jurisdiction over 'civil debts recoverable summarily'.[5] In South Australia (and, by derivation, the Northern Territory) this was not necessary, as the Local Courts were divided into courts of 'limited' and 'full' jurisdiction (depending on the jurisdictional amount). Western Australia and Tasmania were small enough settlements to make do with a simple two-tier system — in Western Australia until 1969, in Tasmania to this day. In the result, the division between inferior civil and criminal courts, which was a feature of the English system, was maintained there but not in Victoria, New South Wales, or Queensland.[6]

In the century or so since the establishment of District, County, and Local Courts, the purposes of 'inferior' civil courts have changed. At first, they were intended to operate cheaply and flexibly, like the Courts of Requests they replaced. For example, the South Australian Local Courts were to decide 'according to equity and good conscience and the substantial merits of the case', a formula which attracted a deal of professional criticism.[7] As their jurisdictional limits were increased, the courts became more like intermediate courts of law with the function of lightening the workload of Supreme Courts. Traces of the earlier approach remain, for example in the small debts jurisdiction of Queensland Magistrates Courts.[8] But the tendency towards a three-tier structure of civil courts was markedly reinforced by the reconstitution of District Courts in Queensland in 1958, and in Western Australia in 1969, and the expansion of the jurisdiction of the South Australian Local Court of Full Jurisdiction (now called the District Court[9]) in 1969. Only Tasmania and the two territories retain a dual system, with emphasis on the Supreme Court for all larger civil cases.

The call for flexible procedures remains, however, and has led to new 'small claims' courts and tribunals in each jurisdiction — a development which to a degree parallels the early attempts at minor civil jurisdiction in Australia, and which is discussed in Chapter 12.[10]

(1) The personnel of inferior and intermediate civil courts

All but four inferior and intermediate civil courts also exercise criminal jurisdiction, and their personnel have been described in Chapter 5. The exceptions are the Local Courts in South Australia, Western Australia, and the Northern Territory, and the Tasmanian Courts of Requests. These are formally separate courts with only civil jurisdiction, but in most cases their personnel are shared with parallel criminal courts. In South Australia, qualified persons are appointed as Local and District Criminal Court judges. In Western Australia and the Northern Territory, and in South Australian Local Courts of limited jurisdiction, magistrates sit. In Tasmania, Courts of Requests are staffed by commissioners appointed by the Governor: in practice, the Supreme Court Master and every magistrate is a commissioner.[11]

In all four jurisdictions lay justices have only a very minor civil role. In South Australia, they can sit only in Local Courts of special jurisdiction, and then only if no magistrate or special justice is available.[12] They rarely, if ever, sit in Western Australia and the Northern Territory.[13] In Tasmania, a commissioner who is not legally qualified has jurisdiction only up to $100.[14]

It has long been said in Australia that lay justices should not exercise civil jurisdiction. Burton J, writing in 1883 of a proposal to establish Courts of Requests staffed by untrained police magistrates, could not

> recommend that the administration of justice, even in the Courts of Requests should be committed to persons less skilled in the law. Although the hearing and determination of cases in the Courts of Requests is summary, yet for the determination of questions which daily arise, legal knowledge is as necessary as in the higher courts; the same law is to be administered in both; and the same questions may arise, although in the one case to be determined summarily, and without appeal; from which if any argument can be raised, it would appear to me to be more in favour of the Commissioner being a person possessing competent legal knowledge than the other way. Respecting the several Police Magistrates throughout the territory . . . I must . . . unequivocally deny their competency to act as Commissioners of Courts of Requests.[15]

On what basis justices could be excluded from exercising any form of civil jurisdiction while being empowered to impose fines and to imprison in criminal cases is not clear. In fact lay justices are increasingly excluded from hearing criminal cases, as was pointed out in Chapter 5. But differences in approach to inferior civil as opposed to criminal jurisdiction are still reflected in a number of ways, as will be seen.

(2) The civil jurisdiction of intermediate civil courts[16]

Under the formal classification of superior and inferior courts, each of the courts discussed in this chapter is strictly an inferior court, though all are 'courts of record'. The term 'intermediate' is used to refer not so much to status as to jurisdiction. For present purposes the County and District Courts can be described as intermediate civil courts.[17]

The jurisdiction of these courts extends principally to personal actions in which damages or specified ('liquidated') claims are made: for example, claims for breach of contract or in tort (injuries from road accidents, etc.). The maximum claim varies from $40 000 in Queensland to $100 000 in New South Wales and South Australia.[18] An important exception to the limitation of jurisdiction is the unlimited jurisdiction of the Western Australian District Court over motor vehicle injury claims.[19] Where there is a maximum, it is expressed in each case as the claim after any agreed set-off or allowance, or on the balance of an account. There is also jurisdiction in a variety of other matters to varying amounts: legacies under a will (or shares on an intestacy), actions for recovery of possession of land (ejectment), replevin (the recovery of goods seized under a disputed claim), and so on. All intermediate courts have a certain, sometimes limited, equitable jurisdiction.

Apart from limitations inherent in the jurisdictional specification some courts are expressly denied competence to determine (except incidentally) title to land or the validity of a will.[20] In New South Wales, claims for less than $1000 cannot be brought in the District Court except by leave.[21]

Each court is also given jurisdiction under a variety of other state Acts. For example, the Victorian County Court has the former jurisdiction of Courts of Mines and there are a further seventy statutes under which the Court exercises some jurisdiction.[22]

(3) The civil jurisdiction of inferior civil courts[23]

For present purposes, the 'inferior' civil courts in Australia are the Magistrates Courts in the Australian Capital Territory, Victoria, and Queensland; Local Courts in New South Wales, South Australia, the Northern Territory, and Western Australia; and the Tasmanian Courts of Requests.

As with the intermediate civil courts, their jurisdiction is primarily over money claims or claims (such as to the detention of goods) which can be expressed as money claims. But in most cases the extent of restrictions or exclusions from jurisdiction is wider. Section 19(1) of the Local Courts (Civil Claims) Act 1970 (NSW) represents the possible range of exclusions: it excludes cases where the validity or effect of wills or settlements or the title to land is in question, actions for passing-off, breach of patent or copyright, false imprisonment, malicious prosecution, defamation, and the repossession of goods under a hire purchase agreement.[24]

Subject to a range of such exceptions, these courts have jurisdiction over personal actions up to a maximum which ranges between $500 in Northern Territory Local Courts of limited jurisdiction to as much as $20 000 in Victorian Magistrates' Courts.[25] Except in the Northern Territory (where there has been no change in jurisdictional limits since 1979), the jurisdictional limits of these courts have at least doubled in every jurisdiction since 1982. (In Victoria the increase — from $3000 to $20 000 — is particularly marked.) These increases are much greater than the rate of inflation. Nonetheless the primary jurisdiction of inferior civil courts is over debt claims, minor accident claims, and contractual disputes. Minor claims or not, the ordinary law (including the law of evidence) applies, although the procedure is more or less summary. In cases where a specific, liquidated sum is claimed (ordinary debt claims) a plaintiff can, by a default summons, require the defendant to take steps to assert a defence, in default of which the plaintiff will win the case. Many cases are dealt with in this way.[26] In Victoria special procedures now exist for the hearing of uncontested damages cases by a magistrate in chambers, in a similarly summary way.[27]

(4) Invested federal jurisdiction in civil cases

Subject to particular jurisdictions made exclusive to other courts, inferior state courts are given general federal jurisdiction by s39 of the Judiciary Act 1903.[28] But the most important instance of federal civil jurisdiction is that conferred by the Family Law Act 1975. Section 39(6) of that Act invests state and territory courts of summary jurisdiction with jurisdiction over ancillary family matters — proceedings for maintenance, custody of or access to children of a marriage, and other related matters.[29] (In the Perth metropolitan area these matters are, however, dealt with by the Western Australian Family Court.) Appeals from decisions of courts of summary jurisdiction go not to the Supreme Court but to the Family Court.[30] In this respect the courts of summary jurisdiction form part of an 'integrated' system of family law: for example, they have power to vary decisions of the Family Court on matters of maintenance, custody, etc.[31]

6.2 Some Problems of Limited Civil Jurisdiction

(1) Limited equitable jurisdiction

How far some inferior civil courts fall short of being courts of general jurisdiction, even within their overall monetary limit, is shown by their often defective equitable jurisdiction. The basic principles of the 'Judicature Act' system, outlined in Chapter 4, require the concurrent administration of law and equity. These principles operate only in an attenuated way in most inferior, and even some intermediate, courts.

The problem arises principally because the limited civil jurisdiction of lower courts is usually expressed in terms of money claims (liquidated or unliquidated). In every case, inferior courts are given power to take into account incidental equities and equitable defences, and to give appropriate remedies in place of the primary money claim.[32] But some equitable claims are primarily claims to specific performance or some similar order, with money awarded only incidentally or in substitution for the order. A standard example is a claim for rent due under an agreement for a lease where the lease has not been formally drawn up. In such a case, if the court has no equitable jurisdiction to specifically enforce the agreement for the lease, then it may have no jurisdiction over the claim for rent.[33] The only remedy is for the litigant to bring the case in a higher court, or for Parliament to give lower courts full jurisdiction, legal and equitable, within their overall monetary limit. There is undoubtedly a movement in this direction, especially in intermediate courts: for example, South Australian District Courts[34] and the Victorian County Court.[35] Other intermediate courts have a more limited equitable jurisdiction: the New South Wales District Court (up to $5000)[36] and the Queensland District Courts (up to $40 000).[37] Some lower courts have at least a limited equitable jurisdiction: for example, Tasmanian Courts of Requests (in the case of claims not exceeding $1000)[38] and the Australian Capital Territory Magistrates Court.[39] Other lower courts have only a minor or ancillary equitable jurisdiction.[40]

That position can perhaps be defended on the ground that equitable claims are inherently more difficult, and thus more appropriate for a higher court, than common law claims for debt or damages. But the primary reason for lower civil courts is to enable smaller claims to be settled swiftly and at reasonable cost, and this applies as much to equitable as to legal claims. The difficulty of a claim may be a reason for removing an action into a higher court: it is no reason for requiring all equitable actions to be started there. The basic point is that legal and equitable rules can interact in particular cases in a number of ways, and it is unsatisfactory to give lower courts only partial jurisdiction in such cases. Indeed, it can be a difficult question working out whether a particular claim is an equitable one.[41] Purity of doctrine may require us to recognize the separateness of law and equity even under the Judicature Act system, but multiplicity of proceedings and jurisdictional uncertainty in lower courts is too high a price to pay.

Courts of limited jurisdiction have difficulty in granting remedies which are not directly quantifiable in money terms — for example, declarations and injunctions. When South Australia introduced a specific declaratory action in the Local Court in 1969, careful provision was made to ensure that the case in which a declaration is sought is not worth more than the Local Court jurisdictional limit.[42]

(2) Avoiding jurisdictional limits

As the discussion so far might indicate, with minor exceptions the jurisdiction of civil courts below Supreme Court level is characterized by strict, and in many cases arbitrary, limits. But parties may wish to sue in a particular court for a variety of reasons: for example, lower costs in a lower court, or the increased publicity or higher level of judicial competence in a higher court. The devices for forum selection are more various in civil than in criminal cases, as the following survey indicates.

(A) SUING IN THE 'WRONG' COURT

In the first instance, at least, a plaintiff can choose the court in which to commence. With some exceptions, the jurisdiction of higher civil courts incorporates that of all civil courts below, so a plaintiff who through uncertainty as to the amount recoverable or for some other reason wishes to proceed in a higher court may do so. There are a number of risks in this procedure. The action might be remitted to a lower court, as will be seen. More important is the risk that the plaintiff will recover no more costs than would have been recovered in the lower court (with its lower scale of costs). There are provisions to this effect in many Australian jurisdictions. An unusually explicit example is s74(2) of the District Court of Western Australia Act 1969 (WA):

When an action is brought in the Court that might have been brought in a Local Court without the consent of the defendant, the plaintiff is not entitled to recover a greater sum by way of costs than he could have recovered had the action been brought in a Local Court, unless the District Court Judge hearing the action certifies —
(a) in the case of an action founded in tort, that in his opinion it was proper to bring the action in the Court instead of the Local Court; and
(b) in any other case, that by reason of some important principle of law being involved, or of the complexity of the issues, or of the facts, the action was, in his opinion, properly brought in the Court.[43]

On the other hand, there are now large claims within the jurisdiction of some courts below Supreme Court level. Most Supreme Court damages awards now fall within the jurisdictional limit of intermediate courts in the state in question.[44] Perhaps for this reason the Victorian provision (introduced in 1986 at the same time as the increase in jurisdiction of the County Court) only singles out for costs penalties, actions in which the amount recovered is less than half the relevant jurisdictional limit.[45]

(B) ABANDONING THE EXCESS
These costs penalties apply when a party sues in a higher court for a claim within the jurisdiction of a lower court. But the converse situation carries its own penalties in costs, of a less formal kind. When a party claims an amount only slightly greater than the lower court jurisdictional limit, to recover the excess is likely to be disproportionately expensive, since legal fees and costs in the higher court will be on a higher scale. One common provision in all Australian jurisdictions, while it prevents a plaintiff from splitting a claim so as to bring each part within the jurisdictional limit, allows him to abandon any excess above that limit so as to bring the case in the lower court. For example, s74(1) of the District Courts Act 1967 (Qld) provides that

A plaintiff shall not divide a cause of action for the purpose of bringing two or more actions in a District Court; but a plaintiff having a cause of action for more than the amount for which a plaint might be entered under this Act may abandon the excess (which abandonment shall be stated in the plaint), and thereupon the plaintiff may, on proving his case, recover to an amount not exceeding the limit specified by this Act and the judgment of the Court shall be in full discharge of all demands in respect of the cause of action, and entry of the judgment of the Court shall be made accordingly.

Thus the plaintiff can give up part of his claim to take advantage of the lower scale of costs.

(C) DISTRICT COURT OF WESTERN AUSTRALIA ACT 1969 (WA) S51(1)

Another provision, in the District Court of Western Australia Act 1969 (WA), has quite the opposite effect. Section 51(1) provides that

> Where . . . a verdict is returned for or a judgment is given for . . . an amount in excess of $80,000 but not exceeding $120,000, the Court shall find and record the amount of the verdict or judgment . . . and the claimant shall be entitled to recover the full amount of the verdict or judgment . . . notwithstanding that the full amount . . . is greater than the amount sought to be recovered.

The effect of s51(1) is that a plaintiff can recover up to 50 per cent more than the jurisdictional limit: this makes allowance for larger than expected judgments or verdicts, the calculation of which is often an estimate rather than an exact figure. This could avoid the need to transfer a case into the Supreme Court when it became clear that more might be recovered than the District Court jurisdictional limit.[46]

(D) CONSENT JURISDICTION

In all five intermediate civil courts it is possible for the parties to circumvent limited jurisdiction by consenting to the court hearing a larger claim. Consent once formally notified is irrevocable (though it would not prevent removal of the case into a higher court under the provisions described below). In Queensland and Western Australia, such consent can overcome all jurisdictional limits, not just limits as to the size of the claim.[47] On the other hand in New South Wales, Victoria, and South Australia, consent only overcomes limitations 'as to the amount of the claim', and other jurisdictional restrictions still apply.[48]

The only inferior civil courts with unlimited consent jurisdiction are the Northern Territory, South Australian, and Western Australian Local Courts.[49] In view of the comprehensive provisions for removal of cases, it is difficult to see why all civil courts should not have an unlimited jurisdiction by consent.[50]

(E) COUNTER-CLAIMS

Even when the plaintiff's claim falls within the jurisdictional limit, the defendant may have a counter-claim which does not.[51] This problem is dealt with in different ways. In the first place, the parties may consent to the court determining the excess, under the general provisions referred to already or (in a Western Australian Local Court) under a specific provision to deal with this situation.[52] Alternatively, the defendant may abandon the excess counter-claim, and proceed as to the rest. If neither alternative is accepted, then in some states the court is still authorized to decide the whole case, except for the excess.[53] In other states, apparently, it is without jurisdiction, at least on the counter-claim.[54] But the position in the Queensland District Courts is different. Where a counter-claim exceeds the District Court jurisdictional limit, a party may apply to a Supreme Court judge to transfer the whole case (or just the counter-claim) into the Supreme Court, but the judge may allow the whole case to proceed in the District Court. If no such application was made, the District Court may proceed to hear the whole case.[55] This admirable provision protects the parties while preventing multiplicity of proceedings. It seems the best solution to the problem of limited jurisdiction and counter-claims.

(3) Increasing jurisdictional limits

When jurisdictional limits are expressed in money terms the real level of jurisdiction decreases with inflation. This has the effect of forcing cases into a higher court, with higher costs likely to be involved. Unless jurisdictional limits can be increased by regulation (a procedure rarely adopted in Australia[56]), frequent amending legislation is required or the jurisdictional limit becomes outdated. For example, in Victoria the County Court jurisdictional limits remained unchanged from 1963 to 1979.

(4) The role of inferior civil courts

Inferior civil courts exist to provide a more economical method of settling smaller civil disputes, and to take the pressure of minor cases from Supreme Courts. There is a clear need for a more uniform and general jurisdiction for such courts, to ease some of the arbitrary jurisdictional restrictions now existing. But it has to be said that in practice much of their work has tended to be in the nature of routine debt collection or insurance claims in accident cases. For example, in South Australia in 1978, there were 5132 verdicts after trial in Local Courts, but as many as 29 147 default judgments. The District Court of Western Australia between 1974 and 1976 averaged 139 judgments after trial, compared with 1989 uncontested judgments. In the Victorian County Court, half the cases commenced in 1981 were for debt (i.e. liquidated claims): of these 51 per cent led to default or summary judgments, and less than 3 per cent were listed for trial.[57]

There is nothing wrong with the use of courts to enforce legitimate claims, but the *de facto* limitation to a few classes of cases has resulted in moves for alternative forums more sympathetic to non-commercial plaintiffs. The most notable example is the development of small claims or consumer claims courts or tribunals and the like, discussed in Chapter 12. Provisions have also been introduced in New South Wales, and proposed elsewhere, for a form of 'court-annexed' arbitration to be ordered in certain cases: this provides yet another alternative to the ordinary procedure of lower courts.[58]

Alongside these developments there have been in recent years marked increases in the jurisdictional levels both of intermediate and inferior civil courts, which can now deal with quite substantial claims.

A marked extension is the unlimited jurisdiction of the District Court of Western Australia over motor accident cases. The more this happens, the less the difference between Supreme Court and lower court civil claims, and the stronger the case for a homogeneous civil procedure— indeed, for a single court of civil jurisdiction.[59]

6.3 Relations Between Courts Exercising Civil Jurisdiction

In the meantime, quite elaborate provisions govern the relations between the two or three levels of civil courts in each state and territory. These are of three main classes — remittal to lower courts, removal to higher courts, and appeal and review. In the two former classes, the provisions are much more comprehensive than for the corresponding criminal jurisdictions — reflecting the pressure of increased criminal business and, perhaps, a lack of confidence in lower civil courts which is not felt (or cannot be afforded) in criminal cases.

(1) Remittal of cases to lower courts

When a case is commenced in a higher court which a lower court has jurisdiction to hear, one possibility is for the higher court to remit the case to the lower court, where, presumably, it can be dealt with more quickly and cheaply. There is no obvious explanation for the fact that in some states this power is generally available, while in Victoria and the Northern Territory it exists in a restricted way and in the Australian Capital Territory not at all.

Thus, in all five states with separate intermediate civil courts, a Supreme Court judge can order a case to be transferred to the intermediate court, usually on the application of a party but in New South Wales and Western Australia, of the judge's own motion.[60] Similarly in four of these five states cases can be transferred from the intermediate court to the inferior court (Victoria is the exception).[61] In only four states can the Supreme Court remit a case directly to the inferior civil court.[62] In the Northern Territory, remittal is possible only where the case involves $2000 or less: with larger claims the plaintiff has an effective choice of forum.[63] On the other hand, there are now general powers in the Australian Capital Territory to transfer cases between Magistrates Court and the Supreme Court.[64]

Where there is power to remit it is discretionary, although in some cases the court is directed to remit unless sufficient reason appears not to. A good example of the considerations involved is s77 of the District Courts Act 1967 (Qld), which allows the judge to remove a case into a District Court unless a party shows

> (a) that unnecessary delay would be caused by a trial in a District Court; or

(b) that, either by reason of the probable cost of trial in a District Court, or by reason of the questions of the law involved in the action, or because there is reason to believe that a fair trial cannot be had in a District Court, the case ought to be tried in the Supreme Court.[65]

This would usually be difficult to do.

(2) Removal to higher courts

Compared with these slightly patchy provisions for remittal, the power to remove cases to higher courts in each jurisdiction is unusually comprehensive. With few exceptions,[66] the power is exercised by a judge of the higher court. Where the case is not within the lower court's jurisdiction, removal is required (though in a few cases the Supreme Court can authorize the case to proceed below), but in most cases removal is discretionary.[67] On the other hand, sometimes cases involving very small amounts of money cannot be removed, or require security for costs to be given.

In New South Wales and Victoria, a case within the jurisdiction of the Courts of Petty Sessions or Magistrates' Courts cannot be removed directly into the Supreme Court, although in Victoria a magistrate may, if the case is 'a fit subject for determination by a superior court', refuse to decide it, thus forcing the parties to relitigate in another court.[68]

Provisions for transferring civil cases between courts are undoubtedly necessary. Whether they need take their present diverse form is another matter: a simple power to transfer cases, within or outside jurisdiction, to another appropriate court would be a more economical method.

(3) Appeal and review

Compared with the variety of methods of appeal and review from inferior and intermediate courts, surveyed in Chapter 5, the avenues of appeal from inferior and intermediate courts exercising civil jurisdiction are relatively straightforward. In a number of cases appeals are restricted or do not exist. In Queensland and South Australia it is possible for the parties to waive any right to appeal altogether: this is also possible in the Victorian County Court, the New South Wales District Court, and Western Australian Local Courts.[69] In the absence of such statutory provision an agreement not to appeal would be unenforceable because it would oust the jurisdiction of the appeal court.

Quite apart from waiver, in some cases there is no appeal at all: for example, decisions of the Queensland Small Debts Court (except as to jurisdiction)[70] and of New South Wales Local Courts (except on questions of law).[71] There is no appeal as of right in a variety of 'smaller' cases: interlocutory decisions (in most jurisdictions),[72] or claims below a specified sum ranging from $60 in the Northern Territory to $5000 in the New South Wales District Court.[73] In such cases, it is necessary to show that there is some special reason why leave to appeal should be granted, usually some reason of general importance rather than personal to the parties.[74]

Where an appeal does lie, the usual structure is that appeals from intermediate courts are heard by the Full Supreme Court or Court of Appeal; of inferior courts by a single judge of the Supreme Court (in South Australia, New South Wales, and the two territories) or of the District or County Court (in Queensland, Western Australia, and Victoria). The exception is Tasmania: all appeals from Courts of Requests are heard by a single Supreme Court judge in chambers.[75]

In only one jurisdiction, Victoria, does the alternative statutory machinery of the application to review exist. There is in fact no appeal from decisions of Victorian Magistrates' Courts under the Magistrates' Courts Act 1971; the order to review, under Part XI of the Act, is the only form of redress. However, a number of other Acts confer jurisdiction on Magistrates' Courts and provide for an appeal to the County Court. Where they do so, appeal and the order to review are alternatives, in the same way as for criminal cases heard by Magistrates' Courts.[76]

Provision is also made, in some cases, for orders in the nature of prohibition, certiorari, and mandamus,[77] for points of law to be reserved,[78] and for applications for a new trial.[79] The common law supervisory jurisdiction of the Supreme Court is sometimes excluded, sometimes not.

Notes

[1] Castles, 64–5, 70–1, 76, 79, 89–93, 96–7, 104–5; Bennett & Castles, 96, 108–12, 126–30, 156–60, 177–88, 215.

[2] See Hewitt, *Judges through the Years* (1984).

[3] NSW District Courts exercising only civil jurisdiction existed until 1973, when they were replaced by the present District Court. See Holt, *A Court Rises* (1976). On separation, Queensland continued the District Courts until 1921: Castles, 111.

[4] Strictly speaking, the Local Courts Act 1896 (Tas.) ss12, 13(b) provided both for Courts of Requests and courts of general sessions (the latter composed of justices of the peace with limited jurisdiction). Courts of general sessions have rarely been used, and the Tasmanian Law Reform Commission has recommended their abolition: Report 45, *Local Courts* (1985) 10.

[5] Bennett & Castles, 159–60.

[6] SA Local Courts at first had criminal jurisdiction, but this was held 'unconstitutional' in *R v Neville* ('The Register', 26 June 1865) and repealed. See Hague, 'Mr Justice Boothby', 235–40; Bennett & Castles, 186. The WALRC has proposed the merger of Courts of Petty Sessions and Local Courts in a new Magistrates Court: WALRC, *Working Paper on the Local Courts Act . . . Jurisdiction, Procedures and Administration* (1983) 21–36.

7 This 'extraordinary enactment' was also declared 'repugnant to the law of England' by the majority of the Supreme Court in *Dawes v Quarrel* (1865) Pelham's R 1; Bennett & Castles, 183–5. This was one of the decisions which led to the Colonial Laws Validity Act 1865. The 'equity and good conscience clause', thus validated, survived until 1886. Its deletion then was opposed as 'not in the interests of suitors' but was defended by Attorney-General Downer: the phrase was 'too vague' and left Local Courts too much power. The formula was replaced by a requirement to administer law and equity — not at all the same thing. See SA, *Parl Debs (H of A)*, 21 Sept. 1886, 1054.
8 Magistrates Courts Acts 1921 (Qld) s10(1).
9 Local and District Criminal Courts Act 1926 (SA) s5ab(1) (inserted 1981).
10 Tasmania was the last jurisdiction to introduce a small claims procedure: Court of Requests (Small Claims Division) Act 1985 (Tas.).
11 Local Courts Act 1896 (Tas.) s8; Burkett, *SMA Papers*, 10; Tas. LRC, Report 22, *Reform of Civil Procedure* (1978) 7–8; Tas. LRC, Report 45, *Local Courts* (1985) 10. Provision has also been made for part-time special commissioners under the Court of Requests (Small Claims Division) Act 1985 (Tas.) s8A (inserted 1987).
12 Local and District Criminal Courts Act 1926 (SA) s23. The function of Local Courts of special jurisdiction is to enforce unsatisfied Local Court judgments: s32b.
13 Local Courts Act 1904 (WA) s12; Hogg, *SMA Papers*, 3; Local Courts Act 1941 (NT) s19; Galvin, *SMA Papers*, 2. This is the position throughout Australia: cf. Magistrates' Courts Act 1971 (Vic.) s51(1).
14 Local Courts Act 1896 (Tas.) s13(1). See above n3.
15 In Bennett & Castles, 109.
16 A major — in some jurisdictions, the only — source on these courts is the various practice books: see *Bourke & Neesham's Practice of the County Court of Victoria* (3rd edn, 1980): *Jacobs' County Court Practice* (6th edn, 1980); Chippindall & Sharp, *District Court Act & Rules. NSW* (1973); O'Grady, *District Court Practice* (1974); *Hannan's Local and District Criminal Courts Practice* (3rd edn, 1980). On the Victorian County Court, see also Civil Justice Committee, *Preliminary Study concerning the Administration of Civil Justice in Victoria* (1984) 134–65; Civil Justice Committee, *Report concerning the Administration of Civil Justice in Victoria* (1984) 36–43.
17 The jurisdiction of NT Local Courts of full jurisdiction is only $10 000, well within the range of 'inferior' civil courts in Australia. It is accordingly not treated as an 'intermediate court'.
18 1987 jurisdictional limits (with 1981 limits in brackets) are: NSW District Court, $100 000 [$20 000 (personal actions at law)/$10 000 (partnerships, accounts, legacies)]; Queensland District Courts, $40 000 [$15 000]; SA District Courts, $100 000, and $150 000 in motor vehicle cases [$20 000]; Victorian County Court, $50 000, and $100 000 in personal injury cases [$12 000 and $25 000 respectively]; WA District Court, $80 000 [$20 000]. The QLRC has proposed increasing the jurisdiction of the District Court to $50 000, and $250 000 in personal injury cases: QLRC WP 29, *The Civil Jurisdiction of the District Court of Queensland* (1985) 28–9.
19 District Court of Western Australia Act 1969 (WA) s50(2). In Victoria motor vehicle claims are covered by a statutory compensation scheme

(Accident Compensation Act 1985 (Vic.)), under which decisions are made by an Accident Compensation Tribunal, from which there is an appeal on questions of law only to the Supreme Court (s68). A somewhat similar scheme now exists in NSW. Under it, claims are made to the Government Insurance Office, with appeals (other than on issues of medical assessment) going to the District Court and thence (on questions of law only) to the Supreme Court: Transport Accident Compensation Act 1987 (NSW) ss184, 193.

[20] This limitation now applies only in Queensland (s66(2)) and NSW (s43(2),(3) (where the land is worth more than $100 000, with jurisdiction in possession actions limited to $10 000: ss48(4), 133)).

[21] District Court Act 1973 (NSW) s48(1) (provided the claim could have been brought in a Local Court).

[22] *Bourke & Neesham's Practice of the County Court of Victoria* (3rd edn, 1980) 346–52. Intermediate courts in NSW, Victoria, and Queensland also have appellate jurisdiction.

[23] See further Jackson & Byron, *Local Courts (Civil Claims) Practice* (2nd edn, 1980); Springvale Legal Service, *Lawyers Practice Manual (Victoria)* (1985) ch. 3. On WA inferior courts see WALRC, *Working Paper on the Local Courts Act . . . Jurisdiction, Procedures and Administration* (1983). On the Victorian courts, Civil Justice Committee, *Preliminary Study concerning the Administration of Civil Justice in Victoria* (1984) 166–92; Victoria, Attorney-General's Advisory Committee, *Report on the Future Role of Magistrates' Courts* (1986).

[24] Only Tasmanian Courts of Requests have no such exclusions. The only restriction in the ACT is in proceedings 'in which title to land is genuinely in question': Magistrates Court (Civil Jurisdiction) Act 1982 s10. Cf. Magistrates' Courts Act 1971 (Vic.) s51(2).

[25] The 1987 jurisdictional limits (1981 figures in brackets) are: ACT Magistrates Court, $10 000 [$2500]; NSW Local Courts, $5000 [$2000]; NT Local Courts of limited jurisdiction, $500, full jurisdiction $10 000 [no change]; Queensland Magistrates Courts, $5000 [$2500]; SA Local Courts of limited jurisdiction, $7500 [$2500]; Tasmanian Courts of Requests, $5000 [$1500]; Victorian Magistrates' Courts, $20 000, and $5000 for personal injury claims [$3000]; WA Local Courts, $6000 [$3000]. In general the limits do not include costs or interest on damages: *Turley v Saffin* (1975) 10 SASR 463. As with intermediate civil courts, jurisdiction is also conferred on the courts by a number of other Acts.

[26] See Kelly, *Debt Recovery in Australia* (1977) 144–57; ALRC 36, *Insolvency: Consumers in Debt* (1987) para. 42–4, 58–60.

[27] Magistrates (Summary Proceedings) Act 1975 (Vic.) ss9–9G (inserted 1979).

[28] The scope of the Federal Court's exclusive federal jurisdiction is outlined in Chapter 8. It is probable that inferior civil courts have no admiralty jurisdiction, either *in rem* or *in personam* (but cf. Navigation Act 1912 (Cth) s328). If the recommendations of the Australian Law Reform Commission in its Report 33, *Civil Admiralty Jurisdiction* (1986) are implemented, state lower courts will be given general *in personam* admiralty jurisdiction, within the limits of their ordinary civil jurisdiction, but will not be given *in rem* jurisdiction: see id., para. 233–4, 240–1.

[29] Family Law Act 1975 (Cth) s39(6), in conjunction with s4(1).

30 Section 96 (except in WA, where they go to the Family Court of WA). Section 46 provides for remittal into the Family Court. Section 96(4) was substituted in 1979 to make it clear that the appeal is by way of a hearing *de novo*.
31 Cf. s47, & Watson, in *SMA Papers*, 6. See further Chapter 11.
32 E.g. Local Courts Act 1941 (NT) ss32–32E.
33 See Meagher, Gummow & Lehane, *Equity, Doctrines and Remedies* (2nd edn, 1984) 58–62 and cases cited.
34 Local and District Criminal Courts Act 1926 (SA) ss35a–f (general claims up to the jurisdictional limit) 259 (special equitable jurisdiction to $40 000).
35 The earlier limited equitable jurisdiction (County Court Act 1958 (Vic.) ss41–2) was repealed by the Courts Amendment Act 1986 (Vic.). Under County Court Act 1958 (Vic.) s37 the County Court now has jurisdiction to determine all cases 'regardless of the type of relief sought', provided the 'value of the subject matter' is within the jurisdictional limit. The only exceptions are prerogative writs and actions upon Supreme Court judgments (s37(2)(c) & (d)). Cf. also Supreme Court Act 1986 (Vic.) s31.
36 District Court Act 1973 (NSW) s134 (little used in practice). A Supreme Court judge may allow equity proceedings above $5000 to continue in the District Court: s147(1)(d). See Morison, 295–7.
37 District Courts Act 1967 (Qld) ss68–9; cf. Judicature Act 1876 (Qld) s2.
38 Local Courts Act 1896 (Tas.) ss13(1)(a)(ii), 74. Cf. also Supreme Court Civil Procedure Act 1932 (Tas.) s178, allowing inferior courts to be invested with part of the Supreme Court's equity jurisdiction by Order in Council (there has been no such Order).
39 Before the Magistrates Court (Civil Claims) Ordinance 1982, the ACT Court of Petty Sessions (as it was called until 1985) had no equitable jurisdiction at all. This was remedied by the 1982 Ordinance: s6 now gives it power to grant the same relief as the Supreme Court may grant in any case within its jurisdiction. But, apart from nuisance (s8), that jurisdiction is limited to cases where 'the amount claimed' does not exceed $10 000.
40 On the unsatisfactory nature of lower court equitable jurisdiction see WALRC, *Working Paper on the Local Courts Act . . . Jurisdiction, Procedures and Administration* (1983) 60–4; Victoria, Attorney-General's Advisory Committee, *Report on the Future Role of Magistrates' Courts* (1986) 59–60; Hallenstein, 'Equitable Jurisdiction and Remedies' id., 137; Crennan (1985) 59 *Law Inst J* 574; Tas. LRC, Report 45, *Local Courts* (1985) 12–14.
41 E.g. *Foster v Reeves* [1892] 2 QB 255; *Homburg v Fromm* [1951] SASR 97. Cf. *Marsh v Mackay* [1948] StR Q 113; *Hondros v Chesson* [1981] WAR 146; *Dunlop Olympic Ltd v Ellis* [1986] WAR 8, on appeal from (1984) 2 SR(WA) 68. But see Owen-Conway (1979) 14 *UWALR* 150.
42 Local and District Criminal Courts Act 1926 (SA) s35f. On the other hand the County Court Act 1958 (Vic.) s37(2)(a) merely refers to the value of the subject matter of the claim.
43 See also Qld SCR 091 r2; NSW SCR Part 52 r24(2). See e.g. *Philip Morris Ltd v Ainley* [1975] VR 345.
44 See Cranston, Haynes, Pullen & Scott, *Delays and Efficiency in Civil Litigation* (AIJA, 1985) 32, 188.
45 Victoria, General Rules of Procedure in Civil Proceedings 1986 Part I O63 r24.

46 Before 1986 there was a rather similar provision in Victoria (County Court Act 1958 (Vic.) s37A), which allowed judgment to be entered for any amount but only where the 'amount sought to be recovered' was within the County Court jurisdictional limit. On s37A see *Incorporated Nominal Defendant v Donelan* (1973) 47 ALJR 138; *Domenicos v Mead* [1975] VR 225. On the effect of its repeal, Jacobs, 41.
47 District Court of Western Australia Act 1969 (WA) s50(1)(e); District Courts Act 1967 (Qld) s73 (to the extent of Supreme Court jurisdiction). But consent could not attract jurisdiction given exclusively to a court (other, perhaps, than the Supreme Court).
48 Local and District Criminal Courts Act 1926 (SA) s33; District Court Act 1973 (NSW) s51 ('by reason only of the fact that the amount claimed exceeds $100 000'); County Court Act 1958 (Vic.) s37(2)(a) & (b).
49 Local and District Criminal Courts Act 1926 (SA) s33; Local Courts Act 1947 (NT) s29 ('without any limitation as to the amount of the claim'); Local Courts Act 1904 (WA) s39. The SA and NT provisions apply to Local Courts of full and limited jurisdiction.
50 The Tasmanian Law Reform Commission so recommended in respect of Courts of Requests: Report 45, *Local Courts* (1985) 14.
51 A counter-claim is a claim by a defendant against a plaintiff which can reasonably be heard together with the initial claim. It contrasts with a set-off, a compensating money claim between the parties which reduces or eliminates the initial claim.
52 Local Courts Act 1904 (WA) s34(2)(b).
53 Local Courts Act 1904 (WA) s34(1); District Court of Western Australia Act 1968 (WA) s58. Similar provisions exist in Victoria (Magistrates' Courts (Summary Proceedings) Act 1975 s91; County Court Act 1958 s51).
54 The Magistrates Court Ordinance 1930 (ACT) ss46–7 precludes a cross-claim for more than the jurisdictional limit unless the defendant expressly abandons the excess in the notice of cross-claim. The NSW and SA provisions, although less explicit, are probably to the same effect: Local Court (Civil Claims) Act 1970 (NSW) s15; Local and District Criminal Courts Act 1926 (SA) s38.
55 District Courts Act 1967 (Qld) s86.
56 For the exceptions see Court of Requests (Small Claims) Act 1985 (Tas.) ss3, 12, 13 (inserted 1987); District Courts Act 1967 (Qld) s60 (proclamations withdrawing criminal jurisdiction from District Courts); Local Courts (Civil Claims) Act 1970 (NSW) s36(1) (proclamations increasing minimum sum for which costs payable).
57 Victoria, Civil Justice Committee, *Report concerning the Administration of Civil Justice in Victoria* (1984) 38.
58 For the NSW provisions see Local Courts (Civil Claims) Act 1970 (NSW) s21H; District Court Act 1973 (NSW) s63A; Arbitration (Civil Actions) Act 1983 (NSW); Jackson & Byron, 112/8–18. For recommendations and discussion see Cranston, Haynes, Pullen & Scott, 200–4; Victoria, Attorney-General's Advisory Committee, *Report on the Future Role of Magistrates' Courts* (1986) 41–7; WALRC, *Working Paper on the Local Courts Act . . . Jurisdiction, Procedures and Administration* (1983) 31–5. For the problem of court–annexed arbitration in matters of federal jurisdiction (Judiciary Act 1903 (Cth) s39(2)(d) as amended in 1984) see Chapter 3.
59 See the brief discussion in Victoria, Civil Justice Committee, *Report con-*

cerning the Administration of Civil Justice in Victoria (1984) 15–21, and for further discussion see Chapter 14.

[60] E.g. District Courts Act 1967 (Qld) s77; District Court Act 1973 (NSW) s143.

[61] E.g. District Courts Act 1967 (Qld) s78; Local Courts (Civil Claims) Act 1970 (NSW) s21F.

[62] Qld RSC 096 r2; Local and District Criminal Courts Act 1926 (SA) s40; Supreme Court Civil Procedure Act 1932 (Tas.) s28; Local Courts Act 1904 (WA) ss87, 88. The WA Supreme Court can also transfer cases between Local Courts: s38A.

[63] Local Courts Act 1941 (NT) s36.

[64] Magistrates Court (Civil Claims) Ordinance 1982 (ACT) ss279–81.

[65] A strange provision in NT, SA, Victoria, and WA allows remittal of Supreme Court cases in tort (or, in Victoria, contract) where the plaintiff is without 'visible means' of paying the defendant's costs: e.g. Local and District Criminal Courts Act 1926 (SA) s35. Cf. also s41.

[66] E.g. District Court of Western Australia Act 1969 (WA) s77 (allowing a District Court judge to remit in difficult or important cases).

[67] In Queensland the Crown can require removal of a case in which it is a party: District Courts Act 1967 (Qld) s28. In NSW there is special provision for removal in equity cases: District Court Act 1973 (NSW) s147(2). Generally see Nash, *Magistrates Courts* (1975) 100–1.

[68] Magistrates (Summary Proceedings) Act 1975 (Vic.) s171.

[69] E.g. Magistrates Courts Act 1921 (Qld) s11(3)(b); District Courts Act 1967 (Qld) s94.

[70] Magistrates Courts Act 1921 (Qld) s11(6).

[71] Local Courts (Civil Claims) Act 1970 (NSW) s69(2). Appeals from Courts of Requests below the appealable amount are possible only on grounds of law or wrongful admission or rejection of evidence: Local Courts Act 1896 (Tas.) s123(3). The Tasmanian Law Reform Commission recommended repeal of this restriction: Report 45, *Local Courts* (1985) 19.

[72] The distinction between a 'final' decision and an interlocutory decision for these purposes has been the subject of much case-law: see e.g. *Hall v Nominal Defendant* (1966) 117 CLR 423; *A. Hudson Pty Ltd v Legal & General Life of Aust. Ltd* (1985) 59 ALR 505. There is an appeal as of right from 'any judgment or order' of the Victorian County Court: County Court Act 1958 (Vic.) s74(2).

[73] The amounts are: ACT $2000; NSW District Court $5000; NT $60 (in most cases); District Court $2500; Queensland Magistrates Courts $600; SA $1000 or any equity case.

[74] E.g. *SA v Muirhead* (1979) 23 SASR 316. Cf. Magistrates Courts Act 1921 (Qld) s11(3)(a) ('some important principle of law or justice').

[75] Local Courts Act 1896 (Tas.) s123(1). An appeal from a WA Local Court to the District Court may be removed into the Supreme Court: Local Courts Act 1904 (WA) s107(5).

[76] Magistrates' Courts Act 1971 (Vic.) ss88–9; Nash, *Magistrates Courts* (1975) 136–7.

[77] E.g. District Court of Western Australia Act 1969 (WA) ss80–4. Under s81 certiorari operates as a remittal; under s83, prohibition as an appeal.

[78] E.g. Local and District Criminal Courts Act 1926 (SA) s57.

[79] Magistrates Courts Acts 1921 (Qld) s11(2), District Court Act 1973 (NSW) ss126–7.

CHAPTER 7

State and Territory Supreme Courts

7.1 The Structure and Personnel of Supreme Courts

Central to the administration of justice in each state and territory is its Supreme Court. After earlier vicissitudes, a Supreme Court was established in New South Wales in 1824,[1] and thereafter in each state upon its foundation. (Western Australia was the exception: settled in 1829, its Supreme Court was not established until 1861.[2]) Subsequent Supreme Court Acts have continued, rather than reconstituted, these Supreme Courts, which thus have a continuous history of 100 to 150 years.

There are many differences between the court systems in the different states: in the extent to which jurisdiction is exercised by the Supreme Court, by intermediate courts, or by specialist courts and tribunals; in the methods of trial (especially, as we have seen, civil trial); and in their size and complexity of organization, reflecting the differences between the states. But the underlying structure of each Supreme Court is similar: a single superior court of general jurisdiction, which is the intermediate appeal court in state and most federal matters, and the body primarily entrusted with the supervision of state law, state legal institutions, and the local legal profession. Much the same is true of the two mainland territories,[3] although in the case of the Australian Capital Territory Supreme Court the intermediate appellate function is exercised by the Federal Court.[4] Though they present a similar pattern, and though much of the law they administer is similar or the same, Supreme Courts are essentially local institutions. To an extent their 'locality' is emphasized through provision for decentralization of judges or for circuit courts.[5]

(1) Judges and other personnel

Each Supreme Court consists of a Chief Justice and a number of other judges, in some states called puisne judges.[6] The number of judges varies markedly between states (37 in New South Wales, 6 in Tasmania), but population is no great determinant: the smaller jurisdictions have, with one exception, more Supreme Court judges per 100 000 people than the larger ones.[7] The number of Supreme Court judges increased markedly in the fifteen years from 1964 (68) to 1979 (105), although it has since increased at a much slower rate (116 in 1986). During this time only Western Australia resisted the temptation to add to the number of its Supreme Court judges, which was unchanged from the early 1960s for twenty years. It is difficult to say whether the marked increase in the number of judges has coincided with a decline in the standard of superior court judges: certainly, it has led to appointments at a much earlier age, with consequent effects upon the Bar.[8] In addition, states provide for the appointment of acting judges as required.[9]

As well as the judges, each Supreme Court has a number of judicial-cum-administrative officers who play an important part in the running of the court. These are variously titled — Masters, Registrars, Prothonotaries, and so on.[10] The principal such officer in most cases is the Master; apart from his administrative duties, he decides a large number of minor judicial matters — in particular, interlocutory applications and taxation of costs.[11] In both Queensland and Western Australia the Master's position has been reinforced, with greater emphasis on ancillary judicial functions. Indeed, in some states the Master, Prothonotary, or Registrar is part of the Supreme Court, and in Western Australia the Master has full judicial tenure.[12]

(2) Administration and regulation of Supreme Court business

In the administration of Supreme Court business the Masters, Registrar, and other officers act under the general direction of the Chief Justice. But no state Supreme Court has the formal administrative and financial autonomy of the High Court under the High Court of Australia Act 1979. The provision of facilities and staff for the courts remains a matter for the relevant government department under the Attorney-General or Minister for Justice, although there have been developments in some states towards a greater degree of administrative autonomy for Supreme Courts, and the High Court model is often cited as a desirable one for them.[13]

A very significant power that is possessed by the judges is that of making rules of court, regulating their practice and procedure, and in some cases, more substantive matters besides. The rule-making authority consists either of the judges or a rules committee or (in Queensland) the Governor in Council acting with the concurrence of at least two judges. The rules are a form of delegated legislation and are subject to parliamentary scrutiny and possible disallowance, which in practice is rare.[14] The rules must not conflict with the Supreme Court Act itself; subject to that, they have statutory force. Parliament itself, of course, retains overall authority to enact procedural and substantive rules, but the delegation of power to the judges or a rules committee seems to work reasonably well in practice.[15]

Whether adequate machinery exists for the more general oversight of 'judicial administration' in Australia is another matter. There is long-standing provision, in several states, for a council of the judges to meet annually to consider defects in law or procedure, and the administration of the Court generally,[16] but this provision seems to have been nugatory. There are much better developed systems in the United States[17] and Canada[18] (and to a lesser extent in England[19]) for reviewing the working of the courts, and there is now general agreement that something more is needed in Australia.[20] This is partly the result of the work of the Australian Institute of Judicial Administration, established in 1982,[21] which has sponsored work on delay in the courts and on other issues of judicial administration.[22] There has also been a thorough review of the working of the courts at various levels in Victoria,[23] involving among other things the adoption in 1986 of a revised Supreme Court Act and Rules.[24]

7.2 The Original Jurisdiction of Supreme Courts

(1) Supreme Courts — superior courts of general jurisdiction

The principal characteristic of Supreme Courts, unlike any other trial courts in Australia, is that they are courts of general jurisdiction. Inferior courts, and federal courts such as the High Court, the Federal Court and the Family Court, have original jurisdiction only to the extent specified in or implied by their statutory (and, in the case of the High Court, constitutional) grants of jurisdiction. By contrast, every matter is within the jurisdiction of a Supreme Court unless expressly excluded. Even where a statute establishes a remedy available only in another court, the Supreme Court may have jurisdiction to enforce the underlying rule by means of the general remedies (damages, declarations, injunctions and other orders) available to it.[25]

The generality of Supreme Court jurisdiction is established in different ways in the legislation. In six of the eight states and territories the jurisdiction is defined in an ambulatory way, by reference to all the jurisdiction that was or could have been exercised by the English superior courts of common law and equity before 1875, with certain additions. A good example is s17 of the Supreme Court Act 1935 (SA):

(2) There shall be vested in the court —
(a) the like jurisdiction, in and for the State, as was formerly vested in, or capable of being exercised by, all or any of the courts in England, following:—
  (i) The High Court of Chancery, both as a common law court and as a court of equity:
  (ii) The Court of Queen's Bench:
  (iii) The Court of Common Pleas at Westminster:
  (iv) The Court of Exchequer both as a court of revenue and as a court of common law:
  (v) the courts created by commissions of assize:
(b) such other jurisdiction, whether original or appellate, as is vested in, or capable of being exercised by the court:
(c) such other jurisdiction as is in this Act conferred upon the court.

Section 18 then confers the probate jurisdiction of the English Court of Probate (1857–75), together with all probate jurisdiction which 'is vested in or capable of being exercised by the court'. Similarly, s19 confers the matrimonial jurisdiction of ecclesiastical courts in England, and all matrimonial jurisdiction 'vested in or capable of being exercised by the court'.[26] The only substantial exclusion is the jurisdiction of the English Court of Admiralty. This was excluded because admiralty jurisdiction — also defined by reference to the jurisdiction of the pre-1875 English Court — was then and is still conferred on Supreme Courts by a paramount Imperial Act, the Colonial Courts of Admiralty Act 1890 (UK).

As the formula 'vested in or capable of being exercised by the court' in ss17–19 indicates, the reference to English jurisdiction is not intended to be restrictive or exclusionary: when the Supreme Courts were first established it was a natural way of expressing the greatest extent of jurisdiction that common lawyers could think of as vested in a court. Along with other provisions in the Acts referring to English forms and procedures, it emphasizes the extent of English influence in the legal system of the states. But it is a curious way of defining the powers of a court, to refer to those of seven courts of another country which were abolished over a century ago. New South Wales and Victoria have replaced the definition by a much shorter and more elegant one, with substantially the same effect. The Victorian Supreme Court has

jurisdiction in or in relation to Victoria its dependencies and the areas adjacent thereto in all cases whatsoever and shall be the superior Court of Victoria with unlimited jurisdiction.[27]

Similarly, the New South Wales Supreme Court is 'the superior court of record in New South Wales', with 'all jurisdiction which may be necessary for the administration of justice in New South Wales'.[28]

The jurisdiction of Supreme Courts, unlike that of inferior civil courts, is not limited by the amount of money at stake in a case. In cases worth more than the lower court jurisdictional limit, the Supreme Court is the only state court with civil jurisdiction, but (with limited statutory exceptions) in cases worth less than that limit the Supreme Court and the lower courts have concurrent jurisdiction. A case can be bought in the Supreme Court to claim 5 cents or $5 million: the only restrictions on suing for trivial amounts in the Supreme Court are the power to remit cases to lower court, penalties in costs, and the inherent power to prevent an abuse of the court's process. These were outlined in Chapter 6.

The notion of the inherent power of a court itself reinforces the generality of Supreme Court jurisdiction. At common law all 'courts' properly so-called have certain 'inherent' powers — that is, powers attributed to the court by virtue of its being a court, which exist unless specifically excluded by statute.[29] But the common law distinguished further between superior courts (or superior courts of record) and inferior courts (whether or not courts of record).[30] A number of important consequences attached to the classification 'superior court'. Only a superior court could punish summarily any contempt of court, without express statutory provision.[31] A superior court had inherent power to regulate its own procedure,[32] to regulate the right of audience before it (including removing a barrister from the roll), and to grant bail (though most of these matters are now covered by statute).[33] Except possibly in extreme cases, a decision of a superior court, unlike a decision of an inferior court, could not be void, but had to be set aside by the appropriate method (writ of error or appeal).[34] This rule applied even to decisions of such a court as to its own jurisdiction, which in the absence of proceedings by way of writ of error or appeal were unimpeachable.[35] Superior courts were not (at least generally) amenable to the writs of certiorari, prohibition, or mandamus, by which decisions of inferior courts, tribunals, and administrators were reviewed.[36] And there is a strong presumption that the jurisdiction of a superior court is not ousted by the conferral of statutory jurisdiction on another court or tribunal.[37]

In principle these rules still apply to Australian superior courts, but a further distinction has evolved between superior courts of general and of defined (or statutory) jurisdiction. Though declared by statute to be superior courts, the Federal Court, the Family Court, and similar bodies are courts of defined jurisdiction. The limitations on their jurisdiction are partly statutory, but partly constitutional. Thus the attributes of superior courts at common law are restricted or excluded by the need to restrain the jurisdiction within its statutory and constitutional limits. Certiorari, prohibition, and mandamus will lie against such courts under s75(v) of the Constitution,[38] and the presumptions protecting the jurisdiction of such a court may not apply, or may be more readily rebutted.[39] By contrast Supreme Courts are courts of general jurisdiction for these purposes, and they attract the full protection of the various rules and presumptions.

Although the Supreme Courts are unified courts of general jurisdiction, in some states provision is made for the exercise of jurisdiction in divisions. The point is not to exclude any of the powers of the court or the remedies available but to allow a degree of judicial specialization and the more convenient handling of business. The New South Wales Supreme Court has as many as nine divisions;[40] other Supreme Courts have fewer or none.

(2) Common law and equity

In Chapter 2 the English development of equity as a separate body of rules administered by the Court of Chancery was described. The Judicature Acts of 1873 and 1875 (UK) brought about the 'fusion', or concurrent administration, of law and equity in a single High Court.

When courts were established in the Australian colonies, there was no warrant for separating law and equity in different courts: the Supreme Courts established after 1824 were courts of general jurisdiction. But local practitioners and judges were so attached to English models that each court was treated as notionally divided into a court of law and a court of equity, with appropriate remedies available only when the judge was wearing the appropriate 'hat'.[41] This unnecessary refinement meant that, after England had adopted the Judicature Act system, the Australian colonies had to decide whether to accept a reform which only their previous copying of English practices required. Both Samuel Griffith and W.E. Hearn, in proposing Judicature Acts for their respective colonies, stressed that they merely restored the status quo of forty years earlier.[42]

In fact the general enactment of the Judicature Act system was a slow, disputatious progress.[43] Adopted fairly rapidly by Queensland (1876), South Australia (1878), Western Australia (1880), and with rather more dissent, Victoria (1883), the concurrent administration of law and equity was not achieved in Tasmania until 1932. More remarkably, New South Wales rejected the system outright: the Equity Act 1880 (NSW) was a movement in the opposite direction, towards the formal separation of equitable jurisdiction, and although the New South Wales legislature thought the 1880 Act only a temporary expedient before the rapid introduction of general reform, the separation lasted ninety years, being defended to the last by equity practitioners.[44]

In each state and territory now the fundamental principle is that equitable rules and remedies should be accessible to judges exercising jurisdiction in any court. In case of conflict, equitable rules prevail. Each court is enjoined

to grant . . . as shall seem just . . . all such . . . remedies whatsoever as any of the parties . . . may appear to be entitled to in respect of any and every legal or equitable claim . . . so that as far as possible all matters so in controversy . . . may be completely and finally determined and all multiplicity of legal proceedings . . . avoided.[45]

No longer need one court restrain proceedings in another; no longer must litigants sue several times to achieve a single result. At least, not on grounds of the separation of law and equity.

(3) Admiralty jurisdiction of Supreme Courts

The growth of admiralty jurisdiction in England, and the subsequent conflict with the common law courts over the rich field of shipping disputes, were also referred to in Chapter 2. The merits of the conflict seem to have been largely with the Admiralty Court, but nothing so trivial as the wishes of litigants concerned common lawyers such as Coke CJ. By the eighteenth century the instance jurisdiction of admiralty had been reduced to a thing of shreds and patches, and despite certain statutory additions, it remained that way until this century.[46]

The colonial Supreme Courts were not at first given admiralty jurisdiction: because of the international implications of prize, and of seizure of and adjudication over foreign ships, and the need for imperial uniformity, the British government sought to retain some degree of control. Instead Vice-Admiralty Courts were established, although the Supreme Courts exercised concurrent criminal jurisdiction over maritime offences such as piracy.[47] These arrangements were not very satisfactory, and in 1890 the Colonial Courts of Admiralty Act (UK) was passed. The Act provided that

> every court of law in a British possession, which is for the time being declared . . . to be a court of admiralty, or which, if no such declaration is in force . . . has original unlimited civil jurisdiction, shall be a . . . Colonial Court of Admiralty

with the same statutory and non-statutory jurisdiction in admiralty as the English High Court then had.[48] Remarkably enough, the 1890 Act is still the basis for the admiralty jurisdiction of state and territory Supreme Courts and the High Court.[49] Questions as to the exact status of the 1890 Act, and of the systems of appeal embodied in it, are of appalling difficulty. Since the admiralty jurisdiction is likely to be replaced by new federal admiralty jurisdiction (based on a report of the Australian Law Reform Commission[50]) only the briefest of summaries of the present position is necessary.

The jurisdiction of colonial courts of admiralty extends to a range of matters: certain claims for seamen's wages, salvage disputes, bottomry bonds,[51] certain claims for damages done to and by ships, certain disputes relating to the possession or ownership of ships; some claims to limit liability for damage done to or by ships, some cargo claims. An important characteristic is the power to arrest a ship or cargo by an action *in rem*: this attracts jurisdiction over the cause of action (and over a defendant shipowner who appears to contest the case[52]), and the ship or cargo becomes available as security to meet any judgment. The 1890 Act requires any court which deals with a matter arising outside the land territory or internal waters of a state and which could be a matter of admiralty jurisdiction to deal with it as such (s2(4)): to this extent, concurrent jurisdiction invested by state law is ineffective.[53]

There is no general declaration now in force under s2(1) of the 1890 Act, and the better view is that all state Supreme Courts are therefore colonial courts of admiralty.[54] The difficulty is that s39(2) of the Judiciary Act 1903 (Cth) seems to invest state courts with 'admiralty and maritime' jurisdiction, and it is arguable that this investment, on terms flatly inconsistent with the 1890 Act, overrides the imperial jurisdiction. But three judges in the High Court have suggested that s39(2) should be construed so as not to include the matters arising in the jurisdiction of Colonial Courts of Admiralty, and it may be that this is the better view.[55]

These are just some of the complexities of admiralty jurisdiction in Australia. Repeal of the 1890 Act and its replacement by more adequate provision for civil jurisdiction in admiralty — such as exists in New Zealand and the United Kingdom[56] — is long overdue.[57]

(4) Other jurisdictions

Supreme Courts as courts of general jurisdiction have access to the whole body of the law unless it is specifically denied them: there is no need for special investment. But in fact the number of provisions denying Supreme Courts jurisdiction in particular matters, state as well as federal, continues to increase. State Supreme Courts have now no jurisdiction to supervise the performance of federal administrative action.[58] They have no jurisdiction under the Family Law Act 1975 (Cth), or under a range of other federal Acts: as will be seen in Chapter 8, the relationship between federal and state courts has become a correspondingly controversial issue. At state level, the extent to which they can hear appeals from, or otherwise supervise, industrial tribunals is restricted. In some states, jurisdiction over small claims is exclusive to the small claims court. Hence the increasing importance of the Supreme Court's supervisory jurisdiction over inferior courts and tribunals, which is discussed in Chapter 13.

7.3 Supreme Courts as Courts of Appeal

(1) The organization of appeals

The more important arrangements which developed in England for review of or 'appeal' from judgments in civil and criminal cases were briefly described in Chapter 2. A regular form of appeal by way of rehearing was not established for common law (as distinct from equity) cases until the Judicature Acts 1873 and 1875 (UK) established the Court of Appeal. In criminal cases, it was not established until 1907. Partly as a result of this history, there is no common law 'right' to appeal: appeal on the merits (as distinct from judicial review) is a purely statutory creation. A further consequence was that when the state Supreme Courts were established, they acquired an array of methods of challenging trial decisions — writs of error, motions in arrest of judgment or for a new trial, appeals by way of case stated, demurrer, and so on.[59] To some extent these have now been abolished, or at least superseded, by provisions for a more flexible appeal by way of rehearing.

Different arrangements exist for the hearing of appeals within the Supreme Courts. In all states but New South Wales, appeal from decisions of intermediate courts, other superior courts or the Supreme Court itself at first instance are heard by a Full Court, that is, by three of the judges. In this way, appellate work is rotated among the judges, in both criminal and civil matters; a system which is like that of a Divisional Court in England rather than the Court of Appeal. Only New South Wales, which is the largest Supreme Court in Australia, has a specialist Court of Appeal, consisting of the Chief Justice, the President, and up to nine Judges of Appeal.[60] This system, established in 1965, enables the judges to specialize in hearing appeals, and may increase the quality of decisions, at the expense, no doubt, of the judges of the court who have no opportunity but to sit on civil appeals.[61] But criminal appeals in New South Wales still go to a Court of Criminal Appeal, consisting of three or more judges of the Supreme Court nominated from time to time by the Chief Justice.[62] The need for trial experience in criminal appeals is greater than in civil cases, so the distinction may be a sensible one.[63]

So far no other Supreme Court has a separate Court of Appeal, although the Queensland Law Reform Commission has recommended such a Court (to hear both civil and criminal appeals) in that state.[64] Opposition to a separate Court of Appeal, based partly on the view that continuing trial experience is necessary for members of an intermediate appeal court, and partly on concern by members of Supreme Courts at the potential loss of the opportunity to hear appeals, is entrenched,[65] and it is unlikely that the New South Wales system will be adopted elsewhere, except as part of some overall plan for an 'Australian Court of Appeal' below the High Court.[66]

While hearing appeals is the most important function of Full Courts, it is not their only one. The supervisory jurisdiction of Supreme Courts is usually exercised by a Full Court, pursuant to the Rules of Court; the Full Court also considers references or cases stated on questions of law under a variety of Acts.

(2) Appellate jurisdiction of Supreme Courts

Unlike the High Court, the appellate jurisdiction of Supreme Courts is not guaranteed in any constitutional sense; indeed, it is not set out in any single Act but in a diffuse way in the Acts establishing the courts and tribunals from which appeals lie.[67] Partly as a result, the appellate jurisdictions of the various Supreme Courts differ quite widely. In all states there is an appeal from most decisions of a single judge of the Supreme Court in civil and criminal cases, interlocutory and final.[68] Only in Tasmania is there an appeal from an acquittal by a jury,[69] although provision has been made in four states for the reference by the Attorney-General of questions of law involved in an acquittal. Such a reference does not affect the decision in the case itself, and is in the nature of an advisory opinion.[70] Provision has also been made for appeals by the Crown against inadequate sentences.[71] Formerly, only a convicted defendant could appeal (whether as of right or by leave) in serious criminal cases.

The position of appeals from other courts is much more variegated. As was pointed out in Chapters 5 and 6, there is usually a general right of appeal from decisions of lower courts, but the forms of 'appeal' are various and in some cases appeal may be by leave only. In the case of specialist courts and tribunals, appeal is frequently restricted to questions of law only: in the industrial jurisdictions, the provisions for appeal are even more restrictive. It is more convenient to describe these provisions when dealing with the courts and tribunals in question.

(3) The functions of intermediate appeal courts

The various devices developed by the common law to avoid the finality of trial decisions demonstrate the need for some form of review or appeal, and the availability of a full appeal is now well accepted.[72] In a hierarchy with (at least) two stages of appeal, one might have expected some coherent theory of the respective roles of intermediate and final appeal courts to emerge, but strangely this does not seem to have happened yet, at least in Australia. Perhaps the most plausible idea is that intermediate courts should be general courts of appeal in all (or potentially all) cases concerned to do justice according to law and thus competent to review decisions on grounds of fact as well as law.[73] (This is subject to due respect for the trial judge's assessment of witnesses, which the appeal court has not seen, and to the great difficulty of impeaching the verdict of a jury.[74]) On the other hand, a final appeal court has as its main function the development of the law and the general oversight of the legal system. But this does not mean either that intermediate appeal courts are, or can be, restricted to applying existing settled rules of law, or that courts of final appeal can decide questions of law in isolation from the facts of the case in hand. The former view would deprive intermediate appeal courts of their very real functions of legal development, functions which cannot in practice be denied;[75] the latter artificially separates the law from the facts, contrary to the basic premises of judicial common-law-making. The High Court's function is to concentrate on issues of basic principle, but those issues can usually only be properly appreciated in their context: if the High Court does intervene, it should examine the whole case, not just some issue abstracted from it.

During the 1970s, however, the High Court developed theories of appellate restraint in several contexts, which in 'inhibiting appeals have changed the effective operation of the appellate system'.[76] The primacy attributed to the trial judge by these theories of restraint had a tendency to reduce intermediate courts to courts of review rather than appeal, with reduced concern for the proper assessment of facts or exercise of discretion. The High Court was then left either to duplicate the appellate function or to decide abstract legal questions.[77] To some extent these developments were brought about by the pressure of the High Court's workload and the unsatisfactory appeal rules; to some extent also, by the maintenance of civil jury trial in the two largest states, which markedly inhibits scrutiny on appeal. Changes in the former have now been made and civil jury trial is in slow but steady decline. Perhaps as a result, the High Court has tended to adopt a more discriminating theory of appeals, allowing greater room for intermediate appellate courts to intervene in cases where no issue of credibility of witnesses is involved.[78]

7.4 Some Problems of Practice and Procedure

Enough has been said to demonstrate the importance of Supreme Courts as the Australian superior courts of general jurisdiction, and also to show the striking differences between them, due in part to the widely divergent sizes and resources of the states, but even more to the considerable differences in structure and operation. It would have been helpful to have been able to compare the caseloads of the different courts, but comprehensive figures are not available in comparable form. Even the Chief Justice of Australia was unable to compile such figures,[79] emphasizing again the need for better information about the court system.

(1) Procedure in Supreme Courts

This is not a book on civil procedure,[80] but some brief reference to those problems is required. In this context, an innovation in the United Kingdom and some Australian states is a separate commercial causes list, of cases involving 'ordinary transactions of merchants and traders'.[81] The point of the list is to speed up the trial and to reduce costs and extraneous procedures. Normally cases are tried without jury: the court has a general power to give directions for 'the speedy determination of the real questions between the parties' and to dispense with pleadings, or even the law of evidence.[82] The parties may agree that the decision of the court is final, in which case there is no appeal. The courts have taken a liberal view of the procedure, for example by rejecting as inadmissible on appeal arguments which were not made to the lower court.[83] There have also been developments in commercial arbitration, whereby the courts can refer a case to arbitration rather than deciding it themselves.[84]

The commercial causes list is undoubtedly a valuable arrangement, but it does involve special treatment for one class of litigants. This may be justified, in that commercial cases sometimes involve relatively well- defined issues of law or the construction of documents, without the more diffuse or wide-ranging questions at stake in other civil litigation. But it may be as plausible to suggest that commercial litigants are better placed to see deficiencies in the ordinary operations of the courts and to exert pressure for reform on their behalf. The need for special methods in such cases may reflect not so much their special character as the unsatisfactory nature of the procedures in ordinary civil litigation, the parties to which are not so well placed. The New South Wales Law Reform Commission, in proposing a general revision of the Rules of Court to accompany the 1970 Act, refrained from more radical reforms not out of conviction but so as to get the basic Judicature Act system into operation.[85] Commentators on Australian civil procedures in the past twenty years have agreed on the need for change — though not on what changes should be made. Suggestions have included more stringent adherence to time-limits for the various stages of a case, with an automatic penalty in costs, reduction in interlocutory procedures such as discovery of documents and interrogatories, increased specialization of judges in particular areas of law, compulsory pre-trial conferences aimed at settlement, increased judicial control over cases in preparation (through the use of Masters), restriction of civil jury trial to the very few cases, such as defamation, which really warrant it, and reform of the law of evidence (especially the hearsay rule).[86]

(2) A *unified civil jurisdiction?*

One promising idea involves abolishing the present distinctions between intermediate and superior trial courts, establishing a uniform process and a more flexible form of case management. In England, the Beeching Commission proposed a single Crown Court to try indictable offences, with flexibility in the use of High Court or Circuit Court judges depending on the nature of case, and greatly improved methods of judicial management.[87] The Commission also discussed a similar proposal for civil jurisdiction:

Since we wished to simplify the structure of the courts, to make them more comprehensible and more flexible in use, we were led to consider, as a counterpart to the single criminal court which we recommend, the establishment of a single civil court of wide jurisdiction and uniform procedure in which the only important variable would be the powers of the judge. We also considered a more modest suggestion which was put to us by several witnesses, including the Law Society, that all civil proceedings might be started in common form, and that, at an appropriate stage in the proceedings, an officer of the court should, after hearing the parties, decide whether the case should be heard by a High Court or a County Court judge. This proposal was not without its attractions because it would provide a straightforward method of deciding by whom cases in the middle range should be tried. We concluded in the end, reluctantly for the most part, that it would be impracticable for us to give effect to either of these possibilities. A partial or total assimilation of the Rules of the Supreme Court and the County Court Rules would have been needed, and this would have involved us in a study for which we are ill-qualified as a body and which would have seriously delayed our report.[88]

The assimilation of the rules of the Supreme Court and of the intermediate civil courts, which is a prerequisite to such a proposal, is itself surely desirable: provided the rules are flexible enough, it would be simpler and more efficient to have the same rules for all civil litigation (other than small claims) within a jurisdiction. Even under the present system, cases can be transferred between Supreme Court and lower courts, and similarity in the relevant rules would be an advantage. An experienced Australian commentator has suggested that

> thought should be given to the question whether litigation should not originate in a common tribunal and continue in a single stream until it appears that, because of the fact that the particular matter is to go to trial or for some other reason, it is necessary that its course should be diverted into the channel proper for its ultimate resolution by the appropriate judicial officer.[89]

A proposal along these lines, for all civil cases to originate by uniform process in the Supreme Court and to be decided by Supreme Court judges or by commissioners, was made by the Tasmanian Law Reform Commission in 1978.[90] Obviously what would suit a jurisdiction with 420 000 people may not be appropriate to one with twelve times as many, but the Beeching Commission's suggestion related to a jurisdiction much larger than all the Australian states together. And it was only echoing the English Judicature Commission in 1872, for whom the Judicature Acts were only the beginning, not the end, of desirable reform in civil jurisdiction.[91] *Plus ça change, plus c'est la même chose*?[92]

Notes

[1] See Bennett, *History*, 30–56.
[2] The colonists had more urgent things to worry about, such as starvation. On the early WA Supreme Court see Edwards (1963) 6 *UWALR* 173. Generally see Bennett & Castles, s.v. 'Court'.
[3] On the other hand the history of the mainland territories differs markedly from the states. On the transfer of the ACT to the Commonwealth, the High Court acted as the superior court for the territory, and NSW inferior

courts retained their jurisdiction. A local Supreme Court was only established in 1933. The SA Supreme Court retained jurisdiction in the NT for a year after its transfer in 1910, when a NT Supreme Court was established. After various changes that Court was replaced in 1961: Northern Territory Supreme Court Act 1951 (Cth). The replacement was itself replaced by the present Court, established by the Supreme Court Act 1979 pursuant to the Northern Territory (Self Government) Act 1978 (Cth); cf. Northern Territory Supreme Court (Repeal) Act 1979 (Cth).

4 Federal Court of Australia Act 1976 (Cth) s24(1)(b). This applies to all territories except the NT: s24(6).

5 The Supreme Courts of Queensland and Tasmania have specific provisions for decentralization: Supreme Court Act 1895 (Qld) (Central and Northern Courts); Supreme Court Civil Procedure Act 1932 (Tas.) s21(3) (sittings in Hobart and Launceston). All the state Acts make provision for Circuit Courts at least in criminal cases: e.g. Supreme Court Act 1935 (WA) s46. Such jurisdiction may be exercised by a judge or a senior practitioner acting as commissioner.

6 Though pronounced 'puny' this does not refer to strength or ability, merely to the fact that puisne judges are formally junior (French *puis-né*).

7 The present number of judges is as follows (approx. ratio to populations in brackets): NSW, 37 [1:148 000]; Victoria, 22 [1:187 000]; Queensland, 19 [1:134 000]; SA, 14 [1:97 000]; WA, 9 [1:157 000]; Tasmania, 6 [1:74 000]. Figures for the two territory Supreme Courts (excluding 'additional judges') are: NT, 6 [1:24 000]; ACT, 3 [1:84 000].

8 The increase in numbers coincides with the establishment of the Federal and Family Courts and the expansion of state intermediate courts.

9 In Victoria there is now also provision for 'reserve' judges (i.e. judges who retire early but are available to sit on request): Constitution Act 1975 (Vic.) s80A, inserted by Courts Amendment Act 1986 (Vic.).

10 For the history of some of these see Bentham & Bennett (1959) 3 *Syd LR* 47, and (1961) 3 *Syd LR* 504.

11 On the English Masters, Ball (1961) 77 *LQR* 33; Diamond (1960) 76 *LQR* 504. On their Australian equivalents, Brettingham-Moore (1963) 1 *U Tas LR* 842; Morison, 268–9; Lee (1981) 11 *Qld L Soc J* 115.

12 Masters and similar officers are part of the Supreme Court in WA (Supreme Court Act 1935 s7(c) (WA) (inserted 1979)), SA (Supreme Court Act 1935 (SA) ss7, 10 (inserted 1981)) and Victoria (Constitution Act 1975 (Vic.) s75(2) (inserted 1983)). To lesser effect Supreme Court Act 1867 (Qld) s39A; cf. SCR 086. These provisions were adopted partly because of the High Court's decision in *Kotsis v Kotsis* (1970) 122 CLR 69 that Masters could not exercise federal jurisdiction because they did not constitute part of the state court. That decision has since been overruled: *Commonwealth v Hospital Contribution Fund* (1982) 150 CLR 49, but the enhanced status of Masters has not been reduced as a result, except in part in Victoria: Supreme Court Act 1986 (Vic.) s104.

13 See the discussion in Victoria, Civil Justice Committee, *Report concerning the Administration of Civil Justice in Victoria* (1984) 293–309, 332–8 (which, however, proposes a 'partnership' model rather than the separate administration of the courts under judicial control).

14 See Campbell, *Rules of Court: A Study of Rule-Making Powers and Pro-*

cedures (1985); Morison, 254–5; Senate Standing Committee on Constitutional and Legal Affairs, *Report on Parliamentary Scrutiny of Rules of Court* (PP 45/1979) 3–7. On the other hand federal bankruptcy, family law, and federal industrial rules are made by executive regulation.
15 Senate Standing Committee on Constitutional and Legal Affairs (1979) 8–16; but cf. *Hass v R* (1975) 133 CLR 120.
16 E.g. Supreme Court Act 1986 (Vic.) s28.
17 See e.g. Fiss (1983) 92 *Yale LJ* 1442; Priest & Klein (1984) 13 *J Leg St* 1; Goldman, *The Federal Courts as a Political System* (3rd edn, 1985); Posner, *The Federal Courts: Crisis and Reform* (1985); and the essays in (1985) 37 *Rutgers LR* 217.
18 Millar & Baar, *Judicial Administration in Canada* (1981); Estey, in AIJA, *Seminar on the Constitutional and Administrative Responsibilities for the Administration of Justice: The Partnership of Judiciary and Executive* (1986) 19.
19 See Donaldson & Scott, in AIJA (1986) 43.
20 Senate Standing Committee (1979) 17–23; Willis & Sallmann (1977) 51 *Law Inst J* 498.
21 (1982) 56 *ALJ* 387.
22 See esp. Cranston, Haynes, Pullen & Scott, *Delays and Efficiency in Civil Litigation* (1985); Cranston (1983) 57 *ALJ* 8.
23 Victoria, Civil Justice Committee, *Preliminary Study concerning the Administration of Civil Justice in Victoria* (1984); Civil Justice Committee, *Report concerning the Administration of Civil Justice in Victoria* (1984) — as to which see Scott (1985) 59 *ALJ* 466; Victoria, Law Department, Courts Management Change Program, *Consultation Report* (1986).
24 Supreme Court Act 1986 (Vic.); General Rules of Civil Procedure Part I 1986; Supreme Court (Rules of Procedure) Act 1986 (Vic.). See Williams (1985) 4 *Civil Justice Q* 49, 150.
25 E.g. *R v Paddington Valuation Officer, ex p Peachey Property Corp. Ltd* [1966] QB 380, 400.
26 Cf. to similar effect: Supreme Court Act 1867 (Qld) ss21–2, 24; Supreme Court Act 1935 (WA) s16; Supreme Court Civil Procedure Act 1932 (Tas.) s6; Supreme Court Act (NT) s14; Australian Capital Territory Supreme Court Act 1933 (Cth) s11 (the last 3 by reference).
27 Constitution Act 1975 (Vic.) s85(1). Section 85(2) rather spoils the simplicity of s85(1) by providing that the Court has 'such jurisdictions, powers and authorities as were had . . . by any of the superior Courts in England'. See also s85(3) (inserted 1986).
28 Supreme Court Act 1970 (NSW) ss22–3.
29 E.g. *Taylor v Taylor* (1979) 25 ALR 418 (inherent jurisdiction to set aside orders where party not served or absent without fault). Cf. *Bailey v Marinoff* (1971) 125 CLR 529 (no inherent power to deal further with an appeal already dismissed by formal order). On the category 'judicial', see *de Smith's Judicial Review of Administration Act* (4th edn, 1980) 77–89 (absolute judicial immunity from suit, etc.).
30 On the characteristics (now of little relevance) of a 'court of record' see Holdsworth, 5 HEL 157–60.
31 *Ex p Bishop of Norwich* [1932] 2 KB 402; *A-G v BBC* [1981] AC 303 (although the contempt might be of an inferior court).

32 But not, the High Court has held, to dispense with the Rules of Court (in the absence of express power to do so): *Doyle v Commonwealth* (1985) 60 ALR 567.
33 Cf. *Ex p Davis* (1963) 63 SR (NSW) 54; *Forrest v Huffa* [1968] SASR 341; *R v McCarthy* (1975) 12 SASR 288. On the limits of the inherent jurisdiction to grant bail, *R v Rademeyer* (1985) 59 ALR 141. Generally on inherent powers see Mason (1983) 57 *ALJ* 449; Cairns (1985) 4 *Civil Justice Q* 309; de Jersey (1985) 15 *Qld L Soc J* 325.
34 *Scott v Bennett* (1871) LR 5 HL 234, 245; *Sanders v Sanders* (1967) 116 CLR 366. Cf. *Cameron v Cole* (1944) 68 CLR 571.
35 *Mayor of London v Cox* (1867) LR 2 HL 239, 260–3 (Willes J).
36 Aronson & Franklin, *Review of Administrative Action* (1987) 566.
37 Id., 671–708.
38 *R v Watson, ex p Armstrong* (1976) 9 ALR 551, 565; *A-G (Qld) v Wilkinson* (1968) 100 CLR 422, 425; *R v Commonwealth Court of Conciliation and Arbitration, ex p Ozone Theatres (Aust.) Ltd* (1949) 78 CLR 389, 399–400; *Re Ross-Jones, ex parte Green* (1984) 56 ALR 609. Cf. *R v Forbes, ex p Bevan* (1972) 127 CLR 1. But cf. the comments of Deane & Dawson JJ in *Re Gray; Ex parte Marsh* (1985) 62 ALR 17, 42–6, 48–50, criticised by Aronson & Franklin, 562–3.
39 *R v MTEA, ex p AEU (Australian Section)* (1951) 82 CLR 208.
40 Morison, 275–87. Of these, the Family Law Division is defunct. The most recent addition is the Commercial Division, added in 1985: Starke (1986) 60 *ALJ* 430, 446–7.
41 Bennett, *History*, 97.
42 Bennett (1970) 9 *UWALR* 211, 228; Bennett & Castles, 147.
43 Bennett (1970) 9 *UWALR* 227; Bennett & Castles, 145–55; Castles, 106–9.
44 E.g. McLelland (later CJ in Eq) (1951) 25 *ALJ* 344, 351–2, echoing Williams J 70 years earlier: Bennett & Castles, 146. On the NSW system before 1970 see Bennett, *History*, 94–109. The Supreme Court Act 1970 (NSW) was preceded by reports strongly supporting the change: see NSWLRC Report No. 7, *Supreme Court Procedure* (1969).
45 Judicature Act 1876 (Qld) s4(8). See also SA: Supreme Court Act 1935 ss20–8, Local and District Criminal Courts Act 1926 ss35a–36; WA: Supreme Court Act 1935 ss24–5, 34; Victoria: Supreme Court Act 1986 ss29–31; NT: Supreme Court Act ss61–70; Tasmania: Supreme Court Civil Procedure Act 1932 ss10–11; ACT: Australian Capital Territory Supreme Court Act 1933 (Cth) ss17–26; NSW: Law Reform (Law and Equity) Act 1972, Supreme Court Act 1970 ss57, 63, District Court Act 1973 s134. See further Morison, 270–1, 276–8.
46 The 'instance' jurisdiction was the general civil and criminal jurisdiction, compared with that in prize. Generally see O'Hare (1979) 6 *Monash ULR* 91, 195; Cowen & Zines, 63–72, 228–33; Zelling (1982) 56 *ALJ* 101, and esp. ALRC 33, *Civil Admiralty Jurisdiction* (1986) chs 2–4.
47 See Bennett, *History*, 153–67; Castles, 28–9, 51, 110; Bennett & Castles, 174–5.
48 53 & 54 Vic c27 s2(1). That the Act 'froze' admiralty jurisdiction as at 1890 is established: *The Yuri Maru* [1927] AC 906; *F. Kanematsu & Co. Ltd v The Ship 'Shahzada'* (1956) 96 CLR 477; *Co-Op Dried Fruit Sales Pty Ltd v The Ship 'Terukawa Maru'* (1972) 126 CLR 170.

49 Query whether the Federal Court of Australia, which has 'unlimited civil jurisdiction' (e.g. under the Trade Practices Act) so as to be a Colonial Court of Admiralty: McPherson (1981) 55 *ALJ* 71.
50 ALRC 33, *Civil Admiralty Jurisdiction* (1986). See (1987) 61 *ALJ* 211.
51 A pleasant name for a dull thing: bottomry bonds are mortgages of a ship to secure provisions etc. for a voyage.
52 *The Dictator* [1892] P 304; ALRC 33, para. 142–3.
53 There is no express reference to admiralty jurisdiction in the Supreme Court Acts, but the general terms of the NSW and Victorian Acts certainly encompass it.
54 The Supreme Court Civil Procedure Act 1932 (Tas.) s4 declares the Supreme Court a Colonial Court of Admiralty under s2(1) of the 1890 Act (cf. s9(5)). Although Australia is one 'possession' for this purpose (*John Sharp & Sons Ltd v The Ship Katherine Mackall* (1924) 34 CLR 420) no one has ever argued that this deprived other courts of admiralty jurisdiction. But a similar Commonwealth provision (in force 1914–39) may have done so: Cowen & Zines, 67–8. Section 3(b) of the 1890 Act allows inferior courts to be given limited admiralty jurisdiction: the only case is the Broome Local Court Admiralty Jurisdiction Act 1917 (WA), the jurisdiction of which has not been exercised within living memory.
55 *McIlwraith McEacharn Ltd v Shell Co. of Aust. Ltd* (1945) 70 CLR 175, 206–10 (Dixon J); *China Ocean Shipping Co. v State of South Australia* (1979) 27 ALR 1, 40–7 (Stephen J), 55–7 (Aickin J). In the latter case Gibbs J thought the question 'completely open'; Murphy J thought the 1890 Act superseded by the Constitution and Commonwealth legislation: id., 24–5, 47–51 respectively. The argument from s39 is maintained, tentatively, by Cowen & Zines, 228–33.
56 The 1890 Act has been repealed in Canada and New Zealand, but only the latter has effectively replaced it. On Canadian admiralty jurisdiction see Kerr (1979) 5 *Dalhousie LJ* 568; on New Zealand, Admiralty Act 1973 (NZ); on the UK, Jackson, *Enforcement of Maritime Claims* (1985).
57 The ALRC's recommendations would involve a comprehensive federal Admiralty Act and Rules, with jurisdiction *in rem* given concurrently to the Federal Court and Supreme Courts: ALRC 33, chs 6–11. The criminal jurisdiction of admiralty courts is almost as troublesome: see *R v Robinson* [1976] WAR 155; *Oteri v R* [1976] 1 WLR 1272. These problems have been partly overcome by the Crimes at Sea Act 1979 (Cth) and associated state legislation; but see Saunders (1979) 12 *MULR* 158.
58 Administrative Decisions (Judicial Review) Act 1977 (Cth) s9 (which excepts only writs of habeas corpus).
59 Bennett, 168–77, 182–3; Castles, 80–2, 108–10.
60 Supreme Court Act 1970 (NSW) ss42–8, 75A, 101–8; Young (1965) 6 *Aust L* 119.
61 Morison, 264–7, 284–90.
62 Criminal Appeal Act 1912 (NSW) s3.
63 But a similar distinction in England between the Courts of Appeal and the Court of Criminal Appeal was abolished in 1966: Jackson, 203–8. Criminal appeals are now heard by the Court of Appeal (Criminal Division) on which, however, High Court judges do still sit.
64 QLRC 32, *Civil Proceedings in the Supreme Court* (1982) 25–37. That

proposal was strongly supported by the Bar and as strongly opposed by the Supreme Court.

[65] E.g. Connolly (1981) 11 *Qld L Soc J* 176, 179–81; Victoria, Civil Justice Committee, *Report concerning the Administration of Civil Justice in Victoria* (1984) I, 105–8.

[66] As proposed as part of an 'integrated court system' by the former Constitutional Convention, Judicature Sub-Committee: *Report on an Integrated System of Courts* (1984) 18–24. See further Chapter 14.

[67] Until 1985 appeals from the two mainland territory Supreme Courts went to the Federal Court of Australia or (by special leave) directly to the High Court. NT appeals are now dealt with within the Supreme Court under the Supreme Court Act (NT) ss51–60: cf. Federal Court of Australia Act 1976 (Cth) s24(6).

[68] NSW: Criminal Appeal Act 1912 ss5–5E, Supreme Court Act 1970 ss101–4; Queensland: Criminal Code 1899 ss668A–D, Judicature Act 1876 ss7–10; SA: Criminal Law Consolidation Act 1935 s352, Supreme Court Act 1935 ss49–50; Tasmania: Criminal Code Act 1924 ss400–1, Supreme Court Civil Procedure Act 1932 ss39–44; Victoria: Crimes Act 1958 ss567–67A, Supreme Court Act 1986 ss10, 14; WA: Criminal Code 1913 ss687–8, Supreme Court Act 1935 ss58–61.

[69] Criminal Code Act 1924 (Tas.) s401(2)(b).

[70] Criminal Appeal Act 1912 (NSW) s5A(2); Criminal Law Consolidation Act 1935 (SA) ss350–1a; Criminal Code 1913 (WA) s693A; Criminal Code 1899 (Qld) s669A(2).

[71] E.g. Crimes Act 1958 (Vic.) s567A.

[72] For the distinction between strict appeals and appeals by way of rehearing cf. *Meakes v Dignan* (1931) 46 CLR 73, 107–11 (Dixon J).

[73] This distinction is adopted by the American Bar Association Commission on Standards of Judicial Administration, *Standards relating to Appellate Courts* (1977) 4–5. On the role of intermediate appeal courts in the US see Hopkins (1975) 41 *Brooklyn LR* 459; Carrington, Meador & Rosenberg, *Justice on Appeal* (1976); Howard, *Courts of Appeal in the Federal Judicial System* (1981); Kaplan (1985) 70 *Mass LR* 10. On the application of the US experience to Australia, Victoria, Civil Justice Committee, *Report concerning the Administration of Civil Justice in Victoria* (1984) 106–7.

[74] There is, and should be, no appeal from a criminal jury on any issue of fact, although the question whether it was open to the jury on the evidence to return a guilty verdict is a question of law: *Chamberlain v R* (1984) 51 ALR 225.

[75] Compare the essays on the SA Supreme Court under Bray CJ in (1980) 7 *Adel LR* 1; and cf. McHugh (1987) 11 *Syd LR* 183. Another, more heterodox, view, suggested by an observation of Elwyn-Jones LC ((1976) 7 *Cambrian LR* 31, 34), is that the final appeal court's function is to decide, from the innovations thrown up in the court of appeal, which ones are of permanent value. This accurately described the position in England while Lord Denning MR presided over the Court of Appeal, but is of limited value in Australia. For one thing, there are eight intermediate appeal courts. For another, none has a Lord Denning!

[76] Hutley, in Tay & Kamenka, eds, *Law-making in Australia* (1980) 179. The leading case expressing this view was *Edwards v Noble* (1971) 125 CLR 296.

77 Hutley, 197–205.
78 *Warren v Coombs* (1979) 142 CLR 531; *Trevey v Grubb* (1984) 44 ALR 20; *Brunskill v Sovereign Marine & General Insurance Co. Ltd* (1985) 62 ALR 53. But certain decisions are still classed as 'discretionary', and the scope for intervention on appeal is correspondingly restricted. This has created problems especially in the field of property division in family law: *Mallet v Mallet* (1984) 52 ALR 193; *Norbis v Norbis* (1986) 65 ALR 12. See further Chapter 10.
79 Barwick (1977) 51 *ALJ* 495; (1979) 53 *ALJ* 487 (giving up the attempt).
80 See Cairns, *Australian Civil Procedure* (2nd edn, 1985); Aronson, Reaburn & Weinberg, *Litigation, Evidence and Procedure* (3rd edn, 1982).
81 In NSW, elevated to a division: Supreme Court (Commercial Division) Amendment Act 1985 (NSW).
82 Supreme Court Act 1970 (NSW) ss38(b)(ix), 41(1)(g), 53(1), 53(3E) (inserted 1985); Commercial Causes Act 1910 (Qld); Supreme Court (Commercial List) Rules 1985 (Vic.). Cf. Baxt (1980) 54 *ALJ* 751; Rogers (1982) 56 *ALJ* 570; Macfarlan (1973) 1 *ABLR* 192; O'Bryan (1985) 17(3) *Commercial Lawyers Assoc of Aust Bull* 51. On the English system see Colman, *The Practice and Procedure of the Commercial Court* (2nd edn, 1986).
83 *Saffron v Société Minière Cafrika* (1958) 100 CLR 231, 240.
84 E.g. Arbitration (Civil Actions) Act 1983 (NSW); Dawson (1985) 23 *Law Soc J* 507; Cranston, Haynes, Pullen & Scott, *Delays and Efficiency in Civil Litigation* (1985) 200–4.
85 NSWLRC 7 (1969) 9.
86 The most comprehensive examination of these issues is Victoria, Civil Justice Committee, *Report concerning the Administration of Civil Justice in Victoria* (1984); and Cranston, Haynes, Pullen & Scott, *Delays and Efficiency in Civil Litigation* (1985). See also Manning (1965) 5 *Syd LR* 1; Blackburn, (1975) 49 *ALJ* 374; Davies, id., 380; Brennan, id., 672; Norris (1976) 50 *Law Inst J* 227; Barwick (1958) 1 *U Tas LR* 1; Burbury (1963) 6 *UWALR* 163; VLRC, Report No. 4, *Delays in Supreme Court Actions* (1976); Mahoney (1985) 59 *ALJ* 494. On reform of the law of evidence see ALRC 38, *Evidence* (1987).
87 Beeching Report (1969), implemented by the Courts Act 1971 (UK); Jackson, 75–80; Zander, *Cases and Materials on the English Legal System* (4th edn, 1984) 20–32.
88 Beeching Report 73.
89 Norris, 231.
90 Tas. LRC, Report No. 22, *Reform of Civil Procedure* (1978) 6–8, 10–11. The Report is apparently still 'under consideration'. Cf. also NZRCC, 309–11.
91 Judicature Commission, *Second Report* (1872) I, 12–13 (C. 631), cited Norris, 231.
92 Australian discussions of 'vertical' integration of the courts have been cursory and negative: the only considered discussion (still negative in its conclusions) is Victoria, Civil Justice Committee, *Report concerning the Administration of Civil Justice in Victoria* (1984) I, 19–21, 110–8. For proposals for 'horizontal' integration of superior federal and state courts (a much less sensible idea) see Constitutional Commission, Committee on the Australian Judicial System, *Report* (1987) ch. 3; and see further Chapter 8.

CHAPTER 8

The Federal Court of Australia

8.1 The Establishment of the Federal Court of Australia

Chapter III of the federal Constitution envisages that federal jurisdiction will be exercised by the High Court, by 'such other federal courts as the Parliament creates', and by state courts invested with federal jurisdiction. The last possibility was not open under the US Constitution, and from 1789 there has been a separate system of federal courts.[1] By contrast, in Australia, only a few federal courts were established in the first 75 years of federation: the most important were the Industrial Court in its various forms, and the Federal Court of Bankruptcy (operating in Victoria and New South Wales).

When new jurisdictions were established by federal statute, the Parliament thus had the choice of giving them to the High Court or to state courts. The latter was not always done, so that the High Court acquired a very miscellaneous jurisdiction in a range of matters not appropriate to a final court of appeal. In some cases, jurisdiction was conferred on the Australian Industrial Court, as the only other federal court operating in all states. Many of these jurisdictions were not 'industrial', so that the Industrial Court itself risked becoming a court of general jurisdiction, with its special industrial responsibilities obscured.

(1) The Federal Court controversy

As a result, successive Commonwealth Attorney-Generals, beginning with Sir Garfield Barwick in 1964, proposed that a new federal court should be created to exercise many of these miscellaneous jurisdictions.[2] Proposals to this effect were introduced into Parliament in

1967, 1973, and 1974, but either lapsed or were defeated.[3] In fact these Bills were not based on a single conception of a federal superior court. There were instead two distinct strands of thought. The first, represented by proposals made by Byers and Toose in 1963,[4] and by the Labor Bills of 1973-4, saw the problem primarily in terms of the inadequacy of investing state courts with federal jurisdiction. There were complaints about delays, differences in interpretation or application (especially in matters of procedure, which would not in many cases reach the High Court for scrutiny[5]), and lack of Commonwealth administrative control over court-room facilities and over the number and appointment of judges.[6] According to this conception, what was needed was a federal court to administer the great bulk of federal law, leaving only incidental or ancillary matters to state courts.[7] On the other hand there was strenuous criticism that this would reduce the status of Supreme Courts, that the new structure would be cumbersome and expensive, and that it would produce unnecessary jurisdictional disputes, as well as duplicating judicial facilities.[8]

The second approach, represented by the Barwick proposal of 1964, rejected the 'federal courts for federal law' argument, and emphasized instead the need to relieve the High Court of its burden of original jurisdiction, inherent and invested. The federal superior court would be given co-ordinate or exclusive jurisdiction over matters previously within the High Court's original jurisdiction, and perhaps some specialized federal and appellate jurisdiction. The 1967 Bill adopted this view in its entirety: the Court was to be given original jurisdiction over most of the matters within the High Court's original jurisdiction, and specialised jurisdiction in taxation and industrial property.[9] But it was to have only a very restricted appellate jurisdiction, not even extending to appeals from territory Supreme Courts. Matrimonial causes jurisdiction was to be retained by state Supreme Courts.

The view that prevailed when the Federal Court was eventually established by the Federal Court of Australia Act 1976 (Cth) implied an acceptance of the arguments for a restrictive rather than extensive jurisdiction for the Court.[10] No attempt was made to confer jurisdiction concurrent with the original jurisdiction of the High Court under s75 of the Constitution. Nor was it given general jurisdiction (exclusive of or concurrent with that of state Supreme Courts) over matters of federal law, such as was contemplated by the Bills of 1973-4. Instead, the Federal Court took over from the Australian Industrial Court and the Federal Court of Bankruptcy their 'functional' jurisdiction under a variety of laws. Relief for the High Court was provided, not by the assumption of original jurisdiction, but by the conferral of appellate jurisdiction from territory Supreme Courts, and from single judges of state Supreme Courts in certain matters. In relation to its appellate jurisdiction the Act quite closely reflected the Barwick proposal of 1964. The lack of original jurisdiction, on the other hand, accorded more with the opponents of a federal superior court than any of its previous supporters.

This apparent resolution of the arguments was not, however, a permanent one. Once established, the Federal Court was likely to become a continuing repository of jurisdiction under new federal laws, with adverse effects on state courts. This has indeed happened, with the result that debate over the relationship between federal and state courts, far from subsiding, has increased in intensity (and most of the participants have been Supreme Court and Federal Court judges!).[11] It is first necessary to describe the present structure and jurisdiction of the Federal Court.

(2) The organization of the Federal Court

The Federal Court, which commenced operations on 1 February 1977, consists of two Divisions. The Industrial Division replaced the Australian Industrial Court, and exercises the strictly industrial jurisdiction of the Court. It is a specialist jurisdiction, and will be dealt with in Chapter 12.[12]

The General Division was initially given the non-industrial jurisdiction of the Industrial Court, and the bankruptcy jurisdiction of the Federal Court of Bankruptcy.[13] Since 1976, further jurisdiction has been conferred on it in areas such as administrative law, taxation, and intellectual property.[14]

The Federal Court is a superior court of law and equity, with jurisdiction extending throughout Australia, and with judges resident in each state except Tasmania. Its judges (presently, a Chief Judge and twenty-seven other judges) are designated to serve in either the Industrial or General Divisions or in both. This allows the appointment of specialists to exercise the Court's industrial jurisdiction.[15] Significant use has been made of Federal Court judges in other roles — as presidential members of the Administrative Appeals Tribunal,[16] as judges or 'additional judges' of territory Supreme Courts, and so on.[17]

8.2 The Jurisdiction of the General Division of the Federal Court

(1) Original jurisdiction

No substantive original jurisdiction was conferred on the Court by the Federal Court of Australia Act 1976 itself.[18] Instead such jurisdiction has been conferred by other legislation, in the following areas.

(A) BANKRUPTCY
Under the Bankruptcy Act 1966 (Cth), jurisdiction was formerly exercised by the Federal Court of Bankruptcy and by state courts.

The Federal Court took over the jurisdiction of the Federal Court of Bankruptcy,[19] but at first operated only in New South Wales, the Australian Capital Territory, and Victoria. In the other states, original jurisdiction was exercised by the Supreme Court (in South Australia, the Court of Insolvency),[20] but the Federal Court has now taken over the exercise of bankruptcy jurisdiction in all states. Jurisdiction in bankruptcy involves the court in taking over the property of those who are insolvent (i.e. who cannot pay their debts), supervising the administration of that property and the payment of at least a proportion of the debts, discharging bankrupts (who are then freed from the burden of previous debts), and related matters.[21]

(B) TRADE PRACTICES

One of the most important heads of Federal Court jurisdiction has been its jurisdiction under the Trade Practices Act 1974 (Cth) (formerly exercised by the Australian Industrial Court). The Federal Court has exclusive criminal and civil jurisdiction to enforce the provisions of the Act relating to restrictive trade practices (retail price maintenance, monopolies, and the like), and concurrent jurisdiction with respect to Part V of the Act,[22] which deals with consumer protection (misleading and deceptive conduct, etc.).[23] It can restrain breaches or threatened breaches of the Act by injunction (s80), and award damages to persons injured by any contravention of the restrictive practices or consumer protection provisions of the Act (s82).[24] Until 1987 the consumer protection jurisdiction under Part V of the Act was exclusive to the Federal Court, and many of the cases discussed below, where jurisdictional disputes arose between the Federal Court and state courts, involved claims under Part V. Indeed, some of the consequences of Federal Court jurisdiction under Part V seem not to have been intended: when the Court held that it could hear a defamation claim against a newspaper connected with a claim under Part V, the position was rapidly reversed by statute.[25]

(C) FEDERAL ADMINISTRATIVE LAW

As important as its trade practices jurisdiction is the Federal Court's role in the 'new federal administrative law'. Government departments and agencies make a vast number of decisions affecting the public — entitlements to pensions or benefits, licences to carry on an activity or business, assessment of taxes and charges, and so on. These decisions have to be made in accordance with law, that is, in accordance with the empowering Act and with general principles of administrative law developed by the courts to ensure minimum standards of regularity and fairness. Enforcement of these standards has been largely left to the ordinary courts — most importantly, the Supreme Courts and also (especially in federal matters) the High Court.

This system had a number of disadvantages. Common law rules of administrative review are based on a distinction between the merits of a decision and the power (or jurisdiction) to make it. Normally the courts have no direct power to review an administrative decision on its merits (power to make it is given by Parliament to the administrator, not the courts). All they can do is investigate whether the administrator actually had power to make the decision in the way he has made it. So someone aggrieved by the merits of a decision has only a slight chance of getting it reviewed. And the rules and remedies available to the courts in reviewing administrative acts are complex, confused, and in some respects unsatisfactory.

Following proposals for reform made by a number of committees of inquiry,[26] two major reforms of the system of review of federal administrative decisions were made: these correspond to the two kinds of problem outlined above. First, the Administrative Appeals Tribunal was established in 1975, with jurisdiction to review on their merits many decisions of federal administrators. Secondly, a comprehensive, simplified system of judicial review of most federal administrative decisions was established under the Administrative Decisions (Judicial Review) Act 1977 (Cth). In both areas the Federal Court has important functions. It hears appeals on questions of law from decisions of the Administrative Appeals Tribunal, which can also refer questions of law to the Court before making a decision on a matter before it.[27] And the Federal Court alone has jurisdiction to review decisions under the Administrative Decisions (Judicial Review) Act 1977. Not only is this jurisdiction exclusive, but no state court can review federal administrative decisions to which the Act applies.[28]

Until 1983, the Federal Court's exclusive jurisdiction under the 1977 Act coincided with the exclusive jurisdiction of the High Court to hear any case in which mandamus, prohibition, or an injunction was sought against an officer of the Commonwealth under s75(v) of the Constitution.[29] This was inconvenient, since the two jurisdictions substantially overlapped. In 1983 the Federal Court was given concurrent jurisdiction under s75(v), except for cases where the 'Commonwealth officer' is a member of the Conciliation and Arbitration Commission or the Coal Industry Tribunal, or a judge of the Family Court.[30]

(D) OTHER CIVIL AND CRIMINAL JURISDICTION

Several other Acts confer civil and criminal jurisdiction on the Federal Court.[31] So far as civil jurisdiction is concerned, important additions are made by the Jurisdiction of Courts (Miscellaneous Amendments) Act 1987 (Cth): these include exclusive jurisdiction over federal tax disputes, and concurrent jurisdiction over industrial property cases (copyright, designs, patents, and trade marks). By contrast the criminal jurisdiction of the Court is of a minor or incidental character. There is, for example, no provision for criminal juries in the Federal Court Act: the intention is that no trials on indictment will take place there.[32]

(2) Appellate jurisdiction

The extent and diversity of the Federal Court's appellate jurisdiction already reflects its possible evolution into a general federal court of appeals, below the High Court.

(A) APPEALS FROM A SINGLE JUDGE OF THE FEDERAL COURT

There is, as one would expect, a right of appeal from 'judgments of the Court constituted by a single judge'.[33] Originally this right of appeal extended to interlocutory matters, criminal as well as civil, although the jurisdiction was sparingly exercised.[34] Interlocutory appeals are now by leave only.[35]

(B) APPEALS FROM TERRITORY SUPREME COURTS

The Federal Court is the immediate appeal court from judgments of Supreme Courts of all territories except the Northern Territory (which in 1985 established its own Full Court to hear intermediate appeals).[36] Before 1977 the only appeal from territory Supreme Courts was direct to the High Court: in assuming this jurisdiction the Federal Court relieved the High Court of what had been a significant caseload.[37]

(C) CERTAIN APPEALS FROM STATE COURTS

In the first ten years after the establishment of the Federal Court, it had an important role as the intermediate court of appeal from state courts in certain federal matters: industrial property cases, bankruptcy, and taxation.[38] These were the only matters in which Supreme Courts were deprived of jurisdiction by the legislation establishing the Federal Court.[39] At the time they were justified on the ground that these were specialist questions suitable for a single 'specialist' court.[40] But they may become precedents for a greater use of the Federal Court as the court of appeal in federal matters.[41]

The provision of an exclusive right of appeal from a state court to a federal court[42] is capable of raising constitutional problems, since it is clear that no federal court (other than the High Court) can be given appellate jurisdiction from a state court exercising state jurisdiction.[43] The point is that some actions involving patents or trade marks may also involve related claims (e.g. for passing-off) under state law. This problem occurs also in the court's original jurisdiction: it is dealt with below.

(D) APPEALS IN CRIMINAL CASES

Section 24 of the Federal Court Act confers jurisdiction to hear certain 'appeals', without further specification. This clearly extends to appeals in criminal cases from conviction and sentence, although it does not displace the various techniques of judicial restraint which have been developed by appeal courts in these cases.[44] However, the principle that there should be no appeal from an acquittal is a fairly well established one at common law, and in *Thompson v Mastertouch TV Service Pty Ltd*[45] the Full Federal Court held that the general words of s24 did not displace this principle. There has been controversy over both the correctness and the scope of the *Mastertouch* rule,[46] but the issue was settled by the High Court in *Davern v Messel*, where a conviction before a magistrate was set aside on an appeal by way of rehearing: the Court held that there was no appeal under s24 from an acquittal at first instance, but that if a convicted defendant appealed, the prosecution could bring a further appeal from any decision on that appeal.[47] Thus if Parliament wishes to provide for appeals from acquittal at first instance, it must say so expressly.

(E) CASES STATED AND SIMILAR REFERENCES
The Federal Court Act itself,[48] and a number of other Acts,[49] allow lower courts or tribunals to state a case or refer a question of law to the Federal Court. This power extends even to criminal cases where there would be no appeal if the defendant were to be acquitted.[50]

(F) MISCELLANEOUS APPEALS FROM TRIBUNALS
Various Acts confer on the Court jurisdiction to review decisions of tribunals or boards. By far the most significant is the Administrative Appeals Tribunal.[51] Although expressed to be an 'appeal', this is formally a 'review' of the decision (in what is technically the original jurisdiction of the Court). Under the separation of powers as enunciated in the *Boilermakers' case*,[52] there can be no appeal, in the strict sense, from a non-judicial body to a court. But, as so often with the separation of powers, the restriction is circumvented: there is no objection to judicial review of administrative decisions and little or no limitation on the grounds for such review.[53]

(3) Pendent, 'associated', and 'accrued' jurisdiction

Where a court has general jurisdiction it can determine all the matters in dispute between the parties, whatever their subject-matter. A court of limited jurisdiction is not in the same position: the question arises whether it can determine matters not specifically within its statutory mandate, but which have arisen in conjunction with matters that are. Legally distinct claims between the same parties can arise out of the same factual situation. If one claim is within Federal Court jurisdiction, does the other become so because of this factual connection? Is the situation different if the 'related' claim is a counter-claim against a third party? This legal issue has become a highly controversial one, associated with the more general policy debate over federal courts and their impact on the status and jurisdiction of state courts. In the event, answers to the legal questions can now be given, as a result of extensive litigation in the High Court and elsewhere. The policy issues, of course, remain, and are discussed later in this chapter.

A distinction needs first to be drawn between matters of federal jurisdiction which are related to a claim within the Federal Court's jurisdiction, and matters of state jurisdiction or of common law which are not in themselves matters of federal jurisdiction but which are related to a Federal Court claim. The former category is known (from the language of s32 of the Federal Court Act) as 'associated' jurisdiction, the latter as 'accrued' jurisdiction. Together it is useful to describe the two categories by the generic title of 'pendent' jurisdiction.

(A) ASSOCIATED FEDERAL JURISDICTION
The Federal Court has jurisdiction only under specified federal laws. But a trade practices claim might be associated with a claim under some other federal law, or which is within federal jurisdiction for some other reason (e.g. because it involves residents of different states, or a claim against the Commonwealth or arising under the Constitution[54]). The Federal Court of Australia Act 1976 (Cth) s32 provides that

To the extent that the Constitution permits, jurisdiction is conferred on the Court in respect of matters not otherwise within its jurisdiction that are associated with matters in which the jurisdiction of the Court is invoked.[55]

It is now settled that this refers not to jurisdiction under state law or the common law, but to the question of associated federal jurisdiction. The introductory phrase to s32 has been read as referring to all the legislative powers of the Commonwealth, and as indicating an intention to confer further federal jurisdiction where another federal matter is 'associated' with a primary claim within jurisdiction. On this point, at least, the High Court was agreed in the leading cases, *Philip Morris Inc. v Adam P. Brown Male Fashions Pty Ltd*; *United States Surgical Corporation v Hospital Products International Pty Ltd*.[56] In the *United States Surgical Corporation* case, the plaintiff sought injunctions against the defendant on a variety of grounds, including deceptive conduct under the Trade Practices Act 1974 (Cth) s52, breach of a distributorship agreement, passing-off, breach of copyright, and breach of confidence. The gist of the claim was the defendant's use of information and written material which he gained while employed as the plaintiff's Australian distributor of surgical goods. The High Court held unanimously that the Federal Court had jurisdiction to determine the breach of copyright claim (a matter of federal law but one which was not at that time within the Federal Court's original jurisdiction), if it was found to be 'associated' with the trade practices claim; although no definition of 'associated' was given. Section 32 was, therefore, successful as an ambulatory formula attracting other *federal* jurisdiction.[57]

(B) ACCRUED JURISDICTION UNDER THE COMMON LAW OR STATE LAW
More difficult is the question whether the Federal Court can exercise accrued jurisdiction in matters of state law or common law. This problem arose in *Adamson v West Perth Football Club*,[58] where Adamson claimed that the Club's refusal to grant him a clearance to play

interstate violated s45 of the Trade Practices Act 1974 (Cth) as well as the common law restraint of trade rule; in *Philip Morris*, where the defendant's use of the term 'Marlboro' on clothes was said to be misleading and deceptive conduct under the Trade Practices Act 1974 (Cth) s52 as well as passing-off at common law; and, as we have seen, in *United States Surgical Corporation*. It has since arisen in many other cases. The outcome, thrice affirmed by a majority of the High Court, is that the Federal Court (like the High Court itself) has jurisdiction over all claims which are part of a single 'matter' for the purposes of ss75 and 76 of the Constitution. The question first arose in the context of High Court jurisdiction: in a series of cases, the High Court had upheld its jurisdiction to determine the entire case where one ground invoked was within jurisdiction.[59] The prerequisites have been that the primary claim should be material and made in good faith, not simply to invoke the court's jurisdiction over the associated claim; and that the other claim should not be 'entirely severable' and distinct.[60] But there is no requirement that the primary claim should succeed, or even that it should be a strong one, so long as it was fairly raised on the facts.

The analogy with Federal Court jurisdiction is close, but it is not exact. High Court jurisdiction, in these cases, was defined by reference to 'matters' — the United States equivalent in 'cases'.[61] The Federal Court's jurisdiction is defined much more precisely — as jurisdiction to grant specified relief on particular grounds (not including restraint of trade, passing-off, or breach of confidence at common law). And this jurisdiction is required by s76(ii) to 'arise under' a Commonwealth law. As Aickin and Wilson JJ, dissenting, pointed out, the common law claims in *Philip Morris* and *United States Surgical Corporation* did not directly arise under federal law.[62] But this was, the majority held, to take too narrow a view of the jurisdiction conferred by the Trade Practices Act, or of the meaning of 'matter' in s76. Where a claim arises under federal law, then the whole inseverable matter to which the claim relates similarly 'arises'. As Mason J, delivering the leading judgment, said:

Once it is accepted, as it must be, that there is no special magic in the scope of those matters which involve the interpretation of the Constitution, the lesson to be learned from the authorities is that the Court having jurisdiction to determine a matter falling within ss75 and 76 giving rise to the exercise of federal jurisdiction has jurisdiction to decide an attached non-severable claim. The classification of a claim as 'non-severable' does not necessarily mean that it is, or must be, united to the federal claim by a single claim for relief, though this is a common illustration of a non-severable claim. The non-severable character of the attached claim may emerge from other aspects of the relationship between the federal and the attached claim. For example, it may appear that the resolution of the attached claim is essential to a determination of the federal question. Likewise, it may appear that the attached claim and the federal claim so depend on common transactions and facts that they arise out of a common substratum of facts. In instances of this kind a court which exercises federal jurisdiction will have jurisdiction to determine the attached claim as an element in the exercise of its federal jurisdiction.[63]

This broad definition of a 'matter' for the purposes of federal court jurisdiction was approved in *Fencott v Muller*[64] and *Stack v Coast Securities (No. 9) Pty Ltd*.[65] In *Fencott v Muller* the majority commented:

Whatever formula be adopted as a guide — and the formula of 'common transactions and facts' is a sound guide for the purpose — it must result in leaving outside the ambit of a matter a 'completely disparate claim constituting in substance a separate proceeding' . . . [I]t is a matter of impression and of practical judgment whether a non-federal claim and a federal claim joined in the proceeding are within the scope of one controversy and thus within the ambit of a matter.[66]

The test thus requires a 'common substratum of facts' rather than complete identity of facts.[67] This expansive formula has been applied on many occasions by the Federal Court, not only in the context of several alternative claims by a plaintiff against a defendant, but also in the context of counter-claims and cross-claims under state law or common law,[68] and of claims against third parties (known as 'pendent party' jurisdiction).[69] The result has been a substantial extension to the effective jurisdiction of the Federal Court.

(C) ACCRUED AND ASSOCIATED JURISDICTION ON APPEAL

There are three ways in which questions of pendent jurisdiction can arise on appeal: an accrued or associated claim may arise at first instance in the Federal Court, and an appeal be brought from the decision on that claim; it may be raised for the first time on appeal in the Federal Court; or it may arise at first instance in a state court, and an appeal be brought to the Federal Court on the claim, on the ground that it is related to a claim which is or may be appealed to the Federal Court. In each case the related claim might be a state or common law one which is part of the same matter, or a federal claim attracted by s32. But in the case of associated jurisdiction there is the additional complication of s32(2), which provides that

The jurisdiction conferred by sub-section (1) extends to jurisdiction to hear and determine an appeal from a judgment of a court so far as it relates to a matter that is associated with a matter in respect of which an appeal from that judgment or another judgment of that court, is brought.

In the first of the three situations, whether the Federal Court had jurisdiction over the claim as part of a single 'matter' or as an associated federal matter attracted by s32(1), its decision would simply be a 'judgment' of a single judge subject to appeal in the ordinary way.[70] Similarly, in the second situation the Federal Court on appeal would only have jurisdiction to hear on the merits an associated claim which was part of the 'matter' on appeal or which was attracted then by s32(1). In neither case does s32(2) have any effect.

Appeals from state courts present different problems. For example, a common law passing-off claim may be associated in a Supreme Court with a patent action under federal law. An appeal lies to the Federal Court from the latter but not from the former, considered in isolation. One would have thought that, provided the case below constituted a single 'matter', the only appeal was to the Federal Court. But the difficulty here is that an appeal from a state court to a federal court (other than the High Court) can be conferred only in a matter of federal jurisdiction, and the High Court seems to have held that a case which involved federal jurisdiction at first instance might not do so on appeal if the federal issue was not the subject of the appeal.[71] On this view in the example given, if the appeal related only to the passing-off claim it might not then involve part of a federal 'matter', and the appeal would lie only to the Full Supreme Court. A preferable view might have been that once a case substantially involves a matter of federal jurisdiction it remains federal throughout any subsequent appeals (irrespective of the grounds of appeal).

Whatever the position of common law or state claims, in the case of associated federal claims attracted by s32, s32(2) itself adopts the narrower view, since it requires that the other federal matter be 'associated with a matter in respect of which an appeal . . . *is brought*'.[72] Whether the appeal lies to the Supreme Court or the Federal Court, in these situations, apparently depends on the grounds of appeal. This will usually be clear enough, but problems can readily be imagined: the amendment of the grounds of appeal, for example, or a cross-appeal by the other party to the other court.[73]

8.3 The Federal Court and Conflict with State Courts

As this account demonstrates, the establishment of the Federal Court has brought with it difficult jurisdictional problems, with cases potentially divided between jurisdictions and with the possibility of direct conflict between state and federal courts.[74] Proposals have been made to address the specific legal and jurisdictional difficulties (which have been more serious in the Family Court than in the Federal Court) and also to settle the more basic issue of the proper role of federal courts *vis-à-vis* state courts. It is necessary to deal with these issues separately.

(1) Resolving jurisdictional conflicts between state and federal courts

Assuming the coexistence of federal and state courts, the most obvious way of avoiding jurisdictional conflict is to ensure that, in areas of potential overlap, the federal court's jurisdiction is concurrent rather than exclusive. This allows litigants to choose their forum having regard to the issues which they believe will be the main ones. (It also allows cases to be transferred to the appropriate court if problems later arise.) Unfortunately one of the main areas of overlapping jurisdiction in the case of the Federal Court has been the consumer protection provisions of the Trade Practices Act 1974 (Cth), especially s52, dealing with misleading and deceptive conduct of trading corporations. Many common law causes of action arise out of or involve misleading and deceptive conduct, but this jurisdiction was exclusive to the Federal Court until 1986.[75]

It it is thought desirable to confer exclusive jurisdiction on a federal court, then the jurisdiction should be as broad as possible: in the case of the Federal Court this has largely been achieved, through the combination of a broad interpretation of the accrued jurisdiction and the associated jurisdiction under s32 of the Federal Court of Australia Act 1976 (Cth). By contrast, the Family Court's jurisdiction has been limited by the interpretation given to the relevant constitutional powers, and by limitations in the Family Law Act 1975 (Cth) itself: as a result severe demarcation problems have arisen in the fields of child custody and property distribution. These problems, and the various measures which have been taken to deal with them, are described in Chapter 10.

In addition to statutory changes, a more comprehensive solution to the jurisdictional problems has been proposed, in the form of a co-operative legislative scheme involving all states, the Northern Territory, and the Commonwealth, for mutual cross-vesting of jurisdiction between the Federal Court, the Family Court of Australia, and state and territory Supreme Courts. Cross-vesting is to occur under the Jurisdiction of Courts (Cross-vesting) Act 1987 (Cth) and cognate state and Northern Territory legislation. It is planned to come into force in 1988.[76]

Assuming that the cross-vesting scheme is constitutionally valid,[77] it will vest in these courts what might be described as general residual jurisdiction. For example, s4 of the federal Act vests in state and territory Courts all the jurisdiction of the Federal Court and the Family Court. The Act does not in terms require that a proceeding be commenced in what would otherwise be the 'correct' court (although according to the preamble to the Act, this is what is intended). Instead it provides for the court in which a case is commenced to decide (on application by an Attorney-General or a party or of its own motion) whether some other court is the more appropriate court to hear the case. The Act sets out criteria for making this decision (which is not subject to appeal):[78] one criterion is which court would 'normally' deal with the case. Apart from appeals,[79] the only 'protected' jurisdiction of any court under the scheme is the jurisdiction of the Federal Court over 'special federal matters': these include federal administrative law matters and certain trade practices claims.[80]

A 'special federal matter' must be transferred to the Federal Court on application by the federal Attorney-General, and the state court's discretion to hear a 'special federal matter' is more restricted than its discretion to exercise cross-vested jurisdiction. Family law disputes are not included in the category of 'special federal matters'. Nor does the scheme deal with criminal jurisdiction or (except in one respect) with the jurisdiction of inferior courts.[81]

How the cross-vesting scheme will work in practice will depend on the way in which the discretions to hear or transfer proceedings are exercised: the absence of any appeal from those decisions means that other measures (judicial or extra-judicial) may need to be taken to ensure reasonable consistency. Where related proceedings are pending in two courts, the legislation is likely to assist in having the proceedings dealt with fully by a single court (although, since applications to transfer might be made by different parties at the same time to both courts, even here some co-ordination will be required). With a proceeding pending in a federal court, the discretion to transfer to a state court is most likely to be exercised where the 'accrued' jurisdiction of the federal court is judged to involve 'the substantial part of the relevant proceeding': the converse is true for Supreme Courts. There is a real possibility of differential assessments of the importance of state versus federal claims — as experience with the accrued jurisdiction has shown. In marginal cases it would not be surprising to find courts tending to retain rather than transfer jurisdiction: if so the principal effect of the legislation may well be to increase still further the capacity for forum-shopping and forensic manoeuvres.[82]

(2) The debate over the merits of the Federal Court

As the preamble to the cross-vesting legislation itself suggests, actual conflicts between state and federal courts have (except in the area of family law) occurred 'occasionally' rather than frequently. Nonetheless the growth of the jurisdiction of federal courts has been highly controversial. Campbell's argument is representative of much of the adverse comment. In his view

> the establishment of a dual court system in Australia in its present form is largely unnecessary . . . will create serious jurisdictional problems, and will produce damaging and far reaching effects on the status and reputation of the Supreme Courts of the states.[83]

On the other hand, the first Chief Judge of the Court has strongly defended its role. In his view, few conflicts have occurred in practice, since

> the factors which have in the past prevented the 'dual' system from operating in a manner contrary to the interests of litigants and the public still continue to operate.[84]

It is difficult to assess the relative costs and benefits of a new court. The case for bringing together existing specialist jurisdictions in the one court, and for providing an intermediate appeal court for the territories, was strong. But this assumes that the Federal Court is intended to be essentially a specialist court with limited and well-defined jurisdiction. Another view is that the Federal Court will inevitably tend to become a general federal court, dealing with most federal civil jurisdiction. The addition of taxation and industrial property to its existing jurisdiction over federal administrative law is a significant step in that direction, but the turning point would undoubtedly be the conferral of jurisdiction under a new federal Companies and Securities Act, if such an Act were to replace the present co-operative scheme.[85] Fear of developments such as these,[86] leading to the progressive weakening of state Supreme Courts, has been a major factor in proposals for some form of 'integrated', or at least 'co-ordinated', Australian court system: these proposals are discussed in Chapter 14. The cross-vesting legislation itself was in part the product of proposals for more basic structural change, proposals which would, it was hoped, secure the existing general jurisdiction (especially the appellate jurisdiction) of state courts and judges.[87] But the aims of the cross-vesting scheme are considerably more limited: the scheme is not intended to 'detract . . . from the existing jurisdiction of any court',[88] and the Commonwealth has made it clear that it is not committed to upholding the existing division of jurisdiction between federal and state courts.[89] On the other hand the states are not without their own weapons in this conflict: in particular the Commonwealth has no desire to take over, or to fund, the growing area of federal criminal law, which the states are presently committed to applying, without specific federal reimbursement.[90] Despite the cross-vesting scheme (and co-operation with some states in respect of family law powers[91]), the underlying conflicts remain unresolved.

Notes

[1] On US federal courts, see Wright, *The Law of Federal Courts* (3rd edn, 1976); Goldman & Jahnige, *The Federal Courts as a Political System* (3rd edn, 1985); Posner, *The Federal Courts: Crisis and Reform* (1985); Surrency, *History of the Federal Courts* (1987). For the proposed federal intermediate court of appeals, see Note (1974) 27 *Rutgers LR* 904; Howarth & Meador (1979) 12 *U Mich JLR* 201. There is apparently 'an emerging negative consensus' on the proposal: Gazell (1986) 6 *N Ill ULR* 1.
[2] (1964) 1 *FLR* 1.
[3] Superior Court of Australia Bill 1967; Superior Court of Australia Bill 1973; Superior Court of Australia Bill (No. 1) 1974; Superior Court of Australia Bill (No. 2) 1974.
[4] (1963) 37 *ALJ* 308.
[5] Id., 314.

6 Byers & Toose set out the arguments: id., 313–16.
7 Id., 319–29.
8 E.g. Burt (1963) 37 *ALJ* 323; Editorials in (1974) 3 *ATR* 1; (1974) 12 *NSW Law Soc J* 121; Senator Wright, 63 *Parl Debs (Senate)* (26 Feb. 1975) 452–6. And see esp. Sawer (1964–5) 8 *JSPTL* 301, 311–14.
9 Bowen (1967) 41 *ALJ* 336; Lane (1969) 43 *ALJ* 148; Editorial (1967) 41 *ALJ* 69.
10 Bowen (1977) 8 *Syd LR* 285; Ellicott (1977) 1 *Crim LJ* 2; Editorial (1977) 51 *ALJ* 55; Cowen & Zines, 104–44. Generally on the 1976 reforms see Lane (1980) 54 *ALJ* 11.
11 The literature is already vast. See e.g. Smith, *ABC Guide to the Federal Court of Australia* (1986); Morison, 236–47; Durack (1981) 55 *ALJ* 778; Renfree, 379–472; Camilleri, *Practice and Procedure of the High Court and Federal Court of Australia* (1978) vols 2, 3; CCH, *Australian High Court and Federal Court Practice* (1980) vol. 2, and the works cited below.
12 The Industrial Relations Bill 1987 (Cth) proposed the establishment of a new specialist industrial court, the Labour Court, at the expense of the Industrial Division of the Federal Court. The Bill was withdrawn in May 1987, but may be reintroduced in modified form. See further Chapter 11.
13 Neither the Federal Court of Bankruptcy nor the Australian Industrial Court was then abolished. They retained jurisdiction over 'proceedings the hearing of which had commenced' before 1 Feb. 1977 and which were not transferred to the Federal Court: Conciliation and Arbitration Amendment Act (No. 3) 1976 (Cth) s3; Bankruptcy Amendment Act 1976 (Cth) ss5, 7; Federal Court of Australia (Consequential Provisions) Act 1976 (Cth) s4. The two courts are not to be abolished until 'no person holds office as a Judge' of them: Conciliation and Arbitration Amendment Act (No. 3) 1976 (Cth) ss4, 5; Bankruptcy Amendment Act 1976 (Cth) ss8, 9. The point of these provisions was that two judges with life tenure but aged over 70 were not appointed Federal Court judges. The avowed intention was to 'encourage' their retirement as their work disappeared. This was a violation of the spirit of the 1977 constitutional amendment providing for retirement of judges, which was expressly not made retrospective.
14 E.g. by the Jurisdiction of Courts (Miscellaneous Amendments) Act 1979 (Cth), substantially removing the High Court's miscellaneous statutory jurisdiction, and the Jurisdiction of Courts (Miscellaneous Amendments) Act 1987 (Cth), conferring substantial additional jurisdiction on the Court.
15 At present, one judge (Gray J) is assigned exclusively to the Industrial Division; 5 exclusively to the General Division; the remaining 22 (including the Chief Judge, *ex officio*) to both. See Federal Court of Australia Act 1976 (Cth) s13.
16 Administrative Appeals Tribunal Act 1975 (Cth) ss6(2), 7A. But Federal Court judges are now sitting much less frequently in the AAT. See further Chapter 13.
17 Federal Court of Australia Act 1976 (Cth) s15(2), (3).
18 Federal Court of Australia Act 1976 (Cth) s19.
19 Bankruptcy Amendment Act 1976 (Cth) s4.
20 Bankruptcy Act 1966 (Cth) s27. All state Supreme Courts are invested with bankruptcy jurisdiction, but in practice they do not exercise it. The SA Court of Insolvency was a curiosity — a state court established by a public Act of restricted application (The Insolvent Act 1886) it apparently

exercised no state jurisdiction at all. It ceased to exercise federal bankruptcy jurisdiction after 1 Feb. 1982. For the Victorian Court of Insolvency see Insolvency Act 1928 (Vic.) (repealed 1982).

[21] On bankruptcy jurisdiction in Australia see *McDonald, Henry & Meek's Australian Bankruptcy Law and Practice* (5th edn, 1977). Proposals have been made to replace the cumbersome procedures of bankruptcy with less formal machinery: see ALRC, Report No. 6, *Insolvency: The Regular Payment of Debts* (1977) esp. 1–19. Any change would not necessarily deprive the Federal Court of jurisdiction, since Commonwealth power extends to 'bankruptcy and insolvency' (Constitution s51(xvii)), the latter a very wide term.

[22] Concurrent jurisdiction will be vested in state courts under Part V when the new s86 of the Trade Practices Act 1974 (Cth) (substituted by Jurisdiction of Courts (Miscellaneous Amendments) Act 1987 (Cth)) is proclaimed. Section 87A (also inserted by the 1987 Act) allows transfer of matters from the Federal Court to state courts.

[23] For criminal jurisdiction see Trade Practices Act 1974 (Cth) s79. Sections 76 and 77 provide what is described as a 'civil action' for 'pecuniary penalties': one consequence of the classification is that the civil burden of proof (proof on the balance of probabilities as distinct from beyond a reasonable doubt) applies.

[24] But the Federal Court has no jurisdiction over a civil action for breach of a term implied into a contract by the Trade Practices Act (except under s32): *Zalai v Col Crawford (Retail) Pty Ltd* [1980] 2 NSWLR 438; *Arturi v Zupps Motors Pty Ltd* (1981) 33 ALR 243 and cf. *Polgardy v AGC Ltd* (1981) 34 ALR 391, or over cases where s86 is relied on as a defence: *Bargal v Force* (1983) 49 ALR 193. On the trade practices jurisdiction generally see Taperell, Vermeesch & Harland, *Trade Practices & Consumer Protection* (3rd edn, 1983); Donald & Heydon, *Trade Practices Law* (2 vols, 1978).

[25] *Australian Ocean Line Pty Ltd v West Australian Newspapers Ltd* (1983) 47 ALR 497, (1985) 58 ALR 548. The effect of the decision was reversed (so far as it concerned 'prescribed information providers', i.e. the media) by Trade Practices Act 1974 (Cth) s65A, inserted by Statute Law (Miscellaneous Provisions) Act (No. 2) 1984 (Cth).

[26] See Commonwealth Administrative Review Committee, *Report* (Kerr Committee) (Cth PP 1971 No. 144); *Final Report of the Committee on Administrative Discretions* (Bland Committee) (Canberra, 1973); *Prerogative Writ Procedures. Report of Committee of Review* (Ellicott Committee) (Cth PP 1973 No. 56).

[27] Administrative Appeals Tribunal Act 1975 (Cth) s44 (appeals), s45 (reference of questions of law).

[28] Administrative Decisions (Judicial Review) Act 1977 (Cth) ss8, 9, but cf. s10. Review by way of habeas corpus is not excluded (s9(2)) but this is a rarity. And cf. s19. On the equivalent jurisdiction of the Canadian Federal Court see Mullan, *The Federal Court Act: Administrative Law Jurisdiction* (1977); Fera (1973) 6 *Ottawa LR* 99; Fera (1977) 8 *Manitoba LJ* 529. See further Chapter 13.

[29] Made exclusive to the High Court by Judiciary Act 1903 (Cth) s38(e).

[30] Judiciary Act 1903 (Cth) s39B. See FCR O54A; *Re Hassell; ex parte Pride* (1984) 52 ALR 181.

31 These are conveniently set out in CCH vol. 2, 50-013ff, and in the Jurisdiction of Courts (Miscellaneous Amendments) Act 1987 (Cth).
32 Federal Court of Australia Act 1976 (Cth) ss39–41 deal only with civil juries. Constitution s80 prevents criminal trials on indictment except by jury.
33 Federal Court of Australia Act 1976 (Cth) s24(1)(a).
34 *McNamara v R* (1978) 29 ALR 98; *Brambles Holdings Ltd v TPC* (1979) 28 ALR 191; *TWU (Aust.) v Leon Laidely Pty Ltd* (1980) 28 ALR 589.
35 Federal Court of Australia Act 1976 (Cth) s24(1A) (inserted 1984).
36 Section 24(1)(b), and cf. s25 (composition of Court). The NT is excluded by s24(6).
37 Cf. Barwick (1964) 1 *FLR* 1, 5–7.
38 Federal Court of Australia Act 1976 (Cth) s24(1)(c); cf. also s32A(2) (chambers appeals). Appeals are provided for by a large number of Acts: see e.g. Bankruptcy Act 1966 (Cth) s38; Copyright Act 1968 (Cth) s131C; Patents Act 1952 (Cth) s148; Trade Marks Act 1955 (Cth) s114. Where leave is required it has been fairly liberally granted: *FCT v Forsyth* (1979) 29 ALR 124.
39 The Jurisdiction of Courts (Miscellaneous Amendments) Act 1987 (Cth) confers concurrent original jurisdiction on the Federal Court in industrial property matters, and retains its exclusive appellate jurisdiction. Federal taxation matters will be exclusively within Federal Court jurisdiction.
40 E.g. Bowen (1979) 53 *ALJ* 806, 809, 813.
41 E.g. Petroleum Retailing Marketing Franchise Act 1980 (Cth) s26(4) (which falls into none of the previous categories); Shipping Registration Act 1981 (Cth) s82.
42 That is, exclusive of Full Supreme Courts. The right to apply direct to the High Court for special leave was retained in the case of income tax, patents, and trade marks, but not in bankruptcy.
43 That is, by Commonwealth legislation: *Collins v Charles Marshall Pty Ltd* (1955) 92 CLR 529. The effect of the cross-vesting legislation is discussed below.
44 *R v Tait & Bartley* (1979) 24 ALR 473 (appeals from sentence); *Duff v R* (1979) 28 ALR 663 (appeals from conviction).
45 (1978) 19 ALR 547 (Deane J, with whom Smithers & Riley JJ agreed).
46 *Burgess v John Connell-Mott* (1979) 25 ALR 467, 479 (Evatt J), 479–80 (Keely J); *Henderson v Pioneer Homes Pty Ltd* (1979) 25 ALR 179, 201 (Northrop J); *Wood v City of Melbourne Corporation* (1979) 26 ALR 449 esp. 451–2 (Northrop J).
47 (1984) 53 ALR 1. See further *Keating v Gresham* (1985) 63 ACTR 19.
48 Federal Court of Australia Act 1976 (Cth) s25(6) (Federal Court), s26 (other courts).
49 E.g. Copyright Act 1968 (Cth) s161; Income Tax Assessment Act 1936 (Cth) s198; Court-Martial Appeals Act 1955 (Cth) ss51–5. Cf. *Pearce v FCT* (1978) 20 ALR 354.
50 *Henderson v Pioneer Homes Pty Ltd* (1979) 27 ALR 229 (HC).
51 Administrative Appeals Tribunal 1975 (Cth) s44. See further Chapter 13.
52 (1956) 94 CLR 253. See Chapter 3.
53 *Shell Co. of Aust. Ltd v FCT* (1930) 44 CLR 530; *Farbenfabriken Bayer AG v Bayer Pharma Pty Ltd* (1959) 101 CLR 652.
54 E.g. *Allied Mills Industries Pty Ltd v TPC* (1981) 34 ALR 105, 116–18;

Superstar Australia Pty Ltd v Coonan & Denlay Pty Ltd (1981) 40 ALR 183; *Mobil Oil Australia Pty Ltd v Brindle* (1984) 56 ALR 541, on appeal on other grounds (1985) 62 ALR 89. Matters of federal jurisdiction are those listed in ss75 and 76 of the Constitution. They are outlined in Chapter 9.
55 Federal Court of Australia Act 1976 (Cth) s32(1). There is an equivalent in Family Law Act 1975 (Cth) s33, which has, however, not been used to any degree in practice. See further Chapter 10 on the accrued and associated jurisdiction of the Family Court.
56 (1981) 148 CLR 457.
57 But s32 does not confer jurisdiction in respect of a claim merely because the Commonwealth has power to regulate it, if it has not exercised that power: *Minister for Health v Ancient Order of Foresters Friendly Society . . . (No. 2)* (1985) 61 ALR 302.
58 (1979) 27 ALR 475.
59 See e.g. *Carter v Egg & Egg Pulp Marketing Board (Vic.)* (1942) 66 CLR 557; *R v Bevan, Ex p Elias & Gordon* (1942) 66 CLR 452; *Hopper v Egg & Egg Pulp Marketing Board (Vic.)* (1939) 61 CLR 665; Cowen & Zines, 72–5.
60 In *Carter's case* the plaintiff claimed that certain Victorian legislation was invalid, but alternatively claimed an account of money paid by him under the Act. The latter claim was held to be entirely distinct and separate, and not within the High Court's jurisdiction. Cf. also *Moorgate Tobacco Co. Ltd v Philip Morris Ltd* (1980) 31 ALR 161.
61 On the US position see *UMWA v Gibbs* 383 US 715 (1966), extending the rather more restrictive position taken in *Hurn v Oursler* 289 US 238 (1933). Cf. Wright, 72–7; Note (1982) 95 *Harvard LR* 1935. On analogous problems in Canada see e.g. Evans (1981) 59 *Can BR* 124; Hogg (1981) 30 *UNBLJ* 9; Scott (1982) 27 *McGill LJ* 137.
62 (1981) 33 ALR 465, 522, 530 respectively.
63 Id., 504. Stephen J agreed. And see id., 474 (Barwick CJ).
64 (1983) 46 ALR 41, 68–9.
65 (1983) 49 ALR 193.
66 (1983) 46 ALR 41, 68–9 (Mason, Murphy, Brennan, Deane JJ). However, the federal claim must be a substantial as distinct from trivial part of the controversy for jurisdiction to extend to the whole 'matter': id., 69. It must also be a 'genuine' claim: *Francis C. Mason v Citicorp Australia Pty Ltd* (1984) 57 ALR 130. Moreover, the common law or state law claims, though part of the accrued federal jurisdiction, are not within the exclusive jurisdiction of the Federal Court: whether the Court should decide them is a matter within its discretion: *Stack v Coast Securities (No. 9) Pty Ltd* (1983) 49 ALR 193.
67 The Australian position is close to the US formula, 'a common nucleus of operative fact'. In *Philip Morris*, Mason J thought that 'some support' was provided by the US decisions: (1981) 33 ALR 465, 504. For discussion of the Australian position see Gummow (1979) 10 *FLR* 211; Lane (1980) 54 *ALJ* 159; Rogers (1980) 54 *ALJ* 285; Gibbs (1981) 12 *U Qld LJ* 3; Renfree, 387–94; O'Brien (1985) 13 *ABLR* 77.
68 *Coward v Allen* (1984) 52 ALR 320; *Kennedy v Australian Coal & Shale Employees' Federation* (1983) 50 ALR 735; *Duff v McCulloch* (1985) 65 ALR 677; *McMahon v Smith* (1986) 69 ALR 527; *Hughes v WA Cricket

Assoc. (Inc.) (1986) 69 ALR 660. *Fencott v Muller* (1983) 46 ALR 41 was itself a pendent party claim.

69 *Stohl Aviation v Electrum Finance Pty Ltd* (1984) 56 ALR 716; *Obacelo Pty Ltd v Taveraft Pty Ltd* (1985) 59 ALR 571.

70 E.g. *Mobil Oil Australia Pty Ltd v Brindle* (1985) 62 ALR 89.

71 *Collins v Charles Marshall Pty Ltd* (1955) 92 CLR 529, 541; *Cockle v Isaksen* (1957) 99 CLR 155, 164–5.

72 Emphasis added. For an example of the limited effect of s32(2) in this context see *F.J. Bloemen Pty Ltd v FCT* (1981) 35 ALR 104, 108.

73 As Bowen, 815–16, has pointed out, a fairly simple amendment would cure these problems.

74 For examples of Federal Court injunctions restraining Supreme Court proceedings see *Denpro Pty Ltd v Centrepoint Freeholds Pty Ltd* (1983) 48 ALR 39; *Turelin Nominees v Dainford Ltd* (1983) 47 ALR 326; *Novasonic Corp. Pty Ltd v Hagenmeyer (A/Asia) BV* (1983) 8 ACLR 303. Such injunctions were a standard method of enforcing the supremacy of equitable over legal remedies before the Judicature Acts.

75 Cf. *Broadlex Pty Ltd v Computer Co. Pty Ltd* (1983) 50 ALR 92.

76 For discussion see Australian Constitutional Convention, Judicature Sub-Committee, *Report on an Integrated System of Courts* (1984) 10, 14–17; Constitutional Commission, Australian Judicial System Committee, *Report* (1987) para. 3.113–15. For the cognate state legislation see e.g. Jurisdiction of Courts (Cross-vesting) Act 1987 (NSW).

77 The Commonwealth Parliament has power to cross-vest all federal jurisdiction in state courts, and territory jurisdiction may be vested in federal courts, but it is not clear on what basis state legislation can vest state judicial power in federal courts, or that territory courts can exercise federal jurisdiction in respect of matters not connected with the territory. See Chapter 3 for discussion of these issues.

78 Jurisdiction of Courts (Cross-vesting) Act 1987 (Cth) ss5, 13(a).

79 The vesting of 'additional jurisdiction' by s4 extends to appellate jurisdiction, but s7 restricts the institution of appeals to the court that would normally hear the appeal. Section 7 would, however, cure the problem of partial appellate jurisdiction where an appeal was brought on both a federal and state ground.

80 Id., s3(1) (definition of 'special federal matter'), s6.

81 Apart from state Family Courts (as to which see Chapter 10), the only 'inferior' courts affected by the cross-vesting scheme are state or territory courts which have jurisdiction over a matter which includes a claim under the consumer protection provisions of the Trade Practices Act 1974 (Cth): such a case can be remitted to that court by the Federal Court or any Supreme Court: s10. See also Trade Practices Act 1974 (Cth) s86A (inserted 1987).

82 One likely area for manoeuvre is the special choice of law provision (s11(1)(b)), and the extraordinarily broad power to determine the 'appropriate' rules of evidence and procedure to apply (s11(1)(c); there is no appeal from such decisions: s13(b)).

83 (1979) 11 *UQLJ* 3, 3. To similar effect, Rogers (1981) 55 *ALJ* 608; Street (1978) 52 *ALJ* 434; Helsham (1978) 52 *ALJ* 466 (all Supreme Court judges). Gibbs CJ has expressed the same view: (1981) 55 *ALJ* 677. For an example of potential conflict (application for Federal Court injunction restraining

Supreme Court action) see *St Justins' Properties Pty Ltd v Rule Holdings Pty Ltd* (1980) 40 FLR 282. And cf. the disagreement between Mason J and Wilson J in *Philip Morris*: (1981) 33 ALR 465, 505, 534.

[84] Bowen, 812, attempts a point-by-point refutation of Street CJ's views. See also (supporting the Federal Court) Durack (1981) 55 *ALJ* 778; Byers (1984) 58 *ALJ* 590. Walker (1981) 55 *ALJ* 312 suggests that competition between courts is actually desirable.

[85] For the present scheme see Companies Act 1981 (Cth) and cognate state and NT legislation; National Companies and Securities Commission Act 1979 (Cth). There is considerable dissatisfaction with it, and comprehensive federal legislation is by no means unlikely, even in the short term; in the longer term it seems inevitable. See e.g. Senate Standing Committee on Constitutional and Legal Affairs, *The Role of Parliament in relation to the National Companies Scheme* (1987).

[86] Another area of concern has been the replacement of the existing admiralty jurisdiction by new federal legislation. There was strong opposition from state governments and judges to any proposal for exclusive Federal Court jurisdiction in admiralty, either at first instance or on appeal. In the event the ALRC recommended concurrent jurisdiction at both levels: see ALRC 33, *Civil Admiralty Jurisdiction* (1986) para. 235–9, and cf. id., para. 220–1 for a summary of the Australian debate on federal and state courts.

[87] E.g. Parker, in AIJA Seminar, *An Integrated Court System for Australia* (1983) 4. See further Chapter 14.

[88] Jurisdiction of Courts (Cross-vesting) Act 1987 (Cth) preamble.

[89] E.g. Jurisdiction of Courts (Miscellaneous Amendments) Act 1987 (Cth).

[90] State courts have no option but to exercise federal jurisdiction vested in them under Constitution s77(iii), and the states are committed by s120 to house federal prisoners. In neither respect is there any specific federal reimbursement (comparable to that provided for state Family Courts under Family Law Act 1975 (Cth) s41(1)).

[91] See e.g. Commonwealth Powers (Family Law) Act 1986 (SA), a reference of power pursuant to Constitution s51(38). See further Chapter 10.

CHAPTER 9

The High Court of Australia

9.1 The Establishment and Constitution of the High Court[1]

As was pointed out in Chapter 3, proposals for a general court of appeal for Australia had been current since the mid-nineteenth century. The need for such an appeal court, combined with the demands of a federal constitution, made the establishment of a 'Federal Supreme Court' a basic tenet of the federal movement. That Court would therefore combine a specifically federal jurisdiction (like that of the US Supreme Court) with the jurisdiction of a general court of appeal (like the Appellate Committee of the House of Lords).[2]

Section 71 of the Constitution states that the judicial power of the Commonwealth 'shall be vested in a Federal Supreme court, to be called the High Court of Australia', and the Court's basic jurisdiction is conferred by the Constitution itself. But the Constitution did not actually establish the Court: this was done, after heated debate, by the Judiciary Act 1903 (Cth).[3] At first, the High Court consisted of a Chief Justice and two justices. In 1907 it was increased to five members, and in 1912 to seven, its present number.[4] This compares with nine Lords of Appeal in Ordinary[5] and nine US and nine Canadian Supreme Court judges.

The administration of the High Court since 1903 has not been without special difficulties. Before 1980 the principal seat of the Court was Sydney and the bulk of its work was done in Sydney and Melbourne, but it was always intended that it be transferred to Canberra, the 'seat of government'. In the meantime, accommodation and other facilities were sometimes of a makeshift kind — even more so on the High Court's annual visits to the smaller capital cities.[6]

The establishment of the High Court in a specially designed building in Canberra was accompanied by the setting up of a form of separate administration for the Court, giving it a formal autonomy of operation which no other Australian court enjoys.[7] There were initial disputes over the powers of the Chief Justice, as distinct from the Court as a whole, in this new system, and over the architectural merits of the Court's new building. In the longer term these have been overshadowed by controversies over the Court's role, and over the danger of its becoming remote from the 'real life' lived in Australian capital cities.[8] The Court's role is indeed an important issue; but it is necessary first to describe its constitutional and statutory jurisdiction.[9]

9.2 The Jurisdiction of the High Court

Consistently with the two main reasons for its establishment, the High Court has a substantial original jurisdiction in 'federal' matters, and comprehensive jurisdiction as the final court of appeal for Australia.

(1) Original jurisdiction

The High Court's original jurisdiction falls into two classes: that conferred by s75 of the Constitution itself (sometimes described as inherent jurisdiction) and that conferred by legislation under s76, its invested jurisdiction. Although detailed analysis is not possible here, a brief account of the categories of original jurisdiction is necessary.[10]

(A) ORIGINAL JURISDICTION UNDER S75

(I) MATTERS ARISING UNDER ANY TREATY (S75(i))
Like a number of the heads of jurisdiction in ss75 and 76, this provision was taken directly from the US Constitution, without sufficient regard to its application in Australia. Under the US Constitution treaties approved by the Senate take effect as part of the law of the land, if their terms are of a legislative (self-executing) character.[11] In Australia, as in England, treaties with other countries require no legislative approval, but in consequence have no domestic law-making effect. In general, if a treaty requires some change to be made in Australian law, legislation must be passed to implement it.[12] In most cases, therefore, a matter would not 'arise' in the High Court under a treaty, but under the legislation giving effect to the treaty.[13]

(II) MATTERS AFFECTING CONSULS OR OTHER REPRESENTATIVES OF OTHER COUNTRIES (S75(ii))
Like s75(i), this was inserted to ensure that matters of international concern could be litigated in the High Court. Like s75(i) there have been no cases under it.[14]

(III) MATTERS IN WHICH THE COMMONWEALTH, OR A PERSON SUING OR BEING SUED ON BEHALF OF THE COMMONWEALTH, IS A PARTY (S75(iii))

This is an important provision, guaranteeing access to the High Court whenever the Commonwealth or one of its agencies is involved. The effect is that no legislation can exclude the High Court's jurisdiction in such a case.[15]

To a limited extent, jurisdiction under s75(iii) has been made exclusive to the High Court: s38 of the Judiciary Act 1903 (Cth) provides that the High Court is the only forum for suits by the Commonwealth (or a person suing or being sued on behalf of the Commonwealth) against a state, or person being sued on behalf of a state, and vice versa.[16]

(IV) MATTERS BETWEEN STATES, OR BETWEEN RESIDENTS OF DIFFERENT STATES, OR BETWEEN A STATE AND A RESIDENT OF ANOTHER STATE (S75(iv))

In the same way as the High Court is the most suitable forum for litigation between the Commonwealth and the states, so it is the most suitable forum for suits between states, which frequently involve important questions of constitutional law and inter-governmental relations. Section 38 of the Judiciary Act 1903 (Cth) similarly makes this jurisdiction exclusive.[17]

But the jurisdiction between a state and a resident of another state, or between residents of different states, known as diversity jurisdiction, is another matter. It was copied from the US Constitution where it was inserted because of distrust of the parochialism of state courts.[18] There was no good reason for its inclusion in s75. Matters in diversity jurisdiction rarely involve significant or difficult questions of law appropriate to the High Court: most usually they involve traffic accidents between drivers from different states. Litigants have used s75(iii) for procedural reasons (especially to avoid restrictive state time-limits for bringing proceedings), or so as to benefit from the complex choice of law rules applicable. The High Court has done its best to deter them by the use of its remittal power, by adverse awards of costs, and by holding that corporations cannot be residents for this purpose.[19]

(V) MATTERS IN WHICH A WRIT OF MANDAMUS OR PROHIBITION OR AN INJUNCTION IS SOUGHT AGAINST AN OFFICER OF THE COMMONWEALTH (S75(v))

Rather like s75(iii), s75(v) was inserted to entrench the High Court's power to supervise the performance, or non-performance, of public duties by Commonwealth officers. Until 1983, the power to grant orders of mandamus or prohibition (but not injunctions) against a Commonwealth officer was exclusive to the High Court under s38(e) of the Judiciary Act 1903 (Cth). The Federal Court has now been given concurrent jurisdiction (subject to certain exceptions) under s75(v).[20]

Jurisdiction under s75(v) is important in the review of administrative action by federal officials and of decisions of tribunals and judges of federal courts,[21] but its principal importance is that Parliament cannot exclude it by making such actions or decisions unreviewable.[22] On the other hand, the selection of the three named remedies is eccentric. The draftsmen could not have been expected to anticipate the growth of the declaration as a remedy in these types of case, but leaving out certiorari and other established remedies was strange.[23]

(B) INVESTED JURISDICTION UNDER S76
Before 1976 the High Court had a very considerable invested jurisdiction, both original and appellate. After much complaint,[24] a general reform of the position was undertaken in 1976 and 1979, and the High Court's invested jurisdiction has been much reduced.[25] Section 76 allows the Parliament to confer original jurisdiction on the High Court in four classes of case; that is, in matters

(i) Arising under the Constitution or involving its interpretation:
(ii) Arising under any laws made by the Parliament:
(iii) Of Admiralty and maritime jurisdiction:
(iv) Relating to the same subject-matter claimed under the laws of different states.

Three categories of jurisdiction remain under s76.

(I) CONSTITUTIONAL MATTERS
Constitutional issues often arise in the High Court's original jurisdiction under s75(iii), (iv), and (v), but they also arise in cases between private parties. It is consistent with the High Court's function as constitutional interpreter that it be given original jurisdiction in constitutional cases. This was done by s30(a) of the Judiciary Act 1903 (Cth), which gives the High Court jurisdiction 'in all matters arising under the Constitution or involving its interpretation'. But no part of this jurisdiction is now exclusive. Constitutional questions can be decided in any court (except a court composed of lay justices).[26] It should be noted that s76(i) extends not only to matters arising under the Constitution but also to matters involving its interpretation. The distinction between the two is not entirely clear, but taken together they ensure that whenever a constitutional issue is genuinely raised in a case, it will bring the case within federal jurisdiction.[27]

(II) MATTERS ARISING UNDER A FEDERAL LAW
Potentially s76(ii) would allow the High Court to be given exclusive jurisdiction under all federal laws whatsoever. But this would not be appropriate, and original jurisdiction actually conferred on the High Court under s76(iii) now includes only a few matters. The only ones of any importance are the High Court's role as the Court of Disputed Returns for Commonwealth elections,[28] and its jurisdiction to hear trials of indictable offences against Commonwealth law.[29] The latter

is not an exclusive jurisdiction: whether a case is heard in the High Court will depend on the decision of the prosecutor in presenting the indictment. Only a very few criminal cases have been heard in the High Court in this way,[30] none in recent years. In virtually all cases (including all cases of indictable offences), federal crimes are prosecuted in state or territory courts.

(III) ADMIRALTY AND MARITIME JURISDICTION
The Parliament has extensive power over navigation and maritime matters under s51, and it has sometimes been suggested that the power over admiralty and maritime jurisdiction under s76(iii) does not add much to the power under s76(ii) to confer jurisdiction under federal laws dealing with such matters.[31] However, many cases of admiralty and maritime jurisdiction arise under foreign law or are not regulated by federal laws. It is desirable that the whole field of admiralty and maritime jurisdiction be within federal jurisdiction, and s76(iii) allows such jurisdiction to be conferred.[32]

However, the admiralty jurisdiction of the High Court at present arises not under s76(iii) but because the High Court is a 'colonial court of admiralty' under the Colonial Courts of Admiralty Act 1890 (UK).[33] This imperial jurisdiction — which is likely to be superseded by new federal admiralty — is held concurrently with the Supreme Courts, and has been described in Chapter 7.[34]

(2) Appellate jurisdiction

More important than the complexities of its original jurisdiction is the High Court's position as the final court of appeal for Australia, in state as well as federal matters. This appellate jurisdiction is established by s73 of the Constitution, which provides that

The High Court shall have jurisdiction, with such exceptions and subject to such regulations as the Parliament prescribes, to hear and determine appeals from all judgments, decrees, orders, and sentences —
(i) Of any Justice or Justices exercising the original jurisdiction of the High Court:
(ii) Of any other federal court, or court exercising federal jurisdiction, or of the Supreme Court of any state, or of any other court of any state from which at the establishment of the Commonwealth as appeal lies to the Queen in Council:
(iii) Of the Inter-State Commission, but as to questions of law only:
and the judgment of the High Court in all such cases shall be final and conclusive.

But no exception or regulation prescribed by the Parliament shall prevent the High Court from hearing and determining any appeal from the Supreme Court of a state in any matter in which at the establishment of the Commonwealth an appeal lies from such Supreme Court to the Queen in Council.

Clearly the High Court's appellate jurisdiction was intended to be comprehensive,[35] and any 'exceptions' or 'regulations' under s73 cannot prevent the High Court determining any matter if an appeal lay from a Supreme Court to the Privy Council in 1900 in such a matter. This has been held to include appeals by special leave of the Privy Council itself; since there was an appeal by special leave to the Privy Council from decisions by Supreme Courts at first instance, it follows that the High Court cannot be deprived of the power to hear appeals from decisions of state Supreme Courts, whether composed of a single judge or a Full Court.[36] On the other hand, there is no guarantee of an appeal to the High Court from federal or territory courts, because they did not exist 'at the establishment of the Commonwealth'.

The High Court's present appellate jurisdiction is broadly as follows.

(A) APPEALS FROM A SINGLE JUDGE OF THE HIGH COURT
There is an appeal 'from all judgments whatsoever of any Justice or Justices, exercising the original jurisdiction of the High Court whether in Court or Chambers'.[37]

(B) APPEALS FROM STATE SUPREME COURTS
Before 1976, appeals lay in certain circumstances as of right from a single Supreme Court judge to the High Court. Since 1976 such appeals may be brought only with the special leave of the High Court.[38] Similarly since 1984 appeals from Full Supreme Courts or Courts of Appeal are by special leave only.[39] The validity of these provisions depends on the power to prescribe 'exceptions' to and 'regulations' of the appellate jurisdiction of the High Court from state Supreme Courts. Section 73 has been interpreted as imposing two distinct restrictions on this power. First, unlike the term 'limiting' in s74,[40] the 'exceptions' and 'regulations' of s73 preclude exclusion of all appeals, and probably the exclusion of any one of the separate heads of s73.[41] Secondly, s73(2) requires that an appeal lie to the High Court by leave or special leave from decisions of a single judge of a state Supreme Court. It was for this reason that the appeal by special leave was retained,[42] although a more constructive use of s73(2) will be suggested.

The abolition in 1984 of rights to appeal from intermediate appeal courts was vigorously opposed by the legal profession but strongly supported by the High Court itself.[43] There have since been complaints that access to the High Court on appeal is uncertain and inadequate: partly in response, the Court has begun again to hear special leave applications in Sydney and Melbourne.[44] In deciding whether to grant special leave, the Court is directed to have regard, among other things, to:

(a) whether the proceedings . . . involve a question of law—
   (i) that is of public importance, whether because of its general application or otherwise;
   or

(ii) in respect of which the decision of the High Court, as the final appellate court, is required to resolve differences of opinion between different courts, or within the same court, as to the state of the law; and

(b) whether the interests of the administration of justice, whether generally or in the particular case, require consideration by the High Court of the judgment to which the application relates.[45]

Given the generality of these criteria the issue is effectively left to the Court itself.

(C) APPEALS FROM STATE COURTS EXERCISING FEDERAL JURISDICTION
Under s39(2)(c) of the Judiciary Act 1903 (Cth) there is an appeal by special leave of the High Court 'from any decision of any Court or Judge of a state [exercising federal jurisdiction] notwithstanding that the law of the state may prohibit any appeal'.

(D) APPEALS FROM TERRITORY SUPREME COURTS
Under s24 of the Federal Court of Australia Act 1976 (Cth), appeals from Supreme Courts of territories other than the Northern Territory go as of right (subject to restrictions imposed by any other Act) to the Full Federal Court. The previous right to appeal direct from a territory Supreme Court to the High Court (like its equivalent in relation to state Supreme Courts) has become a right to seek special leave to appeal.[46]

(E) APPEALS FROM THE FEDERAL COURT OF AUSTRALIA
Appeals from the General Division of the Federal Court of Australia to the High Court are restricted in the same way as those from state Supreme Courts, except that there is no appeal from a single judge of the Court, even by special leave, except as provided by another Act.[47] Thus the only appeal to the High Court is by special leave from decisions of the Full Federal Court. The High Court's appellate jurisdiction from the Industrial Division is even more limited. Where an appeal lies it is by special leave only, but in important respects decisions of the Industrial Division are final and without appeal.[48] These differences reflect the fact that there is no constitutional guarantee (similar to that for state Supreme Courts under s73) of an appeal to the High Court from decisions of any federal court.

(F) APPEALS FROM THE FAMILY COURT OF AUSTRALIA AND OTHER COURTS EXERCISING FEDERAL FAMILY JURISDICTION
Section 95 of the Family Law Act 1975 (Cth) provides:

Notwithstanding anything contained in any other Act, an appeal does not lie to the High Court from a decree of a court exercising jurisdiction under this Act, whether original or appellate, except —
(a) by special leave of the High Court; or
(b) upon a certificate of a Full Court of the Family Court that an important question of law or of public interest is involved.[49]

The power of the Family Court to certify that a matter is worthy of the consideration of the High Court is novel in Australia. But a certificate under s95(b) goes further than this, since its effect is to confer a right of appeal, a right which the High Court itself cannot withdraw.[50] In fact the Family Court has granted a certificate under s95(b) in only one case.[51] Most High Court cases involving the Family Court have been commenced in its original jurisdiction under s75(v), rather than being brought by way of appeal.[52] This situation is, as the High Court is starting to realize, an undesirable one.[53]

(G) APPEALS FROM THE SUPREME COURT OF NAURU
The Nauru (High Court Appeals) Act 1976 (Cth) purports to invest appellate jurisdiction in the High Court from decisions of the Supreme Court of Nauru, pursuant to an agreement between the governments of Australia and Nauru.[54] There are a number of similar arrangements for the highest court of a former administering power to act as court of appeal from a newly independent territory, but this is the High Court's first experience of such arrangements.[55]

(3) Removal and remittal of cases
One way in which the High Court can manage its caseload, ensuring that it deals only with sufficiently important cases, is by the use of statutory powers of removal and remittal. Powers of removal of cases into the High Court are conferred by Part VII of the Judiciary Act, which allows the removal of cases from federal courts, territory courts, and state courts exercising federal jurisdiction.[56] Removal may be ordered at the request of a party, or the Commonwealth or a state Attorney-General. In a constitutional case, an Attorney-General has a right to have a case removed; otherwise, removal is at the discretion of the Court.[57] The basic remittal power is contained in s44(1) of the Act:

> Any matter other than a matter to which sub-section (2) applies that is at any time pending in the High Court, whether originally commenced in the High Court or not, or any part of such a matter, may, upon the application of a party or of the High Court's own motion, be remitted by the High Court to any federal court, court of a State or court of a Territory that has jurisdiction with respect to the subject-matter and the parties, and subject to any directions of the High Court, further proceedings in the matter . . . shall be as directed by the court to which it is remitted.[58]

In addition, ss44(2) and 44(2A) allow the Court to remit to the Federal Court (or, with certain exceptions, any state or territory court) matters over which the High Court has exclusive jurisdiction.[59] Section 44 applies to territory as well as to state courts, and to cases of appellate as well as original jurisdiction (although there is less likelihood that there will be an appropriate lower appellate court). It allows the High Court to act on its own motion, without the consent of any party. To a High Court determined to reduce the burden of its original jurisdiction, s44 has been a potent weapon. Referring to motor accident cases in its diversity jurisdiction, Sir Garfield Barwick stated:

> The Court has begun the practice of remitting all such cases, at least so soon as they are set down for hearing, but also . . . at earlier stages of the litigation, to a state court for disposal. In addition, there are other causes of action between residents of different states which are sought to be litigated in the original jurisdiction of the High Court. These can also now be remitted to state courts.[60]

The practice of the Court is to remit all cases in its original jurisdiction which involve disputes as to matters of fact to a lower court for the facts to be found, even if the matter will then be returned to the High Court for it to deal with the legal issues.[61]

Two points should be made about s44. First, its constitutional validity is not obvious. Section 75 of the Constitution might well have been read as conferring rights upon plaintiffs in diversity cases to choose the High Court rather than a state court. Any such right could not be taken away either directly by Commonwealth legislation, or indirectly pursuant to s44. This was the view previously taken by the US Supreme Court.[62] On the other hand, the Supreme Court has since asserted the power to decline to hear cases on the ground of *forum non conveniens*,[63] and it is arguable that s44 is merely declaratory of the common law position, and therefore valid.[64] In other respects s75 has been held not to create substantive rights, as distinct from conferring jurisdiction,[65] and the High Court has consistently treated s44 as valid. Indeed members of the Court have argued that s44 does not go far enough:[66] even as amended s44 stops short of conferring a general discretion to remit to the most appropriate court (whether or not it would otherwise have had jurisdiction over the case).

The power s44 gives to remit to the appropriate lower court has to be exercised with care. Problems of federal conflicts of laws can make the choice of a lower court decisive of the result of a particular case. For example, in a road accident case, is the matter to be remitted to the court of the defendant's residence, or the court of the state where the plaintiff was resident or where the accident occurred? Each court would apply its own substantive law,[67] which may be different. What if there are two defendants, residents of different states? The High Court has established a preference for the court where the accident occurred, but this is not invariable and in any disputed case an assessment of the most appropriate forum needs to be made.[68]

(4) Accrued jurisdiction in the High Court

The problem of accrued jurisdiction was discussed in Chapter 8. As with the Federal Court, it is settled that the High Court has jurisdiction to decide the whole case, or 'matter', before it, provided that one of the grounds on which it is asked to act is within its jurisdiction, that that ground is bona fide and material, and that it is not completely separate and distinct from the issues or claims not within its jurisdiction.[69] This liberal attitude enables the Court to comply with the injunction, in ss31 and 32 of the Judiciary Act 1903 (Cth), to do 'complete justice' between the parties so as to avoid 'multiplicity of legal proceedings'.[70]

9.3 Changes in the High Court's Jurisdiction and Composition

(1) Further reform of the High Court's jurisdiction

(A) APPELLATE JURISDICTION
The changes made to the High Court's jurisdiction in 1976, 1979, and 1983 were based on two premisses: that the Court should be able to concentrate on important matters of constitutional law or of general legal principle, to the exclusion of less important cases in either original or appellate jurisdiction; and that there should always be an intermediate appeal as of right before a matter reaches the High Court.[71] Both propositions call for comment.

The system for hearing constitutional cases seems now to be satisfactory. Important constitutional cases are likely to commence in the High Court under s75 of the Constitution or s30(a) of the Judiciary Act 1903 (Cth), or to be removed there under Part VII of the Judiciary Act. Improved provision for intervention by Commonwealth or state Attorney-Generals has also been made.[72]

So far as the High Court's non-constitutional appellate functions are concerned, the abolition of rights to appeal is, as noted already, more controversial. Australian lawyers seem to have become used to having, in any major case, two rights of appeal, and it has been argued that the absence of a single intermediate court of appeal requires more secure access to the final appeal court.[73] These arguments are not persuasive. No doubt the amount at stake in an appeal may be relevant to the granting of special leave, but there is no compelling reason for granting a right to appeal, even on a trivial or straightforward point of law, merely because a specified sum of money is involved,[74] and there is no other criterion available for defining in advance the class of cases which should be heard by the High Court. Both the House of Lords and the Canadian Supreme Court hear cases only by way of a system equivalent to special leave: in practice, so does the US Supreme Court.[75] As the Constitutional Commission's Committee on the Australian Judicial System concluded, the case for a different system in Australia has not been made out.[76]

However, consideration should be given to a system by which the intermediate appeal court could either grant leave to appeal, or at least certify a case as involving a point of law of general public importance meriting the grant of special leave to appeal. The English Court of Appeal has both powers, and they are combined in a single procedure under s95(6) of the Family Law Act 1976 (Cth) (which has rarely been used). There is little support at present for allowing intermediate appeal courts to grant leave, though that is the best long-term solution.[77] In the meantime a certification procedure should be introduced, with the certificate being a relevant matter for the High Court to take into account in granting leave under s35A of the Judiciary Act 1903 (Cth).[78]

The notion that there should always be an intermediate appeal before a matter reaches the High Court has been strongly supported by members of the Court,[79] but also requires examination. It may well be helpful for the High Court to have 'the benefit of the views of the Full Court or Court of Appeal of the state', but from the point of view of the litigant, the precedent his case is establishing is usually of secondary importance: what is important is its resolution. A party successful in both lower courts but defeated on a close vote in the High Court may not think highly of the 'benefit of the views' of the lower appeal court. The main reason for a second appellate court such as the High Court is the development and review of the law, not the resolution (whether in agreement with or dissent from lower courts) of a relatively few disputes. A.P. Herbert wittily criticized an equivalent position in England before 1969:

The institution of one Court of Appeal may be considered a reasonable precaution; but two suggest panic.[80]

As a result of this kind of criticism, a limited 'leap-frogging' scheme was introduced by the Administration of Justice Act 1969 (UK). Certain cases involving points of substantial public importance can now be taken direct to the House of Lords, avoiding the Court of Appeal. Such arrangements are valuable, for example, where the issue depends on a precedent binding the intermediate appeal court.[81] Either 'leap-frogging' provisions, on the English model, could be introduced, or the High Court could announce its willingness to give special leave in particularly important cases so as to avoid a second appeal. If it is thought desirable to have an intermediate appeal in all cases, then adequate financial provision should be made: there is now an appeal costs fund for the High Court,[82] and legal aid should also be readily available. The advantages of a second appeal are essentially public, and arrangements for costs should reflect this.

All the changes so far suggested to the High Court's appellate jurisdiction can be achieved under s73 as it now stands. One matter which does require constitutional amendment, on the other hand, is the formula guaranteeing an appeal to the High Court from certain lower courts. As we have seen, this is expressed as a guaranteed appeal in any case where in 1901 there was an appeal to the Privy Council. The effect is that there is no guarantee of appeal from any federal or territory court, nor from any new state court created since 1901. Privy Council appeals from all Australian courts were abolished in 1986, so that the reference to such appeals in s73 is now an anachronism. One possibility would be to substitute for that reference a list of courts from which, or of cases in which, an appeal would be guaranteed.[83] But the Judicial System Committee of the Australian Constitutional Commission in 1987 went considerably further, recommending that the High Court be guaranteed the power to grant special leave to appeal from a decision of any Australian court.[84] As well as permitting 'leap-frogging' in any case, this would prevent parliaments (whether state or federal) providing for unappealable decisions of any courts (as distinct from tribunals).

(B) ORIGINAL JURISDICTION
Since 1976 virtually everything that could be done by statute to reform the High Court's original jurisdiction has been done. What remains is the reform of ss75 and 76 themselves. The two constitutional reform bodies which have examined this issue in recent years have reached very different conclusions. The Australian Constitutional Convention proposed the deletion of many of the heads of federal jurisdiction altogether (viz., present ss75(i) and 75(iii) (except for matters between states), and s76(iv)).[85] The Constitutional Commission's Committee on the Australian Judicial System, by contrast, proposed that each of these provisions be retained, within a structure in which most matters of original federal jurisdiction could be taken away from the High Court and vested in other federal courts.[86] But the pressure for reform of the Court's original jurisdiction has largely disappeared, with the ready use of the remittal power and with the repeal of most of the Court's invested original jurisdiction. The fate of these proposals is no doubt tied up with the future of constitutional reform itself: changes to the Australian Constitution have proved so difficult that one can only be pessimistic.

(2) Advisory opinions
As was pointed out in Chapter 4, one of the basic assumptions of British and, by derivation, Australian law is the adversary system — the decision of legal questions only when these are in dispute between parties with a 'sufficient interest' in them. In the case of private as distinct from government litigants, what is a 'sufficient interest' is fairly strictly defined.[87] In *In re Judiciary and Navigation Acts*,[88] the High Court held that the term 'matters' in ss75 and 76 of the Constitution itself implied the adversary system, and prevented the Parliament granting it jurisdiction to hear advisory opinions as to the validity of legislation. The Court held that

there can be no matter within the meaning of [s76] unless there is some immediate right, duty or liability to be established by the determination of the Court . . . [W]e can find nothing in Chapter III of the Constitution to lend colour to the view that Parliament can confer power or jurisdiction upon the High Court to determine abstract questions of law without the right or duty of any body or person being involved.[89]

Although the attempt to confer an advisory jurisdiction in constitutional cases failed, there is little difference between such an advisory opinion (with adequate provision for intervention by interested parties and, if necessary, the provision of counsel to argue as *amicus curiae*) and an action for a declaration between a state Attorney-General and the Commonwealth. Under the present system an invalid Act may be applied for years before someone appears with the interest and desire to challenge it: regulating the consequences of things done under such legislation in the meantime can be a complex matter. There has been no great support in Australia for a High Court advisory jurisdiction in non-constitutional cases,[90] but for reasons such as these it has been proposed from time to time that the Constitution be amended to allow the High Court to be granted an advisory jurisdiction in constitutional cases.[91] Indeed one such proposal was actually passed by the Parliament, but lapsed under s128 of the Constitution when it was not put to a referendum within the required period of six months after its passage.[92] The proposal was vigorously opposed by the High Court itself, and seems unlikely to be revived.[93]

The High Court's dislike of abstract 'opinions' extends beyond its original jurisdiction in ss75 and 76. It has also held — in cases such as *Minister for Works for Western Australia v Civil and Civic Pty Ltd*[94] — that a decision of a state Supreme Court in the exercise of an advisory jurisdiction under state law is not a judgment, decree, order, or sentence within the meaning of s73, so that there can be no appeal from such a decision to the High Court. Whatever may be the merits of the High Court's self-denial of jurisdiction in *In re Judiciary and Navigation Acts*, its extension to the High Court's appellate jurisdiction in state matters is unfortunate. A distinction could have been drawn between the term 'matter' in s76 and 'judgment' in s73, so that the *Civil and Civic* rule was not compelled by authority. The central point is that the High Court's constitutional function is to develop and unify the law for Australia, in state no less than federal matters. It is most undesirable that decisions of state courts on state law should escape the appellate supervision of the High Court, in any case where, whatever the formal status of the Supreme Court decision, it is in reality authoritative.[95] Ironically, the High Court was prepared to penetrate the form of the Appeals and Special References Act 1973 (Qld), in *Commonwealth v Queensland*,[96] so as to deny the Privy Council jurisdiction, but has not been prepared to do the same so as to give itself a jurisdiction which its position as a general court of appeal requires.

(3) Appointments to the High Court

Issues of judicial appointment were discussed in Chapter 4. These questions have an added importance in the case of the High Court, and most of the controversies that have arisen over judicial appointments in Australia have been over High Court appointments.[97]

There have been a total of 42 High Court appointments, of 37 persons (five of whom were appointed first as justices, then as Chief Justice). The vast majority of appointees were male, from middle and upper-middle class backgrounds, and most were educated at private schools.[98] Of the 37 appointees, eleven had substantial political experience, thirteen had been Supreme Court or federal judges,[99] and only one (Sir Samuel Griffith) had both judicial and political experience. The other twelve were appointed from the Bar.[100] No less than 29 of the 42 appointments were made by non-Labor governments; only thirteen (including Piddington, who never sat) by Labor governments.

A significant difference in appointments practice has occurred since the late 1930s. Of the first fifteen appointees (up to and including Latham), nine had some substantial political experience; only three had any judicial experience (including Dixon, who was an acting judge of the Victorian Supreme Court). The 22 appointees since 1940 have included only two (Barwick and Murphy) with substantial political experience, but as many as twelve with judicial experience. The balance has changed decisively in favour of the latter, reflecting the predominantly technical legal emphasis of the High Court over the past half-century.[101]

It is sometimes argued that judicial promotion is undesirable, because it undermines judicial independence. But this view is evidently not adhered to in Australia, any more than it is in the United Kingdom.[102] The chances of a judge 'tailoring' his decisions to suit the executive and succeeding in obtaining promotion are slight, and there is no evidence that this has happened in Australia (judicial promotion for the performance of sensitive extra-judicial functions may present more of a risk). A greater danger is that 'safe' but unimaginative appointments will be made from persons successful at the Bar but without the attributes of perception, intelligence, and scholarship required in an appellate judge. There is much to be said for appointing persons who, in state or federal courts, have shown they have these qualities: examples of successful appointments of this type include Dixon, Fullagar, Walsh, Gibbs, Stephen, Mason, and Jacobs. The more recent appointments of Brennan, Deane, and Toohey (all Federal Court judges) are also of this type. By the same token, no one avenue of appointment should be exclusive.[103]

In a federation the geographical distribution of appointments is liable to be a sensitive matter. In Canada there is a clear understanding on the proper composition of the Supreme Court,[104] but nothing of the kind exists in Australia. In fact, 29 of the 37 High Court appointees have come from New South Wales and Victoria; before 1979, none at all from South Australia, Tasmania, or Western Australia.[105] It may be significant that the introduction of a procedure of consultation between the Commonwealth and the states led to the first such appointment.[106] Other things being equal, it is better to appoint from a wider field. But the primary factor must be merit, and one danger in even an advisory appointments system is that it will encourage lobbying on irrelevant geographical grounds.[107]

9.4 The Role of the High Court

The High Court is the most visible, and arguably the most important, court in Australia. This is not so much because of the number of cases it decides or (at least in non-constitutional cases) because of the effect of its orders on litigants.[108] It is because of the indirect effects of its judgments, as precedents determining the result of other cases in other courts, as authoritative statements of the law (it takes eight Acts of Parliament to reverse the effect of a single High Court decision on a matter of common law over which the Commonwealth Parliament has no authority), as an expression of position on sensitive political or social questions.

To carry out its role as final court of appeal the Court needs to have a sufficiently varied caseload, large enough to enable it to review the different areas of law and practice, but not so large as to overwhelm it with work. In the period 1965–9 the Court decided, on average, approximately 179 cases per year; in 1970–4 this rose to 205 cases per year. In 1975–9 the average fell to about 160 per year, but this obscures the important changes in High Court jurisdiction which took effect in 1977. In 1976 the Court gave 221 judgments of which 102 were unreserved (that is, given orally without much deliberation at the end of argument). In 1977 the Court decided 172 cases; in 1978, 109. The 1978 figures were the lowest for any year since 1945, reflecting a considerable decline in the Court's original jurisdiction. The number of unreserved judgments on appeal also fell, from 66 in 1977 to 26 in 1978. Since 1979 there has been some tendency for the number of matters heard to increase (from 156, all categories, in 1979 to 243 in 1985), with an average of 196 per year during this period.[109] However, many of these 'matters heard' represent special leave applications: the number of reserved judgments in 1979–85 remained relatively stable (averaging 89 per annum). The real change between 1974 and 1985 is not so much the number of matters heard, but that cases which in 1974 would have been heard on appeal with an unreserved judgment given are now likely to be the subject of an unsuccessful special leave application.

It is difficult to compare the High Court's caseload with those of other final appeal courts. Very many factors affect caseload, and population is among the least of them. The House of Lords, for example (serving a population about four times that of Australia), heard an average of only 32 appeals in the years 1952–70.[110] This is not enough to allow the House to carry out its proper functions as a court of final appeal.[111] Probably the most important factor is the extent to which issues are justiciable within the particular system: the United States, with its Bill of Rights and with, by English or Australian standards, an extraordinary tolerance for judicial determination of controversial questions, is one of the most litigious societies in the world. Its Supreme Court (with a jurisdiction not extending to general state law) had 4704 cases filed before it in its 1977 term, each of which required some form of scrutiny.[112] The pressure of this work is one factor in the markedly different procedures of the Supreme Court: the decline of oral argument, the predominance of single majority opinions, the intense selectivity of the cases actually discussed or decided, and the extensive use of law clerks as assistants to the justices.[113] None of these yet finds any Australian parallel.

A better example is the Canadian Supreme Court, which is a general, not merely a federal, court of appeal, in a country less than twice as populous as Australia, and with a legal system with many resemblances. The Supreme Court has a negligible original jurisdiction: in its appellate jurisdiction it decides about 115 cases per year.[114] It can be suggested that a final appeal court in a jurisdiction such as Canada or Australia needs a sufficiently varied case-load of about 80 to 120 cases a year to fulfil its functions.[115] This can be achieved only by giving the Court control over the cases it decides, leaving it to deal only with cases of some difficulty or general importance. The reforms in the High Court's jurisdiction since 1976 suggest that this aim is now being achieved.

What then are the functions of a final appeal court? The response differs between constitutional and non- constitutional cases.

(1) The High Court in constitutional cases

The High Court is the primary custodian of the Constitution, as the arrangements for constitutional cases in its original and appellate jurisdiction indicate. Its function is to develop a coherent body of constitutional doctrine consistent with the terms of the Constitution and, as far as possible, appropriate to the needs of the community. Assessment of its success or otherwise in this role is outside the scope of this work,[116] but a few comments are in order.

In its constitutional role the High Court inevitably has to decide sensitive political questions — some of them major issues of dispute between the political parties.[117] The Court's decisions, though in some sense tied to the constitutional text, require assessment and evaluation, the orthodox approach to which was stated by Dixon CJ:

Federalism means a demarcation of powers and this casts upon the Court a responsibility of deciding whether legislation is within the boundaries of allotted powers. Unfortunately, it is not sufficiently recognised that the Court's sole function is to interpret a constitutional description of power or restraint upon power and say whether a given measure falls on one side of a line consequently drawn or on the other, and that it has nothing whatever to do with the merits or demerits of the measure. Such a function has led us all to believe that close adherence to legal reasoning is the only way to maintain confidence of all parties in Federal conflicts. It may be that the Court is thought to be excessively legalistic. I should be sorry to think that it is anything else. There is no other safe guide to judicial decisions in conflicts than a strict and complete legalism.[118]

But this is ingenuous. Dixon himself had very clear ideas of the proper structure and functioning of a federation, for example. The decision in the *Boilermakers' case*,[119] for example, was not compelled by the language of the Constitution: any decision to overrule it would be just as much an exercise of evaluation. I prefer Dixon's equally gnomic — this time, judicial — comment in the *State Banking case*:

The Constitution is a political instrument. It deals with government and governmental powers . . . It is not a question whether the considerations are political, for nearly every consideration arising from the Constitution can be so described, but whether they are compelling.[120]

The assumption — an assumption inherent in all attempts at reasoning in the social sciences — is that there are better or worse reasons for decisions, that arguments, even in hard cases, can be more or less convincing (what other assumption could a court adopt?). This assumption, and the requirement of judicial impartiality, together validate the High Court's constitutional authority — or do so to the extent that the requirements are satisfied in its decisions.

The illusion of a 'value-free' position is sustained to an extent by the Constitution itself. It contains no Bill of Rights, and its few guarantees of civil liberties have been of little significance.[121] In determining questions of legislative authority, or inconsistency of laws, the Court has had good reason to adopt a predominantly formal, technical approach: in both areas, the Australian Constitution is much more explicit than that of the United States. Evaluative problems have been more prominent in areas such as the structure of Parliament and the constitutional prohibitions, and most significantly in s92, which provides that interstate trade and commerce shall be 'absolutely free'. The Court is not much closer to a resolution of approaches here than it was in the 1930s, although the dominant trend seems to have been a certain judicial withdrawal, a deference to deliberate legislative judgment. But when such a withdrawal requires the Court to decide whether a national legislative scheme, approved by every Parliament is Australia, is 'the only practical and reasonable course open in present circumstances'[122] or whether the restrictions it imposes are 'no greater than are reasonably necessary in all the circumstances',[123] the claim to a strict and complete legalism wears pretty thin.

(2) The High Court as a general court of appeal

Important though they are, constitutional cases account for less than 10 per cent of the High Court's caseload, which is predominantly in the area of general private law, administrative law, and taxation. Here the High Court now acts substantially as a second court of appeal, the case already having been considered by a Full Court of one of the Supreme Courts, the Federal Court, or the Family Court.

As was argued in Chapter 7, the principal function of a first appeal is to correct errors that can be shown to have been made by the trial court. The notion — very widely accepted — that every litigant is entitled to one appeal is based on the power of the first appeal court to scrutinize the trial decision as far as possible on its merits, whether or not the appeal is formally by way of rehearing.[124] A second appeal has no such obvious justification. A Full Court of three judges can, of course, be wrong, but so too can a High Court or a Privy Council. There is little point in repeating scrutiny for 'error': each repetition carries its own risk of error; no case is decided until after a second (or even third) appeal, and the wealthy or determined litigant has a decided advantage in what becomes trial by exhaustion. If there should be one appeal of right to a multiple-judge court, there should be not more than one.[125]

It follows that the functions of a final appeal court are rather different. In the case of the High Court they seem to be four: the embodiment of the unity of the common law of Australia, the development of that law, the determination of the case in hand in accordance with proper principles of appellate review, and the general supervision of the machinery of justice. The first function — the embodiment of the unity of the common law — needs little comment. It is well established that decisions of the High Court on appeal from any jurisdiction bind all courts in Australia. Probably the existence of a general appeal court is a precondition to the continuing unity of the common law: in the United States there are as many systems of 'common law' as there are separate jurisdictions.[126]

The development of the common law for Australia is of equal importance. That courts develop, or 'make', law is clear, though they do not operate in the same way as legislatures. As Barwick CJ explained, the High Court

> has become the final court of appeal, not merely in matters of federal jurisdiction but as to the principles of the common law applicable throughout Australia . . . The capacity of the judiciary to declare the common law is a notable feature of the common law system . . . It is for the final court of appeal in each juristic unit administering the common law ultimately to declare what is the common law . . . What ought the approach of this court to be

when, for the first time, it is asked to declare the principles of common law in some particular area of human activity? It seems to me the court cannot act as if it were bound by declarations of the common law not made in its own juristic system. It must . . . closely examine the principles of the common law and determine for itself whether or not such prior declarations correctly declare the common law. If, of course, the court concludes that the common law is in accordance with such declarations, then the court should . . . itself make a like declaration . . . the court cannot alter the common law which it is satisfied has been correctly declared. Any such change must be left to the appropriate legislature. If, however, the court is convinced on its examination of principle that the declaration already made is erroneous, then it seems to me the court is bound to declare the common law for Australia that sense which the court thinks is correct.[127]

In face of such freedom, the assertion that the common law exists already, whatever its psychological value, has a certain unreality — or rather, its reality depends on the strength of the often conflicting reasons on which the court acts. The balance of considerations in favour of a particular result is often a very fine one; but a result there must be, and to that extent at least the common law is taken to exist even in the hardest case.[128]

The court is not a legislator also because it decides the law only by deciding the case before it, and only to the extent that the case requires. Even on a second appeal, it is necessary for the court to examine the whole case, and as far as possible from the material to exercise its judgment upon it. In doing so, the court should provide, through its comments and decisions, guidelines for the practice and procedure of lower courts in deciding other cases.

Surprisingly, for each of the last three functions the principles on which the Court should act are not clear or uncontroversial: in each there is a certain dichotomy of approach, of restraint versus activism. The High Court, which is no longer bound by the decisions of any other courts (or for that matter by its own previous decisions), declares the law for Australia, but it can fail to overturn rules which are wholly inappropriate to Australian conditions or to any defensible view of what the law should be.[129] It decides appeals by way of rehearing, but whether it should exercise 'restraint' in failing to reverse decisions, even when it thinks they were 'wrong' has been the subject of a divided case-law.[130] It has left questions as important as denial of legal representation in serious criminal cases to be decided by lower court discretions.[131]

Probably these rules or practices of restraint or non-intervention were, in part at least, the product of a system of appeal as of right. Now that the Court can select its cases with more discrimination it can be expected to decide the cases it does deal with in a more committed way.[132] The balance between restraint and activism may perhaps shift towards the latter, with the increase in the Court's control over its case-load. But that shifting balance is a perennial feature of common law appellate decision-making, dependent principally upon the temper of the court at the time, which rules can only marginally affect.

Notes

1 Generally see Bennett, *Keystone of the Federal Arch* (1980); Sawer, *Australian Federalism*, chs 4, 5; Morison, 203–29.
2 For the debate see Bennett, *Keystone*, 3–20, 133–9; Norris, *The Emergent Commonwealth* (1975) 14–15. But cf. Howell, 226–9, for a different view.
3 Bennett, *Keystone*, 21–5.
4 Suggestions for further increases in the number of justices have been opposed (e.g. Barwick (1976) 59 *ALJ* 436); instead the High Court's workload has been relieved by the transfer of jurisdiction to state courts and the Federal Court. Cf. Lane (1980) 54 *ALJ* 11. In a Full Court, normally 5 or 7 justices sit; a bench of 3 may hear special leave applications or less important appeals. Only one Full Court sits at any one time. At least 5 judges should sit in constitutional cases: Judiciary Act 1903 (Cth) s23(1).
5 Although retired Law Lords do still sit on occasion in the House of Lords and the Privy Council. This is not possible at federal level in Australia, Canada, or the US. The Australian Judicial System Committee of the Constitutional Commission rejected a proposal to introduce a system of 'reserve' justices along the lines of the Victorian arrangement (Constitution Act 1975 (Vic.) s80A): *Report* (1987) para. 5.39–42.
6 Bennett, *Keystone*, 99–105. On the continuance of the High Court sittings outside Canberra see High Court of Australia Act 1979 (Cth) s15; (1980) 54 *ALJ* 55.
7 High Court of Australia Act 1979 (Cth) (replacing Judiciary Act 1903 (Cth) Part II, and High Court Procedure Act 1903 (Cth)). See Gibbs, in AIJA, *Seminar on the Constitutional and Administrative Responsibilities for the Administration of Justice: The Partnership of Judiciary and Executive* (1986) 101.
8 There has also been controversy over the extent of the Court's accountability to Parliament for its administration under the 1979 Act: see Senate Standing Committee on Constitutional and Legal Affairs, *Report on High Court of Australia — Annual Report for the Period 1984–1985* (1986), which sets out the correspondence between the Court and the Committee; Senate Standing Committee on Constitutional and Legal Affairs, *Report on High Court of Australia — Annual Report for the Period 1985–1986* (1986) 7, which reports a 'satisfactory conclusion to the Committee's consideration of the matter'. Gibbs CJ has commented that the 1979 Act has no more than 'a symbolic significance so far as the independence of the Court is concerned': (1983) 10 *Syd LR* 1, 4.
9 As to the other complaints, it is an Australian custom to argue the demerits of expensive public buildings; if there is a risk of remoteness in Canberra, a cynic might say that it was merely the substitution of one risk for another. But see Bennett, *Keystone*, 105–15. The question of responsibility for High Court administration was — rightly — settled in favour of collegiality:

10 High Court of Australia Act 1979 (Cth) s17. Cf. Marr, *Barwick* (1980) 297–8 (which contains much of interest on the High Court since 1964).
10 See Cowen & Zines, 1–103; Howard, 206–30; Lane, 581–716; Renfree, 158–239 for fuller treatment.
11 US Constitution, Art. II s2(1) (making of treaties); Art. VI s2 (legal effect of treaties).
12 *A-G (Canada) & A-G (Ontario)* [1937] AC 326, 347–8 (Lord Atkin); *Bradley v Commonwealth* (1973) 128 CLR 557; *Kioa v Minister for Immigration and Ethnic Affairs* (1983) 62 ALR 321.
13 Section 38(a) of the Judiciary Act 1903 (Cth) makes the High Court's jurisdiction exclusive in respect of matters 'arising directly under a treaty'. On the orthodox interpretation, a matter can only 'arise' directly, and on this basis Cowen & Zines, 27–30, argue that there can never be a matter arising under a treaty. Decisions of common law courts can certainly involve the interpretation of a treaty. See further Crawford & Edeson in Ryan, ed., *International Law in Australia* (2nd edn, 1984) 71, 85–134.
14 Cowen & Zines, 30–2.
15 Cf. *Bank Nationalization Case* (1948) 76 CLR 1.
16 Section 38 was passed under Constitution s77(ii). On what bodies are included in the 'Commonwealth' or a 'State' for this purpose see *Crouch v Commissioner for Rys (Qld)* (1985) 62 ALR 1; *A-G (NSW) v Commonwealth Savings Bank* (1986) 65 ALR 74. That the High Court has jurisdiction in disputes between states does not mean that all disputes between states are justiciable (i.e. raise issues capable of judicial determination). Cf. *South Australia v Victoria* (1911) 12 CLR 667; *South Australia v Commonwealth* (1962) 108 CLR 130; Campbell (1971) 6 *Syd LR* 309.
17 Cf. Cowen & Zines, 32–46.
18 On US diversity jurisdiction (exercised by federal courts, not the Supreme Court) cf. Hart & Wechsler, ch. 7. On Australian diversity jurisdiction see Cowen & Zines, 82–103.
19 *Australian Temperance Assurance Soc. Ltd v Howe* (1922) 31 CLR 290; *Cox v Journeaux* (1934) 52 CLR 282. Cf. also *Watson v Cameron* (1928) 40 CLR 446; Cowen & Zines, 90–2. On the remittal power see further below.
20 Judiciary Act 1903 (Cth) s39B (inserted 1983).
21 Federal judges are 'officers of the Commonwealth' for the purposes of s75, but not state judges exercising federal jurisdiction: *R v Murray & Cormie* (1916) 22 CLR 437; *R v Anderson, ex p Bateman* (1978) 21 ALR 56. (But the High Court has invested jurisdiction over state courts exercising federal jurisdiction: Judiciary Act 1903 (Cth) s33(1)(a), (b).) There is a presumption that superior courts have not exceeded their jurisdiction, so as to be amenable to prohibition under s75(v) (e.g. *R v Judges of the Federal Court of Australia, ex p Pilkington ACI (Ops) Pty Ltd* (1978) 23 ALR 69), and the court has a discretion not to make an order where appeal would be a more convenient remedy. On the relation between prohibition and appeal see e.g. *R v Adamson, ex p West Perth Football Club* (1979) 23 ALR 439.
22 Cf. *R v Hickman, ex p Fox & Clinton* (1945) 70 CLR 598; Aronson & Franklin, *Review of Administrative Action* (1987) 687–701.
23 Mandamus is a prerogative remedy whereby the court orders the per-

formance of a public duty; prohibition prevents an administrative or judicial authority from acting upon a decision made unlawfully or without jurisdiction. Certiorari enables a court to quash an unlawful decision of an inferior court or tribunal. Unlike these common law remedies, an injunction is a private law remedy developed in equity to restrain illegal acts generally. Generally see Cowen & Zines, 46–56; and see further Chapter 13.

24 Barwick (1976) 50 ALJ 433; *Ritter v North Side Enterprises Ltd* (1975) 6 ALR 125.
25 Crawford, 211; Jurisdiction of Courts (Miscellaneous Amendments) Act 1979 (Cth).
26 For *inter se* questions before 1976 see Crawford, 211–2.
27 *Collins v Charles Marshall Pty Ltd* (1955) 92 CLR 529; Cowen & Zines, 57–63.
28 Commonwealth Electoral Act 1918 (Cth) Part XVIII. Cf. also Referendum (Constitution Alteration) Act 1906 (Cth) Part VI.
29 Judiciary Act 1903 (Cth) s30(a). Such trials must be by jury: Constitution s80.
30 E.g. *R v Snow* (1919) 26 CLR 506.
31 Cowen & Zines, 63–72, are critical of the inclusion of s76(iii). But the Constitutional Convention recommended its retention: *Proceedings . . . Adelaide* (1983) I, 319, II, 25 & Appendix 5; as did the Australian Judicial System Committee of the Constitutional Commission: *Report* (1987) para. 4.18.
32 On the scope of s76(iii) see ALRC 33, *Civil Admiralty Jurisdiction* (1986) ch. 5.
33 *Huddart Parker Ltd v The Ship 'Mill Hill'* (1950) 81 CLR 502; Cowen & Zines, 45–72.
34 In the impending reform of admiralty jurisdiction in Australia the High Court will lose its original admiralty jurisdiction, with admiralty appeals going to it in the ordinary way: see ALRC 33, *Civil Admiralty Jurisdiction* (1986) para. 229, 242.
35 Cf. *Davern v Messell* (1984) 53 ALR 1.
36 Cf. *Parkin v James* (1905) 2 CLR 315. The guarantee is satisfied if the High Court itself can give special leave to appeal: id., 336. On appeals from jury verdicts, see *R v Snow* (1915) 20 CLR 315; *R v Weaver* (1931) 45 CLR 321; *R v Wilkes* (1948) 77 CLR 511; *Shaw v R* (1952) 85 CLR 365 (criminal juries); *BSPU v Heggie* (1906) 3 CLR 686; *Fieman v Balas* (1932) 47 CLR 107, *McDowell & East Ltd v McGregor* (1936) 56 CLR 51 (civil juries).
37 Constitution s73(i); Judiciary Act 1903 (Cth) s34.
38 Judiciary Act 1903 (Cth) s35(2). Leave will be granted only 'in exceptional circumstances': Mason (1975) 49 *ALJ* 576.
39 Judiciary Act 1903 (Cth) s35(2). Earlier rights to appeal had been based on monetary limits ($3000, increased to $20 000 in 1976).
40 Which, it was held, allowed the complete exclusion of appeals to the Privy Council: *A-G (Cth) v T & G Mutual Life Soc. Ltd* (1978) 19 ALR 385.
41 *Cockle v Isaksen* (1957) 99 CLR 135, 165–6; *Collins v Charles Marshall Pty Ltd* (1955) 92 CLR 529; Howard, 200–2.
42 But s35(5) of the Judiciary Act 1903 (Cth) (as amended in 1976) provides for 'special provision made by an Act other than this Act whether passed

before or after the commencement of this section, preventing or permitting appeals from the Supreme Courts of the states in particular matters'. So far only one such 'special provision' has been made: Bankruptcy Amendment Act 1976 (Cth) s6. Its validity depends on whether the proviso in s73 extends only to matters actually existing 'at the establishment of the Commonwealth'. There was then, of course no 'matter' arising under federal bankruptcy legislation, and so no appeal in such a matter to Her Majesty in Council. Since the purpose of the proviso is to guarantee the position of the High Court as a general court of appeal for Australia, such a strict interpretation is not inevitable. Cf. also Judiciary Act 1903 (Cth) s39(2)(c), which may have been *pro tanto* repealed by the specific provision for appeals made by Bankruptcy Amendment Act 1976 (Cth) s6.

[43] E.g. *Clyne v DPP* (1983) 48 ALR 545, 546 (Gibbs CJ); Gibbs (1985) 59 *ALJ* 522, 523. And see the first edition of this book at pp. 151–2. For professional opposition see e.g. O'Bryan (1984) 19(4) *Aust L News* 11.

[44] Gibbs (1985) 59 *ALJ* 522, 523.

[45] Judiciary Act 1903 (Cth) s35A (inserted 1984).

[46] Judiciary Act 1903 (Cth) s35AA (NT; inserted 1984); Federal Court of Australia Act 1976 (Cth) s24(2)(a) (other territory Supreme Courts).

[47] Federal Court of Australia Act 1976 (Cth) s33(2).

[48] Conciliation and Arbitration Act 1904 (Cth) s118B.

[49] There is no appeal from a divorce decree which has become absolute: s93. For the Family Court of Australia and other courts exercising family jurisdiction see Chapter 10.

[50] By contrast the High Court can rescind special leave to appeal granted by itself: e.g. *Williams v Williams* (1985) 61 ALR 215.

[51] *Duff v Duff* (1977) 15 ALR 476.

[52] In the period 1979–84 the High Court heard 59 appeals from the Federal Court and only 6 from the Family Court: Gibbs (1985) 59 *ALJ* 522, 527.

[53] E.g. *Re Ross-Jones; ex parte Green* (1984) 56 ALR 609, 636–8 (Deane J), but cf. the more interventionist view of Gibbs CJ: id., 614.

[54] Nauru (High Court Appeals) Act 1976 (Cth) s5 and Schedule. Under the Agreement, an appeal lies as of right in a wide variety of cases: otherwise the High Court may grant special leave. See also HCR 070A (Nauru Appeal Rules). In the period 1976–85 there was one appeal from Nauru: *DPP v Fowler* (1984) 55 ALR 175.

[55] On the constitutional validity of the Nauru (High Court Appeals) Act 1976 (Cth) see Crawford, 217–8.

[56] Judiciary Act 1903 (Cth) ss40, 41, 43, 45. Section 42(1) allows removed cases to be remitted to the original court. Section 42(2) requires it, with respect to any 'cause or part of a cause' that turns out not to be within federal jurisdiction.

[57] Section 40(1). See generally Cowen & Zines, 10–14.

[58] Inserted in 1976, replacing s45, and amended in 1983 and 1984. See *Beecham Group Ltd v Bristol Myers Co* (1977) 14 ALR 591.

[59] Matters in which the Commonwealth is a party (Constitution s75(iii)) are to be remitted to the Federal Court: s44(2A). Section 44(2) does not extend to matters under Constitution s75(v).

[60] Barwick (1977) 51 *ALJ* 480, 489. In 1977 the Court remitted 46 matters to state courts (1978: 19). Perhaps as a result, the number of writs issued out of the High Court dropped from 148 in 1977 to 88 in 1978.

61 E.g. *Mabo v Queensland & Commonwealth* (1986) 64 ALR 1 (the Torres Strait Islands land rights case).
62 *Cohens v Virginia* 6 Wheat 264 (1821); similarly, Cowen & Zines, 75–81.
63 *Massachussetts v Missouri* 308 US 1 (1939).
64 Barwick, 10–15. See further Lindell in Zines, ed., *Commentaries on the Australian Constitution* (1977) 151 and authorities there cited.
65 *Werrin v Commonwealth* (1938) 59 CLR 150; and the cases cited by Hogg, *Liability of the Crown* (1971) 216 n9. Contra, *Commonwealth v NSW* (1923) 32 CLR 200.
66 Gibbs (1985) 59 ALR 522, 523. In the meantime the High Court is giving the broadest interpretation to s44: *Johnstone v Commonwealth* (1979) 23 ALR 385; *In re O'Reilly; ex p Bayford Wholesale Pty Ltd* (1983) 151 CLR 557; *BHP Co. Ltd v NCSC* (1986) 67 ALR 545.
67 *Phillips v Eyre* (1870) LR 6 QB 1; *Chaplin v Boys* [1971] AC 356; *Anderson v Eric Anderson Radio & TV Pty Ltd* (1965) 114 CLR 20.
68 See e.g. *Weber v Aidone* (1981) 36 ALR 345; *Pozniak v Smith* (1982) 41 ALR 353; *Foxe v Brown* (1984) 58 ALR 542; *Fielding v Doran* (1984) 60 ALR 342. See further Pryles & Hanks, *Federal Conflict of Laws* (1974) 133–44; Keeler (1972) 4 *U Tas LR* 17; Pose (1976) 50 *ALJ* 110; Sykes & Pryles, *Australian Private International Law* (3rd edn, 1987) 272–84.
69 In fact the rules relating to accrued jurisdiction in the Federal Court were first elaborated in the far less controversial context of the High Court's original jurisdiction. See e.g. Cowen & Zines, 61–3, 72–5; Lane, 546–602.
70 The rule is, however, not dependent upon s31 or s32 but on the interpretation of 'matters' in ss75 and 76 of the Constitution. There is no equivalent for the High Court of Federal Court of Australia Act 1976 (Cth) s32, conferring jurisdiction over 'associated' federal matters. See further Chapter 8.
71 E.g. Mason (1975) 49 *ALJ* 570, 576.
72 Judiciary Act 1903 (Cth) Part XI Division 1A. Division 1A relates only to intervention, not to the standing of state Attorney-Generals to commence proceedings. But for suggestions for general reform of rules of standing in public interest litigation see ALRC 27, *Standing in Public Interest Suits* (1985).
73 See the submissions referred to by the Australian Judicial System Committee of the Constitutional Commission: *Report* (1987) para. 3.85. The Committee rejected these arguments: id., para. 3.90.
74 A good example of a case in which the appellant had a right of appeal but no issue worth a second appeal was raised is *SGIO (Qld) v Russell* (1979) 27 ALR 458. The High Court said that 'as the issue is one of fact there is nothing to be gained from our undertaking another review of the evidence': id., 549.
75 For the English position see Administration of Justice (Appeals) Act 1934 (UK); Blom-Cooper & Drewry, 117–51. A useful brief account of the Canadian Supreme Court's appellate jurisdiction is Crane (1977) 15 *Osgoode Hall LJ* 389. For a thorough account of the present position and proposals for reform of the US Supreme Court's appellate jurisdiction, see Simpson (1978) 6 *Hastings CLQ* 297.
76 Constitutional Commission, Committee on the Australian Judicial System, *Report* (1987) para. 3.85–90.
77 Under this procedure the High Court could always rescind leave to appeal

if it disagreed with the lower court's assessment of the case, or found it unnecessary to decide the point of law in question.
78 As recommended by the Constitutional Commission, Committee on the Australian Judicial System, *Report* (1987) para. 4.10.
79 Barwick (1977) 51 *ALJ* 480, 489; Mason (1975) 49 *ALJ* 570, 576.
80 *Uncommon Law* (1935) 257.
81 Administration of Justice Act 1969 (UK) s12(3)(b). See Blom-Cooper & Drewry, 149–51; Drewry (1973) 89 *LQR* 260.
82 Federal Proceedings (Costs) Act 1981 (Cth). See *Victoria v Australian . . . Builders Labourers' Federation* (1982) 43 ALR 693. Cf. *Davis v Johnson* [1979] AC 264, 344 (Lord Salmon).
83 This was the approach taken by the Australian Constitutional Convention, which recommended a guaranteed appeal: (i) From a judgment, decree, order or sentence of the Supreme Court of a State. (ii) In any matter arising under this Constitution or involving its interpretation. (iii) In any matter arising under, or involving the interpretation of the Constitution of a State. (iv) In any matter between States or between the Commonwealth and any State or States or between any State or Territory. *Proceedings . . . Perth* (1978) 204.
84 Constitutional Commission, Committee on the Australian Judicial System, *Report* (1987) para. 4.6–8, 4.19.
85 *Proceedings . . . Perth* (1978) 204–5.
86 *Report* (1987) para. 4.2–5. The Committee thus proposed a new category of federal jurisdiction, i.e. jurisdiction which must be vested either in the High Court or in some other federal court.
87 See generally Stein, ed., *Locus Standi* (1979); ALRC 27, *Standing in Public Interest Litigation* (1985).
88 (1921) 29 CLR 257.
89 Id., 265–7. The decision was approved in the *Boilermakers' Case* (1956) 94 CLR 254, 272–3; [1957] AC 288, 316. Cf. the explanation by Jacobs J in *Commonwealth v Queensland* (1975) 7 ALR 351, 372–3. See also *Re Tooth & Co Ltd* (1978) 19 ALR 191; *Pearce v FCT* (1978) 20 ALR 354.
90 The Australian position is similar to that in the US, where the term is 'cases and controversies' (US Constitution, Art. III s2); see Radcliffe, *The Case-or-Controversy Provision* (1978) esp. 180–215. But both the Privy Council (Judicial Committee Act 1833 (UK) s4) and the Canadian Supreme Court (Supreme Court Act 1970 (Can.) ss55–6; *A-G (Ontario) v A-G (Canada)* [1912] AC 571) have an advisory opinions jurisdiction, and a limited advisory jurisdiction after criminal acquittals exists in the UK: Criminal Justice Act 1972 (UK) s36. See also Note (1978) 29 *Maine LR* 305.
91 Senate Standing Committee on Constitutional and Legal Affairs, *Report on Advisory Opinions by the High Court* (PP 222/1977); Australian Constitutional Convention, Judicature Committee, *Report to Standing Committee D* (1977) 18–28; *Proceedings . . . Adelaide* (1983) I, 47–66. Cf. Crawshaw (1977) 51 *ALJ* 112.
92 Constitution Alteration (Advisory Jurisdiction of the High Court) Bill 1983. See Evans (1983) 57 *ALJ* 690, 694–8.
93 There was little support for an advisory opinions jurisdiction in the submissions to the Australian Judicial System Committee of the Constitutional

94 (1967) 116 CLR 273. Other cases include *Smith v Mann* (1932) 47 CLR 426; *Saffron v R* (1953) 88 CLR 523, 527–8; *Fisher v Fisher* (1986) 60 ALJR 731, 735; *R v Bridges* (1986) 68 ALR 545. Cf. *Minister for Immigration and Ethnic Affairs v Pochi* (1981) 36 ALR 561.
95 Cf. *ATC v Colpitts* (1986) 67 ALR 301, where the Federal Court looked to the substance of the matter. The Australian Judicial System Committee of the Constitutional Commission recommended that the High Court should have appellate jurisdiction over any 'decision' of a lower court, whatever the formal status of that decision: *Report* (1987) para. 4.7, 4.9.
96 (1975) 7 ALR 351. In *Civil and Civic*, the state decision was in substance adversary. The decision in *Saffron v R* (1955) 88 CLR 523 (Attorney-General's reference after acquittal), whatever its merits, is distinguishable.
97 Controversial appointments have included those of Piddington (see Bennett, *Keystone*, 33), McTiernan (id., 53) and Murphy (see Blackshield, in Evans, ed., *Labor and the Constitution 1972–1975* (1977) 118–20).
98 See Neumann, *The High Court of Australia. A Collective Portrait 1903–1970* (2nd edn, 1973); Fricke, *Judges of the High Court* (1986). See also Blackshield, 121–6, and in Tomasic, ed., *Understanding Lawyers* (1978) 133; Kirby, in Evans, ed., (1977) 127–8. There are biographies of a few High Court judges: e.g. Joyce, *Samuel Walker Griffith* (1984); Rickard, *HB Higgins: The Rebel as Judge* (1984); Cowen, *Isaac Isaacs* (1967); Tennant, *Evatt: Politics and Justice* (1970); Marr, *Barwick* (1980). For the social and professional characteristics of British appellate judges see Blom-Cooper & Drewry, 152; Stevens, *Law and Politics* (1979); Shetreet, 54–78; Griffith, *The Politics of the Judiciary* (2nd edn, 1981); Paterson, *The Law Lords* (1982). For the US judiciary and appointments process see Abraham, *Justices and Presidents. A Political History of Appointments to the Supreme Court* (2nd edn, 1985). For a comparison, Abraham, *The Judicial Process* (5th edn, 1986) 52–93.
99 Since the creation of the Federal Court in 1977, there have been 6 'new' High Court appointments. Of these, 3 (Brennan, Deane, Toohey) were Federal Court judges; 3 (Wilson, Dawson, Gaudron) were state Solicitor-Generals; none were from Supreme Courts. During this period the 2 appointees to Chief Justice (Gibbs, Mason) had been Supreme Court judges before their appointment as justices of the High Court (Gibbs, in a varied career, was also a judge of the Federal Court of Bankruptcy).
100 Their average age at first appointment was 53 years. Excluding Piddington and the judges still in office, their average length of office was 17 years.
101 Only 4 Chief Justices have completed their term of office since 1935 (Latham 1935–52; Dixon 1952–64; Barwick 1964–81; Gibbs 1981–87); but it seems that this pattern has not been repeated at this level. Four of the 9 Chief Justices have had substantial political experience; only one (Knox 1919–30) was appointed direct from the Bar. But the choice of Gibbs J as Chief Justice in 1981, in preference to R.J. Ellicott, involved a direct choice between a 'safe' legal appointment and a controversial political one: see *Age*, 30 Jan. 1981, 1, 6; Galligan, *Politics of the High Court* (1987) 197–9.
102 On judicial promotion in the UK see Shetreet, 78–84.

103 On the 1987 appointments — Toohey and Gaudron (the first woman justice) — see (1987) 61 *ALJ* 102.
104 Lederman (1979) 54 *Can BR* 592, 687. It is proposed to incorporate this in the Constitution.
105 The figures are: NSW — 19; Victoria — 10; Queensland — 6; WA — 2. At least 2 offers were made to South Australians but were rejected: Bennett, *Keystone*, 21, 31. Cf. (1975) 49 *ALJ* 405.
106 For the procedure see now High Court of Australia Act 1979 (Cth) s6. For the appointment of Wilson (WA) see (1979) 53 *ALJ* 471. Some states have suggested a rigid division of appointments between the Commonwealth and the states: a Queensland proposal along these lines was rejected by the Judicature Sub-Committee of the Australian Constitutional Convention: *Second Report* (1985) 8–10.
107 The experience with the consultative procedure so far has been mixed. Concerted state opposition (Ellicott, vice Barwick, in 1981) or support (Dawson, 1981) may well be influential, but substantial control over the process remains in the Commonwealth. The Australian Judicial System Committee of the Constitutional Commission did not support any more formal machinery for High Court appointment, but suggested that s6 should be interpreted as allowing the states to comment on the Commonwealth's proposed candidate, as well as proposing their own: *Report* (1987) para. 5.29–33.
108 In 1974 the total amount of money awarded in High Court judgments was only $212 800.
109 Source: 1965–75, *Australian Bureau of Statistics Official Yearbook*; 1976, Barwick (1977) 51 *ALJ* 497; 1977–8, *Commonwealth Yearbooks*; 1979-84, Gibbs (1985) 59 *ALJ* 522: 1985, High Court of Australia, *Annual Report 1985-6* (Parl. Paper 327/1986).
110 Blom-Cooper & Drewry, 242. Appeals disposed of in the years 1976–9 averaged 53.
111 Blom-Cooper & Drewry, 120, 399–400. For an exhaustive account of the House of Lords' contribution see Stevens, *Law and Politics. The House of Lords as a Judicial Body 1800–1976* (1979).
112 Simpson, 297. Cf. Note (1974) 27 *Rutgers LR* 878. In 1982 the total caseload was 5062: Goldman & Jahnige, *The Federal Courts as a Political System* (2nd edn, 1985) 91.
113 On the US Supreme Court see McCloskey, *The Modern Supreme Court* (1972); Wasby, *The Supreme Court in the Federal Judicial System* (2nd edn, 1984); Abraham (1986) 177–256. A controversial but detailed account is Woodward & Armstrong, *The Brethren. Inside the Supreme Court* (1979). For the debate over the case-load explosion in US federal courts see Posner, *The Federal Courts. Crisis and Reform* (1985); Brennan (1983) 66 *Judicature* 230; Edwards (1983) 68 *Iowa LR* 871; Wasby, 145–70.
114 Since 1975 leave to appeal has been required in the majority of cases. The Court's case-load averaged 155 in 1975–6, but in 1977–80 the average dropped markedly to 114 per year. See Cavarzan (1965) 3 *Osgoode Hall LJ* 431; Weiler, *In the Last Resort: A Critical Study of the Supreme Court of Canada* (1974); Lederman (1970) 8 *Alberta LR* 1; Russell (1968) 6 *Osgoode Hall LJ* 1; Snell & Vaughan, *The Supreme Court of Canada. History of the Institution* (1985).
115 Cf. Martineau (1979) 63 *Marquette LR* 163. Note that the US Supreme

Court delivers a full judgment in only about 150–160 cases each year: Simpson, 297.
116 See Zines, *The High Court and the Constitution* (2nd edn, 1987) esp. chs 1, 14–16; Zines, in Tay & Kamenka, eds, *Law-making in Australia* (1980) 207; Zines (1984) 14 *FLR* 277; Galligan, 249–61; Galligan (1979) 10 *FLR* 367; Sawer, in Mayer & Nelson, eds, *Australian Politics. A Fourth Reader* (1976) 316; Sawer, *Australian Federalism*, 35–90; Evans, in Hambly & Golding, eds, *Australian Lawyers and Social Change* (1976) 13; Sexton & Maher, *The Legal Mystique* (1982) 39–60; Coper (1984) 14 *FLR* 294; Lane (1981) 55 *ALJ* 737; Lane (1979) 1135–205 for a range of approaches and views. Sawer (1957) 6 *J Pub L* 482 usefully compares the US Supreme Court and the High Court at that time. Comments by members of the Court include Gibbs (1983) 10 *Syd LR* 1; Mason (1986) 16 *FLR* 1. See also McWhinney, *Supreme Courts and Judicial Law-making: Constitutional Tribunals and Constitutional Review* (1986).
117 E.g. *Bank Nationalization Case* (1948) 76 CLR 1; *Communist Party Dissolution Case* (1951) 83 CLR 1; Sawer (1957) 500–1.
118 (1952) 85 CLR xiii; *Jesting Pilate* (1965) 247.
119 (1956) 94 CLR 254. See Chapter 3 for discussion of the decision and its present status.
120 (1947) 74 CLR 31, 82.
121 Sawer, *Australian Federalism*, 168–95; Evans (1973) 45 *Aust Q* 4; Zines (1987) ch. 15.
122 *Uebergang v Australian Wheat Board* (1980) 54 ALJR 581, 592–3 (Gibbs & Wilson JJ).
123 Id., 595 (Stephen & Mason JJ). These were two of approximately four positions taken in the case. Cf. also *Clark King & Co. v Australian Wheat Board* (1978) 140 CLR 120; *Permewan Wright Cons. Pty Ltd v Trewhitt* (1979) 27 ALR 182; *Miller v TCN Channel Nine Pty Ltd* (1986) 67 ALR 321.
124 The case against civil appeals is stated, or rather overstated, by Wilner (1968) 56 *Georgetown LJ* 417, proposing instead interlocutory or pre-trial direction or guidance. On the general purposes of appeals, Shapiro (1980) 14 *Law & Soc R* 629. For a comparative review cf. Jolowicz, in Storme & Casman, eds, *Towards a Justice with a Human Face* (1978) 127.
125 To the same effect, Martineau, 173–4; Lederman, 15–16; Elwyn-Jones (1976) 7 *Cambrian LR* 31, 31–2.
126 Jacob, 151–7, 217–20. The US Supreme Court cannot decide issues of state law for itself, in conflict with state decisions, but must defer to the latter: *Erie RR Co. v Tompkins* 304 US 64 (1938); Wright, 249–86. For similar proposals for Canada, Abel (1965) 4 *Alberta LR* 39; Lederman (1979) 57 *Can BR* 687.
127 *Cullen v Trappell* (1980) 29 ALR 1, 4. And see *MLC Assurance Co. Ltd v Evatt* (1968) 122 CLR 556, 563; *Grant v Downs* (1976) 11 ALR 577; *Viro v R* (1978) 18 ALR 257 for other instances.
128 See e.g. Cardozo, *The Nature of the Judicial Process* (1921); Allen, *Law in the Making* (7th edn, 1964); Cross, *Precedent in English Law* (3rd edn, 1977) 153–233; Llewellyn, *The Common Law Tradition: Deciding Appeals* (1960) Devlin, *The Judge* (1980) 1, 84–116; Atiyah (1980) 15 *Israel LR* 346; Stone, *Precedent and Law: Dynamics of Common Law Growth* (1985. An Australian assessment is Fox, in Tay & Kamenka (1980) 139.

129 *SGIC v Trigwell* (1979) 26 ALR 67; *Dugan v Mirror Newspapers* (1978) 22 ALR 439, respectively. On the High Court's freedom from binding precedent see Morison, 123-8; *Parker v R* (1963) 111 CLR 610; *Viro v R* (1978) 141 CLR 88: *Atlas Tiles Ltd v Briers* (1978) 21 ALR 129. On that of lower courts see *Cook v Cook* (1986) 61 ALJR 25; *Cole v Cunningham* (1983) 49 ALR 123; *Hawkins v Clayton* (1986) 5 NSWLR 109, 136-7.

130 Compare *Edwards v Noble* (1971) 125 CLR 296; *Cashman v Kinnear* [1973] 2 NSWLR 495; *Livingstone v Halvorsen* (1978) 22 ALR 213; *Warren v Coombs* (1979) 23 ALR 405; *McCoomb v Butcher* (1974) 25 ALR 543; *Gronow v Gronow* (1979) 29 ALR 129. The difficulties of lower courts in the face of this conflict are clear from *Ryan v Carstensz Properties Pty Ltd* (1979) 26 ALR 543. Cf. Morley (1979) 53 *ALJ* 4, and for a vigorous critique, Hutley, in Tay & Kamenka (1980) 179.

131 *McInnis v R* (1979) 27 ALR 449. The excessive formalism of the majority is demonstrated clearly in the contrast with *Johns v R* (1979) 25 ALR 573.

132 Cf. Hutley, 203-4. More recent civil cases suggest a greater commitment to appellate intervention: see e.g. *Commonwealth v Introvigne* (1982) 41 ALR 577; *Taylor v Johnson* (1983) 45 ALR 265; *Muschinski v Dodds* (1985) 62 ALR 429. But in criminal cases the position is less satisfactory: see e.g. the majority decisions in *Lowe v R* (1984) 54 ALR 193; *Liberato v R* (1985) 61 ALR 623; *McDonald v R* (1985) 62 ALR 223; *Smith v R* (1985) 71 ALR 631. See further Chapter 7.

PART 3

Specialist Courts and Tribunals

CHAPTER 10

Family and Children's Courts

An increasingly important feature of the Australian legal system is the large number of specialist courts and tribunals. There are so many of these that detailed treatment of all of them is not possible in a work of this kind. Instead, three important classes will be discussed in some detail — family and children's courts, industrial tribunals, and small claims courts and tribunals. In Chapter 13 the other main specialist bodies will be briefly surveyed, and the relations between specialist courts and tribunals and the ordinary courts outlined.

10.1 The History of Family Jurisdictions in Australia

Modern family law has a curious, even bizarre, history. The relevance of that history now is minimal, but its interest is not — and it demonstrates the decisive break with tradition made by the Family Law Act 1975 (Cth).

Before the English Reformation a full 'divorce' (strictly speaking, an annulment of marriage which was invalid for some reason) could be obtained only in the rarest cases and only from the Pope. The Pope's failure to annul Henry VIII's first marriage led to the decapitation of the English Church (perhaps we should now say, a head transplant). One result was that no authority existed who could grant a divorce *a vinculo matrimonii* (from the chains of matrimony), allowing the parties to remarry. But except as to persons, the English Reformation was a conservative one, and the pre-existing law of marriage and 'divorce' was retained, with minor statutory additions and dispensations, until 1857.[1]

Under that law, a valid marriage was indissoluble. The ecclesiastical courts, whose jurisdiction in this area had long been recognized, could grant what would now be called a judicial separation, divorce *a mensa et thoro*: this dissolved the obligation of the parties to live together, but not the marriage itself. The marriage could only be dissolved by private Act of Parliament, through a curious and expensive procedure available only to the very rich. The first divorce was obtained in 1669: thereafter until 1857 there were 317 such private Acts, four of them obtained by women.[2] An alternative procedure was annulment of a marriage which was void, i.e. legally non-existent: this could be obtained from the ecclesiastical courts on fairly restricted grounds such as consanguinity or affinity.[3] (The position in Scotland was, as usual, different and more sensible.[4])

In the mid-nineteenth century, Victorian religiosity met Victorian reform head-on over proposed changes to this system, and the result was a compromise. The Matrimonial Causes Act 1857 (UK) abolished the jurisdiction of the ecclesiastical courts, and established a judicial divorce by decree which, though expensive, was now within the reach of the upper-middle classes. But the grounds for divorce remained substantially what they had been before: a husband had to prove his wife's adultery; a wife, her husband's adultery combined with cruelty or some other 'offence'. The double standard was obvious.

In Australia, as we have seen, the ecclesiastical courts were not received, and there was thus no way in which even the limited divorce *a mensa et thoro* could be obtained (the only attempt at a private Act failed).[5] The Supreme Courts were deliberately not given a matrimonial jurisdiction of any kind, despite frequent complaints. However, after 1857 the colonies were urged to adopt legislation similar to the English Act, and from 1860 (Tasmania) to 1873 (New South Wales) they did so.[6] The legislation, though it followed the general pattern of the 1857 Act, allowed divorce in rather more cases, and was not uniform throughout the colonies.

This lack of uniformity created difficulties for people travelling between the colonies, and the need for a single Australian law of marriage and divorce was generally accepted during the Convention debates of the 1890s. The earliest draft of the federal Constitution gave the Commonwealth Parliament power over marriage and divorce, and a later attempt to restrict this to interstate recognition of divorces obtained under state law failed: 'the sense of the desirability of uniform laws of marriage and divorce prevailed.'[7] Thus the Parliament was given power to legislate for 'marriage' (s51(xxi)) and 'divorce and matrimonial causes; and in relation thereto, parental rights, and the custody and guardianship of infants' (s51(xxii)).

Despite these substantial federal powers, matters of marriage and divorce, with very minor exceptions, continued to be governed by state laws, with a consequent lack of uniformity. In 1961 the Matrimonial Causes Act 1959 (Cth) came into force, displacing state law and jurisdiction in matters of divorce and of custody, property, and maintenance ancillary to divorce.[8] State law continued to govern these questions when they arose independently of divorce, thus creating an unfortunate duality of rules and powers. But duality of jurisdiction was avoided by investing Supreme Courts with federal jurisdiction under the 1959 Act.

The fourteen grounds for divorce under the 1959 Act were a consolidation of those previously available under state law. Most were based on a requirement of matrimonial fault (e.g. adultery, cruelty, desertion), with its accompanying apparatus of rules about collusion, condonation, and discretion statements.[9] However, separation for five (later reduced to three) years was an independent ground, not based on fault, which had previously applied only in Western Australia. Most divorces were obtained on one or some of these four grounds: if a spouse was not prepared to wait three years for a divorce, adultery or desertion or some other 'offence' had to be established (or successfully contrived).

The Matrimonial Causes Act was regarded as a considerable advance at the time, but it was not to last long. The requirement of a matrimonial offence was much criticized; and whatever underlying theory of marriage the law embodied, in practice it did not work well.[10] After much debate the 1959 Act was replaced by the Family Law Act 1975 (Cth),[11] which for the first time established a comprehensive divorce law based on a single ground — irretrievable breakdown of the marriage, evidenced by a year's separation, without regard to the fault of either party. At the same time a new Family Court was established, to exercise jurisdiction under the Act — at first concurrently with the Supreme Courts but later exclusively.

10.2 The Family Court of Australia[12]

(1) The scope of federal family law power

As this brief account demonstrates, the history of family law owes much to the Christian view of marriage as a lifelong union. That view is reflected in the Family Law Act only in the directive principles in s43, which require the Court to have regard, among other things, to 'the need to preserve and protect the institution of marriage as the union of a man and a woman to the exclusion of all others voluntarily entered into for life'. These principles have only an indirect and variable effect in the Court's practice.[13] But another conception of marriage and of its role in society was equally important in the history of English law: marriage (and therefore, so far as it was permitted, divorce) played a crucial part in arrangements for the accumulation and inheritance of property and the control of children. In this aspect family law was closely connected with large areas of private law.

This dual aspect of family law does not cause problems in a unitary system. In a federal system such as Australia or Canada, where legislative power over marriage and divorce is separated from power over 'property and civil rights', it causes acute problems of demarcation. The Family Law Act has since 1976 caused a correspondingly acute division of opinion in the High Court on constitutional issues of property and custody, the effect of Family Court orders on third parties, and the relationship of federal to state law and jurisdiction. It is not possible in a work of this sort to discuss the case-law in detail. But an outline of the divisions in the High Court since 1976 is necessary: the role and powers of the Family Court cannot be understood without it.

(A) THE INITIAL DIFFICULTY: *RUSSELL v RUSSELL*
As we have seen, the Matrimonial Causes Act 1959 (Cth) was based primarily on s51(xxii) of the Constitution, and dealt only with issues of property and custody so far as they were ancillary or incidental to ('in relation' to) divorce or similar proceedings (known as 'proceedings for principal relief'). The Family Law Act 1975 (Cth) adopted a bolder strategy: it gave the Court power over maintenance and property of the parties to a marriage and over the custody of a child of marriage, independently of proceedings for principal relief. This extension of power could not be justified under the matrimonial causes power, s51(xxii). Instead it was based on the marriage power, s51(xxi). Thus the limitations on ancillary issues, inherent in s51(xxii), were avoided.

The High Court upheld this strategy, by a bare majority, in *Russell v Russell; Farrelly v Farrelly*.[14] The difficulty was that, if s51(xxi) extended to enforcing property and custody disputes between separated spouses, s51(xxii), with its careful limitations on such matters, was unnecessary. On the other hand s51(xxi) had already been held not to be restricted to the act of marriage, as distinct from its consequences.[15] The majority (Mason, Stephen, and Jacobs JJ) avoided the difficulty, in accordance with established constitutional principle, by treating s51(xxi) as an independent source of power from s51(xxii). The minority (Barwick CJ, Gibbs J) thought that s51(xxii) controlled and limited the scope of s51(xxi).[16] But the majority's decision did not mean that the 1975 Act was entirely valid. Disputes over the property of married persons, even between themselves, may have nothing at all to do with marriage. A husband and wife may be happily married, but disagree over the running of a partnership or company they are involved in. Similarly, disputes between third parties over the custody of a child of a marriage may have nothing to do with the marriage (e.g. the parents may be dead). So it was necessary to read down these provisions of the Act.[17] The custody jurisdiction would be valid if the dispute arose between the parents: it could be read down under s51(xxi) in that way. But this was not possible for the property jurisdiction, as the example given above shows. This jurisdiction had therefore to be read down under the matrimonial causes power, s51(xxii). As a result, the Court could deal with property disputes only in relation to proceedings for principal relief.[18]

This process of 'reading down' has sometimes been misunderstood. Mason J did not say that no independent property jurisdiction could be conferred under s51(xxi), or that no custody dispute could validly include or bind third parties. But it was not possible for the Court to read into the Act the limitations necessary to achieve these results — that would be a legislative, not a judicial process.[19] Whether the Parliament understood this or not, in fact the Act was amended in 1976 to incorporate the restrictions inferred by Mason J, rather than any broader limits which Commonwealth power might have sustained. Since then the Act has been amended to expand the jurisdiction of the Family Court more or less to the limits of constitutional power — in several cases beyond those limits. Although there have been disagreements in the High Court over the validity of various amendments, all subsequent decisions have been based on the decision in *Russell's case*, which is now established.[20]

(B) THE SCOPE OF THE MARRIAGE POWER: IMPRESSIONS OF A DIVIDED COURT

Once it was clear that the principal source of power for the Family Law Act was the marriage power, the problem became how to determine which of the provisions establishing property, custody, and similar jurisdiction in the Act were 'marriage' kinds of laws. Here the historical duality of marriage, referred to already, has caused difficulty and division. The difficulty was well put by Jacobs J in *Russell's case*:

Paragraphs (xxi) and (xxii) of s51 are the only subject matters of Commonwealth power which are not related to what may be broadly described as public economic or financial subjects but which are related to what are commonly thought of as private or personal rights. The reason for their inclusion appears to me to be twofold. First, although marriage and the dissolution thereof are in many ways a personal matter of the parties, social history tells us that the state has always regarded them as matters of public concern. Secondly, and perhaps more importantly, the need was recognized for a uniformity of legislation on these subject matters throughout the Commonwealth. In a single community, throughout which intercourse was to be absolutely free, provision was required whereby there could be uniformity in the laws governing the relationship of marriage and the consequences of that relationship as well as the dissolution thereof. Difference between the states in the laws governing the status and the relationship of married persons could be socially divisive to the harm of the new community which was being created. But because these subject matters enter so deeply into the field of personal and private rights, a field largely left within the legislative power of the states, it is difficult to resist the tendency in oneself to regard the Commonwealth power as an intrusion into an area solidly filled by state laws on a variety of subject matters which govern personal and private rights. The tendency to minimize the unique intrusion by a narrow characterization of the subject matters so that as far as possible the framework of state laws governing personal and property rights is preserved must be resisted.[21]

But this has been said to be (and in one respect at least was) a dissenting judgment,[22] and some other members of the Court have not so much resisted as embraced the tendency to restrict federal power in this way. Since 1976 some justices have continued to accept the general consequences of this broader conception of marriage.[23] Others have taken a much more restrictive view, emphasizing the limited impact of marriage on other matters such as property and custody — emphasizing, in Wilson J's striking phrase, 'the private world of relationships grounded in marriage'.[24] In the middle Gibbs CJ, accepting (as some members of the Court have not[25]) the majority view in *Russell*, has taken an eclectic position. He has required in each case 'a close connection with the marriage relationship',[26] now finding such a connection (as with the right of a third party to seek custody of a child of the marriage after the death of a parent[27]), now not finding one (as with the power of the Family Court to override by its custody order the protective custody of a state social welfare officer[28]). The result has been an erratic, uncertain jurisprudence.[29] But first the structure and functions of the Family Court itself must be explained.

(2) The Family Court of Australia

Like small claims courts (discussed in Chapter 12), family courts or domestic relations courts derive from experiments in the United States dating from early in this century. Family law is almost entirely a state matter there, and there is no uniformity in the arrangements for family courts.[30] But certain common elements do emerge: the family court is a unified court with as wide a jurisdiction over family matters as possible; it is a 'helping court', which provides counselling facilities to persons with family troubles, whether or not they are litigants; it is a specialist court, with judges who are aware of and responsive to its special needs; it is organized to be widely available within the community, and to function with a minimum of formality and delay. In the Finer Committee's not entirely approving words, it is 'as much a therapeutic agency as a judicial institution'.[31]

Initial proposals for a Family Law Act in Australia would have conferred jurisdiction not on a family court but on the proposed federal superior court.[32] However, a Senate Committee Report in 1974 strongly supported the family court ideal, predicting that 'the establishment of a Family Court and the simplified substantive provisions in the Bill will reduce the scope for legal disputation.'[33] This hopeful recommendation was accepted, and the principal judicial agency under the Family Law Act 1975 (Cth) was a new specialist court, the Family Court of Australia.

The Family Court is a superior court of record, consisting of a chief judge, senior judges, and other judges. At present there are 46 judges, making it by far the largest superior court in Australia. In a number of ways the Act tries to achieve the ideal of the family court, referred to already. The judges, if appointed since 1977, retire at 65; an attempt apparently to avoid outworn judicial attitudes, although no one has yet measured the rate of judicial deterioration between 65 and 70.[34] A prospective judge must be 'by reason of training, experience and personality . . . a suitable person to deal with matters of family law' (s32(2)(b)). The Act makes extensive provision for counselling and reconciliation, with court counsellors appointed as officers to the Court's staff and welfare officers also available. In custody proceedings a judge may order the parties to attend a conference with a counsellor or welfare officer, and in divorce proceedings within two years of marriage counselling is compulsory: otherwise it is voluntary, and the extent to which it is fact available varies between registries in different states.[35] By the time a case actually comes to court the chances of reconciliation are often slight, but court counsellors have been able to achieve a significant level of negotiated settlements on some or all issues, thus saving court time and improving the chances of the settlement actually working.[36]

Once a contested case reaches the Court, the judge acts in a judicial role rather than as a conciliator, although under s14(2) the judge may adjourn to attempt conciliation. One important element in the Family Court ideal was a reduction in adversary proceedings, but the High Court swiftly intervened to re-establish the adversary method. Watson J, an influential proponent of the family court ideal, had remarked that family proceedings were not adversarial: this, the High Court held,

indicated a basic misconception as to the position of the court . . . A judge of the Family Court is given a wide discretion but he must exercise it in accordance with legal principles. He exercises judicial power and must discharge his duty judicially.[37]

In subsequent cases the High Court has not intervened so readily, but it clearly adheres to the adversarial model.

In its procedure the Court is enjoined to act 'without undue formality' and without wigs or robes.[38] Initially Family Court proceedings were heard in closed court: this provision was, after much controversy, reversed in 1983,[39] but there are still restraints on publication of proceedings.[40]

The Family Court model is also supported by a general rule that the parties bear their own costs (s117). Again the model has tended to be eroded. The power to award costs is not an exceptional one, but merely has to be justified in the 'particular case'.[41]

(3) *The jurisdiction of the Family Court*

More important than these procedural matters is the scope of the family jurisdiction exercised by the Court, and here major difficulties have emerged.[42] Only in Western Australia has the problem of dual jurisdiction been largely resolved through the establishment of the Western Australian Family Court, which exercises both state and federal jurisdiction. Elsewhere, the Family Court's jurisdiction is limited in important ways by the Family Law Act and the Constitution. Limitations under the Act have been successively removed by amendments, especially in 1983.[43] But the constitutional limitations remain as significant obstacles to a 'unified' family jurisdiction. More recently there have been moves to overcome these through reference of legislative power by four states, and through the proposed cross-vesting legislation. Before discussing these proposals, it is necessary to outline the present limits on federal family jurisdiction.

(A) PROCEEDINGS FOR PRINCIPAL RELIEF

Fewest problems arise with proceedings for principal relief: that is, for a decree of dissolution or nullity of marriage or for a declaration that a marriage is valid or void or has been dissolved. Dissolution is based solely on 'irretrievable breakdown' evidenced by twelve months' separation (s48). This may be established even if the parties were compelled to live in the same house, if in fact they lived separately, or even if the separation was interrupted by one unsuccessful attempt at reconciliation (ss49(2), 50). Relatively few applications for dissolution are opposed, and the Court spends only about 5 per cent of its time on proceedings for principal relief.[44]

(B) CUSTODY OF CHILDREN[45]

As we have seen, in *Russell's case* the High Court read down the Family Court's custody jurisdiction to proceedings between the spouses, a limitation that was then embodied in the Act. In the first instance, the Court has jurisdiction over disputes over the custody of a 'child of a marriage', defined as the natural or adopted child of the parties to the marriage.[46] This limitation leads to most unsatisfactory results. For example, it is common for a child of one of the parties (whether ex-nuptial or born of a previous marriage) to be accepted and brought up within the family. In 1983 a wider definition of 'child of a marriage' was inserted, extending to '*de facto* children' of the marriage, but this was held to be invalid.[47] Thus it will often happen that some children within a second marriage will be outside the Family Court's custody jurisdiction.

Another significant limitation is that the Family Court has no general power to entertain a custody application by a third party (e.g. a grandparent), unless the application is brought against a party to a marriage in respect of a child of that marriage.[48] As a result, cases have occurred where the custody of the same child has been disputed by the spouses in the Family Court and by third parties elsewhere. Indeed, in at least two cases the two different custody actions were both held to be in the wrong court.[49] It is hard to imagine a more wasteful, unnecessary example of jurisdictional conflict.[50]

When the Court does have jurisdiction in a custody matter the principles to be applied are set out in s64. The primary consideration is the so-called 'welfare principle', that 'the welfare of the child [is] the paramount consideration' (s64(1)(a)). To that end the Court should have regard to the wishes of the child (especially if aged 14 or more), any welfare report, and the arguments of any separate counsel appointed under s65 to represent the child. The role of separate representation of a child is an interesting one, which is still in the process of evolution.[51] It should be noted that it adds to, rather than qualifying, the adversary character of custody hearings. Indeed, it has been argued that, in the adversary context, the welfare principle is adhered to only in form, that what really happens is a balancing of parental 'rights' and predictions as to the future interests of the child. The phrase 'best interests' is itself so vague that disagreement is inevitable.[52] In effect it confers the broadest discretion, and there is little consensus on the appropriate psychological and social welfare criteria for child placement, or on the extent to which it is proper for Family Court judges to draw on the conclusions of social scientists.[53] On the other hand the 'best interests' formula does have an *exclusionary* effect. The focus is on the child, not on extraneous matters such as the fault of either spouse leading to the breakdown of the marriage.[54]

(C) MAINTENANCE

The Court has jurisdiction over proceedings between spouses for maintenance, which can be in the form of periodic payments or a lump sum, and may be varied from time to time. But the duty of one party to maintain another is qualified and may even be excluded where the other party is able 'to support herself or himself adequately'.[55] Arguments about matrimonial fault in claims for maintenance are excluded: the conduct of the parties is relevant only if it relates to their future financial resources.[56]

It is possible for parties to make a formal maintenance agreement, in addition to or even excluding their rights under the Act. Such agreements, to be effective, must be registered or approved by the Family Court, and, as a result of amendments to the Act in 1983, their enforcement is also a matter exclusively for the Court, rather than for state courts.[57]

(D) PROPERTY DISPUTES

Disputes over the division of property on divorce have been even more complex than those over custody of children. Again only a brief outline of the position can be given.

There is no system of matrimonial property in English or Australian law.[58] Parties to a marriage may acquire and deal with property in their separate names, including property such as the matrimonial home. Under state law there is (with the partial exception of Victoria[59] and Western Australia[60]) no way by which the non-financial contributions of spouses to the acquisition and maintenance of property can be reflected in the division of joint assets, or by which a wife can claim a 'fair share' of assets held in the husband's name.[61] By contrast, the Family Court has extensive power to redistribute property of either party to the marriage (ss79, 80, 85), and as a result of amendments in 1983 these powers extend to proceedings between parties to a marriage 'arising out of the marital relationship', as well as to proceedings 'in relation to concurrent, pending or completed proceedings for principal relief'.[62] The provision for independent property proceedings 'arising out of the marital relationship' appears to be a significant extension of power, although to some extent the substance of that power was already being exercised by the Court by way of injunctions under s114.[63]

In making orders to declare or alter property interests the Court must consider, among other things, the contribution made by the parties to the acquisition or improvement of property, whether that contribution is direct or indirect, financial, or 'in the capacity of homemaker or parent'.[64] Despite the broad definition of property in s4(1), some important interests do not constitute property for these purposes — for example, most future expectations to superannuation or under a discretionary trust (depending on the terms of the particular scheme).[65] In such cases all the Court can do is take the expectation into account in making other property or maintenance orders, or delay a decision until money is received. Since the Court is required, if possible, to 'finally determine the financial relationships between the parties to the marriage and avoid further proceedings between them' (s81), indefinite delay may not be possible.[66]

A major difficulty in this area is the limited power of the Court to enforce its orders against third parties. It can, for example, order a husband to exercise voting rights as a shareholder in a private company in the wife's interests, but cannot do the same to third-party directors who are bound under the general law to consider the interests of the other shareholders.[67] It cannot, as a state court can, appoint a receiver to a business partnership between husband and wife, even though such an appointment may be necessary to determine finally their financial relationship and claims.[68] These limitations create uncertainty and opportunities for evasion.[69]

Important questions arise as to the principles to be applied by the Court in property cases. The Act confers a broad discretion, and the High Court has insisted that the discretion is not to be fettered by the application of rules or presumptions not expressed in the Act (e.g. the presumption of equality of entitlement to property acquired during the marriage).[70] This insistence on a broad discretion in turn limits the power of the Family Court on appeal to maintain some consistency in property decisions.[71] The impression of 'palm-tree justice' is thereby strengthened.

(E) ACCRUED AND ASSOCIATED JURISDICTION OF THE FAMILY COURT
The scope of accrued federal jurisdiction was discussed, in the context of the Federal Court, in Chapter 8. There would seem to be no reason why the Family Court should not have a similar jurisdiction, since it derives from the meaning of the term 'matter' in s76(ii) of the Constitution, which is the source of all jurisdiction arising under federal laws. If there was any doubt, it would seem to have been removed by the recasting of the Family Court's jurisdiction, in 1983, in terms of 'matters' arising under the Family Law Act 1975 (s31(1)). Similarly the Family Court has an 'associated jurisdiction' under s33 of the Act, in similar terms to that of the Federal Court under s32 of the Federal Court of Australia Act 1976 (Cth).

Despite these similarities, it appears that any accrued or associated jurisdiction of the Family Court is of a limited kind, far more so than that of the Federal Court. In part this is due to the character and limits of the Court's property jurisdiction, especially so far as third parties are concerned. In property cases the Court is concerned to redistribute property rights of the parties in the exercise of a broad discretion. It has no direct power to resolve third-party claims.[72] In the leading case, *Smith v Smith*, the High Court held that the Family Court had no accrued jurisdiction to approve a maintenance agreement as effective for the purposes of the Family Provision Act 1982 (NSW), because that Act required the approval of the Supreme Court.[73] The Court did not need to decide whether the Family Court will ever be called on to exercise accrued or associated jurisdiction, but three justices seem to have thought not.[74] It is difficult to see why the special character of family jurisdiction should have such a limiting effect.

(F) ENFORCEMENT OF FAMILY COURT ORDERS
The Court has a variety of enforcement powers, including interim and final injunctions under s114. Much of the work of enforcing maintenance is done by magistrates' courts, with indifferent success.[75] Imprisonment for failure to pay maintenance has been abolished, although the possibility remains in severe cases of contempt.[76] Enforcement of family law orders has always been a problem, and the

Family Court is no exception.[77] The Australian Law Reform Commission, while conceding that enforcement issues are 'inherently intractable', has proposed that existing contempt powers be largely replaced by criminal sanctions.[78]

(G) APPEALS

There is an appeal from decrees of a single judge of the Court (or of a state Family Court exercising federal jurisdiction) to the Full Family Court (s94). Similarly, there is an appeal to the Court from state magistrates' courts exercising jurisdiction under the Act (s96). Appeals are heard by the Appeal Division, established under the 1983 amendments to the Act.[79] Some judges are permanent members of the Appeal Division, while others are assigned to it from time to time.[80] The Full Court's case-load has been a significant one, averaging nearly 167 cases disposed of after hearing, in each year from 1980 to 1984.

There is a further appeal from the Full Court to the High Court, by special leave of the High Court or on a certificate of the Full Court itself, under s95 of the Act. This was described in Chapter 9. The High Court also has supervisory jurisdiction over the Family Court under s75(v) of the Constitution and this jurisdiction has been frequently invoked. It would be an exaggeration to compare the Family Court with the old Court of Admiralty in suffering a deluge of prohibitions, but the High Court on several occasions has had to affirm the desirability of appeal rather than direct, and often premature, intervention on its part.[81] On a number of occasions it has appeared wilfully to ignore its own counsel of restraint.[82]

(4) Other problems of the Family Court

(A) COSTS AND DELAY

Since its establishment the Family Court has attracted a vast, unpredicted case-load, much greater than the equivalent case-load under the 1959 Act. For example in the years 1980–4 it averaged, in round figures, 42 000 dissolution applications, 9400 custody applications, 4600 applications for access, 9400 maintenance applications, 12 300 property applications, and 4800 applications for injunctions. The numbers of dissolution applications have been fairly steady, after the initial rush in the first year or so after the Act came into force.[83] But there have been significant increases in maintenance and especially property cases since 1980.

Even the largest superior court in Australia has not been able to cope with this flood of cases, and significant delays have built up in the hearing of contested cases — as much as two years in some registries.[84] The hopeful prediction that the Act would reduce the scope for legal disputation, while true of dissolution applications, has not been true of other cases, and very considerable problems exist with costs and the restricted availability of legal aid.[85]

(B) AVAILABILITY OF COUNSELLING

A key aspect of the family court ideal, as we have seen, is its emphasis on mediation and conciliation, assisting the parties to agree on matters in dispute, with adjudication of disputes only where conciliation fails or agreement is not possible. This is reflected in the Family Law Act 1975 (Cth) itself, and in the establishment of a counselling service as part of the Court's structure.[86] The Family Law Council has stated that 'settlement by conciliation is at the core of the Family Court's successful functioning'.[87]

However, counselling has not been as freely available as it should be, and in some registries has hardly been available at all.[88] The Western Australian Family Court's experience demonstrates that counselling can be effective in reducing contested cases and, thus, costs and delay. The Parliamentary Joint Committee reported in 1980 that increased provision for counselling was the first priority in tackling these problems, and this continues to be the case.[89]

Apart from questions of resources there are problems over the respective roles of counselling and adjudication under the Act. These have surfaced in disagreements in particular cases over the part to be played by court counsellors (especially in child custody disputes),[90] and in reported confusion among court counsellors themselves over their roles as officers of the court, on the one hand, and counsellors to the parties, on the other.[91] Suggestions have been made that the counselling service be separated from the Court, with its own premises and with a statutory requirement that counselling be attempted before a case comes to court.[92] In the meantime experiments with conciliation in family disputes are continuing, in the form of Family Conciliation Centres in Melbourne and Wollongong.[93]

(C) ATTACKS ON FAMILY COURT JUDGES

In the period 1980–4 three bomb attacks (one on a court building, two on judges' homes) and a shooting resulted in the death of a judge, and a judge's wife.[94] No person has yet been charged with these crimes. The physical security of Court personnel and buildings has become a major problem.

(D) CONFLICT BETWEEN FEDERAL AND STATE JURISDICTIONS

It will already be clear that there have been significant conflicts of jurisdiction between the Family Court and Supreme Courts in areas such as custody, property, and maintenance. One particular area of difficulty is the relation between the Family Court's custody jurisdiction and the custody of state welfare authorities over children who are delinquent, deserted, or in 'need of care and control'. Section 10(3) of the Act, which provided that the Court may in special circumstances override such official custody by a custody order of its own, was held by the High Court to be invalid. In this case Gibbs J sided with Barwick CJ and Aickin and Wilson JJ in failing to find sufficient connection with marriage: the minority (Stephen, Mason, and Murphy JJ) had no such problem.[95] The difficulty with the majority's position is shown by the fact that the state officer could in effect award possession of the child to a parent the Family Court had decided was unfit to care for the child, so long as the officer retained the formal shield of guardianship under state law. In this way, the Family Court's considered custody decision (which might be the only judicial decision on the point) would be subverted.[96] Co-operation between state and federal authorities is the only remedy.

(5) *Proposals for additional Family Court jurisdiction*
In fact a number of different proposals have been made to deal with these problems, by conferring additional jurisdiction on the Court.

(A) THE CROSS-VESTING LEGISLATION
The cross-vesting legislation was discussed in Chapter 8. It applies to the Family Court and to state Family Courts, and (assuming that it is valid) will close many of the gaps in federal family jurisdiction.[97] However, the substantive law applicable to a case will remain the relevant state law,[98] so that the scheme does not involve the extension of the powers and provisions of the Family Law Act itself to state cases of custody or property.

(B) THE REFERENCE OF POWER OVER CHILD CUSTODY
An even more fundamental change will be made as a result of the reference by four states of power over maintenance, custody, and guardianship of children.[99] As a reference of legislative power under s51(xxxviii) of the federal Constitution, this will allow the substantive provisions of the Family Law Act 1975 (Cth) to be extended to children who are not children of a marriage as presently defined. Neither Queensland nor Western Australia is a participant in the reference of power. In the case of Western Australia this is of limited significance, since the Western Australian Family Court has power over both 'federal' and 'state' children. Queensland's non-participation is more significant, although, since state jurisdiction over children depends on presence within the jurisdiction rather than residence or domicile, it may be possible to bring an ex-nuptial child within the scope of the Family Law Act 1975 by taking the child to another state.

(C) POSSIBLE CONSTITUTIONAL AMENDMENT
There was some discussion within the Constitutional Convention of a possible constitutional amendment to give the Commonwealth more ample power over family law (including family property disputes).[100] This contributed to the decision to refer power over child custody, as well as to the terms of that reference. But the Convention's proposed power over family property was in such limited terms that it

would have added little or nothing to the existing powers under s51(xxi) and (xxii), and may even have been counter-productive.[101] The cross-vesting scheme and reference of child custody powers cover most of the remaining matters in the Constitutional Convention's proposals, and a constitutional amendment to expand federal family law powers is thus unlikely to proceed, at least for the time being.[102]

(6) Assessment

In two quite different ways, attacks on the Family Court in the 1980s have created the impression, and to some degree the reality, of a court under siege. The physical attacks on judges and court buildings have already been referred to. But there have also been attacks on the prestige and professionalism of the Court, exemplified by these extra-judicial comments of Gibbs CJ in 1985:

> It may have been a mistake to establish a separate court to administer the Family Law Act . . . [T]he creation of that Court has made it difficult to maintain the highest standards in the making of judicial appointments . . . Although many judges of considerable ability have been appointed . . . it would be hypocritical to pretend that the jurisdiction of that Court, which is limited in scope and likely to be emotionally exhausting, is such as to attract many of the lawyers who might be expected to be appointed to the Supreme Courts or to the Federal Court. The consideration which I have had to give to judgments of the Family Court has led me to conclude that . . . there is a present need to provide a new and more effective avenue of appeals from its decisions.[103]

There has been a tendency within the legal profession to segregate family law from other areas of legal practice, and to regard family law as a 'less prestigious' area of practice.[104] The poor quality of many family court buildings and facilities, and the lower salaries of judges, have contributed to this tendency. On the other hand there is still strong support, within the Court and outside it, for the family court ideal.[105] The Commonwealth, having committed itself to that ideal, has the responsibility to create the conditions which will allow it to be achieved. It has accordingly undertaken a program of 'renovation' of the Court,[106] with improved facilities and buildings, greater delegation of cases to registrars and magistrates,[107] and the measures (discussed already) to resolve many of the jurisdictional problems which have dogged the Court.

It remains to be seen whether these reforms will resolve the problems, or whether they are of a more basic, structural kind. Very different views are held as to whether the Family Law Act encouraged the flood of divorces, or merely reflected the number of unhappy marriages for which the old law provided no remedy.[108] Whichever view is held, there is now little support for a return to 'matrimonial fault', and in any event, such arguments relate to the grounds for dissolution of marriage rather than the success of the Court. The

Court has had its successes: these include the provision of counselling, simplified procedures for dissolution, the reduced formality of proceedings, and, perhaps, the growth of a specialist judiciary and legal profession. The defects are equally clear: excessive delay in some registries, jurisdictional gaps and uncertainties greater than any other Australian court, and marked unevenness of operations between states. It has been suggested that these defects reveal the failure of the family court ideal itself, and that the Court should be transformed either into a division of the Federal Court, or into a federal trial court at District Court level. But there is strong opposition to both proposals, including from the judges of the Federal Court and the Family Court itself.[109] Instead the Commonwealth has undertaken its program of 'renovation', on the success or failure of which the future of the Court may well depend.

10.3 State Family Jurisdictions

(1) The Family Court of Western Australia

An important innovation under the Family Law Act 1975 is the possibility of state family courts exercising both federal and state jurisdiction over the whole range of family law matters. Such courts are to be established by agreement with the Commonwealth, on the following terms:

- 'the Commonwealth Government will provide the necessary funds for the establishment and administration of those courts (including the provision of counselling facilities for those courts)' (s41(1));
- 'arrangements [should be] made under which Judges will not be appointed to that court except with the approval of the Attorney-General of the Commonwealth' (s41(4)(a));
- 'Judges appointed to that court are by reason of training, experience and personality, suitable persons to deal with matters of family law and cannot hold office beyond the age of 65 years' (s41(4)(b)); and
- 'counselling facilities will be available to that court' (s41(4)(c)).

Although each state was given the opportunity to establish a family court, only one such court has been established, in Western Australia pursuant to the Family Court Act 1975 (WA).[110] In addition to its federal jurisdiction the Court has extensive state jurisdiction (to the exclusion of the Western Australian Supreme Court) in matters such as adoption, affiliation, and the custody of ex-nuptial children.[111] In the exercise of state jurisdiction the Court has the same powers and applies many of the same procedures as the Family Court of Australia. In some cases it has more extensive powers: for example, separate representation of children is not limited to custody claims.[112] Its counselling operations have been a notable success.[113] But the main advantage with the Court is that it avoids at first instance most of the jurisdictional difficulties facing the Family Court of Australia. It can deal with children whatever their status; it has a wardship jurisdiction which enables it to act in respect of 'state' children; its Registrar, sitting as a stipendiary magistrate, can handle minor matters more efficiently than in other states.[114]

The main formal difficulty occurs on appeal. Appeals under the Family Law Act 1975 (Cth) go to the Full Family Court of Australia, while appeals in matters of state jurisdiction go to the Full Supreme Court of Western Australia.[115] The difficulty was cited by the Joint Parliamentary Committee as a reason for not preferring state family courts as the best solution to the jurisdictional problem.[116] However, no such conflict has yet occurred in practice, and the other advantages of a co-operative family court greatly outweigh this objection.

(2) Other state family jurisdictions[117]

A detailed examination has been made of the Family Court of Australia, both because of its interest as an experiment in judicial administration, and because it is a model of the difficulties the federal system throws in the way of a coherent court system. A briefer account can be given of the parallel state jurisdictions.

(A) THE ROLE OF STATE AND TERRITORY SUPREME COURTS

Supreme Courts retain important family law powers in areas not covered by the Family Law Act 1975 (Cth). This is particularly true in relation to custody and maintenance of children not children of a marriage as defined in the Act, and of many independent property proceedings between spouses. In each state the Supreme Court can, under testator's family maintenance legislation, make provision for the family of a deceased person who has not provided adequately for them by will.[118]

A significant residual jurisdiction of Supreme Courts is the so-called prerogative or wardship jurisdiction, deriving initially from a delegation by the King to the Chancellor of power to act as custodian of the persons and property of children without guardians. This very general power enables the Supreme Court to make a child a ward of court and to supervise the child in a wide variety of situations.[119] A Family Court custody order, while it may reduce the scope of the wardship power, does not exclude many of its supervisory elements.[120] State courts also exercise jurisdiction under state maintenance and affiliation legislation.

(B) ADOPTION COURTS

Traditionally, the adoption of children in England and Australia has required a judicial order, after a court has considered the welfare of the child and determined that the parent's consent has been duly given (or can properly be waived). In seven of the eight Australian jurisdictions this is still so, but the actual arrangements vary widely. Jurisdiction is exercised by the Supreme Court in the two territories and New South Wales,[121] by the Supreme Court or the County Court in Victoria, by the state Family Court in Western Australia, by the Children's Court, a District Court, or a specially constituted court of summary jurisdiction in South Australia, and by a magistrate in Tasmania.[122] Only Queensland has an administrative adoption: orders are made by the Director of the Department of Children's Services (although only the Supreme Court can dispense with parent's consent or set aside an adoption order once made).[123]

(C) COURTS OF SUMMARY JURISDICTION
In addition to their family jurisdiction under state law, courts of summary jurisdiction have invested federal jurisdiction under the Family Law Act 1975 (Cth) in respect of proceedings other than proceedings for principal relief. They are the usual forum for the enforcement of maintenance awards, but they can also act in property and custody disputes. However, in custody cases or cases involving property exceeding $1000 in value, if the case is contested it must be transferred to the Family Court unless the parties consent.[124]

The original intention was to phase out the jurisdiction of courts of summary jurisdiction under the Act, but the workload of the Family Court makes this unlikely, at least for the time being. There has, however, been criticism of the handling of family law cases by these courts.[125] The Parliamentary Joint Committee proposed that they be retained, but that only selected and specially qualified magistrates be entitled to act.[126] The question whether the Commonwealth could validly select specific state magistrates in this way was discussed in Chapter 3.

(D) ADMINISTRATIVE JURISDICTIONS
In addition to these judicial jurisdictions dealing with family problems, each state and territory has legislation for the protection of children by administrative means. Typically, the Director-General of Community Welfare Services or an equivalent officer can, with the consent of the child's custodian, assume care and custody of a child who is neglected, ill-treated, or has no suitable guardian.[127] Apart from review procedures established by the legislation itself, there is a strong presumption that the Supreme Court's protective or wardship jurisdiction is not ousted by this administrative custody.[128] As we have seen, the Family Court of Australia cannot by its custody order override a Director-General's statutory custody. This leads to the curious situation that the Family Court order can override the Supreme Court's wardship jurisdiction, which can in turn override the state statutory custody, but that the Family Court cannot override the latter directly.

10.4 Children's Courts

Although some versions of the family court ideal would require it to incorporate the protective and criminal jurisdiction of juvenile or children's courts, in fact children's courts are separate in each state and territory, and are likely to remain so.[129]

(1) The philosophy and functions of children's courts

At common law, a child over the age of 7 charged with a criminal offence was liable to be tried in the ordinary courts and, if it could be shown that the child was aware of the wrongfulness of the act charged, could be convicted and sentenced in the same way as any adult.[130] But ideas of reforming child offenders through special and separate treatment developed, alongside similar humanitarian reform movements in England and America in the nineteenth century, and the establishment of separate juvenile courts, in South Australia by 1895 and Illinois in 1899, was a natural progression from these ideas.[131] The ideal was a juvenile court with a primary focus on the reform through 'treatment' of child offenders. The developing social welfare and therapeutic disciplines were to be central to this goal. 'Adult' notions of crime and punishment, responsibility and retribution, were regarded as misplaced.

Nearly a century later, the consensus is that this ideal has failed, and 'new' methods of treating young offenders have been introduced, themselves with mixed success, since the mid-1960s.[132] A catalyst in this development was a series of decisions of the US Supreme Court applying due process standards — natural justice, onus of proof, double jeopardy — to juvenile courts.[133] Previously these proceedings had been characterized as 'civil' or 'remedial', and thus exempt from the minimum standards of a criminal trial. At least one improvement in recent reform has been the abandonment of such euphemisms, which glossed over the real impact of juvenile court sentences.[134] As the Supreme Court pointed out, the earlier emphasis on welfare had led to extensive, often arbitrary, discretionary powers, depriving children of their freedom for periods of time which were wholly disproportionate to the offence charged. (In many cases, these were 'status' offences — acts which were criminal only when committed by juveniles.) Such a result could be tolerated only if the welfare aims of the juvenile courts really were fulfilled — but the rate of recidivism (i.e. re-offending) remained high, and there was no evidence that the juvenile court helped any proportion of those it dealt with. In the words of one authority:

> the juvenile court . . . too often . . . seeks to do things best not done; it undertakes ambitious tasks without available means and it fails to apply means at hand to clearly defined ends . . . [It] aggravates many problems . . . and in some cases . . . furthers delinquent careers.[135]

So the crisis of the juvenile court reflected the crisis of theory in the social welfare professions.

Recent developments, then, have been towards the separation of the criminal jurisdiction of the juvenile or children's courts (as they are now called throughout Australia) from their remedial or welfare jurisdiction, reinforcement of procedural safeguards (though these were never as neglected as in some parts of the United States),[136] and the development of formal programmes of diversion of minor offenders away from courts. For the most serious or persistent offenders there is the possibility of diversion in the other direction, to the ordinary criminal courts and the prospect of real custodial sentences. How much actual difference these 'reforms' will make to the status quo is not altogether clear: for one thing, attitudes are harder to change than institutions, and in any event, these developments are by no means uniformly reflected in Australia: they have been explicitly adopted only in South Australia and Western Australia.[137]

(2) Children's courts in Australia

In each state and territory there is a children's court or courts. Usually these are constituted by special or stipendiary magistrates who are not full-time children's court judges, although there is provision for special appointments, not always used.[138] The close link between children's courts and courts of summary jurisdiction is underlined in Tasmania and the Australian Capital Territory by a provision that the court of summary jurisdiction exercising jurisdiction under the relevant Act is to be 'known as the Children's Court' — rather like a rose of another name.[139] The exception is South Australia, where the Children's Court is presided over by a specialist judge in the District Court, although magistrates act in minor matters.[140]

In each state and territory children's courts have either primary or exclusive jurisdiction over offences committed by children and young persons up to the age of 17 or 18. This includes all summary offences (in South Australia, traffic offences are excluded) and most indictable offences. Trial is summary, without a jury, in a court from which the general public is excluded. As with the Family Court, privacy of children's court proceedings has been criticised, and in some states has been reduced by recent amendments.[141] Publication of court proceedings is restricted, in an effort to prevent the stigma of a criminal conviction attaching to a young offender.

In the exercise of its criminal jurisdiction, the children's court, like any other court, is required to find the defendant guilty 'beyond a reasonable doubt': otherwise, procedures tend to be somewhat less formal and more inquisitorial.[142] A defendant is entitled to legal representation, but it is uncommon in practice. A Victorian survey found only 6 per cent of children represented.[143] In the great majority of cases the defendant pleads guilty, and the real question for the court is one of disposition or sentencing. Before deciding on sentence the court will often (and may be obliged to) call for a 'social background report' on the child, prepared by a social worker: this is admitted under an exception to the rules of evidence, and will often be influential in the sentencing decision.[144] The court's sentencing powers are significantly restricted: it can impose bonds or limited fines, suspend sentencing for a period to allow a defendant to show good behaviour, impose a probation order or a custodial sentence in institutions operated by the Department of Community Welfare or its equivalent, or decide to record no offence or penalty. Probation is by far the most usual order in cases where some penalty is imposed. The court does not, with very limited exceptions, have power to commit a young offender to prison.

Appeals from children's courts tend to go in the same way as for the equivalent court of summary jurisdiction — in most cases to the Supreme Court, in Victoria to a County Court.[145]

In addition to their criminal jurisdiction, children's courts play an important role in the process of placing children under state control. In Victoria, the only way in which this may occur is by a children's court order; elsewhere, if the custodians of the child do not consent, a court hearing is necessary.[146] But the children's court retains supervisory power over custody, and may vary its terms or order the child's release. There is an appeal to the Supreme Court (in Victoria the County Court) from children's court orders in this protective jurisdiction. But the inherent wardship jurisdiction of the Supreme Court is not excluded.[147]

Children's courts exercise a variety of other functions: maintenance applications on behalf of state wards or generally, certain cases involving parents, offences by adults against young children, and so on. However, numerically and otherwise their criminal jurisdiction is the main part of their work.

(3) *Diversion of young offenders from judicial process*

It has been said that children's courts have had limited success in their reformative aims. Consequently the value of diverting children from judicial processes has gained a deal of acceptance. It is ironic that, the juvenile court having been established to avoid the stigma of criminal convictions, machinery now has to be devised to avoid the stigma of juvenile court convictions. In any case, the police have always had informal ways of diversion, through a 'warning' system and by decisions not to prosecute. In Scotland and in two Australian states, panels have been established (consisting, for example, of a police officer and a social welfare officer) to discuss a child's case with the child and his or her parents. Panels have no power to impose sanctions, though they may require a child to enter into an undertaking as to future conduct, breach of which may entail penalties or a children's court appearance for the original or subsequent offences. Appearance before a panel is voluntary, and depends on the child admitting the offence.[148] The Western Australian panel system is considerably more formal and limited than the South Australian one: the required admission of guilt is equivalent to a guilty plea, and there is an appeal to the children's court from a panel decision.[149]

Different views have been expressed as to the success of diversion through panel proceedings. The South Australian system is said to be working well, though it may be that it has only replaced the informal police warning system with a more formal procedure to the same effect.[150] Students of the evolution of juvenile justice may not be surprised that the panel system itself has been criticized for its 'coercive' elements and for involving children in the stigma of official proceedings against them.[151] It seems that the only thing the state can do is nothing!

(4) Young offenders and the ordinary courts

In all jurisdictions except the Northern Territory, children's courts have no power to determine a few most serious offences (e.g. homicide). In addition, in most jurisdictions, the defendant may elect trial by jury either for any indictable offence or in more limited cases, and the court itself has a discretion to refer the case to the appropriate higher court.[152] In South Australia, as a result of the recommendations of a 1977 Royal Commission, the Attorney-General may apply to the Supreme Court for an order that a young offender be tried in an adult court (and thus be liable to the appropriate adult penalty).[153] The 'adult' courts also have the sentencing powers of children's courts, including probation and admitting to state custody.

Where the Supreme Court or the intermediate criminal court has jurisdiction the children's court will act as the committing court under the procedures for committal discussed in Chapter 5.

Notes

1. Baker, 110–15, 391–410; Holdsworth, 1 HEL 580–632; Radcliffe & Cross, 229–41.
2. UK, *Report of the Committee on One-Parent Families* (1974, Cmnd 5629) (Finer Report) II, 92–6.
3. Finer Report, 86–8.
4. Finer Report, 152–201.
5. Currey (1955) 41 *JRAHS* 97.
6. Bennett, 143–52; Russell, 51–2, 167–8.
7. Quick & Garran, 608; cf. 610.
8. Finlay, *Family Law in Australia* (3rd edn, 1983) 14–18. The Act was sponsored by Attorney-General Barwick: see Marr, *Barwick* (1980) 141–6.
9. On these rules see Finlay & Bissett-Johnson, *Family Law in Australia* (1972) 345–84.

10 E.g. Finlay, 17–18; Finlay (1971) 4 *FLR* 287.
11 The Family Law Act 1975 (Cth) was sponsored by Attorney-General Murphy: Finlay, 16–17.
12 On the Family Court and the system of family law it administers see e.g. Australia, Joint Select Committee on the Family Law Act, *Family Law in Australia* (2 vols, Parl. Paper 1980/150–1); Broun, Fowler & Dickey, *Australian Family Law and Practice Reporter* (3 vols, 1982); Chisholm, Foreman & O'Ryan, *Australian Family Law* (3 vols, 1987); Dickey, *Family Law* (1985); Gamble, *Law for Parents and Children* (2nd edn, 1986) chs 2–4; Finlay, Bradbrook & Bailey-Harris, *Family Law. Cases and Commentary* (1986). Other general accounts of the Act include Gurvich, *For Better or Worse* (1983); Nygh, *Guide to the Family Law Act 1975* (4th edn, 1986).
13 Cf. Bates (1981) 55 *ALJ* 181.
14 (1976) 134 CLR 495; 9 ALR 103. Generally on s51(xxi) and (xxii) see Sackville & Howard (1970) 4 *FLR* 30; Lane, 191–214; Finlay, 47–98.
15 *A-G (Victoria) v Commonwealth* (1962) 107 CLR 529.
16 For Barwick CJ, s51(xxi) would not have extended to the enforcement of rights upon the breakdown of a marriage anyway, a distinction Mason J (delivering the leading judgment) found 'arbitrary': (1976) 9 ALR 103, 114, 137. But Quick & Garran, 609, adopted something like Barwick CJ's view.
17 (1976) 9 ALR 103, 140 (Mason J, with whom on these matters Stephen J agreed). Jacobs J took a broader view of s51(xxi) in this context: id., 146–7. In the result, Mason J's judgment was taken to be the judgment of the Court.
18 Id., 140 (Mason J; 148–9 (Jacobs J).
19 Id., 140 (Mason J) citing *Pidoto v Victoria* (1943) 68 CLR 87.
20 The Court in *R v Lambert ex p Plummer* (1981) 32 ALR 505 refused to reconsider *Russell*.
21 (1976) 9 ALR 103, 143–4, echoed by Murphy J in *Plummer* (1981) 32 ALR 505, 524, accusing the majority of reading the marriage power down 'to fit the interstices of state law'.
22 The ALR headnote has Jacobs J in the majority with Stephen & Mason JJ. The CLR headnote has him as a sole dissentient. But on no issue relevant to those matters in the two cases was Jacobs J in dissent. The ALR headnote is clearly right. But cf. *R v Lambert ex p Plummer* (1981) 32 ALR 505, 539 (Wilson J). On the closed court question, of course, Jacobs J did dissent.
23 E.g. Mason, Murphy & Deane JJ (and to a lesser extent Brennan J). There are differences between them: Murphy J's view was significantly wider (e.g. id., 522–6), as is Deane J's (e.g. *Re Cook; ex p Cook* (1985) 60 ALR 661, 668–73). Mason CJ is now tending to this broader view: e.g. *Re F, ex p F* (1986) 66 ALR 193, 203–4 (Mason, Deane JJ, dissenting).
24 Id., 539.
25 E.g. Wilson J who, having refused to re-examine *Russell's case*, proceeded to find Barwick CJ's views there 'helpful to a resolution of the present problem': id., 537, despite the fact that Barwick CJ's position in *Russell* was by far the most restrictive. And cf. Dawson J's comments in (1984) 14 *MULR* 353, 360–1.
26 *R v Lambert, ex p Plummer* (1981) 32 ALR 505, 512.

27 *Vitzdamm-Jones v Vitzdamm-Jones*; *St Clair v Nicholson* (1981) 33 ALR 537, 558–9.
28 *R v Lambert, ex p Plummer* (1981) 32 ALR 505, 511–13.
29 The most remarkable example is *Gazzo v Comptroller of Stamps (Vic.)* (1981) 38 ALR 25, where the majority upheld the right of a state to tax a party's compliance with a Family Court order. Cf. *Re Fisher* (1986) 67 ALR 513, 523, where Mason & Deane JJ described the decision as 'fundamentally unsound'. FLA s90 was amended in 1983 to undo as far as possible the damage done in *Gazzo*, and state tax exemptions were enacted as to the remaining issues: see Chisholm, Foreman & O'Ryan, 1635.
30 For comparative surveys see Glendon, *State, Law and Family* (1977); Eekelaar & Katz, *The Resolution of Family Conflict* (1984). On Canada see e.g. Baxter (1979) 29 *U Tor LJ* 199, Payne (1985) 4 *Can J Fam L* 355; Gifford (1985) 4 *Can J Fam L* 385; on the UK, Eekelaar, *Family Law and Social Policy* (2nd edn, 1984), Barnard, *The Family Court in Action* (1983), Scott (1986) 5 *Civil Justice Q* 8, Hoggett (1986) 6 *Leg St* 1; on the US, Fried & Walker (1985) 18 *Fam LQ* 389, (1986) 19 *Fam LQ* 331.
31 *Report on the Committee on One-Parent Families* (2 vols, 1974, Cmnd 5629) I, 173. But the Committee proposed their own version of a unified family court: id., 170–6. Similarly NZRCC, 146–85 (a particularly enthusiastic account); Canada LRC, WP 1, *The Family Court* (1974); *Report on Family Law* (1976) 7–12. The NZ proposals were implemented by Family Courts Act 1980; Family Proceedings Act 1980. See also Scott (1977) 8 *VUWLR* 436.
32 Family Law Bill 1973 (Cth) cl. 19.
33 Senate Standing Committee on Constitutional and Legal Affairs, *Report on . . . the Family Law Bill, 1974* (Parl. Paper 1974/133) 29; cf. 10–15. See also Finlay (1974) 9 *MULR* 567.
34 On the constitutional provisions for retirement of federal judges see Chapter 3. Another justification, perhaps more valid, for early retirement of Family Court judges is the 'wear and tear' of the jurisdiction: Family Law Council, *Administration of Family Law in Australia* (1985) 51–2 (hereafter *Administration of Family Law* (1985)).
35 FLA Part III, s62; *Family Law in Australia* I, 130–3, 164–84. Even at a compulsory conference under s62 there is no duty on a party to disclose facts: *R v Cook, ex p Twigg* (1980) 31 ALR 353.
36 See further Singer & Preston (1978) 52 *L Inst J* 175; Finlay, 28–32; Family Law Council, *Administration of Family Law in Australia* (1985) ch. 3.
37 *R v Watson, ex p Armstrong* (1976) 9 ALR 551, 560–1 (Barwick CJ, Gibbs, Stephen & Mason JJ). Jacobs J dissented, persuasively: cf. id., 589, 592. See also *R v Cook, ex p Twigg* (1980) 31 ALR 353; *Re JRL; ex p CRL* (1986) 66 ALR 239. And cf. *Re Winter* (1979) 23 ALR 211, 227 (Murphy J).
38 The 'wigs and gowns' provision (FLA s97(3)(4)) has been singularly divisive: see *Administration of Family Law* (1985) 27–34 (recommending no change).
39 FLA s97(1). See *Family Law in Australia* I, 157–63; and cf. Missen's dissent, id., 210–12. Generally see Wade (1978) 27 *ICLQ* 820.
40 FLA ss97(2), 121. See Chisholm, Foreman & O'Ryan, 1847–8.
41 *Penfold v Penfold* (1980) 28 ALR 213; Peterson (1980) 54 *ALJ* 269; *Family Law in Australia* I, 185–98. Section 117(2) (as amended in 1983) expressly

so provides. Cf. *Collins* (1985) 9 Fam LR 1123; Chisholm, Foreman & O'Ryan, 1828–35.
42 So far the Court has not even had general jurisdiction in the territories, although this will change, so far as the NT, the ACT, and Norfolk Island are concerned, when FLA s31(l)(c) (as amended in 1983) is proclaimed; cf. *Family Law in Australia* I, 145–7.
43 See Bailey (1984) 58 *ALJ* 369; Jessup & Chisholm (1987) 1 *AJ Fam L* 169.
44 See Finlay, 161–201; Dickey, chs 6–7. The grounds for nullity of a marriage are now contained in the Marriage Act 1961 (Cth) ss22–3.
45 Generally on custody disputes see Goodman (1976) 50 *ALJ* 644; Finlay, ch. 6; Broun & Fowler I, 13001–19451; *Family Law In Australia* I, 44–68; Dickey, ch. 13; Jessup & Chisholm (1985) 8 *UNSWLR* 152.
46 FLA s4(1) 'matrimonial cause' para. (c)(ii). The definition of 'child of a marriage' is in s5.
47 *Re Cormick, ex p Salmon* (1984) 56 ALR 245; *Re Cook, ex p C* (1985) 60 ALR 661. However, a narrower definition, based on '*de facto* adoption', might survive scrutiny: *Re F, ex p F* (1986) 66 ALR 193.
48 FLA s4(1), definition of 'matrimonial cause' para. (ce) (as amended in 1983). This provision was upheld in *V v V* (1985) 60 ALR 522. Cf. also *Fountain v Alexander* (1982) 40 ALR 441.
49 This was the result in *Vitzdamm-Jones v Vitzdamm-Jones*; *St Clair v Nicholson* (1981) 33 ALR 537 (where the Court split into different 4–3 majorities in the two cases).
50 Cf. *Re F, ex p F* (1986) 66 ALR 193, 199 (Gibbs CJ, referring to the 'lamentable results' of the case).
51 On separate representation see *Wotherspoon v Cooper* (1981) FLC 91-029; *Schmidt* (1979) 28 ALR 84; *Family Law in Australia* I, 50–2; Finlay, 253–6; Broun & Fowler I, 19003–24; Barblett (1980) 54 *ALJ* 489, 494–7; Kobienia (1978) 6 *Adel LR* 466, and for comparative perspectives, Stone, *The Child's Voice in the Court of Law* (1982); Giller & Maidment, in Eekelaar & Katz, 405; Lyon, in Freeman, ed., *Essays in Family Law 1985* (1986) 1.
52 A particular problem is that of custody in cross-cultural marriages, especially involving Aboriginal children: e.g. *Goudge* (1984) 54 ALR 514. The ALRC has recommended an 'Aboriginal child placement' principle to reflect the special needs of such children, and its view is reflected in some state and territory legislation: Community Welfare Act 1983 (NT) s69; Adoption Act 1984 (Vic.) s50. See ALRC 31, *The Recognition of Aboriginal Customary Laws* (1986) ch. 16; Gamble, ch. 12.
53 The classic critique of family court practice is Goldstein, Freud & Solnit, *Beyond the Best Interests of the Child* (1973). An Australian example of the 'weighing of interests' they condemn in *E v E (No. 2)* (1979) FLC 90645, and cf. *Raby* (1976) 27 FLR 412; *Waters* (1985) 8 *UNSWLR* 137.
54 *Smythe* (1983) 48 ALR 677.
55 FLA s72. See further ss73–7, 82–3; Finlay, 274–90; Broun and Fowler I, 20001–7592; *Family Law in Australia* I, 69–92.
56 *Soblusky* (1976) FLC 90-124; *Ferguson* (1978) FLC 90- 500.
57 FLA ss86–9. For the position before 1983 see *Perlman* (1984) 51 ALR 317. Legislation is planned to establish a national maintenance enforcement system, operating primarily through administrative means: see Aus-

tralia, Report of the National Maintenance Inquiry, *A Maintenance Agency for Australia* (1984).
[58] See ALRC 39, *Matrimonial Property* (1987), for a comprehensive discussion of the present position, and modest proposals for reform. See also *Family Law in Australia* I, 101–8; Hardingham & Neave, *Australian Family Property Law* (1984); Bailey (1980) 54 *ALJ* 190; Canada LRC, WP 8, *Family Property* (1975).
[59] Marriage Act 1958 (Vic.) s161; Finlay, 313–17; Hardingham & Neave, 264–75.
[60] Family Law Act 1975 (WA) s30; Hardingham & Neave, 275–8.
[61] However, there is state legislation establishing limited powers to vary property rights of *de facto* spouses: see NSWLRC 36, *De Facto Relationships* (1983); Hardingham & Neave, ch. 11.
[62] FLA s4(1) 'matrimonial cause' para. (ca)(i)–(iii). There is no reason to doubt the constitutionality of these provisions, although the interpretation of para. (ca)(i) remains an open question: see Dickey, 508–13.
[63] Cf. *Re Dovey, ex p Ross* (1979) 23 ALR 531.
[64] FLA s79(4)(b). Cf. *Rolfe* (1979) FLC 90-629.
[65] Cf. *Mullane* (1983) 45 ALR 291. On superannuation see *Bailey* (1978) 20 ALR 199; *Crapp* (1979) FLC 90-615; *Murkin* (1980) FLC 90-806; *Family Law in Australia* I, 95–7; Chisholm, Foreman & O'Ryan, 1479–83. On family companies and trusts, id., 1483–90; Palk & Bailey (1977) 6 *Adel LR* 131.
[66] Section 79(5), inserted in 1983, expressly allows an adjournment if there is likely to be a significant change in the circumstances of the parties 'in the reasonably near future'.
[67] *Ascot Investments Pty Ltd v Harper* (1981) 33 ALR 631.
[68] *R v Ross-Jones, ex p Beaumont* (1979) 23 ALR 179; *Re Ross-Jones, ex p Green* (1984) 56 ALR 609. On the position of third parties cf. *Re Dovey, ex p Ross* (1979) 23 ALR 531; *Sanders* (1967) 116 CLR 366; *Antonarkis v Delly* (1976) 51 ALJR 21. On sham transactions cf. *Abdullah* (1981) FLC 90-003.
[69] On the property jurisdiction see also Wade (1977) 5 *U Tas LR* 248; Walker (1979) 10 *FLR* 1; Broun & Fowler I, 30001–5062; Finlay, ch. 8; McCall, in *Family Law and Property. Three Essays* (1980) 1; Dickey, id., 53–85; Dickey, ch. 21; Kovacs (1983) 13 *FLR* 201; Kovacs (1985) 8 *UNSWLR* 21; Hardingham & Neave, chs 13–15.
[70] *Mallet* (1984) 52 ALR 193; *Norbis* (1986) 65 ALR 12.
[71] Cf. *Williams* (1985) 61 ALR 215. See also Goodman (1982) 13 *FLR* 131.
[72] *Re Prince* (1984) 54 ALR 467; *Re Ross-Jones, ex p Green* (1984) 56 ALR 609; *Re McKay* (1984) 59 ALR 117.
[73] (1986) 66 ALR 1. Approval under the NSW Act was necessary to prevent claims for family provision against the estate of a deceased spouse.
[74] Id., 14–18 (Gibbs CJ, Wilson, Dawson JJ). Mason, Brennan & Deane JJ left the point open: id., 27.
[75] Kovacs (1973) 47 *ALJ* 725, and (1974) 1 *Monash ULR* 67; *Family Law in Australia* I, 84–91, 147–55; Family Law Council, *Fourth Annual Report* (1980) 17–18.
[76] *In re Helliar* (1980) 28 ALR 604, 607. Cf. the disagreement between Barwick CJ and Murphy J on the point in *Ascot Investments Pty Ltd v Harper* (1981) 33 ALR 631, 636, 651–2.

77 Chesterman & Waters (1985) 8 *UNSWLR* 106; ALRC 35, *Contempt* (1987) chs 13–14.
78 Id., lix.
79 As recommended in *Family Law in Australia* I, 126–9.
80 FLA s22(2AA), (2AB).
81 *R v Ross-Jones, ex p Beaumont* (1979) 23 ALR 179; *R v Baker, ex p Johnston* (1980) 33 ALR 660.
82 E.g. *Re Ross-Jones, ex p Green* (1984) 56 ALR 609.
83 Family Law Council, *Annual Report 1984–85* (1986) contains the statistics, and also details 'serious problems' in collecting statistics under the Act: id., 69–70.
84 *Administration of Family Law* (1985) 35–45; *Family Law in Australia* I, 125–6.
85 *Family Law in Australia* I, 196–8; cf. Missen, id., 206, 209; Family Law Council (1980) 28–30; *Administration of Family Law* (1985) 88–92.
86 FLA ss14–19, 62–62A; Dickey, 79–82.
87 *Administration of Family Law* (1985) 59.
88 *Family Law in Australia* I, 131–4, 142–3, 179.
89 Ibid.; *Administration of Family Law* (1985) 57–8.
90 See e.g. the disagreement between the majority and minority of the High Court in *Re JRL, ex p CRL* (1986) 66 ALR 239.
91 *Administration of Family Law* (1985) 61.
92 Constitutional Commission, Australian Judicial System Committee, *Report* (1987) para. 3.139. For the Family Law Council's proposals see *Administration of Family Law* (1985) 612–13.
93 Truex (1984) 58 *Law Inst J* 1448; Greenwood & Hooper (1986) 11 *LSB* 77. Generally on conciliation in family law see Horwill (1983) 18 *Aust Psychologist* 39; Finlay (1983) 10 *Syd LR* 61; Davies & Bader (1985) 15 *Fam L* 42, 82; Kiel & Kingshott (1985) 10 *LSB* 2; Goodman (1986) 1 *AJ Fam L* 28.
94 Abrahams (1986) 1 *AJ Fam L* 67.
95 *R v Lambert ex p Plummer* (1981) 32 ALR 505.
96 In *Lambert* the Director-General had granted care of the child to the husband, but on certain conditions. The difficulty with the majority position was exposed in Stephen J's brilliant dissenting judgment: (1981) 32 ALR 505, 515–16. Section 10(3) was amended in 1983 to reflect the Court's decision.
97 Jurisdiction of Courts (Cross-vesting) Act 1987 (Cth) and counterpart state legislation. For the validity of the latter see Chapter 3.
98 Subject to the limited choice of law provisions in s11. The cross-vesting scheme is reciprocal, and since Family Law Act matters are not 'special federal matters' under s6, it will in theory allow dissolutions of marriage to be granted by Supreme Courts.
99 Commonwealth Powers (Family Law) Act 1986 (NSW), and similar Acts in SA, Victoria, and Tasmania.
100 Constitutional Convention, *Proceedings . . . Melbourne 1975*, 172; *Proceedings . . . Hobart 1976*, 203–4. The 1985 debate was inconclusive: *Proceedings . . . Brisbane 1985*, 170–204.
101 As pointed out by Crawford: see Judicature Sub-Committee, *Second Report* (1985) 15.
102 But see Constitutional Commission, Distribution of Powers Committee,

Report (1987) ch. 4 for discussion of possible amendments.
103 Gibbs (1985) 59 *ALJ* 522. For criticism of Gibbs' criticisms see Chisholm & Jessup (1985) 1 *Aust Fam L* 1. Other criticisms of the Court include Hutley (1987) 31 *Quadrant* 73.
104 Wade (1985) 8 *UNSWLR* 183. But cf. Evatt, id., vii.
105 For defences of the ideal see e.g. Nygh (1985) 8 *UNSWLR* 62; Fogarty, id., 204; Finlay (1985) 59 *ALJ* 559. See also Sackville (1978) 27 *ICLQ* 127; Davies & Fowler, in *Proceedings and Papers of the Fifth Commonwealth Law Conference* (1977) 531; Evatt, id., 321.
106 A term invented for present purposes by the Constitutional Commission, Australian Judicial System Committee, *Report* (1987) para. 3.137, 3.140. For the Attorney-General's announcement see id., para. 3.138.
107 FLA s37A (inserted in 1983) already provides for extensive delegation to registrars: see O'Ryan (1986) 1 *AJ Fam L* 78.
108 See Jupp, in *Family Law in Australia* II, 22 and the different assessments of it in the Report: I, 27–43, and the Martyr dissent: id., 223–7 (the only thoroughgoing dissent from the principles of the 1975 Act).
109 See the discussion of various suggested options by the Constitutional Commission, Australian Judicial System Committee, *Report* (1987) para. 3.117–141.
110 See Dickey & Davis, *Annotated Family Court Act and Regulations of Western Australia* (1980); Finlay, 91–5; Dickey, 89–91. For the agreement between the Commonwealth and WA for the establishment of the Court see Dickey & Davis, 135–9. The agreement is terminable on 12 months' notice: Art. 19.
111 Family Court Act 1975 (WA) s27(2) & (3); Adoption of Children Act 1896 (WA) ss2, 3.
112 Family Court Act 1975 (WA) s82; cf. also Legal Representation of Infants Act 1977 (WA) s3(c).
113 *Family Law in Australia* I, 131, 179; Family Law Council (1980) 14–15.
114 Family Court Act 1975 (WA) ss23, 74–5. On the Court's jurisdiction over interstate cases see *Allison* (1981) 1 SR (WA) 248.
115 Id., s80 (federal jurisdiction), s81 (non-federal jurisdiction).
116 *Family Law in Australia* I, 17–20 (proposing as one possibility joint federal and state commissions for Family Court judges: cf. id., II, 88–90). Cf. *Hudina* (1981) 7 Fam LR 654.
117 See CCH, *Australian State Family Law Legislation* (2 vols, 1986).
118 Hardingham & Neave, 279–82.
119 For the closely analogous English jurisdiction see Lowe & White, *Wards of Court* (1979).
120 But the wardship jurisdiction cannot be used as a backdoor way of obtaining custody: *Fountain v Alexander* (1982) 40 ALR 441, and this rule has been strengthened by the addition in 1983 of para. (ce)–(ch) of the definition of 'matrimonial cause' in FLA s4(1). See also McKay (1981) 55 *ALJ* 227. There is express provision in WA: Family Court Act 1975 (WA) s85, but the Supreme Court's wardship jurisdiction is probably not excluded: Dickey & Davis, 40–1.
121 Adoption of Children Ordinance 1965 (ACT) s7; Adoption of Children Act 1967 (NT) s7.
122 Adoption of Children Act 1965 ss6, 8 (NSW); Adoption of Children Act 1967 (SA) s5 (the court of summary jurisdiction is to consist of a magistrate

and 2 JPs (at least one a woman)); Adoption of Children Act 1968 (Tas.) s4 (magistrate); Adoption Act 1984 (Vic.) s6(1) (Supreme Court or County Court at applicant's option).

[123] Adoption of Children Act 1964 (Qld) s7. Generally on adoption in Australia see Finlay, ch. 10; Dickey, ch. 16.

[124] FLA ss39(2), (6), (7), 46, 47. The only proclamation excluding the jurisdiction of courts of summary jurisdiction has been made in respect of the Perth metropolitan area, where the Family Court of Western Australia, or its registrar, acts.

[125] *Family Law In Australia* I, 147–55.

[126] Id., 154–5, but cf. Missen's criticisms: id., 207–8. On the constitutional problems cf. id., II, 91–3.

[127] McGregor & Bailey (1978) 6 *Adel LR* 44. Eekelaar (1973) 7 *Fam LQ* 381.

[128] *Carseldine v Director of Children's Services* (1974) 48 ALJR 344; *Johnson v Director-General of Social Welfare (Victoria)* (1976) 135 CLR 92; but cf. *Minister for the Interior v Neyens* (1965) 113 CLR 411, where the resumption was rebutted.

[129] Both the SA Royal Commissioner and the ALRC recommended against giving criminal jurisdiction to a larger family court: *Report . . . into the Administration of the Juvenile Courts Act . . . Pt II* (1977) 16; ALRC 18, *Child Welfare* (1981) para. 307–11. The New Zealand Royal Commission, by contrast, was enthusiastic about the idea: NZRCC, 158–60, and cf. Gordon (1975) 14 *J Fam L* 1. Not even the Family Court of Western Australia has this expanded jurisdiction, but cf. Family Court Act 1975 (WA) s27(3) (a limited addition).

[130] McNiff, *Guide to Children's Courts Practice in Victoria* (1979) 72–3.

[131] A good account is Parker (1976) 26 *U Tor LJ* 140.

[132] On the UK see Bottoms, McLean & Patchett [1970] *Crim LR* 368, Burney, *Sentencing Young People* (1985); on Canada, Fox (1977) 26 *ICLQ* 445; generally, Ketcham (1966) 6 *J Fam L* 191; Morris & Giller, eds, *Providing Criminal Justice for Children* (1983); Pratt (1986) 25 *How J Crim Jus* 33. The best articulation of the newer ideas is the US Juvenile Justice Standards Project: Morris [1978] *Crim LR* 529. And see ALRC 18, ch. 5.

[133] *Kent v US* 383 US 541 (1966); *In re Gault* 387 US 1, 12–31 (1966) (the leading case); *In re Winship* 397 US 358 (1970); *Breed v Jones* 421 US 519 (1975). But jury trial is not required: *McKeiver v Pennsylvania* 403 US 528 (1971), and pre-trial detention is permissible under certain safeguards: *Schall v Martin* 52 USLW 4681 (1984).

[134] Such euphemisms still exist in some Australian Acts: e.g. Child Welfare Act 1960 (Tas.) s4. Cf. *J v Lieschke* (1987) 69 ALR 647, 658 (Deane J).

[135] Lemert, *Instead of Court. Diversion in Juvenile Justice* (1971) 15. See also Ryerson, *The Best-Laid Plans. America's Juvenile Court Experiment* (1978); Stamm (1979) 4 *LSB* 51; Shireman & Reamer, *Rehabilitating Juvenile Justice* (1986); Krisberg, Schwartz, Laitsky & Austin (1986) 32 *Crim & Del* 5. Defenders of the original ideal include Nicholas (1961) 1 *J Fam L* 151; Hahn, *The Juvenile Offender and the Law* (2nd edn, 1978) 277–335.

[136] See e.g. *J v Lieschke* (1987) 69 ALR 647 (parent's right to be heard in 'neglect' proceedings against child not excluded by NSW Act).

[137] In SA the Juvenile Courts Act 1971, itself regarded as 'progressive', was replaced by the Children's Protection and Young Offenders Act 1979,

following a Royal Commission Report substantially influenced by the idea of due process and diversion. See Seymour, *Juvenile Justice in South Australia* (1983); Bailey (1984) 9 *Adel LR* 325. For a defence of the old Juvenile Courts see SA, *Eighth Annual Report on the Administration of the Juvenile Courts Act* . . . (1979) 10–17.

[138] ACT: Children's Services Ordinance 1986 s20 (Children's Court); NSW: Child Welfare Act 1960 s13 (Children's Courts) (to be replaced by Children's Court of NSW when Children's Court Act 1987 (NSW) is proclaimed); NT: Community Welfare Act 1983 s24 (Family Matters Court); Queensland: Children's Services Act 1965 ss18–20 (children's courts); SA: Children's Protection and Young Offenders Act 1979 ss8–11 (Children's Court); Tasmania: Child Welfare Act 1960 s13(3)–(5A) (children's courts); Victoria: Children's Court Act 1973 ss5, 6 (Children's Court); WA: Child Welfare Act 1947 s19 (children's courts). On the Tasmanian courts see Cairns (1975) 49 *ALJ* 275; on the Victorian Court, McNiff; Hiller & Hancock, in Tomasic, ed., *Legislation and Society in Australia* (1980) 299. For proposed reforms in Queensland see O'Connor (1985) 10 *LSB* 76.

[139] ACT, s20; Tasmania, s13(1).

[140] SA, ss8(2), 20(2).

[141] E.g. SA, s92(2) (right of media representatives to attend), but cf. s92(1) (no right to publish information identifying child); WA, ss126–126B.

[142] The only specific provision is Victoria, s20.

[143] Stamm (1979) 4 *LSB* 51. One proposal to remedy this is the creation of a Youth Advocate: cf. NZRCC, 170–1; ALRC 18, 241–53. See ACT ss9–12.

[144] Gamble (1976) 9 *ANZJ Crim* 197; Cairns (1975) 49 *ALJ* 621; ALRC 18, 121–3. Generally on the role of social workers here see Parker, ed., *Social Work and the Courts* (1979).

[145] ACT, s144; NSW, s18; NT, s50; Queensland, s21(2)(b); SA, ss76–7, 80; Tasmania, s13(1); Victoria, s52(1); WA, s19(6). Cf. *Ross v R* (1979) 25 ALR 137.

[146] Victoria, s14(d); cf. Community Welfare Services Act 1970 (Vic.) ss31, 34, 35, 104. Uniquely, this Act provides an Appeal Tribunal to hear appeals against decisions of the Director-General 'in any case-planning matter' relating to a child in Departmental care where there is no appeal to a court: s200B. The Children (Care and Protection) Act 1987 (NSW) Part 8 will establish a Community Welfare Appeal Tribunal to hear appeals from certain decisions under the Act.

[147] Cf. Qld, s102.

[148] On the value of diversion see ALRC 18, 76–89; Canada LRC, WP No. 7, *Diversion* (1975). On the Scottish system cf. Morris (1976) 15 *Howard J Pen* 26; Aubrey [1965] *Crim LR* 641. Panels were introduced in SA by the Juvenile Courts Act 1971 ss11–14, and expanded by the Children's Protection and Young Offenders Act 1979 (SA) to cover all offences except homicide, motor vehicle offences, and truancy: ss25–30 (Screening Panels), ss32–8 (Children's Aid Panels). See Seymour, chs 3–4. Panels were introduced in WA in 1976: Child Welfare Act 1947 ss70–8.

[149] WA, ss75–6. The system applies only to certain first offenders: ss70(2), 72.

150 Extension of the panel system was recommended by the 1977 Royal Commission, which stated that the 'overwhelming weight of evidence' favoured the panels: *Report*, 19–23. On balance, this verdict of Sarri & Bradley (1980) 26 *Crim & Del* 42 is also favourable; and cf. Sarri, in Morris & Giller, 52. Panel systems have been proposed for NZ: NZRCC, 182–3, NSW: Department of Youth and Community Services, Children's Courts Project Team, *Review of the Child Welfare Act 1939* (1974) 6–12, and the ACT: ALRC 18, 79–89. The Community Welfare Act 1982 (NSW) ss130–1 provided for a system of Children's Panels, but was never proclaimed. It will be superseded by the Children (Criminal Proceedings) Act 1987 (NSW), which adopts a more punitive attitude to young offenders.
151 E.g. Gamble (1976) 50 *ALJ* 68. Cf. Sarri & Bradley, 59–62; Fox, 461–2; Morris, 265; ALRC 18, 78–9. The ALRC's recommendation for a panel system was not adopted in the Children's Services Ordinance 1986 (ACT).
152 E.g. Victoria, s15(1), (3).
153 SA, s47; *In re Szekely* (1980) 25 SASR 112.

CHAPTER 11

Industrial Courts and Commissions

11.1 The History of Industrial Jurisdictions in Australia

The movement to specialized family jurisdictions is common to many parts of the world: by contrast, the various industrial jurisdictions which have existed in Australia throughout this century are unique. In no other comparable country, except New Zealand, is there formal legal machinery for determining the terms and conditions of employment, as distinct from enforcing terms and conditions agreed on by employees and employers through negotiation and direct action (collective bargaining). Within Australia, too, there is no system of specialist tribunals which shares the complexity, the coverage, or the importance of the industrial tribunals. In their effects on the everyday life of Australian workers they are much more important than the 'ordinary' courts. They are widely regarded as maintaining minimum living standards for many employees who would lack bargaining power in a system of collective bargaining. They certainly maintain many a small or 'weak' union, functioning not through direct action but as an administrative agent of the system.[1]

If the industrial tribunals support union weakness, they had their origins in such weakness (and, perhaps conversely, are themselves at their weakest in times of union strength, with labour shortages and full employment). The crushing defeat of the maritime and shearers strikes in the 1890s, both in Australia and New Zealand, led to the substitution of legal forms for direct action. Higgins called it 'a new province for law and order':

The process of conciliation, with arbitration in the background, is substituted for the rude and barbarous processes of strike and lock-out. Reason is to displace force: the might of the State is to enforce peace between industrial combatants as well as between other combatants; and all in the interest of the public.[2]

An Arbitration Court was established in New Zealand for the conciliation and arbitration of industrial disputes in 1894. At first the Australian colonies attempted forms of voluntary conciliation, but employers would not co-operate and voluntarism failed.[3] The immediate impulse of the wages boards, first established in Victoria in 1896, was 'sweated' labour in certain industries.[4] Employer participation was compelled, but once convened wages boards operated primarily through negotiation between the employer and employee representatives: the independent chairman could not impose a settlement, but could only resolve deadlock by voting for one position or the other. More formal, autonomous arbitration systems were established in New South Wales in 1901, the Commonwealth in 1904, Western Australia, Queensland, and South Australia in 1912 (in the last three cases, replacing earlier wages board systems). Only Tasmania, in 1910, followed Victoria in establishing and maintaining wages boards.

Despite many alterations and additions the structures of conciliation and arbitration so established remain broadly similar today. The complexities of the seven systems, and the various alternative tribunals for particular industries, cannot be described in detail here.[5] Moreover the federal industrial system has been the subject of a major review, and although the basic structure is likely to be retained, many particular changes have been foreshadowed.[6] What follows is only an outline of the federal arbitration structure, of the industrial tribunals of the states and territories, and of their relations to each other and to the ordinary courts.

11.2 The Federal System of Conciliation and Arbitration

Throughout the federal Constitutional Conventions in the 1890s, the proposal to give the Commonwealth power to establish industrial tribunals was controversial. After earlier rejections Higgins' proposal was narrowly accepted, at the last moment, in 1898.[7] Thus the new Commonwealth could legislate for 'conciliation and arbitration for the prevention and settlement of industrial disputes extending beyond the limits of any one state' (Constitution, s51(xxxv)).

(1) The ambit of federal industrial power
This apparently limited power, inserted to deal with Australia-wide conflicts such as the strikes of the 1890s, turned out to be much wider than even its supporters hoped. The apparently restrictive requirements of a 'dispute' 'extending beyond' a state have largely been

reduced to formalities, readily satisfied. The less obviously restrictive terms 'conciliation and arbitration', and especially 'industrial', have caused much more trouble. Each of these problems should be briefly referred to.[8]

The requirement of a 'dispute' is usually met by one party making a demand against the other which is not accepted. In practice, claims are usually made by unions on behalf of their members (and sometimes non-members) against employers or employer association, or by employers or employer associations against unions in respect of their members.[9] There is no need for direct industrial action (e.g. strikes) to exist or be threatened: the demand and its rejection are enough.[10] Hence the term 'paper dispute': the 'log of claims' which initiates the dispute is well named, since so much paper is required to serve each of the employers and employers associations sought to be bound. For the requirement of a dispute between parties prevents the resulting award being made a 'common rule' for the industry; it can, with minor exceptions, bind only the parties to it (including members of the associations bound).[11] Moreover the Commonwealth can legislate only for 'conciliation and arbitration': this has been taken to exclude forms of settlement not achieved by third-party intervention, and prevents s51(xxxv) being used to enforce agreements reached through direct collective bargaining.[12]

In a rather similar way to the creation of 'disputes', their extension beyond a single state can be achieved by making and refusing demands. There is no requirement, for example, that the employers in different states should have anything in common, beyond being in the same industry with respect to the demands made. Once an award has been made, disputes under it (within its 'ambit') can be dealt with by variation or amendment, without the need to create a fresh interstate dispute, because they derive from the original dispute and its settlement.[13] On the other hand, a sympathy strike in one state over a dispute in another is not a single interstate dispute; the interstate aspect of the dispute must be a 'genuine' one.[14]

Historically the most significant restrictions in s51(xxxv) have related to the requirement that the dispute be an 'industrial' one. From 1929 onwards the High Court took the view that this required the dispute to be in an 'industry', and it has also tended to take a strict view of what is an 'industry' for this purpose. Thus state schoolteachers, university teachers, firemen, and clerical staff engaged in government administration were all held not to be employed in industry.[15] At length the Court, in *R v Coldham, ex p Australian Social Welfare Union*, adopted a much broader approach, one better suited to an economy with a growing 'tertiary' sector (clerical work, education, entertainment, and service industries).[16] The only requirement is that the dispute have an industrial character, broadly defined to include 'every kind of dispute between master and workman in relation to any kind of labour'.[17] Accordingly schoolteachers, social workers, and administrative employees generally are now within the scope of the power.[18]

In the light of this broader approach it remains to be seen how many of the earlier restrictions imposed by reference to the concept of an 'industrial' dispute will survive. No doubt it is still the case that general political and social issues cannot be arbitrated, since the employer has no power to grant what is demanded. But the earlier decisions extend far beyond this obvious point. The opening and closing hours of shops (as distinct from the working hours of shop employees),[19] the deduction of union dues from employees' pay,[20] disputes over the employment of independent contractors,[21] the reinstatement of validly dismissed employees (since dismissal terminates the industrial relation)[22] were all held not to be industrial. The absurd technicality of much of the case-law is demonstrated by the one-man bus cases, where exactly the same demand was twice held not to be industrial, then held industrial when differently formulated.[23] The doctrine of 'managerial prerogatives', reflected in many of these decisions, is questionable in principle, since there is no express reservation of management issues in s51(xxxv). It is likely that the High Court will take a broader view of these questions, as it has already done, since *Coldham's case*, in holding disputes over superannuation,[24] unfair dismissal,[25] and consultation with employees over the effects of technological change[26] all to be 'industrial'.

Despite the broader interpretation of s51(xxxv) now adopted, there remain limitations on Commonwealth power. These can be overcome, in part at least, in a variety of ways.[27] The most significant is through co-operation between federal and state industrial authorities. But the Commonwealth itself may be able to expand the Commission's jurisdiction by using its legislative powers over the Commonwealth public service, or employees engaged in interstate or overseas trade, or within a territory. A further source of power, which could be of great significance, is the corporations power (s51(xx)), presently little used.[28]

The Commission is not necessarily restricted in practice by limits on its jurisdiction. It can make recommendations to the parties on other matters, and quite often acts as a 'private' arbitrator, by agreement — for example in reinstatement disputes.[29]

(2) The Australian Conciliation and Arbitration Commission

The federal arbitration system was established soon after federation, in 1904. The Commonwealth Court of Conciliation and Arbitration, the principal organ, was presided over by a High Court judge until the 1920s, and thereafter by judges specially appointed.[30] But in the *Boilermakers' case* in 1956 the High Court held that the Court could not exercise both the 'quasi-legislative' function of making awards and the judicial functions of interpreting and enforcing them.[31] Two new bodies resulted: to exercise the non-judicial power of conciliation and arbitration, the Australian Conciliation and Arbitration Commission (as it is now called), and the Australian Industrial Court, for the strictly judicial functions. Since 1977 the Industrial Court has been replaced by the Industrial Division of the Federal Court.[32]

The Commission is the most important industrial tribunal in Australia. Its basic function is 'to prevent or settle industrial disputes by conciliation or arbitration' (s18). Through conciliation it can assist the parties to settle their disputes by an agreement which will, when certified, take effect in the same way as an award.[33] Through arbitration it can make awards binding on the parties as to their industrial conditions (hours, pay, work conditions, leave, etc.).[34] In 1974 about 40 per cent of all employees were covered by federal awards: that figure declined to 34.7 per cent in 1983.[35] But the effect of the Commission's decisions is more extensive than this, since in major matters at least its decisions are followed by state authorities ('flow- on' into state awards).[36]

The Commission consists of a president with legal qualifications, deputy presidents who must have legal, industrial, or similar qualifications (in practice, most are industrial lawyers), and commissioners.[37] Presidential members have judicial tenure, but commissioners also have considerable security of tenure.[38] Members of the Commission specialize in particular industries or areas by assignment to one of eight panels, under a deputy president. There is provision for consultation with the deputy president before a commissioner acts in respect of a dispute covered by that panel.[39]

An important distinction exists in the Commission's work between particular disputes and matters of more general concern. The former are usually dealt with by single commissioners or presidential members, and the emphasis is on conciliation and informality — what has been termed 'accommodative arbitration'.[40] On the other hand, certain questions of standard hours of work or pay are required to be decided by a Full Bench (of at least three members including at least two presidential members).[41] This is particularly true of the periodic national wage cases which, though in form related to a particular dispute before the Commission, in practice lay down general principles to guide the Commission (and state tribunals) in all wage-fixing claims. The gap between appearance and reality, common in the field of industrial arbitration by legal process, is particularly evident here. Indeed, the point is very nearly conceded by s31 of the Act, which defines as an exclusively Full Bench matter the making of an award

> making provision for, or altering, rates of wages . . . on grounds predominantly related to the national economy and without examination of any circumstance pertaining to the work . . . or the industry

which is the subject of the dispute. In such cases the Commission settles particular disputes on macroeconomic grounds, without regard to the facts of the case! As Gibbs CJ put it in one case, 'the Commission stands in a special position not directly comparable with that or other administrative or quasi-judicial tribunals'.[42]

Under s51(xxxv) of the Constitution, the Parliament is restricted to providing machinery for conciliation and arbitration of disputes and is therefore restricted in the extent to which it can require the Commission to act on fixed principles. Certain substantive rules are contained in the Act (e.g. forbidding award payments to persons on strike[43]), but in general the Commission is free to establish its own guidelines (e.g. the wage indexation guidelines in effect from 1975 to 1981 and again since 1983).[44] These general principles are, in the first instance, Full Bench matters under s31.

The Commission also hears appeals by leave from determinations of single members, references by the president, and applications by the minister for review.[45] Both the president and the minister have wide powers to intervene on 'public interest' grounds, thus reinforcing the tendency to uniformity flowing from Full Bench decisions. To this extent the economic implications of the Commission's decisions override any special industrial relations elements.

(3) The Federal Court of Australia (Industrial Division)

The establishment of the Federal Court was described in Chapter 8. The Industrial Division has taken over the 'industrial' jurisdiction of the Australian Industrial Court, although the latter retains a residual jurisdiction over matters already commenced there.

The Industrial Division has exclusive jurisdiction over the more important civil, criminal, and supervisory matters arising under the Conciliation and Arbitration Act 1904 (Cth) and related Acts. Most of the original jurisdiction of the Court is exercised by a single judge: these matters include prosecutions for breach of the Act (ss5, 191), injunctions to restrain such breaches (s109(1)(b)), civil proceedings to recover penalties for breach of an award or to recover wages due under an award (ss119, 123), proceedings for the interpretation of an award (s110), inquiries into disputed union elections (s158P and Part IX), a wide variety of powers relating to the internal affairs of organizations (membership disputes and the like), and proceedings for contempt (including failure to comply with 'bans clauses' and other orders under s109(1)(b)).[46] Unlike the position before 1978, there is an appeal to the Full Court under s24 of the Federal Court of Australia Act 1976 (Cth) in almost all matters.[47]

The Full Federal Court (Industrial Division) has original jurisdiction in a few of the more important matters: references by the Commission or the Registrar on questions of law (ss107, 112), declarations of the invalidity of a state law or award for inconsistency with a federal award (s108), and applications for deregistration of an organisation, which is one of the 'sanctions' for union non-compliance with the Act or an award (s143).[48] The long-standing policy that most of these questions be decided finally by the Industrial Court is maintained. The only provision in the Full Court's original jurisdiction under which appeals to the High Court are permitted is s108 (conflict with state law or awards).[49]

The Full Court's original jurisdiction has been reduced but its appellate jurisdiction is considerably expanded. It hears appeals from state courts (other than Supreme Courts) and territory courts exercising jurisdiction under the Act, to the exclusion of any other court (s113). It also has, as has been noted, general appellate jurisdiction from decisions of a single judge of the Court. Since this jurisdiction is conferred by the Federal Court of Australia Act 1976 (Cth), it does not extend to an appeal from acquittal on the merits, unlike the appeal under s113 from state and territory courts, which is quite general.[50] A single judge of the Court may also refer a question to the Full Bench in any case (s118C).

Appeals from the Industrial Division to the High Court are by leave of the High Court only, and are substantially restricted: they include appeals from prosecutions and civil proceedings for penalties or wages.[51] In practice the High Court's review jurisdiction under s75(v) of the Constitution is more important.

In general the Federal Court's jurisdiction under the Act is exclusive, but in a number of respects state and territory courts share enforcement and recovery functions, in particular through industrial magistrates exercising federal jurisdiction.[52]

(4) Other federal industrial forums

On a number of occasions in its history, the Commission's jurisdiction has been challenged by groups seeking improved conditions through special arrangements. A special tribunal may not feel that same responsibility for wage uniformity as the Commission, and may therefore be more favourable to exceptional claims. On the other hand a special tribunal may help to insulate other awards from the flow-on effects of concessions to powerful groups. In 1920 the establishment of special tribunals for the Commonwealth public service and certain strategic industries forced the resignation of Higgins, the Arbitration Court judge.[53] A number of special tribunals still exist, but recent amendments have tended to bind them back in to the general wage-fixing structure of the Commission: this is true, for example, of the Flight Crew Officers Industrial Tribunal.[54] In the case of the Commonwealth public service, earlier special provisions were repealed in 1983, and public servants are now within the jurisdiction of the Australian Commission.[55] In other cases — Commonwealth statutory corporations, the maritime and stevedoring industries and the Snowy Mountains Authority — the Commission retains direct extended authority under other constitutional powers.[56]

11.3 Industrial Regulation in the States and Territories

As we have seen, there are important differences between the states in the provision of industrial tribunals. Historically, these differences were represented by four states with formal arbitration systems and two (Victoria and Tasmania) with wages or industrial boards. However, the arbitration systems have marked differences between themselves, and as a result of new industrial legislation in Victoria (1979) and Tasmania (1984) the distinction has virtually disappeared. In Victoria the Industrial Relations Act 1979 (Vic.) replaced Wages Boards with a combination of an Industrial Relations Commission and Conciliation and Arbitration Boards. The new machinery — which implemented a Report of a Committee of Review in 1976 — adopts features of both the Industrial Board and the arbitral systems.[57] Tasmania has gone even further to a centralized system, with an Industrial Commission exercising both arbitral and judicial powers.[58] In New South Wales and South Australia, conciliation committees continue to exist, although subject (in the same way as the Victorian Conciliation and Arbitration Boards) to the overriding powers of the Commission or Court.

Accounts of Australian industrial arbitration often ignore or minimize the importance of the state machinery. In the field of general wage policy, state tribunals have almost always followed the guidelines of the Australian Commission, especially since 1975. Here the influence of the Commonwealth system has been paramount. But state machinery has still been essential to ensure conformity with the Australian Commission's principles, and to bring about (however automatically) a general flow-on to state awards. In other areas of hours and conditions of work, reinstatement and grievance procedures, the state systems have had an independent role. Again, only a brief account is possible.

The states are almost entirely free of the troublesome constitutional restrictions which dictate the formal structure of Commonwealth arbitration. This is as true of the separation of judicial power (which is not a requirement under state constitutions) as of the limits which have been read into s51(xxxv). Three states (Queensland in 1961, Western Australia in 1963, South Australia in 1966) followed the Commonwealth in separating Industrial Commission functions from those of the Industrial Court,[59] but in no state is the demarcation of powers the same. Indeed, the tendency in the more recent legislation has been to give the Commissions overtly judicial power. For example, the Western Australian Industrial Appeal Court hears appeals and references on questions of law or jurisdiction, but the Western Australian Industrial Relations Commission has general power to interpret and enforce awards.[60] Under the Victorian Act, the president sits alone as the Commissioner in Court Session to hear appeals from magistrates' courts and other matters. In the Commission in full session (which hears, among other things, appeals from decisions of Boards, and applications for the interpretation of awards and agreements) all decisions on questions of law are taken by the president alone.[61] In Queensland the Industrial Conciliation and Arbitration Commission, composed of persons with industrial rather than legal qualifications, can interpret awards and hear certain appeals from industrial magistrates. The Industrial Court's jurisdiction is restricted to criminal, appellate, and supervisory matters.[62] South Australia has a more 'orthodox' distribution of functions, but the members of the Industrial Court are also members of the Industrial Commission: the distinction between their function is thus largely formal.[63]

On the other hand, New South Wales, Victoria, and Tasmania have no separate Industrial Court. In each state the Commission exercises both arbitral and judicial power, with many of the 'court' functions given to the Commission in Court Session (New South Wales, Victoria) or to the Full Commission (Tasmania).[64]

(1) State industrial commissions

Whatever their judicial powers, three of the Commissions are declared to be 'a court of record' (the New South Wales Commission 'a superior court of record'). Members, whether or not legally qualified, have judicial tenure similar to that of Supreme Court judges.[65]

Their jurisdictions are considerably more comprehensive than is that of the Australian Commission. The term 'industrial' is widely defined in each Act, and there is no requirement of a 'dispute'. Commission awards are, or may be made, a common rule.[66] Jurisdiction is extended in a number of other ways. For example, under the Western Australian Act, the Commission in Court Session may declare non-industrial matters to be within jurisdiction if this is consistent with the Act and otherwise desirable. That decision is conclusive, and can only be appealed to the Full Bench of the Commission or the Industrial Appeal Court. One purpose was to allow the Commission to deal with the provision of services (such as electricity or water) in 'company towns'.[67]

In New South Wales the Commission's jurisdiction is extended to certain 'deemed employees', who are formally independent contractors and therefore outside the normal definition of 'industrial' power. This avoids the difficult problem of determining whether a person (e.g. an insurance salesman) is an employee or an independent contractor.[68] The New South Wales and Western Australian Commissions also exercise power to deal with reinstatement of dismissed employees, a major source of disputes. A similar jurisdiction is exercised by the South Australian Industrial Court.[69]

Much of the work of the state commissions involves specific grievances or disputes, which are dealt with by single commissioners or by committees or boards of reference.[70] But the same distinction exists between individual claims and questions of general application as in the federal sphere, and indeed the state Acts are able to emphasize the distinction more clearly, not being confined to the determination of 'disputes'. Thus the Commission in Court Session or its equivalent has the power to issue general determinations of wages and hours which operate across all state awards. In each state, the full Commission has appellate jurisdiction from decisions of single commissioners, committees (in some cases), industrial magistrates, and the registrar, as well as powers relating to registration of unions and the conduct of union affairs.[71]

(2) Conciliation committees and other tribunals

In New South Wales, Victoria, and South Australia the Commission's jurisdiction is complemented by that of Conciliation Committees (in Victoria, Conciliation and Arbitration Boards), with an equal number of employer and employee representatives and a commissioner as chairman. If a Committee cannot agree the chairman has all the powers of the Commission, and is not confined to the proposals of the representative parties.[72] There is a general appeal from committees to the Commission. In practice, committees operate as a forum for registering awards by consent, within the constraints imposed by the 'general economic principles' of the Commission.[73]

In addition to the several hundred Conciliation Committees, the NSW Act provides for various other tribunals, for example, a Retail Trade Industrial Tribunal.[74]

(3) Industrial courts

Powers to determine the validity of awards or orders and to enforce awards is vested in the Industrial Court in South Australia and Queensland, although minor enforcement matters are dealt with by industrial magistrates.[75] The South Australian Court has the most extensive range of powers, but, as we have seen, formal separation is countered by shared personnel. In Western Australia the Industrial Appeal Court has now no original jurisdiction but hears appeals from the Commission on questions of law or jurisdiction.[76]

The Queensland and Western Australian Courts have a status equivalent to that of the Supreme Court. The Western Australian Court is composed of Supreme Court judges and the president of the Queensland Court is also a Supreme Court judge. The point is to exclude the Supreme Court's supervisory jurisdiction over industrial tribunals, a result achieved in part by provisions excluding Supreme

Court jurisdiction, and in Queensland also by the novel device of investing the Industrial Court with

> all the powers and jurisdiction of the Supreme Court for the purpose of ensuring . . . that the Commission and all industrial magistrates properly exercise and do not exercise their jurisdiction under . . . this Act.[77]

It is easier to prevent Supreme Court intervention if the persons exercising the excluded jurisdiction are themselves Supreme Court judges in another guise!

(4) Industrial regulation in the territories

Although separate industrial jurisdictions could be established for the territories, in fact the Conciliation and Arbitration Act 1904 (Cth) has been specifically extended to them. Neither the requirement of 'interstateness' nor that of an 'industry' applies to the Act in its application to the territories. The Commission is specifically empowered to declare a common rule for an industry.[78]

(5) Industrial magistrates

In all jurisdictions, minor penal proceedings for breach of awards, and actions to recover wages or other sums due under awards, are brought either before the ordinary magistrates courts or before industrial magistrates, who are magistrates either acting as such or appointed as industrial magistrates by or under the relevant Act.[79] Appeals from their decisions lie exclusively to the Industrial Court or Commission. In Victoria the Metropolitan Industrial Court (within the Melbourne area) and magistrates outside it exercise minor civil and criminal jurisdiction, with appeals going only to the Industrial Relations Commission in Court Session.[80] State industrial magistrates, and other state courts, have federal jurisdiction in a similar range of matters under the Commonwealth Act.[81]

11.4 The Future of Industrial Arbitration

Since the introduction of compulsory industrial arbitration in its various forms in the 1890s, there has rarely been a time when the industrial tribunals have not been a subject of controversy. Three broad areas of difficulty emerge.

(1) Conflict and co-operation between the federal and state systems

In view of the various restraints on federal industrial power, the relations between the federal and state systems might be expected to be a recurring problem. From time to time this has been so: indeed in 1929 it was one factor in an attempt by the Commonwealth government to vacate the field, leaving it almost entirely to the states.[82] The attempt failed, and since then various formal and informal devices have been adopted to avoid conflict and to advance co-operation between the tribunals. Although conflicts still occur, they tend to be particular or special rather than systemic ones.[83]

To a considerable extent unions, and industries, operate either under federal or state awards.[84] There are various mechanisms which prevent forum-shopping. Once a federal award governs an industry, state awards on the same area are displaced: conversely, a state Commission may withdraw the protection of a state award if application is made to the Australian Commission.[85] The Australian Commission will not act in respect of an industry previously covered by state awards unless there is good reason to do so.[86]

Co-operation is also achieved in more positive ways. Gaps in federal award coverage can be filled by 'counterpart' state awards, in identical terms. Where the Australian Commission lacks a particular jurisdiction which a state authority has, the federal award may be framed so as to leave open that area for state regulation: this has been the case, for example, with reinstatement disputes.[87] There is now general provision in the Commonwealth and state Acts for consultation between authorities, and for joint sittings in areas where both retain jurisdiction.[88] Another example is the special provision made for New South Wales oil industry employees.[89]

The most striking case of co-operation has been the general adherence by state tribunals to the federal indexation guidelines since 1975, in part voluntarily but in part also at state legislative direction. For example, the New South Wales Commission in Court Session is directed to follow decisions of the Australian Commission 'based wholly or partly on economic grounds . . . unless there are good reasons not to do so'.[90]

(2) *Industrial jurisdictions and the ordinary courts*

By contrast, the industrial tribunals, far from co-operating with the ordinary courts, have been as much as possible insulated from their interference. The ordinary courts have sometimes seemed hostile to, or incompetent in dealing with, the special problem of industrial jurisdiction, and in all states the supervisory power of the Supreme Courts is limited or excluded. This is especially true of Commission decisions. For example, the Western Australian Act provides that, with minor exceptions,

no award, order, declaration or proceeding of the President, the Full Bench, or the Commission shall be liable to be challenged, appealed against, reviewed, quashed, or called in question by any court on any account whatsoever.[91]

The extent to which such 'privative clauses' are effective to exclude Supreme Court review is variable. A Commission decision may be manifestly outside jurisdiction, so that it will not be a 'proceeding' or 'decision' which could benefit from the privative clause at all.[92]

However, where some other court is given the jurisdiction instead of the Supreme Court the latter will not usually interfere. In any event the merits of Commission decisions are almost wholly excluded from review. In Queensland and South Australia, there is a limited appeal restricted to jurisdictional error — from the Industrial Court to the Full Supreme Court, but even this is excluded in Western Australia.[93]

In the case of the federal authorities the position is a little different. The High Court retains its supervisory jurisdiction over Commonwealth officers (including members of the Commission) under s75(v), and the Commission cannot, formally at least, act outside the scope of federal constitutional power.[94] But apart from these constraints, decisions of the Commission are final and unreviewable.[95]

In other areas with industrial implications, however, the ordinary courts do have jurisdiction. This is so in some states as to worker's compensation claims,[96] and in all states as to industrial accident claims based upon the employer's negligence or breach of statutory duty. More controversially, the ordinary courts retain jurisdiction to enforce the law of torts against employees engaged in industrial action.[97] Torts such as intimidation and inducing breach of contract may be available in this context, although in practice they have not — or not yet — been much used in Australia.[98] A more significant remedy is provided by ss45D-E of the Trade Practices Act 1974 (Cth), dealing in particular with secondary boycotts. This has been successfully invoked in a number of disputes.[99] The Industrial Relations Bill 1987 would have provided for compulsory conciliation of disputes involving 'industrial matters' before any action could be taken under ss45D-E.[100] This proposal was highly controversial, and was one reason for the withdrawal of the Bill.

(3) The future of industrial arbitration

From time to time proposals have been made to abandon the industrial arbitration systems, converting to some form of collective bargaining (such as in the United Kingdom or the United States).[101] In particular, the period from 1966 to 1975 was a troublesome one for the industrial tribunals. Penal sanctions against unions were discredited;[102] the capacity of the tribunals to maintain industrial 'peace' was challenged by a great increase in strikes, and there was a distinct move towards collective bargaining.[103] The consensus among industrial relations writers was of the undesirability, and lack of realism, of industrial arbitration.[104] In England, judicial settlement of labour disputes was tried and failed.[105] Higgins' 'new province for law and order' was repeatedly debunked, seldom defended.

But the inflation, industrial troubles, and recession of the 1970s led to a gallop back to arbitration.[106] In 1974–5, only 21.2 per cent of the average weekly wage increase was attributable to the national wage case: in 1975–6, with indexation, the figure was 88.5 per cent.[107] Except for the period 1981–2, when wage indexation was temporarily abandoned, similar high figures have been maintained.[108] In a sense, collective bargaining was never really tried, because the arbitration system retained its role as guarantor of minimum standards for the employed, passing on what the strong had earned to the (industrially) humble and meek. Real collective bargaining would cause pronounced changes in wage relativities, which have always been extremely difficult to achieve in Australia.[109] Some critics of industrial arbitration have accepted the point, proposing mixed forms of bargaining and arbitration with the tribunals acting only in a secondary role.[110] Indeed, that is not far from Higgins' own conception (the problem of penal sanctions against trade unions apart).[111] At the same time many of the supposed defects of the system have been reassessed in more favourable terms — the 'legalism' of the Australian Commission, for example.[112] These 'revisionist' interpretations culminated in the endorsement of the principles of conciliation and arbitration by the Hancock Report, which concluded that

> In the submissions we received, no strong case for radical change by way of abolition of conciliation and arbitration was apparent . . . After an examination of all the material before us, we reached the conclusion that no substantial case had been made that industrial relations would improve if conciliation and arbitration were abandoned in favour of some other system, such as collective bargaining. Thus, we have concluded that conciliation and arbitration should remain the mechanism for regulating industrial relations in Australia.[113]

On the basis of this somewhat unenthusiastic conclusion, the Report went on to propose substantial re-enforcement and centralization of the arbitration machinery, with the replacement of 'the outmoded patchwork that is the Conciliation and Arbitration Act'.[114] As embodied in the Industrial Relations Bill 1987 (Cth), the new system would involve an Australian Industrial Relations Commission with comprehensive authority over federal industrial disputes, an Australian Labour Court, replacing the Industrial Division of the Federal Court, with judges holding joint commissions as presidential members of the Commission, and provision for joint proceedings with state industrial authorities, and for other forms of co-operation.[115] Whatever the details of the new system when it is eventually introduced, the underlying structure remains very much the same as that developed since 1904, with a continuing need for the industrial tribunals to balance their role as settlers of industrial disputes with their role as central economic agencies, independent arms of government.[116] Short of fundamental constitutional change (which is unlikely to occur),[117] that dual role seems destined to continue — an 'established' province for law and order, perhaps for want of a better!

Notes

1. Howard, in Ford, Hearn & Lansbury, *Australian Labour Relations: Readings* (3rd edn, 1980) 78, 91.
2. *A New Province for Law and Order* (1922) 2.
3. E.g. Conciliation Act 1894 (SA).
4. Chan (1971) 13 *J Ind Rels* 155.
5. An essential compilation is CCH, *Australia Labour Law Reporter* (4 vols, 1986). See also the essays in Ford, Hearn & Lansbury; Isaac & Ford, *Australian Labour Relations: Readings* (2nd edn, 1971); Portus, *Australian Compulsory Arbitration* (2nd edn, 1979); McCallum & Tracey, *Cases and Materials on Industrial Law in Australia* (1980); Macken, *Australian Industrial Laws. The Constitutional Basis* (2nd edn, 1980); Plowman, Deery & Fisher, *Australian Industrial Relations* (1980). See also Bischoff, Mitchell & Steer, *Australian Labour Law. A Selected Bibliography* (1985).
6. Committee of Review into Australian Industrial Relations Law and Systems, *Report* (1985) (hereafter Hancock Report). For discussion see the essays in (1985) 27 *J Ind Rels* 323ff. The principal recommendations in the Report would have been implemented by the Industrial Relations Bill 1987 (Cth), but the Bill was withdrawn, after opposition to certain aspects of it, before the 1987 federal election. It is likely to be reintroduced in some form.
7. Macken, 3–14; Quick & Garran, 645–7.
8. See generally Macken, 40–80; Portus, in Ford, Hearn & Lansbury, 395; Lane, 287–337; McCallum & Tracey, 7–151; 1 ALLR 3591–903; Ford (1985) 16 *UWALR* 191; Zelling (1985) 59 *ALJ* 309; McDonald (1985) 10 *Syd LR* 639.
9. A trade union can create a dispute in relation to the conditions of employment of non-unionists: *Burwood Cinema Ltd v Australian Theatrical & Amusement Employers' Assoc.* (1925) 25 CLR 528; *Metal Trades' Employers Assoc. v AEU* (1935) 54 CLR 387. But employers cannot create a dispute with unions vis-à-vis non-unionists: *R v Graziers Assoc. of NSW, ex p AWU* (1956) 96 CLR 317. Inter-union demarcation disputes can be industrial: *R v Commonwealth Court of Conciliation and Arbitration, ex p Australian Paper Mills' Employees' Union* (1943) 67 CLR 619, but not disputes between employers: *R v Portus, ex p Australian Air Pilots' Assoc.* (1953) 90 CLR 320.
10. E.g. *Re Heagney, ex p ACT Employers' Federation* (1976) 10 ALR 459; *Re Ludeke, ex p QEC* (1985) 60 ALR 641. But a dispute must still be 'genuine', in some residual sense: *R v Gough, ex p BP Refinery (Westernport) Pty Ltd* (1966) 114 CLR 384; *R v Cohen, ex p Doumany* (1981) 38 ALR 129.
11. Decisions excluding a common rule are *Australian Boat Trade Employees' Federation v Whybrow & Co.* (1910) 11 CLR 311; *R v Kelly, ex p Victoria* (1950) 81 CLR 64. Generally on the parties to awards see McCallum & Tracey, 120–40.
12. *Australian Railways Union v Victorian Railways Commissioners* (1930) 44 CLR 319; Thomson (1953) 26 *ALJ* 470. But see Conciliation and Arbitration Act 1904 (Cth) (hereafter CAA) ss172–80 (industrial agreements); McCallum & Smith (1986) 28 *J Ind Rels* 57.
13. On the doctrine of 'ambit' see id., 152–76. Cf. *R v Holmes, ex p Victorian Employers' Federation* (1980) 31 ALR 487; *R v Hegarty, ex p Salisbury*

City Corp. (1981) 36 ALR 275; Re Bain, ex p Cadbury Schweppes (1984) 51 ALR 469.
14 Caledonian Collieries Ltd v A/Asian Coal & Shale Employees' Federation (1930) 42 CLR 527; R v Gough, ex p BP Refinery (Westernport) Pty Ltd (1966) 114 CLR 384.
15 Federated State School Teachers' Assoc. of Australia v Victoria (1929) 41 CLR 569; Pitfield v Franki (1970) 123 CLR 448; R v Holmes, ex p Public Service Assoc. of NSW (1977) 18 ALR 159; R v McMahon, ex p Darvall (1982) 42 ALR 449. Generally see Ex p Professional Engineers Assoc. (1959) 107 CLR 208.
16 (1983) 47 ALR 225. This involved a return to the broad view taken in Jumbunna Coalmine NL v Victorian Coalminers' Assoc. (1908) 6 CLR 309.
17 Id., 366 (O'Connor J).
18 R v Coldham, ex p Australian Social Welfare Union (1983) 47 ALR 225 (social workers); Re Lee, ex p Minister for Justice (Qld) (1986) 65 ALR 577 (schoolteachers).
19 R v Kelly, ex p Victoria (1950) 81 CLR 64.
20 R v Portus, ex p ANZ Banking Group (1973) 127 CLR 353.
21 R v Commonwealth Industrial Court, ex p Cocks (1968) 121 CLR 313.
22 R v Portus, ex p City of Perth (1973) 129 CLR 312; cf. R v Staples, ex p Australian Telecommunications Commission (1980) 30 ALR 533.
23 R v Commonwealth Conciliation and Arbitration Commission, ex p Melbourne & Metropolitan Tramways Board (1965) 113 CLR 228, (1966) 115 CLR 443; Melbourne & Metropolitan Tramways Board v Horan (1967) 117 CLR 78. See Maher & Sexton (1972) 46 ALJ 109.
24 Re Manufacturing Grocers' Employees Federation of Australia, ex p ACM (1986) 65 ALR 461.
25 Slonim v Fellows (1984) 54 ALR 673. Cf. MTIA (Australia) v AMWSU (1983) 48 ALR 385.
26 Federated Clerks Union of Australia v Victorian Employers' Federation (1984) 54 ALR 589. Like Slonim v Fellows, this case involved the interpretation of the term 'industrial dispute' in the Industrial Relations Act 1979 (Vic.), but there is no indication that that term now has a narrower meaning for the purposes of the CAA.
27 Various attempts have been made to amend the Constitution so as to increase Commonwealth industrial power, but without success: Macken, 258–9.
28 O'Donovan (1977) 51 ALJ 234. The only significant use of s51(xx) so far is Trade Practices Act 1974 (Cth) s45D–E, prohibiting 'secondary boycotts'.
29 1 ALLR 4522. Cf. Macken, 244, 257.
30 See generally Healey, Federal Arbitration in Australia. An Historical Outline (1972); Macken, 83–103; Hancock Report, ch. 2.
31 R v Kirby, ex p Boilermakers' Soc. of Australia (1956) 94 CLR 254; aff'd (1957) 95 CLR 529.
32 Aspects of the division of powers between the Commission and Court may still cause difficulty: e.g. CAA s66. Cf. R v Marks, ex p ABLF (1981) 35 ALR 241. For a critique of the impact of the decision see Hancock Report, 380–98. See also Chapter 3.
33 CAA s28. On the relationship between conciliation and arbitration see

CAA s22(2); *R v Gough, ex p Key Meats Pty Ltd* (1982) 39 ALR 507; *Re Bain, ex p Cadbury Schweppes Australia Ltd* (1984) 51 ALR 409, 478–9 (Brennan, Deane JJ); *Re McKenzie, ex p AMIEU* (1984) 53 ALR 399.
34 CAA s30.
35 Hancock Report, 252–7. Increasing numbers of women in the workforce are a major reason for the change: 23.7% of women are covered by federal awards, compared with 50.7% of men.
36 Cf. Hancock Report, 43–9, 256–7; Sykes, in Ford, Hearn & Lansbury, 300, 307.
37 CAA ss6–7.
38 CAA ss7(4), 13–14.
39 On the panel system see CAA ss22A–23. The centralization of presidential authority in a variety of ways has led to protest: see Staples (1979) 51 *Australia Q* 51. But see Hancock Report, 578–9.
40 Isaac, in Hambly & Goldring, eds, *Australian Lawyers and Social Change* (1976) 321, 345–6. Cf. Kirby (1970) 4 *FLR* 1.
41 CAA ss31, 34, 34A.
42 *R v Clarkson, ex p ATPOA* (1982) 39 ALR 1, 10.
43 CAA s25A; Macken, 192. Cf. Staples, 54–6.
44 On wage indexation and the Commission's wage-fixing principles generally, see Niland, ed., *Wage Fixation in Australia* (1986); Portus, 20–78; McCallum & Tracey, 270–331; Yerbury, in Ford, Hearn & Lansbury, 462. On the early development of these principles see Higgins; Macarthy, in Roe, ed., *Social Policy in Australia* (1976) 41.
45 For appeals see CAA s35 (the Commission must determine that the matter is of 'such importance that, in the public interest, an appeal should lie'). For references by the president see s34A(3); for reviews on application by the minister, s36A. On the relationship between appeals to the Full Commission and applications for judicial review to the High Court see *Re Merriman, ex p ABLF* (1984) 53 ALR 440.
46 On the controversial bans clause provisions see McCallum & Tracey, 225–36; Isaac, in Isaac & Ford, 451. In 1977 an Industrial Relations Bureau was created to secure the enforcement of federal industrial law: CAA ss126A–R. It had little impact, and was abolished in 1983: cf. McCallum, in Ford, Hearn & Lansbury, 368–94.
47 The exception is disputed elections under CAA s158P & Part IX: s118B(l)(a); *Marsh v Adamson* (1985) 59 ALR 629.
48 CAA s118A(4B). See also the contempt powers in CAA s118A(4C) and Federal Court of Australia Act 1976 (Cth) s31. On federal and state efforts to deregister the Builders' Labourers Federation see *Victoria v ABLF* (1982) 41 ALR 71; *Re Ludeke, ex p ABLF* (1985) 62 ALR 407; *ABLF v Commonwealth* (1986) 66 ALR 363; *Re AFCC, ex p Billing* (1986) 68 ALR 416.
49 CAA s118B(2).
50 *Burgess v John Connell-Mott, Hay & Anderson Pty Ltd* (1979) 25 ALR 467; *Davern v Messel* (1984) 53 ALR 1. See further Chapter 8. Proceedings for penalties under CAA s119 are civil rather than criminal, so an appeal lies from dismissal of a summons: *Gapes v Commercial Bank of Australia Ltd* (1979) 27 ALR 87.
51 CAA s118B(l)(b), (2).

52 Cf. *Rowell v Child* (1983) 48 ALR 333.
53 Higgins, 162–6, 169–76; Rickard, *H.B. Higgins* (1984) 170–204, 231–57.
54 CAA Part IIIA, enacted in 1967 under Constitution s51(i). Cf. 1 ALLR 4885–902; *R v Commonwealth Conciliation and Arbitration Commission, ex p Associated Airlines Pty Ltd* (1978) 19 ALR 360. There is also a joint Coal Industry Tribunal under the Coal Industry Act 1946 (Cth) and counterpart NSW legislation: 1 ALLR 4923–42. The validity of the Tribunal was upheld in *Re Duncan, ex p Australian Iron & Steel Pty Ltd* (1983) 49 ALR 19.
55 For the earlier provision see Public Service Arbitration Act 1920 (Cth). See now CAA ss70A–K.
56 For separate Commonwealth instrumentalities cf. *R v Staples, ex p Australian Telecommunications Commission* (1980) 30 ALR 533; 1 ALLR 4981–4. See also CAA ss71–5 (maritime industries), ss76–80 (Snowy Mountains area), 81–8 (waterside workers), ss88A–D (Commonwealth projects). On the role of the separate tribunals see Romeyn (1986) 28 *J Ind Rels* 3.
57 Industrial Relations Act 1979 (Vic.) (in force 1981). For the Committee of Review of the Labour and Industry Act 1958, *First Report* (1976) see Fristacky, ed., *Victoria's Industrial System. The Future* (1978) 108–17. For its *Third Report* (1978) on public sector tribunals, see id., 120–5. On the position under the 1979 Act see 1 ALLR 10031ff. On the earlier position see Alley, *Industrial Law in Victoria* (1973); Hince, in Ford, Hearn & Lansbury, 344; Fristacky (1976) 18 *J Ind R* 309. See also Fox (1984) 26 *J Ind Rels* 25.
58 For Tasmania, see Molhuyson (1972) 14 *J Ind R* 132; Plowman (1979) 21 *J Ind R* 477; 1 ALLR 19031ff.
59 Editorial note in Isaac & Ford, 330–1. The SA Commission was created 'because the word "court" has a legal connotation and it would not be proper for lay commissioners to be appointed to a court': SA, 4 *Parl Debs* (1965–6) 3904.
60 Industrial Relations Act 1979 (WA) ss23–4, 90. Some powers are exercised by the Commission in Court Session: e.g. s50.
61 The Act replaces an earlier Act of 1912. To a considerable extent it follows proposals for reform in the Kelly Report (1978); 1 ALLR 17031–2. Generally see id., 17001ff.
62 Industrial Relations Act 1979 (Vic.) ss 11, 12, 15(3), 22(7).
63 Industrial Conciliation and Arbitration Act 1961 (Qld) ss8, 9–13. For earlier legislation see Fry, 123–30; generally, 1 ALLR 13101ff.
64 Industrial Arbitration Act 1940 (NSW) ss14, 30B, 30C, 36. The NSW Commission is stated to be a 'superior court of record': s14(1). The High Court has proceeded on the assumption that the Commission is a court for the purposes of federal jurisdiction: *Gosper v Sawyer* (1985) 58 ALR 13; *Tana v Baxter* (1986) 68 ALR 245, 251–2 (Brennan J). See generally 1 ALLR 7001ff; Mills, *Industrial Laws. New South Wales* (1977).
65 NSW, s14; Queensland, ss9(5)(9); WA, ss 12, 22. The SA Commission is the exception, but in their other capacity as Industrial Court judges the presidential members have judicial tenure (s12(4)) which in effect guarantees their tenure as members of the Commission (s22). But the non-legal commissioners have no such status or tenure: s23. The president of

the Victorian Industrial Relations Commission has modified judicial tenure: Industrial Relations Act 1979 (Vic.) s5. Commissioners and other members have no tenure: s7.

66 NSW, s87; Queensland, s11 (general jurisdiction of Commission to regulate callings), s94 (industrial agreements); SA, s29(1)(f) (special application required); Tasmania, s38 (awards a common rule unless otherwise provided); Victoria, s34 (awards a common rule by definition); WA, ss37, 41(5)–(10) (procedure for declaring consent award common rule).

67 WA, ss7, definition of 'industrial matter', para. (g).

68 NSW, ss5(2)(3), 88E. Cf. also s88B. See *Caltex Oil (Australia) Pty Ltd v Feenan* (1981) 34 ALR 341; *Wilson Parking (NSW) Pty Ltd v FMWUA (NSW Branch)* (1981) 38 ALR 431. On the extraterritorial limits of the NSW jurisdiction see *Gosper v Sawyer* (1985) 58 ALR 13. On the problem of distinguishing employees from independent contractors see e.g. *AMP Soc. v Chaplin* (1978) 18 ALR 385; *Price v Grant Industries Pty Ltd* (1978) 21 ALR 388; Powe (1986) 28 *J Ind Rels* 86.

69 Earlier doubts about the NSW reinstatement jurisdiction were settled by the insertion of s20A in 1978. See 1 ALLR 7921. For SA see s31 (which replaced the earlier provision, s15(1)(e), in 1984); Stewart (1986) 28 *J Ind Rels* 367. For WA, ss23(1)(a), 29(b).

70 The WA Act s48 requires a Board of Reference for each award. Generally on Boards of Reference see de Vyver, in Isaac & Ford, 544; Sykes, in Ford, Hearn & Lansbury, 300, 321–2.

71 Dual union registration, deregistration, union preference, and intervention in union affairs have all been significant sources of difficulty. See generally Martin, in Isaac & Ford, 166; Portus, 119–29; McCallum & Tracey, 334–440.

72 This system (known as 'final offer arbitration') applied under the old Victorian and Tasmanian Acts. The WA Act also expressly allows final offer arbitration by consent of all parties: s26(4). Final offer arbitration is defined as 'arbitration in which the issue is decided by the Commission by awarding, without qualification or amendment that one of the final proposals made by the parties which, viewed in its entirety is the more or the most reasonable' (s7(1)).

73 Under the SA Act the Industrial Commission has no original jurisdiction over an industry for which a Committee exists: s25(3). But there is an appeal from a Committee to the Full Commission in the same way as from a single commissioner: s96, cf. ss101–2. For NSW see 1 ALLR 7252.

74 See 1 ALLR 8301ff. For the Contract Regulation Tribunals in the transport industry see NSW, ss91J-M (inserted 1979); 1 ALLR 8064–5.

75 Queensland, s8; SA, s15.

76 WA, ss86, 90.

77 Queensland, s8(1)(d).

78 Seat of Government (Administration) Act 1910 (Cth) s5; Northern Territory (Self-Government) Act 1978 (Cth) s53. The common rule power is in CAA s49. See *Poulos v Waltons Stores (Interstate) Ltd* (1986) 72 ALR 136.

79 NSW, ss5(1), 120, 226; Queensland, ss24, 27, 36, 42; WA, ss81–4. The SA provisions are rather different: industrial magistrates can, if directed by the president, constitute the Industrial Court itself: s14(2). Industrial magistrates appointed under s13 thereby become magistrates. They have

exclusive jurisdiction over minor industrial offences: s174. The only appeal is to a single judge of the Industrial Court: s94.
80 Victoria, ss12(1), 22, 90–2. There is no special provision for industrial magistrates in Tasmania: s92.
81 CAA ss119, 123, 148, 189. Appeals go as of right and exclusively to the Industrial Division of the Federal Court: s113, and only ultimately, by leave, to the High Court: s118B(l)(b), (2).
82 Macken, 87–8, 249–52.
83 One significant 'particular' dispute was that over the Queensland electricity workers: see *Re Ludeke, ex p QEC* (1985) 60 ALR 641; *QEC v Commonwealth* (1985) 61 ALR 1; *Re QEC, ex p ETUA* (1987) 72 ALR 1.
84 Macken, 209–10; Portus, 78–9.
85 Macken, 203–39; Portus, 79–89 for good surveys of the provisions.
86 CAA s41(1)(d)(ii). See Hall (1984) 13 *UQLJ* 49.
87 McCallum & Tracey, 202–23; *R v Clarkson, ex p GMH Pty Ltd* (1975) 134 CLR 56. This will not work if federal law otherwise regulates dismissal: *ABC v Industrial Court of SA* (1977) 15 ALR 609; *MTA (Australia) v AMWSU* (1983) 48 ALR 385. But a Commonwealth award may not exclude state reinstatement power where the dismissal is based on 'non-industrial' grounds: *Ansett Transport Industries (Operations) Pty Ltd v Wardley* (1980) 28 ALR 449; or where the state jurisdiction is expressly saved: *Belton v GMH Ltd (No. 2)* (1984) 55 ALR 305.
88 E.g. CAA s67; NSW ss38H–M; Victoria, ss46A–F; WA, ss80ZF–ZJ.
89 CAA s4A; NSW, ss38A–G; 1 ALLR 8044 (introduced in 1980).
90 NSW, s57. See Macken, 241–80.
91 WA, s34(4). See also s34(3) (decisions not removable to any court by certiorari or otherwise).
92 See generally Aronson & Franklin, *Review of Administrative Action* (1987) ch. 21. On the effect of NSW, s84 in excluding certiorari for error of law on the face of the record see *Houssein v Under Secretary, Department of Industrial Relations* (1982) 38 ALR 577.
93 Queensland, s8(4)–(5); SA, s92(3); WA, s87(2).
94 The High Court has sought to avoid second-guessing the Commission on jurisdictional facts by imposing a strict onus of proof on applicants for prohibition or mandamus: e.g. *R v Alley, ex p Plumbers and Gasfitters Employees' Union* (1981) 37 ALR 1, and esp. *Re Bain, ex p Cadbury Schweppes Australia Ltd* (1984) 51 ALR 469.
95 CAA s60. On the ineffectiveness of s60 to exclude High Court review under s75(v) of jurisdictional issues see *R v Coldham, ex p AWU* (1983) 49 ALR 259. Review of Commission decisions is excluded from the Federal Court's jurisdiction under Judiciary Act 1903 (Cth) s39B.
96 Only in Queensland and SA is the Industrial Court involved in worker's compensation claims. Elsewhere, these are dealt with by the ordinary courts, by arbitration, or by special boards or tribunals. See 2 ALLR 34501ff; McCallum & Tracey, 497–647; Sykes, *Labour Law in Australia* (1980) I, 150–341.
97 A partial but significant exception is SA s143a (inserted 1984).
98 Sykes, 342–78; Mitchell (1976) 5 *Adel LR* 428.
99 E.g. *AMIEU v Mudginberri Station Pty Ltd* (1985) 61 ALR 635. For criticism of s45D see McHugh & Madgwick, in Evans, ed., *Law, Politics and the Labor Movement* (1980) 18.

100 Industrial Relations Bill 1987 (Cth) ss193–8. The Hancock Report, 642–3, was unable to reach agreement on the point. An earlier amendment to the CAA to similar effect was rejected by the Senate. See also *Co-Op Bulk Handling Ltd v WWF (Australia)* (1983) 51 ALR 79.

101 See Blandy & Niland, eds, *Alternatives to Arbitration* (1986); Ludeke (1984) 58 *ALJ* 157; Gutman (1986) 30 *Quadrant* 56; Blandy (1985) 27 *J Ind Rels* 452; Brown & Rowe, id., 484. For a survey of other systems see Loewenberg et al., *Compulsory Arbitration. An International Comparison* (1976); Hanami & Blanpain, eds, *Industrial Conflict Resolution in Market Economies* (1984); Blanpain, ed., *Comparative Labour Law and Industrial Relations* (2nd rev. edn, 1985). Different views are also held of the NZ system, which shares many characteristics of the Australian one. See Joseph, *The Judicial Perspective of Industrial Conciliation and Arbitration in New Zealand* (1980); Szakats [1980] *NZLJ* 436, 484–94.

102 Isaac, in Isaac & Ford, 451; Rawson, in Tay & Kamenka (eds) *Law-making in Australia* (1980) 290, 291–5.

103 Yerbury, 462–3.

104 E.g. Isaac, in Isaac & Ford, 496, 536–43; Laffer, id., 527; Woodward (1970) 12 *J Ind R* 115; Wootten, id., 130. But some economists were less sure: Hancock, in Isaac & Ford, 514.

105 Weekes et al., *Industrial Relations and the Limits of Law. The Industrial Effects of the Industrial Relations Act 1971* (1975); Jackson, 133–7. For the present position see Clegg, *The Changing System of Industrial Relations in Great Britain* (1979) 290–396, 325–7; Ridout, *Industrial Tribunal Law* (1980); Bain, ed., *Industrial Relations in Britain* (1983). Supporters of legal abstention in this field include Wedderburn (1980) 9 *Ind LJ* 65; Kahn-Freund, *Labour Relations, Heritage and Adjustment* (1979) 77–80.

106 On the return to arbitration see Yerbury, in Isaac & Ford, 123; Lansbury (1978) 117 *Int Lab R* 611.

107 Howard, 92–3; cf. Portus, 68.

108 Hancock Report, 44–9.

109 The 'received wisdom', that there is little difference between the economic effects of the Australian arbitration system and other systems in comparable countries, in terms of the distribution of wages, at least (Hughes (1973) 15 *J Ind R* 1; Norris (1980) 22 *J Ind R* 249), is being reviewed in the light of studies showing that relativities in Australia are more compressed: e.g. Plowman, in Niland (1986) 15, 38–41; Norris, id., 183.

110 Rawson; Niland, *Collective Bargaining and Compulsory Arbitration in Australia* (1978).

111 Throughout *A New Province for Law and Order*, Higgins emphasized the role of consent and conciliation. The role of arbitration, in his view, was to achieve what would, if the right conditions (equality of bargaining power, legal neutrality) had existed, have been agreed through collective bargaining. See id., 25, 40, 44, 47, 55, 98, 109, 138; but cf. 150–1. To similar effect Yerbury, 162–5. For a sensitive reassessment, Isaac.

112 Ibid.; Cupper, in Ford, Hearn & Lansbury, 409; Sykes, id., 334–7; Portus, 141–53. See also Evans, 58, 349.

113 Hancock Report, Summary, 1-2. See also Hancock Report, 241–5, for a fuller account of the Committee's reasons.

114 *Federated Clerks Union of Australia. v Victorian Employers' Federation* (1984) 54 ALR 489, 513 (Deane J).

115 For criticism of the Labour Court proposal see Dabscheck (1985) 27 *J Ind Rels* 511.
116 Isaac (1977/3) *Aust Economic Rev* 16.
117 The Constitutional Commission's Distribution of Powers Committee has recommended that s51(xxxv) be replaced with power over 'industrial relations and employment matters': *Report* (1987) 35, and see id., 31–4, for a review of earlier proposals. Proposals have also been made for a transfer of state industrial powers to the Commonwealth: cf. Ludeke (1980) 54 *ALJ* 88. This seems equally unlikely.

CHAPTER 12

Small Claims Courts and Tribunals

12.1 The Development of Small Claims Courts

One interesting development in the provision of courts is the growth of small claims courts and tribunals.[1] Ordinary civil courts have always had jurisdiction over claims for small amounts arising from the sale of goods and similar transactions. However, those courts simply apply the ordinary law and procedure, with its right to legal representation and to appeal. In practice this creates a situation of severe inequality between commercial and private litigants. Commercial litigants with a large number of claims (e.g. relating to the provision of credit) can take advantage of economies of scale in the use of courts as debt collection agencies. They, or their agents, know the system. The rare contested case might cost more than the debt that is recovered, but their interests extend beyond the occasional defeat. The private litigant, on the other hand, is almost always unfamiliar with the system. He may have kept no records of the particular transaction. He may not be aware of possible defences or counter-claims. He is almost always the defendant. Most of all, the cost of legal representation often exceeds the amount at stake, and he may have no clear idea how much a lawyer will cost. Even if he wins at first instance he faces the expensive possibility of appeal. Especially in cases involving consumer credit, with the plaintiff a large corporation and the defendant a consumer without experience of litigation, the result tends to be that the inferior civil courts become part of the machinery of debt collection.[2]

Some remedies were required to redress the balance. One idea was to create a special jurisdiction, intended to hear cases involving small amounts of money quickly and informally, at minimum cost to the parties.³ Legal representation and the right to appeal, which tend to increase costs and formality, would have to be excluded for all but exceptional cases. In the absence of skilled representation, the judge or referee would have to take a more active role in finding out the truth of the matter. In 1913, the first small claims courts were established along those lines in two American states. By 1975, small claims courts existed in each state of the United States.⁴ In Australia, the innovation is a more recent one. The first small claims tribunals were established in Victoria and Queensland in 1973, and all the other mainland states and territories followed in 1974. Tasmania introduced a small claims jurisdiction in 1985, following repeated proposals in the previous decade.⁵

12.2 Small Claims Courts and Tribunals in Australia⁶

The Australian small claims jurisdictions are of two distinct types. In Queensland, Victoria, New South Wales, and Western Australia, separate small claims tribunals (in New South Wales more accurately called 'Consumer Claims Tribunals') have been established, staffed by specially appointed referees, and available only for hearing claims by consumers against traders in respect of 'consumer transactions', as defined. In South Australia, the two territories, and Tasmania the local courts have been given a special jurisdiction to hear small claims, and are required to follow simplified procedures in doing so. (There are also 'small debts' jurisdictions attached to the ordinary lower courts in Queensland and Western Australia.⁷) As a result, there are marked differences in the structure and (to a lesser extent) the operation of the two types. Three differences may be mentioned.

First, while the tribunals have their own specialist referees, the small claims courts are staffed by existing lower court judges or magistrates. In such cases specialization in the small claims jurisdiction would be a matter for individual enthusiasm and administrative flexibility. Without that, the court model carries a real risk of importing inappropriate 'judicial' attitudes into the informal small claims procedure.⁸ The concentration on small claims work of a full-time referee is intended to bring a greater commitment to the aims (and experience with the problems) of a small claims jurisdiction.⁹

Secondly, that the small claims jurisdiction is vested in an existing court is a reason (based on 'rule of law' considerations) for not excluding traders as plaintiffs from that jurisdiction. In the two territories, South Australia, and Tasmania no restriction is placed on who may bring a small claim, or who may be the defendant.¹⁰ Nor is there any narrow or specific limitation of claims that can be brought: subject to its upper limit, the jurisdiction includes all or most civil claims.¹¹ Indeed in South Australia the small claims jurisdiction is the only Local Court jurisdiction for such claims.

In the tribunal states, on the other hand, access to the jurisdiction is more or less strictly limited to 'consumers' bringing 'small claims' or 'consumer claims' against 'traders'. Thus the Victorian Act defines a 'small claim' as a claim for the payment of money or performance of work under a contract (including a contract of insurance) 'between persons who, in relation to those goods or services or that contract of insurance, are a consumer on the one hand and a trader on the other'.[12] The effect can be to exclude classes of 'small claim' which cry out for similar treatment (e.g. tenancy disputes[13]), or to create uncertainty, and litigation, over the definition of jurisdictional terms such as 'trader'.[14] Moreover, under such definitions traders' claims are left to the ordinary courts, although in some cases traders may encourage claims to be brought against them in a tribunal (with its low cost and informality) rather than instituting proceedings themselves in the courts.[15] Demands from small traders to have their own right of access to a small claims jurisdiction led Queensland in 1984 to extend the jurisdiction to claims by traders against traders, as well as to disputes over boundary fences (s4). Similar pressures led to the establishment of a small debts jurisdiction in Queensland and Western Australia.

Related problems occur, in the restricted jurisdiction of the tribunals, with such matters as recourse against third parties who are not themselves 'traders'.[16] A consumer's real grievance might be with the finance company which financed the purchase of a second-hand car rather than the trader who sold it. It is not clear whether the finance company would be a trader *vis-à-vis* the consumer in such a case. One remedy in this type of case has been to request the registrar or referee to give notice to the manufacturer or finance company as a 'person' with 'a sufficient interest in a resolution of the dispute'. The person notified then becomes a 'party to the proceedings', with the result that an order may be made in favour of the consumer and against the third party, even if the original defendant is exonerated.[17] But in *R v Small Claims Tribunal, ex parte Escor Industries Pty Ltd*, a case involving a claim under a warranty given by the manufacturer of goods sold by a trader, this device was rejected. Having determined that the claimant was not a 'consumer' of the warranty within the Act, McInerney J held that ss23–4 could not be used to extend the tribunal's jurisdiction to disputes with third parties that were neither 'small claims' nor ancillary to small claims.[18] This is unfortunate, since the aim of ss23–4 is to resolve finally 'the dispute to which the claim relates' as between the parties (original or subsequent) to the proceedings. To read in a requirement that the claimant–third-party relationship either be a small claim or be 'ancillary' to such a claim is to frustrate this intent. It should be sufficient for the third-party dispute to 'relate' to the original claim, by arising out of the same facts (including the commercial connection between the original trader and the third party).[19] But McInerney J's restrictive view has since been followed by the Queensland Full Court.[20] Problems such as these are inherent in a limited jurisdiction:[21] they do not occur in the small claims courts, whose jurisdiction is unrestricted as to parties and (with few exceptions) as to subject-matter.

A third difference between small claims tribunals and courts relates to the possibility of appeal from, or judicial review of, decisions. In the four tribunal states (and also in Tasmania), it is expressly provided that decisions of a tribunal are final and without appeal.[22] Judicial review of decisions by way of certiorari or related proceedings is restricted to decisions taken without jurisdiction or in violation of natural justice.[23] This excludes such grounds for review as error of law not going to jurisdiction, or acting against the weight of evidence. The aims of small claims adjudication require that decisions should be, as far as possible, final.[24] This finality may be better achieved in the tribunal states than in those court states where there is appeal by leave or special leave to the Supreme Court,[25] though much would depend on the readiness of the Supreme Court to grant leave.[26]

On the other hand, despite the differences between them, Australian small claims jurisdictions have many common features. Their jurisdictional limits are within the same broad range: initially set at between $450 and $1000, they have been increased in each case, broadly in line with inflation, to a range of $1500–$3000.[27] They are not bound by the law of evidence, but may inquire in much less formal ways into the truth of the matter.[28] Costs are either not available at all, or only in very restricted cases.[29] Legal representation is (with two exceptions) not available except with the consent of all parties and of the court or tribunal (which must be satisfied that there will be no prejudice to any unrepresented party).[30] Officials of the court or tribunal are specifically directed to assist unrepresented parties in filling out forms, filing claims, and so on.[31]

A primary function of the court or tribunal is frequently stated to be to assist the parties in reaching a satisfactory settlement. Only if this is not possible is it to proceed to an adjudication.[32] Fears have been expressed that the conciliation role is inconsistent with subsequent adjudication by the same judge or referee, though in practice this does not seem to have been a problem.[33] Whatever the judge's proper role in bringing about a settlement, once conciliation has failed it is clearly intended that he take an active inquisitorial role, rather than the neutral, distant, and impartial position of a judge in adversary proceedings. This involves detailed questioning of the parties and their witnesses, requests for documentary evidence, and in some cases for the assistance of the Consumer Affairs Department or other government officers with knowledge of the subject-matter in dispute.[34]

This inquisitorial function is perhaps the most radical innovation of those introduced by small claims statutes into the Australian judicial system.

A problem common to all small claims jurisdiction derives from the remarkable reticence of the constituent Acts about the substantive rules to be applied in deciding small claims. The intricacies of the law of commercial transactions might seem irrelevant to the rapid common-sense solution of small disputes. Thus the Small Claims Tribunal Act 1976 (NZ) s15(4) provides that

> The Tribunal shall determine the dispute according to the substantial merits and justice of the case, and in doing so shall have regard to the law but shall not be bound to give effect to strict legal rights or obligations or to legal forms or technicalities.[35]

With one exception, the Australian Acts show little indication of this approach. It is quite clear that the small claims courts are to apply the ordinary law to transactions in dispute, since on appeal the Supreme Court will also apply that law.[36] The same has been held to be true of the Victorian and Western Australian tribunals: in neither state does the Act make any express provision, and express provisions would be required to displace the common law in judicial proceedings in an Australian tribunal.[37] In consumer claims tribunals, the nearest approach to a special 'law' is the provision, common to New South Wales and Queensland, that a tribunal may make such order as is 'fair and equitable' to the parties in dispute.[38] Even here, it seems that the ordinary law is to be applied, with the tribunal's discretion limited to the appropriate order in the circumstances.[39] It is arguable that to allow tribunals or courts to disregard the general law violates notions of the 'rule of law', since it is not possible for the parties to know in advance the rules that will apply to their transaction. On the other hand, this formal consideration may exaggerate the extent to which the parties to small transactions ever concern themselves with the law. In view of the requirement that the small claims tribunals should apply the ordinary law, it is surprising that the Queensland Magistrates Court, in its small debts jurisdiction, is not required to do so. Section 10(1) of the Magistrates Courts Act 1921 (Qld) (inserted in 1975) provides that

> the hearing and determination of an action for a small debt and of any other action in which the sum sued for is less than $300 shall be guided by equity, good conscience and the substantial merits of the case without regard to technicalities or any rules of evidence . . . [40]

The duty of small claims courts and tribunals to apply the ordinary law has clear implications for review of or appeal from decisions. Reasons of law for small claims decisions are unlikely to be given, so that in the absence of specific provision,[41] the Supreme Court might have to guess, for the purpose of reviewing, the probable reasoning of the judge or referee at first instance. Since appeals are rare or nonexistent and since the reasons (if given) are given informally and without deliberation, there is to be considerable 'flexibility' in applying the law.[42]

12.3   Further Reform in Small Claims Jurisdictions

Despite these qualifications the small claims jurisdictions have become a well-accepted and much-used addition to the ordinary system of courts.[43] But such jurisdictions were not introduced as part of any court reform movement so much as what might be termed the procedural second phase of 'consumerism'. It was thought to be not enough to change the law: it was also necessary to create machinery giving genuine remedies to ordinary people to implement those substantive changes. (Legal aid and class actions may be seen in the same light.) On the other hand, from the point of view of advocates of the adversary system, the small claims jurisdiction is welcome only to the point where it starts to impinge on transactions which are thought properly to belong to the ordinary courts (with their stricter procedure, rigorous application of the law of evidence, and rights to representation and appeal). In England the strength of this view has been such that special small claims jurisdictions (as distinct from simplified county court procedures) have never been established on an official basis.[44] In Australia, the small claims jurisdictions are now well established, but these issues surface when proposals are made for the extension of tribunal jurisdiction to non-consumer claims[45] or for increases in jurisdictional limits.[46]

Indeed, as jurisdictional limits increase, either to the limits of inferior court civil jurisdiction or even, as in the case of consumer credit transactions in Victoria, beyond it,[47] there are real questions about how the overlap of minor civil tribunals can be justified. Thus an increasingly important issue is whether the informality of procedures will be allowed to infect other inferior courts. If, with increasing familiarity, the public comes to see small claims procedures as more normal, less exceptional than the legal profession now does, there may well be pressure for the extension of those procedures to other courts.[48] To some extent this may be happening already, with the creation of a small debts jurisdiction in Queensland and Western Australia, and with the introduction in New South Wales of court-annexed arbitration.[49] Nonetheless, in view of the predominant professional influence over the legal system in the past, it would be a brave man who predicted any rapid, or widespread, infection of informality![50]

Notes

1 Earlier analogues have existed: e.g. in England, courts of requests, and in Australia some of the early minor civil courts. See Steele (1981) 6 *Am Bar Found Res J* 293; and see also Chapter 2.
2 Most Local Court actions for debt are undefended, with the result that the plaintiff can sign judgment without having to prove the case, and without there ever having been an independent scrutiny of the facts. In at least some states, a defendant has to file grounds of defence within a limited time (e.g. six days) to prevent judgment in default. See further Ison (1972) 35 *MLR* 18; Great Britain, Consumer Council, *Justice out of Reach: A Case for Small Claims Courts* (1970); Consumer Council, *Simple Justice* (1979).
3 See Pound (1913) 26 *Harv LR* 302 for an influential early statement.
4 See Domanskis (1976) *U Mich JL Reform* 590; Sarat (1976) 10 *Law & Soc Rev* 339; Yngvesson & Hennessey (1975) 9 *Law & Soc Rev* 219 & works there cited. For Canadian small claims jurisdictions see Neilson (1982) 20 *Alberta LR* 475.
5 Consumer Claims Tribunal Bill 1977 (Tas.); Tas. LRC Report 22, *Reform of Civil Procedure* (1978) 8–10.
6 The best account of Australian small claims jurisdictions is Taylor, in Cappelletti & Weisner, eds, *Access to Justice*, vol. 2, *Promising Institutions* (1979) 595. See also Goldring (1976) 2 *LSB* 2, 50; Ellinger (1977) 5 *ABLR* 121. On the Victorian Act see Turner (1975) 2 *Monash ULR* 125. The Australian legislation is as follows: ACT, Small Claims Ordinance 1974; NSW, Consumer Claims Tribunals Act 1974; NT, Small Claims Act 1974; Queensland, Small Claims Tribunals Act 1973; SA, Local and District Criminal Courts Act 1926 (Part VIIA 'Small Claims' inserted in 1974); Tasmania: Court of Requests (Small Claims Division) Act 1985; Victoria, Small Claims Tribunals Act 1973; WA, Small Claims Tribunals Act 1974. The legislation is set out in CCH, *Australian Consumer Sales and Credit Law Reporter* (1985) vols 2–3.
7 Magistrates Courts Act Amendment Act 1975 (Qld); Local Courts Act 1904 (WA) Part VIA (introduced 1982). For a comparison between the two Queensland jurisdictions see Corrin (1985) 13 *ABLR* 127.
8 Cf. Ison, 31–2.
9 E.g. WA, *Annual Report of the Referee, Small Claims Tribunal, for the year ended 30th June, 1977*, printed as an Appendix to WALRC, Working Paper 63, *Small Debts Court* (1978) 40–9. But laymen have no monopoly on enthusiasm and dedication: the SA system, under a Local Court judge, is said to work well: NZRCC, 144. The small claims division of Tasmanian courts of requests is staffed by a Special Commissioner, who may be a part-time appointment: ss7, 8A.
10 For the problems caused by unrestricted access of commercial claimants to small claims jurisdictions in North America, see Axworthy (1976) 22 *McGill LJ* 480. The Small Claims Tribunals Act 1976 (NZ) s10 excludes undisputed debts from the jurisdiction. Similar desires to prevent swamping of small claims tribunals by commercial litigants lie behind the separate establishment of a Small Debts Court in Queensland and WA (following a WALRC recommendation to similar effect): Report, *Small Debts Court* (1979) 8–15. And cf. Goldring, 51.

11 The territory Ordinances exclude cases in which the title to land is in issue or the property in or possession of goods is claimed: ACT, s4(1)(b); NT, s5(2). See *R v O'Neill, ex p Moran* (1985) 58 ACTR 26. The SA Act adopts a broad inclusive definition: pecuniary claims (whether or not liquidated) in contract, quasi-contract, and tort. Tasmania s3 is to similar effect. The SA Act allows the Attorney-General to notify additional causes of action upon which a small claim may be founded: s4. There have been no such notifications.

12 Victoria, s2(1). However, the NSW Act, as a result of an amendment in 1979, provides only that the respondent must have been 'engaged in a business activity' as defined (s4(1)), and s4(3A) extends the notion of 'business activity' to any business of supplying goods or services, whether in the course of a profession, trade or commerce, or otherwise.

13 The Queensland and WA Acts were amended in 1975 to make express provision for landlord and tenant disputes (at least, tenancy bond disputes) to be heard by the tribunals: Qld, s4; WA, s4(1). In a number of states a special tribunal exists for tenancy disputes. For example in South Australia, residential tenancy disputes (involving amounts up to $2500) are within the exclusive jurisdiction of the Residential Tenancies Tribunal, established on lines similar but not identical to a Small Claims Tribunal: see Residential Tenancies Act 1978 (SA) Part III. Where the matter involves more than $1000 there is an appeal to a District Court. Generally on residential tenancies see Bradbrook, *Residential Tenancy Law and Practice: Victoria and South Australia* (1983); Lang, *Residential Tenancies Handbook, New South Wales* (1986); Tarlo (1979) 11 *UQLJ* 71.

14 One problem that has arisen is whether persons engaged in the traditional professions are 'traders' within the statutory definition. In *R v Small Claims Tribunal ex p Gibson* [1973] Qd R 490, a dentist was held not to be a trader under the Queensland Act. The WA Act s4(2) appears expressly to exclude professional claims. In 1976 the NSW Act was amended to include in the definition of services in s4(1), 'work of a professional nature'. Nonetheless Lee J in *Holman v Deol* [1979] 1 NSWLR 640 managed to decide that lawyers, doctors, and dentists were still excluded from the jurisdiction, since they were not engaged in trade or commerce. Parliament promptly reversed the decision, with retrospective effect: Consumer Claims Tribunals (Amendment) Act 1979 (NSW). There is now no doubt that the professions are within the jurisdiction: cf. *Thompson v Consumer Claims Tribunal* [1981] 1 NSWLR 68. On the other hand an ordinary car parking arrangement is a 'contract for services' within the jurisdiction of the Victorian Tribunal: *Walsh (Referee of the Small Claims Tribunal) v Palladium Car Park Pty Ltd* [1975] VR 949, noted O'Connor (1975) 1 *LSB* 308. See also *R v Levine ex p de Jong* [1981] VR 131.

15 Thus the NSW, Queensland, and WA Acts allow claims for relief from payment of money to a trader: in determining such a claim, the tribunal may order that the money is not owing, or that it (or part of it) is to be paid to a 'person specified in the order': NSW, s23(1)(a); Queensland, s20(2)(a); WA, s20(2)(c). The Victorian Act has a more restrictive provision to similar effect, requiring payment to the tribunal of the full amount sought by the trader before the claim is brought: s20A(1)(b).

16 On the application of the definition of 'consumer' in the context of services

provided apart from contract see *R v Small Claims Tribunal ex p Escor Industries Pty Ltd* [1979] VR 635; Scheinkestel (1980) 12 *MULR* 581.
17 NSW, ss14–15; Queensland, ss25–6; Victoria, ss23–4; WA, ss25–6. Cf. Evans (1978) 3 *LSB* 132.
18 [1979] VR 503, 511. McInerney J's decision was reversed on appeal on another ground: [1979] VR 635.
19 Cf. the problem of pendent party jurisdiction discussed in Chapter 8. In other respects Supreme Courts have adopted a broad and beneficial construction of small claims jurisdiction: *Fairey A/Asia Pty Ltd v Joyce* [1981] 2 NSWLR 314; *R v Registrar, Small Claims Tribunals, ex p Consolidated Rutile Ltd* [1986] 2 Qd R 282.
20 *R v Massingham, ex p Majeau Carrying Co. Pty Ltd* [1985] 1 Qd R 349. Cf. Duggan (1979) 4 *LSB* 49.
21 Another example is the problem of set-offs and counter-claims. The tribunal states' legislation contains no express provision for set-offs and counter-claims. Presumably a set-off could be allowed to the extent of the original claim, at least in NSW and Queensland where the Acts require that the order be 'fair and equitable to all the parties': NSW, s23(2); Queensland, s10(2). The position of counter-claims is less clear, though it may be that the same reasoning would apply. In the territories, counter-claims and set-offs are expressly permitted up to the limit of the jurisdiction: ACT, s17; NT, s17. In SA there is no jurisdiction over a counter-claim that is not a small claim: s152f(2), (3). The Tasmanian provision is more flexible. A counter-claim need not be a small claim as defined, the parties may consent to jurisdiction over a counter-claim exceeding the jurisdictional limit, and the special commissioner has a discretion to hear such a counter-claim even if not all the parties consent: s12. See further Taylor, 'Small Claims', 621–3.
22 NSW, s20; Queensland, s18; Tasmania, s33; Victoria, s16; WA, s18. But in Tasmania a case can be stated to the Supreme Court on a point of law of general and public importance: s28.
23 NSW, s21; Queensland, s19; Tasmania, s34; Victoria, s17 (& cf. Administrative Law Act 1978 (Vic.) s4(3)); WA, s19. In two states it is expressly provided that tribunal proceedings are judicial: Queensland, s39; WA, s38. In all four tribunal states the tribunal is directed to apply 'natural justice': NSW, s34; Queensland, s37; Victoria, s34; WA, s36. But failure of a party to appear or give evidence is not itself a denial of natural justice: NSW, s32; Queensland, s34; Victoria, s32; WA, s34. For cases of violation of natural justice, see *R v Small Claims Tribunal ex p Cameron* [1976] VR 427, *APA Life Insurance Ltd v Charles* [1981] 2 NSWLR 252; Taylor, 'Small Claims', 653–4. Failure to give adequate notification to a defendant of the claim does not constitute a violation of natural justice, provided the statutory service requirements are complied with: *McLelland v Amcil Industries Pty Ltd* [1983] 1 NSWLR 615.
24 Supreme Courts have, sometimes reluctantly, given effect to this intent: e.g. *R v Small Claims Tribunal ex p Barwiner Nominees Pty Ltd* [1975] VR 831; *Thomson v Consumer Claims Tribunal* [1981] 1 NSWLR 68; *Jet 60 Minute Cleaners Pty Ltd v Brownette* [1981] 2 NSWLR 232, 237 (Hunt J, referring to 'palm-tree justice'); *APA Life Insurance Ltd v Charles* [1981] 2 NSWLR 252, 358 ('egregious error'); *McLelland v Amcil Industries Pty*

Ltd [1983] 1 NSWLR 615, 618 ('gross injustice . . . founded upon the conduct of the referee; but which it is beyond this Court to rectify').
25 ACT, s33; NT s32 (in both cases, leave is only to be granted for error of law or procedural unfairness to the applicant); SA, s58(3). In SA there is the further possibility of judicial review (s49) or the reservation of a point of law to the Supreme Court (s57) although these rights can be waived in advance: s66a.
26 But decisions of the Queensland Small Debts Court are not appealable, and judicial review is restricted in the same way as for the Tribunal: Magistrates Courts Act 1921 (Qld) s11(6). Generally, see Taylor, 'Small Claims', 668–73.
27 Present limits are: ACT, $2000; NSW, $3000; NT, $2000; Queensland, small claims, $1500, small debts, $1500; SA, $1000; Tasmania, $2000; Victoria, $3000; WA, small claims, $2000, small debts, $2000.
28 ACT, s12; NSW, s31(4); NT, s12; Queensland, s33(3); SA, s152a(1); Tasmania, ss25–6; Victoria, s31(3); WA, s33(3).
29 ACT, ss29, 41(2); NSW, s33; NT, ss29, 40(2); Queensland, s35; SA, s152d; Tasmania, s29; Victoria, s33; WA, s35. See Taylor, 'Small Claims', 566–7.
30 NSW, s30; Queensland, s32; SA, s152b; Tasmania, s23; Victoria, s30; WA, s32. By contrast the territories allow legal representation, but require leave for a non-legal agent to act: ACT, s42; NT, s41.
31 ACT, s44; NSW, s13(2); NT, s43; Queensland, s24(2) Victoria, s22(2); WA, s24(2). The SA Act has only a general provision (s152a(2)) relating to assistance to unrepresented parties in the presentation of their case. In Tasmania the special commissioner has powers of independent inquiry, and can have a report into a case prepared at the Crown's expense: s25(1)(a).
32 NSW, s22 ('best endeavours'); Queensland, s10; Victoria, s9; WA, s10 (all of which use the 'primary function' formula). The SA Act empowers, but does not require, conciliation: s152c. The ACT, NT, and Tasmanian Acts contain no such provisions.
33 *R v Walsh & Taylor ex p Palladium Car Park Pty Ltd* (unreported, Murray J, 1975): see Evans, 135. No reference was made to the issue on appeal: [1975] VR 949. On somewhat different grounds cf. Ison, 30–1. For an assessment of the Australian practice, see Taylor, 'Small Claims', 654–8. In the ACT there is provision for a compulsory conference before the Clerk of the Small Claims Court: ss10A–D (added 1985).
34 ACT, ss11, 12, 14; NSW, s31(4); NT, ss11, 12, 14; Queensland, s33(3); SA, s152a(2); Tasmania, s26(1)(b); Victoria, s31(3); WA, s33(3). For a strong argument in favour of the inquisitorial approach see Ison, 27–9.
35 For criticism see Ellinger, 126. On the NZ Act see generally NZRCC, 141–5; Frame [1982] *NZLR* 250.
36 ACT, ss33(2)(a), 37(1)(b), 40(1); NT, ss32(2)(a), 36(1)(b), 39(1); SA, ss57(1), 63(2); Tasmania, s28.
37 *R v Small Claims Tribunal, ex p Barwiner Nominees Pty Ltd* [1975] VR 831, 835–6 (Gowans J); *Walsh (Referee of the Small Claims Tribunal v Palladium Car Park Pty Ltd* [1975] VR 949, 955.
38 NSW, s23(2); Queensland, s10(2).
39 To similar effect *Jet 60 Minute Cleaners Pty Ltd v Brownette* [1981] 2 NSWLR 232, 236 (Hunt J). The point was left open by the Queensland

Full Court in *R v District Court Judges, ex p Kruger Enterprises Ltd* (1982) 41 ALR 531, but McPherson J 'inclined to the view' that the tribunal was not bound to apply the law: id., 536. In *Cachia v Isaacs* (1985) 3 NSWLR the Court of Appeal held that a tribunal determination could create an issue estoppel.

40 Cf. *Walter Reid & Co. Ltd v Murphy* [1924] QSR 1; Small Debts Recovery Act 1912 (NSW) s7(1); Taylor, 'Small Claims', 602–4, 658–60.

41 In the territories there is specific provision for a report of the reasons for the magistrate's decision: ACT, s37; NT, s36. General provisions may perhaps be used to the same effect in SA: ss63(1)(d), 64. Tasmania, ss11(1)(b), 26(4), requires a summary record to be kept.

42 For complaints about small claims adjudication see Lynch (1983) 8 *LSB* 94, and the cases cited in n24.

43 There were 3447 small claims applications in Victoria in the year 1984–5: Attorney-General's Advisory Committee, *Report on the Future Role of Magistrates' Courts* (1986) 15.

44 See Appelbey, in Cappelletti & Weisner, 683; Turner (1974) 48 *ALJ* 345; Hickman (1977) *NLJ* 856; Hanks (1978) 3 *LSB* 60. For the strengthened 'special procedures' (a form of court-annexed arbitration) see Thomas (1981) 131 *New LJ* 429.

45 The WA Law Reform Commission rejected such an extension, for fear of overloading the tribunal with undefended commercial claims, and instead proposed a special small debts jurisdiction of the Local Court (with a jurisdictional limit of $1000) similar to the Queensland Small Debts Court (but applying the substantive law rather than 'equity and good conscience'): Report, *Small Debts Court* (1979). That recommendation was implemented in 1982: Local Courts Act 1904 (WA) Part VIA.

46 In 1978, a proposal to increase the small claims jurisdiction of the SA Court from $500 to $2500 met with strong opposition from the Law Society and in Parliament. In the event an increase to $1250 was agreed on: see SA, *Parl Debs (H of A)* 21 Mar. 1978, 2403ff. But that amendment never came into force: the present limit of $1000 was inserted by the Statutes Amendment (Jurisdiction of Courts) Act 1981 (SA) s11.

47 Credit Administration Act 1984 (Vic.), conferring on the tribunal jurisdiction over consumer credit disputes up to $20 000.

48 Cf. id., 21.

49 Arbitration (Civil Actions) Act 1983 (NSW). See *Adair v Morahan* (1986) 5 NSWLR 146.

50 See the contrasting treatment of these issues in Victoria, on the one hand by the Civil Justice Committee, which rejected the 'dual system' and recommended that the small claims tribunals be integrated into the Magistrates' Courts, while retaining the advantages of the small claims procedure (*Report concerning the Administration of Civil Justice in Victoria* (1984) 234–40), and, on the other hand, by the Attorney-General's Advisory Committee, which strongly rejected the arguments for such a merger (*Report on the Future Role of Magistrates' Courts* (1986) 20–3). Generally on reform of small claims procedures see Robbins (1982) 7 *LSB* 280, (1983) 8 *LSB* 28.

CHAPTER 13
Other Specialist Courts and Tribunals

13.1 Other Specialist Courts and Tribunals — A Conspectus

Family courts, children's courts, industrial courts, commissions and boards, and small claims courts and tribunals may be the more important specialist courts and tribunals in Australia, but they by no means exhaust the list. Many other courts have been established by statute to perform some special function. Some of these — coroner's courts for example — are English importations with a long history. Others, such as licensing courts or warden's courts, are more distinctly Australian institutions, long established here. But many are relatively recent creations — a Land and Environment Court, a Local Government Court, a Market Court, and so on. Many more administrative tribunals exist, at both federal and state level, performing a wide variety of functions. Residential tenancy tribunals, town planning appeal boards, licensing boards and tribunals for various occupations — the list is even longer. It is not possible, in a work of this scope, to deal with the multitude of administrative tribunals,[1] but some discussion of the relations between specialist courts and tribunals, on the one hand, and the ordinary courts on the other, is required.

It is not always clear why a particular function is assigned to ordinary courts or to a specialist court specially created, or to a tribunal. Requirements of informality and expertise may provide the answer, but the impression of ordinary courts as excessively formal and 'inexpert' is at least reinforced by failure to confer novel jurisdictions on them. This poses problems for a coherent court structure, and it also makes the courts' function of jurisdictional review of tribunals an important and delicate one. But first a brief survey of other specialist courts in Australia will be undertaken.

13.2 Some Examples of Other Specialist Courts

(1) Licensing courts

At common law, 'the multitude of taverns was not mischievous but by accident and was not *malum in se* and not punishable'.[2] In Australia the authorities took a stricter view. The first accounts of European settlement refer to the drunkenness of the 'lower class': some of the first governmental acts — legislative and curial — involved the issue of liquor licences.[3] Liquor licensing, as a form of social control, as a planning device, as a forum for conflict between the temperance movement and its opponents, has a colourful, if unexplored, history.[4]

In four states, separate licensing courts are now established to decide on applications for liquor licences and permits, and similar matters. These are courts of record, constituted by judges or licensing magistrates (the former are lawyers; the latter need not be).[5] There is an appeal, at least on questions of law, to the Supreme Court (in New South Wales, the District Court), and there may also be provision for stating a case to the Supreme Court on questions of law.[6]

The equivalent bodies in Tasmania, Victoria, and the two territories are boards or commissions.[7] Their licensing functions are very similar, but there is less emphasis on legal qualifications for membership than on relevant experience. Divergent provisions for appeal exist, ranging from a full appeal to the Supreme Court on the one hand, to the general exclusion of appeal or review on the other.[8]

The point of formalizing hearings on applications for the various kinds of liquor licence in this way is to enable counter-arguments from competitors or other objectors to be heard, and some balancing of the relevant interests to be made. Why this should be done in separate courts rather than in a specialized tribunal (as in four jurisdictions) or by justices (as in England) is not so clear. The historical and social importance of the problem may account for the present elaborate arrangements for liquor licensing. Whether it justifies them is another matter.

(2) Mining courts

Like alcohol, mining has played an important part in Australia's social and economic history. Like alcohol, its contribution to Australia's well-being has sometimes been doubted. The institution of the warden's court developed as a way of providing summary justice on the spot, in the often turbulent disputes over miners' rights or mining ventures. The emphasis was less on legal procedure than on the technical expertise and experience of the warden.

These elements continue in the present arrangements for warden's courts in six of the eight jurisdictions.[9] There is no requirement that wardens or mining registrars have legal qualifications. The emphasis is on summary procedures for the settlement of disputes, and in general, the jurisdiction of warden's courts is widely defined, including matters such as the ambit of mining claims, disputes over the use of land or water rights under a claim, or arising out of mining ventures, and the forfeiture of mining leases and claims.

The courts have taken a generally benevolent approach to the jurisdiction of warden's courts. As Wells J commented in one case:

It would be absurd to profess ignorance of the character, function and work of Wardens and their Courts, who have been exercising their important jurisdictions, and doing valuable work for many years. They perform for the mining community, to the members of which vociferous quarrels and violent disputes are not unknown, a service not dissimilar to that performed by the old courts of piedpouldre [English market courts]. A mining Warden, too, is expected to know mining and miners, and the customs, expectations, practices and attitudes of those over whom they may be called upon to exercise their jurisdiction. He should be able to deal, decisively, authoritatively, and promptly, with disputes that arise in the field. Unless it is demonstrated on appeal that the Warden whose judgment is called in question has committed some egregious blunder in his findings of fact, or has misdirected himself on the law, I should, I think, be slow to interfere with those parts of his judgment that emanate principally from his knowledge, understanding and assessment of the esoteric world of miners and mining tenements.[10]

However, there are limits to the flexibility with which warden's courts can operate. Minimum procedures must be complied with,[11] and the warden is to apply the substantive common law rather than a form of 'palm-tree' (or even 'gum-tree') justice.[12] The ordinary courts may intervene in matters before the warden to decide issues of law not involving substantial discretions.[13] And there are marked differences between the states, both in the judicial and non-judicial functions of wardens.[14]

In two states, different provision is made. In the Australian Capital Territory mining matters are regulated by the Minister, with provision in certain cases for arbitration and with the general oversight of the administrative process left to the ordinary courts.[15] In Victoria in 1969, warden's courts were abolished, and their jurisdiction transferred to Magistrates' and County Courts. The reason given was the decline in mining activities, which prevented specialization by wardens, meant that no experienced assessors were available, and produced doubt and confusion over mining law and procedure.[16] But an amendment was accepted, requiring courts exercising mining jurisdiction to do so without regard to legal forms and technicalities and in an informal way. This, it was claimed, would 'preserve the inquisitorial nature of the court'.[17] The intention of the Victorian Act was to bring about a change of forum rather than substance.

(3) *Land and environment and local government courts and tribunals*
Regulation of land use has become a feature of governmental activity. Disputes frequently arise from the granting or refusal of consent to

particular uses of land, or about the compensation payable for resumption of land for public purposes. Although primary decisions on these questions are normally made administratively, by central or local government, it is necessary to provide some system of review or appeal in a tribunal or court. This area contains vivid examples of the conflict between the use of specialist courts or tribunals and the role of the ordinary courts.

There is no uniformity in Australian arrangements for these matters. For example, questions of compensation for land acquisition are dealt with by the Supreme Court in a special Division in South Australia,[18] by a Board of Review as an alternative to the Supreme Court in Victoria,[19] by a separate Land Court in Tasmania,[20] and by a specialist tribunal in Western Australia and the Northern Territory.[21] Very different provisions exist for the composition, jurisdiction, and functioning of these bodies, and for appeal from them.

The most interesting arrangement, in terms of the relation between specialist and general courts, is the New South Wales Land and Environment Court, established in 1979. Land compensation, local government, and planning disputes had previously been dealt with in a number of forums, the most important of which were the Land and Valuation Court and the Local Government Appeals Tribunal. As part of a more general reform of New South Wales environmental and planning laws, it was proposed in 1976 to abolish the Land and Valuation Court and to confer its jurisdiction on the Supreme Court and the District Court.[22] This was supported by the local Law Reform Commission, which discussed the case for and against a specialist court in the following terms:

Advantages of having a special court to deal with land and valuation matters have been said to be — (a) greater consistency of decisions; and (b) greater efficiency by reason of a developed expertise of the judge of the court in the complexities of land laws and principles of valuation. The main disadvantage of a special court appears to us to be lack of flexibility in its ability to handle its workload. Insufficient work for the court means that an expensive public utility is not being fully used. Too much work may cause serious hardship to litigants through delays. A single court, for example, can only hear one urgent case at the one time. The great fluctuations in the volume of business of the court over the years demonstrates the seriousness of this criticism. In our view the advantages of consistency of decisions and expertise of the judge of the Land and Valuation Court may be retained otherwise than by the retention of a separate court. If the Supreme Court were invested with the jurisdiction and the work assigned to a Division, a judge of that Division would ordinarily deal with the work and would be available for other work when there was insufficient land and valuation business. On the other hand if there were more urgent land or valuation work than he could manage he would be able to call on other judges for assistance. In our view this would result in better use of judicial time and also of court staff.[23]

After a considerable delay what emerged was a radically different proposal, for the establishment of a new court, of co-ordinate status with the New South Wales Supreme Court,[24] and with a wide jurisdiction over environmental planning and protection appeals, local government appeals, land tenure, valuation, rating and compensation appeals, and civil and summary criminal enforcement in matters of environmental planning and protection.[25] The Court's civil jurisdiction is extended so that it can

hear and dispose of proceedings —
(a) to enforce any right, obligation or duty conferred or imposed by a planning or environmental law;
(b) to review, or command, the exercise of a function conferred or imposed by a planning or environmental law; and
(c) to make declarations of right in relation to any such right, obligation or duty or the exercise of any such function . . . [26]

and s71 makes this jurisdiction exclusive of the Supreme Court.[27] Here is a specialized court with a vengeance, established expressly as a superior alternative to the Supreme Court. But specialization is not its only rationale. Extensive provision is made for the Court to sit with expert assessors, and for an assessor to conduct compulsory preliminary conferences, or, by consent, inquiries, in planning and compensation appeals, reporting to the Court his views and findings, and in certain circumstances disposing of the case entirely.[28]

The emphasis on flexibility and informality is underlined by s38: the appeals jurisdiction is to be 'conducted with as little formality and technicality and with as much expedition as the proper consideration of the matters before the court permit' and the laws of evidence do not apply. (The Land and Valuation Court had been criticised for undue formality and adherence to the rules of evidence.[29]) Parties may be represented not only by a barrister or solicitor but by a non-legal agent.[30] The Court has independent powers to inform itself of matters in dispute and to take the public interest into account.[31] Appeals to the Supreme Court (except in civil and criminal enforcement matters) are on questions of law only.[32]

The Minister emphasized these innovations in justifying the choice of a separate court rather than a new division of the Supreme Court.

The proposed Land and Environment Court Act will not be inferior in status to the Supreme Court. The judges of the new court will be equal in status to those of the Supreme Court. For the first time the jurisdiction of the new court will cover comprehensively the fields of planning, building, pollution, heritage, valuation and land tenure . . . With the enhanced jurisdiction of the new court, I am sure there will be little difficulty in attracting the most eminently qualified personnel to the court. Though it is generally desirable to avoid separate tribunals or courts, an exception has always been made to that principle in areas of specialized or unique jurisdiction. For many years this state has had two such bodies the Industrial Commission of New South Wales and the Land and Valuation Court. When one compares the contribution of the former judges of the Land and Valuation Court with their perceptive insights and consistent development of policies to the development of planning law since 1972 one can and will see the advantages of a separate court. Additionally, the proposed new court is a somewhat innovative experiment in dispute resolution mechanisms. It attempts to combine judicial and administrative dispute-resolving techniques and it will utilize non-legal experts as technical and conciliation assessors. Such a method of operation does not fit harmoniously with the operation of the Supreme Court at present. Nonetheless, I predict that it will not be long before the Supreme Court adopts the novel and innovative structure and method of operation of the Land and Environment Court.[33]

The Land and Environment Court is by far the most comprehensive attempt at rationalization of dispute-settlement machinery in these important fields. In other states a miscellany of courts and tribunals performs similar functions, although some consolidation of machinery was achieved in Western Australia in 1978 with the establishment of Land Valuation Tribunals,[34] and Queensland has a Local Government Court to hear appeals from decisions of local government authorities.[35]

(4) Coroner's courts

In Chapter 5 reference was made to the power of coroners to commit for trial persons suspected of homicide or arson. This is not the coroner's primary function but arises from that function, which is to inquire into violent or unexplained deaths or certain serious or destructive fires. The purpose of inquests (into deaths) or inquiries (into fires) is not to produce a decision as to their cause which is binding on anyone, but to arrive at a verdict, after taking evidence, as to the probable cause of the death or fire, upon which appropriate action may be taken by police, fire-fighting authorities, or government.[36] 'Crowner's quest law' has a long and interesting history,[37] and coronial inquests and inquiries continue to provide an important — often the only — public forum where these matters can be investigated.[38]

(5) Courts of disputed returns

One of the established powers or 'privileges' of each House of Parliament is to determine its own composition: this includes such matters as qualifications for election and the validity of any election.[39] Elections can be challenged on grounds such as bribery or undue influence of voters, or illegalities under the relevant Electoral Act, or mistaken admission or refusal of votes. In all Australian jurisdictions, such disputes have been referred by statute to a court of disputed returns or similar body. In each case the jurisdiction is exercised either by the Supreme Court itself[40] or by a Supreme Court judge.[41] In the case of the Commonwealth, the High Court is the Court of Disputed

Returns.[42] Characteristically, the Court is exhorted to be flexible rather than legalistic, for example to decide according to 'the real justice and good conscience the case, without regard to legal forms and solemnities'.[43] The implication, apparently, is that legal forms and solemnities here are unjust and unconscionable.

(6) Other courts

Even this list does not exhaust the varieties of specialist courts in Australia: indeed, so many different entities are described as separate courts in the legislation of the nine jurisdictions that it would be extremely difficult to locate them all. Other examples include Courts of Marine Inquiry, a sort of maritime equivalent of the coroner, with the duty to inquire into wrecks and maritime accidents, but with certain disciplinary powers over mariners;[44] courts martial, which enforce military discipline;[45] the New South Wales Compensation Court, which hears worker's compensation claims;[46] the Victorian Market Court, which has a very specialized function in enforcing consumer legislation,[47] and so on.

13.3 Proliferation in the Court System — Desirable, Avoidable, or a Necessary Evil?

As this brief account may suggest, the pressure for establishing separate specialist courts and tribunals is a continuing one. A very large number of such bodies exists: in many ways, specialist courts bear more resemblance to tribunals than they do to courts of general jurisdiction — though, described as courts, they may be more nearly integrated into the structure of appeal, and share other organizational elements. Although there have been complaints at the proliferation of jurisdictions and the exclusion of the ordinary courts from new areas of decision,[48] it is not possible to lay down any general rule. As we have seen, specialist courts may be established in areas not traditionally dealt with by ordinary courts, with a high 'public policy' or technical content, or in areas where the law or its administration has become too rigid. They are established to allow the appointment of specialist judges (not necessarily with legal training, or with additional qualifications), or to provide different forms of decision-making (the use of assessors, pre-trial conciliation, and so on), with legal representation excluded or non-legal representation allowed. Above all, they are established to encourage informality and speed in hearing cases, and to avoid some of the costs and delay seemingly inherent in litigation in ordinary courts.

But there are (with minor exceptions confined to the level of federal jurisdiction) no constitutional reasons preventing similar reforms in the ordinary courts, and indeed some of the machinery already exists.[49] It is, for example, doubtful whether small claims tribunals have carried out their novel assignment more efficiently than small claims courts, where these are established as separate divisions of Local Courts or Courts of Petty Sessions.

The establishment of a separate jurisdiction, whatever its advantages, carries with it certain costs and risks. The costs of separate administration — premises, court staff, judges — may be considerable, and will probably be more than the equivalent costs of vesting jurisdiction in courts already established. A more important cost — not borne directly by the state but by litigants — is that of jurisdictional conflict and uncertainty: whenever a case is decided on jurisdictional grounds rather than on the merits, costs are thrown away and time is wasted. The more separate jurisdictions there are, the more such cases there are likely to be. The common law's experience with these problems is long; they led directly to the Judicature Act system, with its emphasis on generality of jurisdiction and finality or proceedings in a single court. Proliferation of courts touches a sensitive nerve: judicial complaints at it cannot be put down entirely to self-interest or self-defence.

If specialist courts are to be established, there is much to be said for establishing them with a consolidated jurisdiction, over as broad a range of cognate matters as can be. In this respect the Land and Environment Court may be a model for the future: the same could be said for the Family Court of Australia, but for the troublesome jurisdictional conflicts discussed in Chapter 10. What must be avoided is the establishment of special courts not on their merits but as a reaction against the inadequacies of the ordinary courts, as an easy way of avoiding necessary reform in court procedures and practices. If pre-trial conciliation is desirable in certain cases, it is desirable in those cases wherever they are decided. If the law of evidence has repeatedly to be excluded by statute in specialist jurisdictions, then the law of evidence needs reforming.[50] If costs and delays are a problem, then measures should be taken to reduce them, wherever they occur. The alternative is that the ordinary courts may become an enclave of formality in a divergent, scattered system, avoided rather than useful, with (relatively) diminishing jurisdiction and correspondingly less relevant to the needs of the community.

13.4 The Relations Between the Ordinary Courts and Specialist Courts and Tribunals

One role which the 'ordinary' superior courts of common law have always had is that of judicial review of the operation of specialist tribunals and courts. At common law there was no inherent right of appeal from one court or tribunal to another: the appeal is an almost wholly statutory creation. This is also the case in Australia, with the exception of the High Court's entrenched appellate jurisdiction over state Supreme Courts, under s73 of the Constitution. Otherwise no appeal need be provided, and many decisions of specialist courts and tribunals are 'final' in this sense. Even where an appeal lies, it is frequently limited to questions of law or matters of general importance.

However, the Supreme Courts have inherited the supervisory jurisdiction of the Court of King's Bench over inferior courts, administrative tribunals, and the executive government generally, and this cannot readily be excluded. It is through judicial review rather than appeal that the ordinary courts maintain their position as the courts of general jurisdiction, and restrict specialist bodies to their particular statutory functions. In this way the formal coherence of the legal system is maintained, and a situation of rival courts asserting general jurisdiction avoided. But the Supreme Courts' role in this area has been markedly qualified by the exclusion of review of federal tribunals and administrative decisions: such review is now in almost all cases the function of the High Court and the Federal Court.

A general account of the administrative law of judicial review is outside the scope of this work.[51] But the common law position, and the recent statutory additions, will be briefly outlined, to fill out this account of the position of specialist courts and tribunals.

(1) Judicial review of decisions of inferior courts and tribunals

There is no single theory which explains, or justifies, the various grounds on which a Supreme Court can act at common law to review a decision of an inferior court or tribunal. Much of the law was developed over several hundred years through the use of the three main prerogative writs of prohibition, certiorari, and mandamus, and to some extent the modern law still bears the marks of the limitations imposed by those remedies. Prohibition enabled the court to prevent an inferior tribunal exceeding its powers; certiorari removed the decision of an inferior court or tribunal into the superior court so that it could be scrutinized for jurisdictional error, breach of natural justice, or manifest error of law; and mandamus enabled the court to order the inferior tribunal or authority to perform its duty, if it refused to do so. More recently the remedies of the declaration and the injunction have also been used: the former, in particular, is of great importance.[52]

Inferior tribunals and courts created by statute have no inherent jurisdiction, and can act only within the limits of their statutory mandate. The first, and primary, role of judicial review is to restrict the inferior court or tribunal to its proper jurisdiction. Thus the court or tribunal must be duly constituted, and any requirements of fact or law which are a necessary precondition to the exercise of jurisdiction ('jurisdictional facts') must in truth exist, or the decision will be vitiated.[53] Examples have already been given: the requirement of an actual or threatened interstate industrial dispute before the Australian Conciliation and Arbitration Commission can act, or of a 'consumer claim' between a 'trader' and a 'consumer' before a consumer claims tribunal can act. Whether a particular element in a decision goes to the tribunal's jurisdiction or not depends on such matters as the statutory context, the extent to which determining its existence is a matter of discretion and judgment for which the tribunal is better fitted, the status of the tribunal, and so on. In some cases the distinction between the jurisdiction of a tribunal and the merits of its decision has seemed almost to vanish, but the distinction is fundamental to the theory of judicial review and has been frequently reaffirmed.[54]

Even when acting within its jurisdiction the tribunal is limited in a variety of ways. It must comply with any statutory procedures, and will also (to the extent that these procedures are not treated as exhaustive) usually have to comply with the common law principles of natural justice. Broadly, these require that the decision-maker not be materially interested in the decision (absence of bias) and that the parties affected be given reasonable notice of the basis of the decision, and the opportunity to be heard.[55] Having satisfied the principles of natural justice, the tribunal must decide the issue at hand for itself (i.e. not under dictation or improper direction from another), having regard to the relevant considerations, and without considering wholly irrelevant or extraneous considerations.[56] Again, non-compliance with these requirements vitiates the decision. Finally, if in the 'record' of the decision of the tribunal there is a material error of law, again the court may intervene (in particular by certiorari) to quash the decision, requiring it to be made again.[57]

In these various ways, a person affected by a decision may obtain by judicial review what might otherwise have been achieved by appeal, had one existed. But appeal and review remain distinct. On appeal the court may substitute its own decision for an erroneous decision appealed from. In an exercise of judicial review it cannot do so. The decision remains exclusively one for the lower tribunal or court, which may (provided it avoids its earlier error) reach exactly the same decision as before.[58] And whereas an appeal exists only when specifically provided for, judicial review exists unless expressly excluded. As we have seen, attempts to exclude the supervisory jurisdiction of the ordinary courts are often made (e.g. in the case of industrial tribunals). But the courts interpret such privative clauses strictly, so that complete exclusion is rarely achieved.[59]

(2) Review of decisions of federal tribunals and courts

(A) THE ROLE OF THE HIGH COURT

In a variety of ways the position of federal tribunals and courts is different. The High Court has jurisdiction, conferred by s75(v) of the

Constitution, over 'matters in which a writ of Mandamus or prohibition or an injunction is sought against an officer of the Commonwealth'. The Court applies the ordinary common law rule of administrative review, and may grant other remedies if these are more convenient than one of the three named remedies (provided the named remedy is plausibly sought).[60] This constitutional (and thus non-excludable) jurisdiction has already been discussed in Chapter 9.

(B) THE FEDERAL COURT AND FEDERAL ADMINISTRATIVE REVIEW
In addition to concurrent jurisdiction over most matters within s75(v) of the Constitution,[61] the Federal Court also has jurisdiction to review a wide range of federal administrative actions under the Administrative Decisions (Judicial Review) Act 1977 (Cth). The grounds for review are set out in the Act (ss5–7): they reflect, and in some areas at least arguably extend, the available grounds at common law.[62] The Act is not only a new and more effective charter of federal administrative review: it also simplifies the procedures for review (a single 'application for review' replaces the nominate remedies) and avoids some of the obstacles to review at common law. In particular, reasons for many decisions can be required, and may form the basis for challenging the decision (ss13–14).[63] And the Act overrides privative clauses contained in earlier legislation (s4).

(C) THE ADMINISTRATIVE APPEALS TRIBUNAL (AAT)
The reasons for the creation of the AAT in 1975 were briefly referred to in Chapter 8. It marks a major development in review of administrative decision, since the AAT's function is not, or not primarily, to determine the legal validity of a federal administrative decision, but to 'review' it on the merits, as an independent authority. The AAT consists of a number of members with legal or administrative qualifications. Presidential members so far have all been judges of the Federal Court (acting, of course, in their personal capacity).[64] Under s25 of the Act, the AAT has to 'review' specified decisions on applications by a person affected. In contrast with the Administrative Decisions (Judicial Review) Act 1977 (Cth), the grounds for review are not specified, and to a considerable extent the AAT is at large. Although it will take note of administrative policy in particular areas it is not bound by such policies (unless they are given statutory force).[65] What it has to determine is whether the decision made is the preferable one, all things considered. It can review the facts of the case, and in many instances much more information becomes available through the arguments and investigations of the parties. It can also review the correctness of the application of the law to the facts, although since the AAT is a non-judicial body it cannot decide questions of law or jurisdiction conclusively.[66] In that respect it is in the same position as the original administrator. It can also give advisory opinions on questions of law where another Act so provides.[67]

As at 30 June 1986 the AAT had jurisdiction to review decisions under a total of 236 Commonwealth Acts and regulations and Australian Capital Territory ordinances,[68] a steep increase from 93 in 1980. The matters over which it does have jurisdiction vary greatly in importance, but they include decisions to deport persons under the Migration Act 1958 (Cth), decisions relating to pilot's licences under Air Navigation regulations, decisions of the Director-General of Social Services which vary decisions of a Social Security Appeals Tribunal, and so on.[69] A major extension in 1986 was the jurisdiction of the former Taxation Boards of Review in federal tax matters, which is now exercised by a Taxation Appeals Division of the AAT.[70] In its first three full years of operation the AAT averaged 288 applications for review annually.[71] For the three financial years from 1983–4 to 1985–6, that average had grown to 2160 (in 1985–6, it was 2555), an enormous increase, due in large part to new areas of jurisdiction.[72]

A good example of an important contentious jurisdiction, which has attracted a steady workload, is the power to review orders of deportation (122 applications, 1982–6). Exceptionally, the AAT here can only affirm the order or recommend that it be varied: the Minister is not bound to accept such recommendations (although so far he has done so in all but one case).[73] Very full reconsideration is given to the facts of each case and to any special factors in the applicant's favour. This important safeguard compares strikingly with the traditional unwillingness of courts to intervene in the area of deportation through judicial review — although there are signs of a more activist approach by the courts even in this sensitive area.[74]

Despite the conferral of jurisdiction over social welfare cases and taxation cases in 1980 and 1986 respectively, the AAT's jurisdiction still falls short of the original proposals made in the Kerr Report in 1971.[75] It is possible that the rather formal approach taken by the AAT in many cases, with a strict adversarial method and frequent use of legal representation, may deter further substantial increases in jurisdiction.[76] Within federal government departments different views are held as to the value of the AAT, at a time of financial restrictions in the public sector.[77] Its first president referred to the 'disparity between intention and execution',[78] though such a disparity is not a novel thing in human affairs! But the AAT is by any account an important experiment in public administration.

Although the AAT is principally a merits-review tribunal, it has jurisdiction over decisions which are 'purported' rather than lawful, so that it can in effect set aside a decision as *ultra vires*.[79] To this extent there is an overlap between the AAT's jurisdiction and those of the Federal Court and the High Court. This is not a disadvantage. Strictly alternative jurisdictions would present problems of choice of forum for someone seeking review of a doubtfully valid decision. And if the original decision was procedurally defective the AAT's own review may remedy the defect, freeing the decision on the merits from threat of collateral challenge in the courts.[80]

There is an 'appeal' on questions of law, under s44 of the Act, to the Federal Court sitting as a Full Court (and thence, under the Federal Court of Australia Act 1976, to the High Court). The appeal lies only from final decisions of the AAT, as distinct from preliminary rulings.[81] Formally the Federal Court is itself exercising 'original jurisdiction', since the AAT is not itself a court,[82] but the proceedings are indistinguishable from an appeal. There could be no appeal under s44 from an advisory opinion given by the AAT under s59,[83] but the Federal Court has heard a number of appeals from 'recommendations' in deportation cases. Since federal courts cannot decide abstract, hypothetical, or non-binding issues, the validity of the appeal in such cases is not self-evident. Perhaps what is at stake is the applicant's right to have the case reviewed by the Minister in the light of the AAT's recommendation — although that would not necessarily be the issue in the Federal Court.[84]

Only in Victoria is there any equivalent to the AAT,[85] although proposals for one have been made in New South Wales and Queensland,[86] and there are now Commercial Tribunals in three states with jurisdiction under various Acts.[87] One argument against an AAT is that the establishment of a centralized tribunal dominated by lawyers leads to excessive legalism and formalism in administration, and tends to assimilate administrative decision-making with judicial decision-making.[88] But such criticism has to meet the point that state tribunals continue to be established in a diffuse and disorganized way. Perhaps what is at issue is not the 'tribunal' form of decision-making, but the independence or lack of it of tribunals in sensitive policy areas.[89] If so the AAT is indeed an important improvement.

Notes

[1] There is no full study, and not even a complete list, of Australian tribunals. The Administrative Review Council compiled a list of 272 federal tribunals (defined according to fairly broad criteria): *Fourth Annual Report* (Parl. Paper 268/1980) 69–94. The WALRC listed 121 administrative appeals in its Report, *Review of Administrative Decisions: Appeals* (1982). On English tribunals see Wraith & Hutchesson, *Administrative Tribunals* (1973); Farmer, *Tribunals and Government* (1974); Frost & Howard, *Representation and Administrative Tribunals* (1977). On state tribunals see e.g. Harris (1972) 4 *Adel LR* 389.

[2] *Thomas v Sorrell* (1696) 1 Freeman 85, 90; 89 ER 53, 55 (Windam J).

[3] E.g. SA Act No. 4 of 1837, disallowed and replaced by Act No. 1 of 1839.

[4] On the system of liquor licensing in Australia see e.g. SA, *Royal Commission into . . . Intoxicating Liquors . . .* (1966) and references. For the NZ experience see Bollinger, *Grog's Own Country* (2nd edn, 1967).

[5] NSW, Liquor Act 1982; Queensland, Liquor Act 1912; SA, Liquor Licensing Act 1985; WA, Liquor Act 1970.

6 NSW, ss146–7; Queensland, ss5C, 5D (questions of law only); SA, ss17–18; WA, s21. On the jurisdiction of licensing courts cf. also *Dalgety Wine Estates Pty Ltd v Rizzon* (1979) 53 ALJR 647.
7 Tasmania, Licensing Act 1976 (Licensing Board of Tasmania); Victoria, Liquor Control Act 1968 (Liquor Control Commission); ACT, Liquor Ordinance 1975 (Liquor Licensing Board); NT, Liquor Act 1978 (Liquor Commission).
8 ACT, s76 (limited right of appeal); Tasmania, s5 (case stated by Board or by order of Supreme Court); Victoria, ss14–16 (case stated by Commission or by order of Supreme Court); NT, s56 (general privative clause).
9 NSW, Mining Act 1973; Queensland, Mining Act 1968; SA, Mining Act 1971; Tasmania, Mining Act 1929; NT, Mining Act 1980. See generally Forbes & Lang, *Australian Mining and Petroleum Laws* (2nd edn, 1987) ch. 11.
10 *Pacminex (Ops) Pty Ltd v Australian (Nephrite) Jade Mines Pty Ltd* (1974) 7 SASR 401, 415.
11 Cf. *Sykes v Collins* [1971] ALR 572 (service of summons).
12 *Georgio v Tanfara* (1976) 13 SASR 306, 309, 311 (Bray CJ) (regretting the result and suggesting alternative devices).
13 *Forster v Jododex Aust. Pty Ltd* (1972) 127 CLR 421; & cf. *Sinclair v Mining Warden at Maryborough* (1975) 132 CLR 473.
14 On appeals from warden's courts cf. *Stow v Mineral Holdings (Aust.) Pty Ltd* (1977) 51 ALJR 672.
15 Mining Ordinance 1930 (ACT) s63.
16 Mines (Abolition of Courts) Act 1969 (Vic.). See Victoria, (1969) 293 *Parl Debs* 3008–11. On abolition of the warden's court in Queensland see Forbes (1985) 5 *AMPLA Bulletin* 51.
17 Victoria, (1969) 294 *Parl Debs* 3715, 4528, 4530–1. See now Mines Act 1958 (Vic.) s207.
18 Supreme Court Act 1935 (SA) Part IIIA (inserted 1969). See also Valuation of Land Act 1971 (SA) ss25–25C.
19 Valuation of Land Act 1960 (Vic.) s14(2) & Part III.
20 Queensland, Land Act 1962 (Land Court & Land Appeal Court) (and see Valuation of Land Acts 1944 s21); Tasmania, Land Valuation Act 1971 Parts V, VI (Land Valuation Court).
21 WA, Land Valuations Tribunal Act 1978 (& cf. Valuation of Land Act 1978); NT, Valuation of Land Act 1963 Part VI (Land & Valuation Review Tribunal). In the ACT the jurisdiction is now exercised by the AAT. For a general account see ALRC 14, *Lands Acquisition and Compensation* (1980); Hyam, *The Law affecting the Valuation of Land in Australia* (1983) ch. 15.
22 See Environmental Planning Bill 1976 cl. 170 (compensation), cl. 173 (offences), cl. 188(5) (enforcement of awards).
23 NSWLRC 23, *Report on the Land and Valuation Court* (1975) 8–9.
24 The Court is a superior court of record (Land and Environment Court Act 1979 (NSW) s5). Its judges have the same status as Supreme Court judges (s9).
25 Id., ss18–21. And see generally Hort & Mobbs, *Outline of NSW Environmental and Planning Law* (1979) 91–104 (a description of the proposals in the 1979 Bill).

26 Land and Environment Court Act 1979 (NSW) s20(2). For the definition of 'a planning or environmental law' see s20(3).
27 Cf. also s24 (exclusive jurisdiction in certain compensation cases).
28 See s34 (preliminary conferences), s35 (inquiries), s36 (delegation to assessors), s37 (assessors sitting with judge). There is an appeal to a judge of the Court from a decision of assessors (s56A), and provision for them to refer questions of law to a judge (s36(5)). But the Land and Environment Court Amendment Bill 1987 will allow assessors to be dispensed with in certain cases.
29 Hort & Mobbs, 101.
30 Land and Environment Court Act 1979 (NSW) s63 (except in the summary criminal jurisdiction). Cf. Land and Valuation Court Act 1921 (NSW) s11.
31 Land and Environment Court Act 1979 (NSW) s39(4). But the Chief Judge of the Court has commented that the absence of budgetary provision for independent inquiries and reports renders this provision ineffective: Cripps, 'Environmental Law' (mimeo, 1986) 8.
32 Land and Environment Court Act 1979 (NSW) s57(1). For civil and criminal appeals see ss 56(b), 58(1); for transfer of cases from the Supreme Court to the Land and Environment Court, s72.
33 NSW, *Parl Debs*, 46th Parl. 2nd Sess. (1979) 3349–50. The Opposition, echoing the NSW Bar Association, criticized the Bill for not conferring jurisdiction on a Division of the Supreme Court: id., 3135–6, 3365.
34 Land Valuation Tribunals Act 1978 (WA). This replaced '20 boards and courts . . . involved in hearing and determining valuation disputes': WA, 220 *Parl Debs (NS)* (1978) 2617–8.
35 City of Brisbane Town Planning Act 1964 (Qld) (extended to other local government areas in 1966). See Row (1980) 10 *Qld Law Soc J* 3 for an account. In other states and the NT, the principal town planning tribunals are as follows: NT, Planning Appeals Committee (Planning Act 1979); SA, Planning Appeal Tribunal (Planning Act 1982); Tasmania, Planning Appeal Board (Local Government Act 1962); Victoria, Planning Appeals Tribunal (Planning Appeals Act 1981); WA, Town Planning Appeal Tribunal (Town Planning and Development Act 1928). There is no equivalent in the ACT because of the special forms of land tenure there: the Supreme Court has jurisdiction to vary land-use provisions in a lease under the City Area Leases Ordinance 1936 s11A. Generally see Fogg, *Australian Town Planning Law* (2nd edn, 1982) chs 12–13.
36 There is no appeal from a coroner's verdict but the courts have statutory and common law powers of review. Generally see Waller, *Coronial Law and Practice in New South Wales* (1973). On the status of coroner's courts as courts of record, *In re O'Callaghan* (1899) 27 VLR 957.
37 Cf. *Hamlet* Act V Sc. I, 123. On the history of coroners see Hunnisett, *The Medieval Coroner* (1961); Gross, ed., *Select Cases from the Coroners' Rolls AD 1265–1413* (1896); McKeough (1983) 6 *UNSWLJ* 191. On the modern English position, Thurston, *Coronership* (1976).
38 Whether coroners in Australia have made appropriate use of their important office is another matter: cf. Harding, *Police Killings in Australia* (1970) s.v. 'Inquests'.
39 *Goodwin v Fortescue* (1604) 2 St Tr 91; *Barnardiston v Soame* (1674) 6 St Tr 1092, (1689) 6 St Tr 1119.

40 Tasmania, Electoral Act 1985 Part VIII; NT, Electoral Act 1980 Part XIII. In Victoria, the Supreme Court is the Court of Disputed Returns: Constitution Act Amendment Act 1958 Part V Division 22.
41 NSW, Parliamentary Electorates and Elections Act 1912 Part VI; Queensland, Elections Act 1983 Part IX (Elections Tribunal); SA, Electoral Act 1985 Part XII; WA, Electoral Act 1907 Part V.
42 Commonwealth Electoral Act 1918 (Cth) Part XXII. The High Court may refer a disputed return to a Supreme Court in the state where the election was held: s354. The Parliament may also refer to the Court any question relating to qualifications of MPs or Senators or any vacancy in either House: s376. See e.g. *In re Senator Webster* (1975) 6 ALR 65. This looks suspiciously like an advisory opinions jurisdiction: perhaps it could be saved on the basis that the High Court is merely acting as *curia designata*!
43 Queensland, s145. Cf. Cth, s364.
44 E.g. Marine Act 1936 (SA) ss28, 38–9, 43, 86 (Courts of Survey), ss106–25 (Courts of Marine Inquiry); Inquiries into Wrecks Act 1864 (WA); Western Australian Marine Act 1982 (WA) Part VII (Local Court as Court of Marine Inquiry); Navigation Act 1901 (NSW) Part III; Navigation Act 1912 (Cth) Part IX. On the role of assessors in federal courts of marine inquiry see *Re TNT Alltrans* (1986) 67 ALR 107.
45 Courts-Martial Appeals Act 1955 (Cth); Defence Act 1903 (Cth) Pt VIII.
46 Compensation Court Act 1984 (NSW).
47 Market Court Act 1978; Pagone & Cunningham (1979) 6 *Monash ULR* 76; Victoria, Civil Justice Committee, *Preliminary Study concerning the Administration of Civil Justice in Victoria* (1984) 237–42.
48 E.g. Street (1978) 52 *ALJ* 594.
49 E.g. Conciliation Act 1929 (SA) providing for judicial conciliation in Supreme Court proceedings.
50 As the ALRC has concluded: ALRC 38, *Evidence* (1987).
51 See generally *de Smith's Judicial Review of Administrative Action* (4th edn, ed. Evans, 1980) and for an Australian statement, Aronson & Franklin, *Review of Administrative Action* (1987).
52 A remedy less often used is habeas corpus, to compel the release of someone wrongly detained. On the development of these remedies see de Smith, 584–603; for the modern law, id., Part III; Aronson & Franklin, chs 16–20.
53 De Smith, 93–155; Aronson & Franklin, 78–82. These principles apply also to 'domestic tribunals' established under the rules of a club, association, trade union, etc.: see e.g. *Cains v Jenkins* (1979) 26 ALR 652.
54 A controversial example is *Anisminic Ltd v Foreign Compensation Commission* [1969] 2 AC 147. If the distinction was ever in doubt, later cases have tended to reinstate it: see e.g. *SE Asia Fire Bricks SB v Non- Metallic Mineral Products Mfg Employees Union* [1981] AC 363; Leigh [1980] *Public Law* 34.
55 De Smith, 156–277; Aronson & Franklin, chs 6–8; Flick, *Natural Justice* (1979).
56 De Smith, 278–356; Aronson & Franklin, 44–54.
57 De Smith, 400–8, 518–21; Aronson & Franklin, 35–41.
58 As in *Green v Daniels* (1977) 13 ALR 1; cf. (1977) 2 *LSB* 251.
59 De Smith, 357–76; Aronson & Franklin, ch. 21. Privative clauses in Victorian Acts before 1978 are overridden by the Administrative Law Act

1978 (Vic.) (in respect of tribunals and inferior courts). See Glick (1980) 12 *MULR* 417.
60 Judiciary Act 1903 (Cth) s32; *Pitfield v Franki* (1970) 123 CLR 448; *R v Cook, ex p Twigg* (1980) 31 ALR 353.
61 Judiciary Act 1903 (Cth) s39B. See Chapter 8.
62 On the Act see Pearce, *The Australian Administrative Law Service* (1979) I, 2091ff; Aronson & Franklin, 241–56; Thynne & Goldring, *Accountability and Control* (1987) 166–87. In general the Act does not extend common law principles of review: *Kioa v Minister for Immigration and Ethnic Affairs* (1985) 62 ALR 321. But those principles are themselves expanding, and the scope of review under the Act expands with them.
63 In 1985 there were 1807 requests for reasons under the Act, only 125 of which were refused: Administrative Review Council, *Tenth Annual Report 1985–86* (1986) 169–71.
64 Administrative Appeals Tribunal Act 1975 (Cth) s7(1); *Drake v Minister for Immigration and Ethnic Affairs* (1979) 24 ALR 577.
65 *Re Georges & Minister for Immigration and Ethnic Affairs* (1978) 22 ALR 667; *Drake v Minister for Immigration and Ethnic Affairs* (1979) 24 ALR 577, 589–91 (Bowen CJ, Deane J); *Minister for Immigration and Ethnic Affairs v Pochi* (1980) 31 ALR 666. See Sharpe, *The Administrative Appeals Tribunal and Policy Review* (1986); Pearce (1980) 11 *FLR* 203.
66 *Re Costello* (1979) 2 ALD 934.
67 Administrative Appeals Tribunal Act 1975 (Cth) s59. The only such provision so far is Ombudsman Act 1976 (Cth) s11.
68 Listed in ARC, *Tenth Annual Report 1985–86* (1986) Appendix 4.
69 On this jurisdiction see ARC 8, *Social Security Appeals* (1981); ARC 21, *The Structure and Form of Social Security Appeals* (1984).
70 Taxation Boards of Review (Transfer of Jurisdiction) Act 1986 (Cth), following the recommendation in ARC 17, *Review of Taxation Decisions by Boards of Review* (1983).
71 ARC, *Fourth Annual Report 1979–80* (1980) 64–8.
72 In 1985–6, 29.5% of cases were social security appeals, 26.0% veterans' appeals, 11.2% freedom of information matters. See *Tenth Annual Report 1985–86* (1986). A significant feature of the jurisdiction has been the way in which new heads of jurisdiction initially attract a very large number of applications, which then reduces in size as the AAT establishes guidelines and principles appropriate to the area. Thus in 1982–3 social security appeals constituted 64.1% of all applications, in 1985–6, only 29.5% (in numerical terms, 1104 compared with 735).
73 A recommendation by the Administrative Review Council that the AAT be able to decide in favour of, rather than recommend, non-deportation was rejected: id., 38. In consequence judicial members of the AAT have been reluctant to exercise the jurisdiction, leading to an ARC recommendation that deputy presidents of the AAT be permitted to do so: ARC 19, *Rights of Review under the Migration Act 1958 and related Legislation — Interim Report on the Composition of the AAT* (1983) 3–6. But the Minister has at least to exercise great care in rejecting an AAT recommendation: *Barbaro v Minister of Immigration and Ethnic Affairs* (1982) 46 ALR 123.
74 Cf. *Re Jeropoulos* (1980) 2 ALD 891 with *R v Brixton Prison Governor, ex p Soblen* [1963] 2 KB 243; *Salemi v MacKellar (No. 2)* (1977) 137 CLR

396. For recent examples of greater activism by the courts: see e.g. *A-G (Hong Kong) v Shiu* [1983] 2 AC 629; *Kioa v Minister of Immigration and Ethnic Affairs* (1985) 62 ALR 321. The ARC has recommended further extensions of the AAT's jurisdiction in this field: ARC 25, *Review of Migration Decisions* (1985).
75 Commonwealth Administrative Law Committee, *Report* (1971) 86–92.
76 See generally Curtis, in Goldring, ed., *The Workings of the Administrative Appeals Tribunal* (1980) 5; Gyles, id., 37; Brennan (1980) 9 *Syd LR* 1.
77 Cf. the different assessments by Skehill, Broome & Davey, in Goldring. For general accounts of different areas of its work see Ross, id., 23; Kirby (1978) 2 *UNSWLJ* 203; Brennan (1979) 4 *Otago LR* 286; Pearce, I, 5023–64; Osborne (1982) 13 *FLR* 150; Hall (1983) 57 *ALJ* 389; Goldring (1982) 13 *FLR* 90; Peiris (1986) 6 *Leg Studies* 303; Aronson & Franklin, ch. 10; Thynne & Goldring, 153–66; Layton (1986) 24 *Law Soc J* 38.
78 Brennan (1980) 2.
79 *Collector of Customs (NSW) v Brian Lawlor Automotive Pty Ltd* (1979) 24 ALR 307; *Deputy Commissioner of Patents v Board of Control of Michigan Technological University* (1979) 28 ALR 551. And cf. *Re Adams* (1976) 1 ALD 251 (Brennan J).
80 On the choice between AAT appeal and administrative review see Administrative Decisions (Judicial Review) Act 1977 (Cth) s10(2)(b)(ii); *Anderson v Commissioner of Employees' Compensation* (1986) 72 ALR 41.
81 *Director-General of Social Services v Chaney* (1980) 31 ALR 571.
82 *Committee of Direction of Fruit Marketing v Australian Postal Commission* (1980) 30 ALR 599, 606 (Mason & Wilson JJ).
83 *Re Reference under s11 of Ombudsman Act* (1979) 2ALD 86, 91 (Brennan J).
84 The High Court declined to hear an appeal from a decision of the Federal Court on appeal from the AAT, on the basis that the Minister would not be bound by any decision: *Minister of Immigration and Ethnic Affairs v Pochi* (1981) 36 ALR 561. The Court assumed, without explaining, the validity of the appeal to the Federal Court from a recommendation.
85 Administrative Appeals Tribunal Act 1984 (Vic.). The Act was in part inspired by a critical review of the working of Victorian tribunals by the Victorian Law Foundation, *Administrative Tribunals in Victoria* (1983), noted (1983) 8 *LSB* 92. On the Victorian Act see Kyrou, *Victorian Administrative Law* (1985).
86 NSWLRC, Report 16, *Appeals in Administration* (1973) 64–70; John (1986) *Qld Law Soc J* 83. But there is a Government and Related Employees Appeal Tribunal in NSW: see Cahill, *Promotion and Disciplinary Appeals in Government Service* (1986). By contrast the WALRC recommended that administrative appeals be heard by administrative divisions of the Supreme Court and Local Court: Project 26(1), *Review of Administrative Decisions: Appeals* (1982) 92–109. No action has yet been taken. A New Zealand equivalent has been in operation since 1968: Wild (1972) 22 *U Tor LJ* 258. For mixed verdicts on it see Northey (1974) 6 *NZULR* 25, and (1977) 15 *Alberta LR* 186; NZRCC, 25–6, 91–3.
87 See Commercial Tribunal Act 1982 (SA), and similar NSW and WA Acts of 1984. The SA Tribunal, for example, has jurisdiction over commercial (as distinct from residential) tenancies.
88 See e.g. Jinks (1982) 41 *AJ Pub Adm* 209.
89 Cf. Hughes, in Tay & Kamenka, eds, *Law-making in Australia* (1980) 263.

PART 4

Prospects for Change

CHAPTER 14

Reform of Australian Courts

14.1 An Increasing Pace of Change

It will have become clear that the Australian courts since 1975 have undergone a remarkable number of changes, unprecedented since the establishment of the first Supreme Courts in the Australian colonies, 100 to 150 years ago. Many of these changes have been at federal level: the High Court's removal to Canberra in 1980 and a sequence of reforms to its original and appellate jurisdiction, the creation of two major courts, the Family Court of Australia and the Federal Court of Australia, with consequent jurisdictional extensions and disputes, and the establishment of two new systems of review of federal administrative action through the Administrative Appeals Tribunal and the Federal Court. But changes are also increasingly widespread at state level: the abolition of Privy Council appeals, large extensions in the jurisdiction of intermediate and inferior civil and criminal courts, the institution of small claims and small debts courts or tribunals, more secure tenure for judges and especially magistrates, the extension of legal aid, and various props to or mitigations of the adversary system (forms of official representation or intervention, pre-trial counselling and other pre-trial procedures aimed at avoiding delay).[1] There have also been continuing experiments with the structure and procedures of industrial tribunals and of children's courts, and, at least in Victoria, a thorough-going review of judicial administration.[2]

Substantial changes are likely to continue to be made, although fluctuations in government, the economy, and prevailing political ideologies make these difficult to predict. Possibilities include further restrictions in trial by jury, in civil cases, and possibly also in criminal trials, consolidation of administrative jurisdictions and in methods of administrative review and appeal (as with the Victorian Administrative Appeals Tribunal), reform in the procedures of and appeals from magistrates courts, and a continuation of the trend to replace lay justices with legally trained magistrates. Possibilities at federal level, as we have seen, include the reform of admiralty jurisdiction, the 'renovation' of the Family Court,[3] and further extensions to the jurisdiction of the Administrative Appeals Tribunal.

Other suggestions are, perhaps, more problematic: unified civil courts at state level, special indigenous courts for Aborigines,[4] consultative machinery on judicial appointments, formal systems of judicial training or education,[5] further extensions in the rules for standing and class actions to allow important matters of public concern to be more easily litigated,[6] improved collection of and access to information about the courts, and further study of and improvements in judicial administration.[7]

14.2 Structural and Constitutional Issues

Improbably, changes in Australian courts are even occurring through federal-state co-operation, in particular through the scheme for cross-vesting jurisdiction between federal and state courts, and through the reference of power (by four states) over child custody and maintenance. There is also substantial co-operation — though falling short of a reference of legislative power — in the area of industrial law.[8]

The climate of change, and the dissatisfaction with the jurisdictional conflicts produced by the establishment of the Federal Court and Family Court, has revived an old debate about a unified system of Australian courts. That argument was first put by Sir Owen Dixon in 1935:

[I]t would appear natural to endeavour to establish the Courts of justice as independent organs which were neither Commonwealth nor state. The basis of the system is the supremacy of the law. The Courts administering the law should all derive an independent existence and authority from the Constitution. Some practical difficulties would occur in carrying such a principle beyond the superior Courts, but it is not easy to see why the entire system of superior Courts should not have been organized and directed under the Constitution to administer the total content of the law. No doubt some financial provisions would be required for levying upon the various Governments contributions to the cost of administering justice. To make judicial appointments and deal with some other matters, it would have been necessary to create a joint committee. But it would not have been beyond the wit of man to devise machinery which would have placed the Courts, so to speak, upon neutral territory where they administered the whole law irrespective of its source.[9]

The proposal was taken up by Sir Garfield Barwick and the then Attorney-General, R.J. Ellicott,[10] and was discussed at successive meetings of the Australian Constitutional Convention.[11] It has also been the subject of vigorous advocacy from a number of Supreme Court judges, with detailed schemes drawn up — and in one case, approved by a sub-committee of the Constitutional Convention — for achieving a uniform system, either at the level of all superior courts, or at least at the level of an Australian Court of Appeal.[12] It has been suggested that unification be effected either by the states conferring state appellate jurisdiction on the Federal Court, which would become the only intermediate court of appeal with general jurisdiction, or by a new arrangement to be entered into pursuant to s51(xxxviii) of the Constitution.[13] The debate has not been fruitless: in particular the cross-vesting scheme is a product of suggestions for a more extensive integration of jurisdictions.[14] But at the more fundamental level the objection to all the proposals, beginning with Dixon's in 1935, is their tendency to deny the basic requirement of political (that is to say, democratic) accountability for the administration of the courts. Although judges must be independent of the executive in exercising their judicial powers, the staffing, structure, and workings of the courts as a system are not, and should not be, 'neutral territory'. As the Judicial System Committee of the Australian Constitutional Commission stated:

judicial power is a branch of governmental power and . . . the other branches of government have functions in relation to the judiciary. It is for legislatures (subject to any constitutional limitations) to determine what courts there shall be, their jurisdiction, their composition . . . Again it is the responsibility of the legislature to determine the conditions of office of the persons constituting the courts, to determine or to provide the means of determining the procedure and rules of those courts, and to make finance available to those courts . . . The Committee accepts that it is possible to devise measures (including constitutional measures) which will make provision for all these matters in order to provide a system which is neither federal nor State, but it feels that no matter what arrangements are made . . . the inevitable practical result is that there would be divided responsibility for such courts, and such divided responsibility cannot but be productive of difficulties . . . Too often the only agreement between governments required to agree will be to leave things as they are.[15]

Consistently with this view, there are only two ways in which a unification of the superior courts might be achieved — either by administrative co-ordination from a separate constitutional base, or by the transfer to the Commonwealth of complete responsibility for the whole system of superior courts. Indeed different members of the Judicial System Committee favoured each of these courses.[16]

A unified federal superior court system is, for the foreseeable future, politically out of the question. But it is also not desirable in principle. Increasingly the courts below Supreme Court level are becoming the courts of first instance, with Supreme Courts as courts of first instance in a comparatively few major cases, and as courts of appeal in all others. Thus the main needs for administrative co-ordination and for efficient case-management occur at the level of the lower courts. To cut these off from the superior courts, as would tend to happen with the unification of the superior courts under federal auspices, would be inefficient and undesirable. If unification is required, it is required at the level of trial courts, that is, at Supreme Court level and below. Yet that form of unification has not been seriously considered so far, as we saw in Chapter 7.

Administrative co-ordination as between federal and state courts is no doubt desirable, and will inevitably tend to increase through the exercise of concurrent jurisdiction, through the operation of the cross-vesting scheme, and in other ways. But it is doubtful whether any very elaborate co-ordinating mechanism is required. Between constitutionally distinct courts there is no room for central direction or control, and less formal kinds of co-ordination can occur on an *ad hoc* basis. Moreover proponents of administrative co-ordination tend to overlook the very real differences of policy and practice between the states, reflected in such matters as the existence of a separate Court of Appeal, of co-ordinate superior courts (such as the NSW Land and Environment Court), of special courts or tribunals not subject to Supreme Court oversight or review, and also of special powers or jurisdictions attached to particular courts (e.g. the contracts review jurisdiction under the Industrial Arbitration Act 1940 (NSW), referred to in Chapter 11). Despite many similarities the state court structures are not homogeneous: their differences are not merely accidental or historical but in many cases reflect real differences in policy and values. For these reasons no fundamental constitutional change is called for.

14.3 Alternative Dispute Resolution and the Future of the 'Ordinary Courts'

Courts are not intrinsically happy places. No more are hospitals, though it is probable that a higher proportion of the clients of hospitals leave contented than of the clients of courts! But the comparison is misleading: a primary purpose of courts is the maintenance of a wider social order, beyond the interests of individual litigants. The conflict is evident, for example, in the disputes over the role of children's courts. Litigation is usually a symptom of discord, which is not necessarily to be encouraged: unlike hospitals, courts may have a certain deterrent value.

Where litigation is inevitable, the tendency is often to seek alternative means of handling the underlying disputes.[17] These can be broadly of three kinds. The first is diversion away from judicial processes to forms of mediation or conciliation, a process we have seen at work in the children's panels and the Family Court, and which is the basis of the New South Wales Community Justice Centres,[18] and of experiments along similar lines in Victoria.[19] There is also a growing tendency to encourage and facilitate court-annexed arbitration, both in small claims[20] and in large commercial cases,[21] although the reasons for arbitration rather than adjudication tend to be different in the two areas. Secondly, specialist administrative tribunals or courts can be established, either on the basis that the ordinary courts are inadequate, or to reduce their workload. This is, as we have seen in Chapter 13, a continuing tendency, which makes the call for a unified Australian court system seem even less realistic or desirable. A third, more drastic method is to exclude established legal machinery altogether, by creating administrative or financial substitutes. The most significant such proposal is the creation of national or state compensation schemes to replace the industrial and road accident litigation which provides such a high proportion of the civil case-load of state courts. A compensation scheme along these lines has been in operation in New Zealand since 1974, with apparent success,[22] and traffic accident compensation schemes of different kinds have been introduced in some Australian states and territories.[23]

In the face of such threats, the extent to which the civil case-load of superior courts will (or should) be maintained may be doubtful.[24] Certainly the increases in the case-load and number of superior judges over the past fifteen years are unlikely to continue.[25] There are presently in Australia more professional judges than in the entire United Kingdom. If federalism means legalism, it also means duplication.

But more positively, federalism also involves the opportunity for local experiment and choice. This may account for the diversity of arrangements for Australian courts and the viability of some, at least, of the continuing developments in the nine jurisdictions.

Notes

[1] Cf. Adams (1974) 12 *Osgoode Hall LJ* 569.
[2] See esp. Civil Justice Committee, *Report concerning the Administration of Civil Justice in Victoria* (1984).
[3] As recommended by the Parliamentary Joint Committee, *Family Law in Australia* (1980).
[4] Daunton-Fear & Freiberg, in Chappell & Wilson, eds, *The Australian Criminal Justice System* (2nd edn, 1979) 89. But the ALRC, after a thorough review of Australian and overseas practice, rejected any system of Aboriginal courts: ALRC 31, *The Recognition of Aboriginal Customary Laws* (1986) chs 27–31, esp. para. 838–43.
[5] A very sensitive subject: cf. Devlin, *The Judge* (1979) 34; Samuels (1980) 54 *ALJ* 581; Note (1984) 58 *ALJ* 127. The NSW Judicial Commission has judicial education among its functions: Judicial Officers Act 1986 (NSW) s9.
[6] ALRC 27, *Standing in Public Interest Litigation* (1985); Barrett (1980) 54 *ALJ* 688.

7 Kilduff [1979] *ACLD* TD247; Victoria, Civil Justice Committee, *Report concerning the Administration of Civil Justice in Victoria* (1984) ch. 8, and see Chapter 4 for the work of the Australian Institute of Judicial Administration.
8 These developments are discussed in Chapters 8, 10, and 11 respectively.
9 (1935) 51 *LQR* 590, 607.
10 Barwick (1977) 51 *ALJ* 480, 490–1; Ellicott (1978) 52 *ALJ* 431. See also Else-Mitchell (1970) 44 *ALJ* 516.
11 Note (1978) 52 *ALJ* 409; Judicature Committee, *Report to Standing Committee D* (1977) 29–31; Saunders' working paper, id., 62; *Proceedings of the Australian Constitutional Convention . . . 1978*, 150–65; Standing Committee D, *Fourth Report* (1982) 12–18; Standing Committee D, *Supplementary Fourth Report* (1983); *Proceedings of the Australian Constitutional Convention . . . 1983*, vol. 1, 9–47; Judicature Sub-Committee, *Report on an Integrated System of Courts* (1984); *Proceedings of the Australian Constitutional Convention . . . 1985*, vol. 1, 137–205.
12 See Burt (1982) 56 *ALJ* 509; Street, id., 515; Neasey (1983) 57 *ALJ* 335; Moffitt (1983) 57 *ALJ* 167; Note (1983) 57 *ALJ* 167, 439; AIJA, *An Integrated Court System for Australia* (1983). The debate is summarized in Constitutional Commission, Committee on the Australian Judicial System, *Report* (1987) 26–45. For equivalent US proposals see Ashman & Parness (1974) 24 *De Paul LR* 1.
13 Cf. Bowen (1979) 53 *ALJ* 806, 814–6.
14 Street (1978) 52 *ALJ* 434, 436.
15 Constitutional Commission, Committee on the Australian Judicial System, *Report* (1987) 38.
16 See id., 40–3 for a summary of the different views.
17 On the growing area of alternative dispute resolution see Shetreet (1979) 17 *UWOLR* 35; Abel, *The Politics of Informal Justice* (1982); Tomasic & Feeley, eds, *Neighbourhood Justice: Assessment of an Emerging Idea* (1982); Cranston (1986) 11 *LSB* 21; Mugford, ed., *Alternative Dispute Resolution* (1987).
18 These were first established on an experimental basis (Community Justice Centres (Pilot Project) Act 1980 (NSW); Chart (1979) 4 *LSB* 152), then made permanent after review. See Schwartzkoff & Morgan, *Community Justice Centres: A Report on the NSW Pilot Project 1979–1981* (1982); Community Justice Centres Act 1983 (NSW); Graycar (1983) 1 *AJ Law & Soc* 134; Faulkes (1985) 59 *ALJ* 457.
19 See Evidence (Neighbourhood Mediation Centres) Act 1987 (Vic.); Bryson (1987) 12 *LSB* 108.
20 See (1986) 60 *ALJ* 594, and see further Chapter 6.
21 See e.g. Commercial Arbitration Act 1984 (NSW); Sharkey, *Commercial Arbitration* (1986).
22 See Ison, *The Forensic Lottery* (1967); Palmer, *Compensation for Incapacity* (1979); Keeler (1975) 5 *Adel LR* 121; Keeler (1981) 7 *Adel LR* 526; NSWLRC 43, *A Transport Accidents Scheme for New South Wales* (1984).
23 E.g. Accident Compensation Act 1985 (Vic.); Transport Accidents Compensation Act 1987 (NSW).

[24] Cf. Palmer (1985) 5 *Windsor Ybk of Access to Justice* 327.
[25] Generally on these changes in judicial case-loads and functions see Brennan (1979) 53 *ALJ* 767; Braybrooke, in *Law under Stress. Future Challenges for the Legal System* (1979) 53, 62–7; Clarkson, id., 80; Milner (1974) 20 *McGill LJ* 521; Fiss (1983) 92 *Yale LJ* 1442; Rogers (1984) 58 *ALJ* 608.

SELECT TABLE OF CASES

(Only cases discussed in some detail are listed.)

Adamson v West Perth Football Club (1979) 143–4
Alexander's case: see *Waterside Workers' Federation of Australia v J.W. Alexander Ltd*
Amalgamated Society of Engineers v Adelaide Steamship Co. Ltd (1928) 39, 50
Attorney-General v Queen (1957): see Boilermakers' case
Australian Ocean Line Pty Ltd v West Australian Newspapers (1983) 139, 151
Barton v R (1980) 98–9
Boilermakers' case (1956) 27–30, 44, 142, 172, 221–2
Capital TV and Appliances Pty Ltd v Falconer (1971) 40–1
Carter v Egg & Egg Pulp Marketing Board (Vic.) (1942) 153
Commonwealth v Hospital Contribution Fund of Australia (1982) 48, 130
Commonwealth v Queensland (1975) 168
Davern v Messel (1984) 142
Felton v Mulligan (1971) 35–6
Fencott v Muller (1983) 145
Gazzo v Comptroller of Stamps (1981) 210
Hilton v Wells (1985) 45–6
Judiciary and Navigation Acts, In re (1921) 167–8
Le Mesurier v Connor (1929) 36
McInnis v R (1979) 63, 174, 184
Melbourne Corporation v Commonwealth (State Banking Case) (1947) 172
Minister for Justice, ex rel ATI (Operations) Pty Ltd v ANAC (1977) 68
Minister for Works for Western Australia v Civil and Civic Pty Ltd (1967) 50, 168, 181
Philip Morris Inc. v Adam P. Brown Male Fashions Pty Ltd (1981) 143–6, 153
Porter v R (1926) 39
Prohibitions del Roy (1607) 4–5
Queen Victoria Memorial Hospital v Thornton (1953) 37
R v Bernasconi (1915) 39–41, 50
R v Coldham, ex p Australian Social Welfare Union (1983) 220–1
R v Joske, ex p Shop Distributive and Allied Employees' Association (1976) 30
R v Kirby, ex p Boilermakers' Society of Australia (1956): see Boilermakers' case
R v Lambert, ex p Plummer (1981) 200, 209, 213
R v Small Claims Tribunal, ex p Escor Industries Pty Ltd (1979) 242–3
R v Watson, ex p Armstrong (1976) 64, 193, 210
Russell v Russell (1976) 36, 190–3, 194, 209
Sankey v Whitlam (1976) 91
Smith v Smith (1986) 197, 212
Southern Centre of Theosophy Inc. v South Australia (1979) 175–6
Spratt v Hermes (1965) 39–41, 50
Stack v Coast Securities (No. 9) *Pty Ltd* (1983) 145, 153

Thompson v Mastertouch TV Service Pty Ltd (1978) 141–2
United States Surgical Corporation v Hospital Products International Pty Ltd (1981) 143–6, 153
Vitzdamm-Jones v Vitzdamm-Jones (1981) 210
Waters v Commonwealth (1951) 39
Waterside Workers' Federation of Australia v J.W. Alexander Ltd (1918) 27–8

INDEX

AAT: *see* Administrative Appeals Tribunal
aborigines, Australian: child custody cases 211; recognition of customary laws 19, 211, 275; special court facilities 272; status of 14, 19
accrued jurisdiction 142–8, 152–4, 164–5, 179, 197, 212, 242–3
Act of Settlement 1700 16, 56
acting judges 58, 62, 70–1, 118
Administrative Appeals Tribunal (AAT) 29–30, 139–40, 142, 150, 261–3, 267–8
Administrative Decisions (Judicial Review) Act 1977 (Cth) 98–9, 139–40, 147–8, 151, 261, 267
administrative law 129–30, 153, 158–9, 258–63, 266–8; *and see* Administrative Appeals Tribunal, Administrative Decisions (Judicial Review) Act 1977 (Cth), judicial review, prerogative
administrative tribunals 140, 142, 251–63, 267–9, 275; *and see* by name
Admiralty Court 11, 120, 123, 198
admiralty jurisdiction: Australian generally 16, 120, 123–4, 132–3; English 11, 123; Federal Court of Australia's 133, 153; High Court's 160, 177; need for reform 124, 177; of intermediate courts 123
adoption courts 203–4, 214–15
adversary system 53–4, 62–4, 167, 193, 195, 240–1, 243–4, 257, 271; *and see* inquisitorial system
advisory opinions 38, 126, 167–8, 180–1, 261, 263, 267, 268
appeal: accrued jurisdiction on 145–6; against sentence 126; contrasted with review 125, 139–40, 142, 159, 176, 224, 260–3; costs of 63, 73; development of 12, 13–14, 65, 125–7; from acquittal 65, 126, 141–2, 152, 224; from administrative tribunals 139–40, 142, 263; functions of first appeal 126–7, 134–5, 165–7, 173; functions of final appeal 165–7, 170–5, 182–4
arbitration: civil 64, 127; court-annexed 48, 108, 250, 275; industrial 221–5, 226–7, 230–1
Ashmore & Cartier Islands 51
assessors 256, 266
assizes 9

associated jurisdiction 143, 145–6, 153, 179, 197
Attorney-General 55, 64–5, 74, 90–1, 97–9, 118, 147–8, 163, 165, 168, 202
Australia: court reform 165–70, 245, 271–7; early constitutional development 22–6; English influence upon 4–5, 14–15, 23, 25, 100, 120, 122; reception of common law and equity 14–15; reception of English institutions 14–16; reception of English statute law 15–16; settlement of 14; *and see* Family Court of Australia, Federal Court of Australia, High Court of Australia, Supreme Courts
Australia Acts (1986) 32
Australian Antarctic Territory 51
Australian Capital Territory: Children's Court 206–7; Court of Petty Sessions 83–7, 95, 100–11; exercise of federal jurisdiction in 38–42; family law jurisdiction 211; history 49, 129–30; industrial jurisdiction 228; small claims jurisdiction 241–50; Supreme Court 39–41, 117–35
Australian Conciliation and Arbitration Commission: composition 221–3; in territories 228; influence on state tribunals 222, 229, 231; jurisdiction 220–1, 221–3; proposed reconstitution 45–6, 219, 231; review of decisions 140; wage-fixing principles 222–3, 229, 231
Australian Constitutions Act 1850 (UK) 15
Australian Courts Act 1828 (UK) 15
Australian Industrial Court 45, 71, 137, 138, 150, 221–2, 223
Australian Institute of Judicial Administration 119, 276
Australian Law Reform Commission 133, 151, 153, 177, 179, 211, 212, 217, 275
Australian Legal Aid Office 63, 73

bankruptcy jurisdiction 129, 137, 138–9, 150–1
Barwick CJ 56, 72, 136–7, 169, 173–4, 175–6, 181, 272
Beeching Report (1969) 128–9, 135
Bigge Reports (1823) 23, 43
Bill of Rights 1688 16

Boards of Reference 227, 236
Boothby J 20, 57, 69, 111–12
Bray CJ 56, 134
Brennan J 61, 62, 169, 181
Broome Local Court 133
Burke's Act (Colonial Leave of Absence Act 1782) 56, 69

Canada: admiralty jurisdiction 133; appointment of judges 55, 68–9, 169–70, 182; Federal Court 153; Supreme Court 156, 165, 169, 171, 180, 182
case stated 86–7, 131–2
certiorari 159, 177, 259, 261
chief justices/judges 60, 72, 127, 143, 181
children's courts: Australian 205–7; children's aid panels 207–8, 216–17; diversion from 206, 207–8, 216–17; ideal of 205–6, 208, 215–17; relation to ordinary courts 208
Christmas Island: 49; court system 51
circuits 9, 71, 130
civil procedure 101–2, 109–19, 127–9, 245, 271
closed courts 36, 48, 193, 210
Coal Industry Tribunal 49, 140, 235
Cocos (Keeling) Islands: 49; court system 51
Coke, Sir Edward 5, 123
Colonial Courts of Admiralty Act 1890 (UK) 16, 120, 123–4, 132–3, 166
Colonial Laws Validity Act 1865 (UK) 15, 20
colonies, Australian: constitutions 22, 93; courts, development of 23; *and see* Australia (and states by name)
commercial causes 127–8, 135
committal proceedings: alternatives to 90–1; changes of plea after 89; children's courts 208; committal by coroner 97; committal for sentence 89–90; costs 91, 98; hand-up brief 89, 97; history and nature 49, 88–91; judicial review of 90–1, 98–9; procedure 83–4, 91, 96–9; reform 89, 91, 99; *and see* criminal prosecution, minor indictable offence
common law: and equity 7–8, 122–3; courts of 8–10; development 3–4, 6–10, 126, 165–6, 173–4; reception in Australia 14–15, 173–4
Commonwealth Constitution 1900: nature of 24; s49 29; s51(i) 68; s51(xx) 68, 221, 233; s51(xxi) 188–9, 190–2, 194–6, 200–1, 209–10; s51(xxii) 138–9, 188–9, 190–2, 200–1; s51(xxxv) 27, 219–21, 232–3, 239; s51(xxxviii) 155, 200, 273; s64 27; Chapter III generally 25–38; s71 26–8, 156; s72 30–1, 39, 41, 57–8, 71–2, 94, 150; s73 32, 40–2, 160–3, 166–7, 168; s74 26, 32, 47, 161; s75 26, 38, 39–40, 133–5,
157–9, 164, 165, 167; s75(i) 157, 167; s75(ii) 157; s75(iii) 158, 159, 167; s75(iv) 33, 158, 159; s75(v) 39, 121, 140, 159–60, 163, 198, 224, 237, 260–1; s76 37, 38, 143–5, 159–60; s76(i) 159; s76(ii) 41, 144–5, 159–60; s76(iii) 160; s76(iv) 167; s77(ii) 33; s77(iii) 33–8, 155; s79 49; s80 24, 31–2, 39, 42, 46–47, 75; s92 172–3, 183; s102 44; s120 155; s122 38–42, 49–51; s128 43, 168
Commonwealth Court of Conciliation and Arbitration 27–8, 221–2
Commonwealth Industrial Court: *see* Australian Industrial Court
Commonwealth of Australia Constitution Act 1900 16, 24–6, 33; *and see* Commonwealth Constitution, federal movement
Community Justice Centres (NSW) 275, 276
Companies Act, proposed federal 155
complaints against judges 59, 71
conciliation in litigation 54, 193, 199, 202, 243–4, 249, 255–6, 257, 274–5
consent jurisdiction 67, 89, 91, 107
Constitutional Commission, Judicial System Committee 24, 31–2, 46, 49, 69, 71–2, 94, 135, 164, 165, 179, 180–1, 182, 213–14, 273
consumer claims courts: *see* small claims courts
contempt of court 93, 121, 131
Coral Sea Islands 49, 51
coroner 65, 75, 97, 256, 265
costs: *see* legal costs
Council: *see* Privy Council
counter-claims and jurisdictional limits 107–8, 145, 242–3, 248
County Courts (English) 11, 100
court martial 29, 257
Court of Appeal (England) 10, 14, 125, 133, 134, 166
Court of Chancery 7, 11, 14; *and see* equity, Lord Chancellor
Court of Common Pleas 9–10, 13
Court of Constable and Marshall 11
Court of Delegates 11
Court of Exchequer 9–11, 13, 17
Court of Exchequer Chamber 13
Court of High Commission 11–12
Court of Insolvency (South Australia) 139, 150–1
Court of Insolvency (Victoria) 151
Court of King's Bench 9–10, 13
Court of Requests 12, 18
courts: abolition of 59, 71, 150; defined 48, 235; inferior 93; intermediate 93; of record 10, 102, 111, 131; role of 3, 52, 53–4, 170–5, 240, 245, 257–9, 274–5; superior 93, 121–2, 176
courts of disputed returns 159, 256–7, 266
criminal prosecution: *ex officio*

information 90–1, 98, 146; of children 206–7; private prosecution 90, 98; procedure on indictment 66, 81–2, 89–92; summary offences 81–2, 84–5; termination of 64–5, 89, 97; *and see* grand jury
cross-vesting scheme 38, 49, 147–8, 149, 154, 200, 213, 274
Crown Courts (England) 82, 119
Curia Regis 8, 9, 12; *and see* Parliament, Privy Council

delay: 129, 198, 202, 275
Denning, Lord 53, 134
Director of Public Prosecutions 64–5, 90, 99
diversity jurisdiction 158, 164, 167, 176
Dixon CJ 28, 56, 169, 171–2, 181, 272

ecclesiastical courts and law: in England 11, 187–8; non-reception in Australia 14–15, 120, 188
English courts, history 3–4, 7–14; *and see* by name
equity: development by Chancellor 4, 7, 11; jurisdiction of inferior courts 104–5, 115; jurisdiction of intermediate courts 103, 104–5, 115; reception in Australia 14–15; relation to common law 6, 7, 17, 122–3; *and see* Judicature Act system
error, proceedings in 13–14
evidence, law of 102, 127, 128, 206, 243, 257–8

Family Court of Australia: accrued jurisdiction 197, 212; appeals from state courts 104, 124, 198, 203; appeals to High Court 162–3, 166, 178; associated jurisdiction 153, 197; attacks on judges of 199; closed court 36, 193; conflict with state courts 194–7, 199–200, 201, 203, 204; cross-vested jurisdiction 147; judicial review of decisions 140; jurisdiction 191–2, 194–7; problems of 191–2, 194–7, 198–200, 201–2; procedure 36, 193–4; proposed new powers 200–1; renovation of 201–2, 214, 272; retirement of judges 46, 193, 210
family courts: concept of 192–4, 195, 199–202, 205, 210, 217; enforcement 197–8; minor civil jurisdiction 104, 204; state family courts 36, 154, 155, 199, 202–4, 214–15; *and see* Family Court of Australia, Family Law Act 1975 (Cth)
Family Law Act 1975 (Cth): s4 211–12, 214; s10(3) 199–200, 213; s23A 46; s31(1) 197, 211; s33 153, 197; s37A 214; s39(6) 104; s41 36, 155, 202–3; s64 195; s95 162–3, 166, 198; s96 114; s114 197, 198, 211

family law powers, reference by states 149, 155, 200
Federal Court of Australia: AAT appeals 140, 142, 262, 268; accrued jurisdiction 142–6, 153–4; admiralty jurisdiction, proposed 155; appeal to High Court 162, 178, 268 ; appellate jurisdiction 141–2, 145–6, 152, 154, 268; conflict with Supreme Courts 99, 137–8, 146–9, 151–5; associated jurisdiction 143, 145–6, 153–4; cross-vested jurisdiction, proposed 147–8, 154; General Division jurisdiction 98–9, 138–46, 150–3, 261–3; Industrial Division jurisdiction 138, 222, 223–4, 234–5; proposals for 136–8, 149–50; review of federal administrative decisions 98–9, 139–40, 142, 151, 158–9, 261–3
Federal Court of Australia Act 1976 (Cth): 137, 138, 142; s24 141–2, 162, 223; s32 143, 145–6, 147, 197
Federal Court of Bankruptcy 71, 136, 137, 138–9, 150–1
Federal Court of Canada 153, 161
federal jurisdiction: appeals in 141–2, 145–6, 160, 198, 224, 263; conflicts of laws in 158, 164, 176, 179; defined 32–3, 157–60; exercise by Masters 118; exercise by registrars 214; exercise by territory courts 38–42, 211; in criminal cases 85–6, 149; invested in state courts 25, 33–8, 85–6, 104, 137, 139, 202–3, 228

federal movement 25–6, 156
federal-state co-operation 37, 38, 146–9, 154–5, 170, 182, 200, 202–3, 221, 225, 228–9, 272–4
felony 81–2
final judgment 126
Flight Crew Officers Industrial Tribunal 224

Gibbs CJ 181, 201, 214
grand jury 65–6, 74–5, 97; *and see* criminal prosecution, jury trial

habeas corpus 16, 21, 266
Hale, Sir Matthew 7, 17, 67
Hancock Report 45, 219, 231, 232
Heard & McDonald Islands 49, 51
Higgins J 218–19, 224, 231
High Court (England) 10
High Court of Australia: administration 60, 156–7, 171, 175–6; appeals to Privy Council 26, 32, 161, 167, 177–8; appellate jurisdiction 24–5, 26, 34, 41, 42, 160–3, 165–7, 177–81, 183–4, 198, 224, 263; as final appeal court 32, 126–7, 134–5, 167, 173–5; court of disputed returns 159, 256–7, 266; functions of Chief Justice 60, 175–6;

judicial appointments 55–6, 69, 169–70, 181–2; jurisdictional reforms 136–7, 165–8; jury trials in 66, 76, 160; nineteenth-century proposals for 24, 44, 156; original jurisdiction 41, 157–60, 167–8; removal and remittal of cases 163–4, 178–9; retirement of judges 30–1; review of federal officers 39, 121, 158–9, 167, 198, 237, 259–61; role under Constitution 24–6, 61–2, 167, 170–5, 179–84, 260–1; special leave applications 73, 161–3, 165–7; workload 136, 170–1, 182–3
High Court of Australia Act 1979 (Cth) 60, 118, 130, 175
House of Lords: Appellate Committee 19, 156, 165–6, 171, 175; development as court 8, 14; reforms of 1875 14, 19; workload 171

indictable offence 31, 81–2, 88–92, 140, 159–60; *and see* minor indictable offences, summary offence
industrial arbitration: Australasian history 27–8, 218–19; federal system of 219–25, 228–31; future of 230–1, 238–9; ideal of 218–19, 231, 238; industrial tribunals and ordinary courts 229–30; in states and territories 219, 225–8; special forums for 224–5, 227, 229, 231, 235; *and see* Australian Conciliation and Arbitration Commission; Federal Court of Australia, Hancock Report
industrial magistrates 141, 226, 228, 236–7
Industrial Relations Act 1979 (Vic.) 225, 226, 235
inferior civil jurisdiction 100–2, 103–9, 240–1, 245
inferior court 81, 93
inferior criminal jurisdiction 81–92
information: *see* criminal prosecution
inherent jurisdiction 131, 119–21
inquisitorial system 54, 243, 249–50, 253; *and see* adversary system
inter se matters 32, 47, 177
interlocutory appeals 141
intermediate civil jurisdiction 100–1, 102–3
intermediate criminal jurisdiction 73–5, 84–5
international law, acquisition of Australia in 14
Irvine memorandum (1923) 61

JPs: see justices of the peace
judges (Australian): acting judges 58, 62, 70–1, 72, 108; appointment 55–6, 68–9, 169–70, 181–2, 202; continuing legal education 71, 272; crimes against 199; dismissal 57–9, 68–9; extra-judicial use of 29–30, 60–2,

72–3, 169–76; increasing number of 118, 130, 175, 193, 275; independence of 56–60; Judicial Commission 55–6, 57–9, 71; loss of tenure through abolition of court 59, 71, 150; promotion of 156; reserve 130, 175; retirement 30, 46, 130, 194, 210; salaries 60, 201; tenure 24, 30–1, 39, 56–60, 69–70, 84, 94
judges (English): appointment 55, 68, 181; independence of 56–7; role in creating common law 3–4, 7, 182
Judicature Act system: adoption in Australia 15, 122–3, 129, 132; adoption in England 4, 10, 19, 122, 129, 258; definition 8; in lower courts 104–5; *and see* equity
Judicature Acts 1873 & 1875 (UK) 10, 15, 19, 122, 124
judicial administration 60, 81, 92–3, 108–9, 127–9, 130–1, 157, 175, 198, 201–2, 241, 272, 274–5
Judicial Commission, proposals for 55–6, 57–9, 71, 170, 182
Judicial Committee: *see* Privy Council
Judicial Committee Act 1833 (UK) 13, 16
Judicial Committee Act 1844 (UK) 16
judicial power: in federal territories 38–42; under Commonwealth Constitution 26–30, 37–8; under state constitutions 23, 29, 32–3, 37–8, 43
judicial review:; of administrative action 17, 139–40, 142, 258–63; of constitutionality of laws 44, 158–9, 171–3; of lower court decisions 13, 17, 86–7, 91–2, 125, 140, 198, 244–5, 248–9, 258–63; *and see* Administrative Decisions (Judicial Review Act 1977 (Cth)), administrative law, High Court of Australia, prerogative writs/orders
Judicial Services Act 1986 (NSW) 58–9, 71
Judiciary Act 1903 (Cth): 156; s23(2)(b) 72; s30(a) 159, 165, 177; s31 165; s32 165; s35 161–2, 177–8; s35A 161–2, 166; s38 34, 158, 176; s39 34–6, 104, 124; s39(2)(b) 47; s39(2)(c) 162; s39(2)(d) 37, 47–8; s39A 47; s39B 140, 151, 176, 237; s44 163–4, 165; s68 47, 85–6; s71A 90
Jurisdiction of Courts (Cross-vesting) Act 1987 (Cth) 147–8, 231
jury trial: civil cases 65–7, 75–6, 117–18, 128, 139; constitutional guarantee of 31–2, 46–7, 75; criminal cases 65–7, 75–7, 91–2, 140, 159–60; development in England 9, 20, 53, 65, 67; future of 66–7, 76–7, 118; introduction in Australia 21, 23, 65–6, 74–5; majority verdicts 32, 66, 75; other forms of 65–6, 67, 74–5; waiver of 66, 75; *and*

see grand jury; minor indictable offence
justices of the peace (Australia):; civil jurisdiction 101–2; criminal jurisdiction 81–91; federal jurisdiction and 37, 47–8; future of 82, 83–4, 93–4; history 16, 67, 81–2; tenure 59; *and see* courts of summary jurisdiction
justices of the peace (England): modern role 82; origins of 10, 16, 82, 93
juvenile courts: see children's courts

Labour Court, proposed 150, 231, 239
Land and Environment Court (NSW) 254–7, 259, 266–7
land courts 253–6, 264–5
Law Officers of the Crown 64–5; *and see* Attorney-General, Director of Public Prosecutions, Solicitor-General
law (French) 17
laymen, participation in judicial process 65–7
legal aid 54, 62–4, 73, 199
legal costs 54, 63, 73, 90–1, 105, 106, 127, 166, 193, 198, 240–1, 243
legal procedure, reform 54, 67, 91, 201–2, 240–1, 245, 257–8
legal profession 53, 62–4, 73–4
legal representation: Family Advocate 216; in small claims courts 63, 243, 249; official forms of 64–5, 73, 74; role of 53, 62–3, 256; separate representation of children 195, 202 ; special leave applications 73
licensing courts 252, 263–4
liquor licensing boards 252, 263–4
Local Court of Appeals 24, 44
local government courts 253–6
Lord Chancellor 7, 11, 55, 68

maintenance, proposed national scheme 213
magistrates: history 81–3; industrial magistrates 141, 226, 228, 236–7; jurisdiction 81–90, 93–7, 101–3, 204, 206–7; tenure 59, 71, 84, 94; *and see* summary jurisdiction
Magna Carta (1215/1297) 8–9, 16, 20
mandamus 158, 176
marine inquiry, courts of 140, 257, 266
Mason CJ 46, 181
Masters (Supreme Court) 48, 101, 118, 130
mining courts: *see* warden's courts
minor indictable offence 84–5, 89, 95
misdemeanour 81–2
Murphy J 30–1, 57–8, 63, 70, 169, 181

Nauru: 49, 163; appeal to High Court 163, 178
New Guinea: *see* Papua-New Guinea
New South Wales: Children's Courts 206–7; Compensation Court 257;
Conciliation Committees 225, 227; Consumer Claims Tribunals 241–50; Court of Appeal 125–7; Courts of Petty Sessions: *see* Local Courts ; development of courts 22–4, 43, 100–1; District Court 82–3, 91–2, 100–1, 102–3; District Courts 100; Industrial Commission 225–7; Judicial Services Commission 59, 71; Land and Environment Court 253–6, 258, 264–5, 274; Local Courts 71, 81–7, 94–6, 101–2, 103–4; Supreme Court 23, 71, 117–35, 204
New Zealand: accident compensation scheme 275; admiralty jurisdiction 133; family court 210; industrial arbitration, history of 218–19, 238; judicial review of administrative acts 269; small claims jurisdiction 244, 249
nisi prius jurisdiction 9, 13
nolle prosequi 64–5, 89
Norfolk Island: 49, 211; court system 51
Northern Territory: Children's Court 206–7; Court of Summary Jurisdiction 81–7; family law jurisdiction 211; history 49, 80, 130; industrial jurisdiction 228; Local Courts 101, 103–4; small claims jurisdiction 241–50; Supreme Court 117–35, 141

Papua-New Guinea 49
paramount force statutes 15–16
Parliament, British 8, 12, 13–14
Parliamentary Commission of Inquiry 57–8, 70
pendent jurisdiction: *see* accrued jurisdiction, associated jurisdiction
persona designata doctrine 29–30, 45–6, 60–1, 261
personal injury litigation 102, 108–9, 112–13, 275, 276
Petition of Right 1628 16
Petrov case 62
petty sessions 9, 81–2
Piddington, A.B. 69, 155
precedent, rules of 15, 53, 153, 171, 178–9, 180, 183
prerogative: creation of courts under 3–4, 7, 12–13, 17, 23, 43; defined 12
prerogative writs/orders 86–7, 121, 158–9, 159–61, 176–7, 198
Privy Council: abolition of appeals 24, 32, 34, 161, 271; Act of 1640 13; advisory opinions 168; Australian jurisdiction 23, 24, 31–20, 123; early history 12–14; Judicial Committee of 13; overseas jurisdiction generally 13–14, 19; problems as final court of appeal 13–14, 24
prohibition 163, 176–7, 259
puisne judge 118, 130

quarter sessions 9, 81–2
Queensland: Children's Court 206–7;

Index • 285

District Courts 71, 82–3, 91–2, 100–1, 102–3; Industrial Conciliation and Arbitration Commission 225–7; Industrial Court 225–9; Local Government Court 256; Magistrates Courts 59, 81–7, 94–6, 101–2, 103–4; Small Claims Tribunals 241–50; small debts jurisdiction 101, 241, 242, 244, 245; Supreme Court 53, 72, 117–135

Registrars (Supreme Court) 48, 118, 130
remittal: *see* transfer of cases
removal: *see* transfer of cases
requests, courts of 18, 100–1, 246
roman law 17
Royal Commissions 60–2, 72–3
rules of court 60, 118–19, 129, 130–1

sentencing:; appeals against 126; guidelines 71
separation of powers: and extra-judicial use of judges 60–2, 72–3; and federal territories 29, 39–42; and state courts 29, 37–8, 43; separation of judicial power 26–30, 31, 44, 221–2, 226, 233
set-off 105, 248
small claims courts/tribunals: Australian 54, 101, 102, 241–50, 257–8; English 245, 250; further reform 245, 250; New Zealand 244, 249
Solicitor-General 64, 74
South Australia: adoption court 204, 214–15; Children's Court 206–7; Conciliation Committee 225, 227; Court of Insolvency 139, 150–1; Courts of Summary Jurisdiction 81–7, 94–6, 214–15, 236; District Courts 82–3, 91–2, 98–9, 100–1, 102–3; Industrial Commission 225–7; Industrial Court 225–9; Local Court of Appeals 24, 44; Local Courts 101–3 ; Residential Tenancies Tribunal 247; small claims jurisdiction 241–50; Supreme Court 117–35
specialized courts and tribunals, proliferation of 187, 251–2, 257–8, 273–4
standing 179
Star Chamber, Court of 12
state constitutions 20, 22–4, 43, 58
Statute of Westminster 1931 (UK) 20
stipendiary magistrates: *see* magistrates
summary jurisdiction, courts of: appeal from 36–7, 96, 110–11, 142; Children's Courts 206–7; family law jurisdiction 104, 198, 204, 206, 214–15; federal jurisdiction of 34, 37, 47–8, 85–6, 204; industrial magistrates 141, 226, 228, 236–7; jurisdiction generally 81–90, 95–6, 103–8, 240; reform of 83–4, 87, 108–9, 245; *and see* justices of the peace (Australia), magistrates

summary offence 81–2, 84–6, 206–8; *and see* indictable offence
superior court 93, 119, 121–3, 176, 235
Supreme Courts: acting judges 58, 62, 70–1, 118; as courts of appeal 125–7, 133–4, 174–5; constitutional provisions for 22–4, 58; decentralization 130; establishment 117–19, 122; family law jurisdictions 188–9, 191–200, 202, 203, 204, 207–8, 213–14; jurisdiction 64, 93, 119–27, 229–30; personnel 117–18; relation to Federal Court 137, 139, 140, 141, 142–9, 150–5; tenure of judges 24, 58–9, 69–70

Tasmania: Children's Courts 206–7; Court of Petty Sessions 81–7, 94–6; courts of requests 100–1, 103–5; history of courts 23; Industrial Commission 225–8; small claims 241–50; Supreme Court 23, 117–35
tenancy disputes 242, 247, 268
territories (Commonwealth) 38–42, 49–51, 58, 129–30, 228; *and see* by name
trade practices jurisdiction 139, 147, 151, 155, 230
transfer of cases: remittal to lower courts 109–10, 116, 154, 163–4, 178–9; removal to higher courts 110, 116, 149, 163–4; under cross-vesting scheme 147–8
transport accidents: *see* personal injury litigation
trial by jury: *see* jury trial

unified Australian court system 135, 149, 272–4
unified civil jurisdiction 108–9, 128–9, 135, 257–61, 272–4; *and see* cross-vesting scheme
United States Constitution: Art. III s2 46, 130; Australian departures from 55, 136; influence on Australia 25, 153, 156, 180, 205, 215; judicial independence under 55, 70–1; pendent jurisdiction under 153
United States courts 126, 131, 136, 149, 205, 241, 246; *and see* United States Constitution, United States Supreme Court
United States Supreme Court 72, 156, 165, 172, 175, 181–2, 205; appointment of judges 55, 157; extra-judicial use of judges 60; jurisdiction 25, 60, 156, 176, 179, 180, 183; workload 171

Van Diemen's Land: *see* Tasmania
vice-admiralty courts 123
Victoria: Children's Courts 206–7;

Conciliation and Arbitration Boards 225, 227; Constitution Act 1975 24, 175; County Court 82–3, 91–2, 100–1, 102–3, 108; Court of Insolvency 138; court reforms 128; Industrial Relations Commission 225–7; Magistrates' Courts 81–7, 94–6, 101–2, 103–4, 250; Market Court 257; Small Claims Tribunals 241–50; Supreme Court 24, 117–35; Wages Boards 219, 225

wages boards 219, 225, 227
warden's courts 252–3, 264–5
wardship jurisdiction 203, 214
Western Australia: Children's Courts 206–7; Courts of Petty Sessions 81–7, 94–6; District Court 81–7, 100–1, 103–4, 107 ; early history 43; Family Court 34, 104, 194, 200, 202–3, 204, 215; Industrial Appeal Court 225–9; Industrial Commission 225–7; Land Valuation Tribunals 256; Local Courts 101–2, 103–4, 241; Small Claims Tribunals 241–50; small debts jurisdiction 241, 242, 245, 250; Supreme Court 24, 117–35
workers' compensation 237, 275